Accession no.
36184306

D0421698

From Penitence to Charity

WITHDRAWN

WITHDRAWN

From Penitence to Charity

Pious Women and the Catholic Reformation in Paris

BARBARA B. DIEFENDORF

LIS - LIBRARY

Date	Fund
17-4-15	i-che

Order No.

2592150

University of Chester

OXFORD

UNIVERSITY PRESS

2004

OXFORD
UNIVERSITY PRESS

Oxford   New York
Auckland   Bangkok   Buenos Aires   Cape Town   Chennai
Dar es Salaam   Delhi   Hong Kong   Istanbul   Karachi   Kolkata
Kuala Lumpur   Madrid   Melbourne   Mexico City   Mumbai   Nairobi
São Paulo   Shanghai   Taipei   Tokyo   Toronto

Copyright © 2004 by Oxford University Press, Inc.

Published by Oxford University Press, Inc.
198 Madison Avenue, New York, New York 10016

www.oup.com

Oxford is a registered trademark of Oxford University Press

All rights reserved. No part of this publication may be reproduced,
stored in a retrieval system, or transmitted, in any form or by any means,
electronic, mechanical, photocopying, recording, or otherwise,
without the prior permission of Oxford University Press.

Library of Congress Cataloging-in-Publication Data

Diefendorf, Barbara B., 1946–
From penitence to charity : pious women and the Catholic Reformation in Paris / Barbara Diefendorf.
    p. cm.
Includes bibliographical references and index.
ISBN 0-19-509582-0
1. Paris (France)—Church history—17th century. 2. Women in the Catholic
Church—France—Paris—History—17th century. 3. Monasticism and religious orders for
women—France—Paris—History—17th century. I. Title.
BR848.P3D54 2004
282'.44361'082—dc22   2003066174

9 8 7 6 5 4 3 2 1

Printed in the United States of America
on acid-free paper

In Memory
Susanna Crane Boonstoppel
(1916–2000)

Acknowledgments

This book was long in the making, and it is a pleasure to acknowledge the many debts of gratitude incurred on its slow path to completion. As ever, I am indebted to Natalie Davis for introducing me to the society and culture of early modern France when I was a graduate student at Berkeley many, many years ago. Her willingness to look beyond the limits that patriarchal society imposed on women to ask how they maneuvered within these limits has profoundly influenced my approach to the study of gender roles. My debt to Denis Richet is nearly as old. Welcoming me as a student to his seminar, he shared his incomparable knowledge of Parisian history and pushed me to refine the questions I asked. The first conversation I had about the problems that lie at the heart of this book was with Denis Richet. Regrettably, it was also my last conversation with him, as he died a few months later.

With time, the dialogues begun with Natalie Davis and Denis Richet became a much broader conversation. Looking back, I see that I presented parts of this research in seminars at Boston College, Brandeis, Catholic University, Cornell, DePaul, Harvard, the Graduate School of the City University of New York, the Institute for Advanced Study at Princeton, the Massachusetts Center for Renaissance Studies at Amherst, the National Humanities Center, Rhode Island College, the Sorbonne, Stanford, and Yale. Invitations to teach semester-long seminars on practices of piety in early modern Europe at the Harvard Divinity School and the Folger Shakespeare Library allowed me to extend and refine my understanding of devout piety in the company of the colleagues and students who took part in these seminars. I also enjoyed the opportunity to talk about this work in plenary sessions of the Western Society for French History and the "Attending to Early Modern Women" symposium sponsored by the Center for Renaissance and Baroque Studies at the University of Maryland, College Park. I am grateful for the invitations and for the valuable comments, references, and suggestions offered on each of these occasions.

I want to thank the John Simon Guggenheim Foundation, the School of Historical Studies at the Institute for Advanced Study in Princeton, and the National Endowment for the Humanities for fellowships that supported research for this book. At Boston University, Dean and Provost Dennis Berkey also encouraged and aided this research. Sister Claudette of the Carmelite Monastery of Concord, New Hampshire, provided a valuable introduction to the French Carmelites and to their historical traditions. The prioresses and archivists at the Carmelite convents of Pontoise and Clamart made me feel welcome and generously shared their resources, as did the archivists at the Capuchins' provincial house and the motherhouse of the Congregation of the Mission in Paris. Without the rich collections of the Archives nationales and Bibliothèque nationale de France, the Bibliothèque mazarine, and the Bibliothèque de Sainte-Geneviève and the aid of the archivists and librarians in these institutions, this work would not have been possible.

I owe a very special debt of gratitude to fellow laborers in the vineyards of early modern France. Philip Benedict, Tom and Katherine Brennan, Denis Crouzet, Robert Descimon, Mack Holt, Orest Ranum, Virginia Reinburg, Al Soman, and Simone Zurawski have been tremendously supportive colleagues and friends for many years. Thanks also to Steven Ozment, Mark Edwards, Jodi Bilinkoff, and the anonymous reader who read the completed manuscript for Oxford University Press. Nancy Lane showed her confidence in the project by signing the book for Oxford when it was still at an early stage. Susan Ferber carried it through to completion. I am grateful to them both. Jeffry Diefendorf remains my first and most patient reader, listener, and sounding board. He has lived with these pious women for far too long and will, I am sure, be glad to have an end of hair shirts, scourges, and fasts. His generous love makes my work as a scholar both possible and worthwhile.

This book about strong-minded and creative women was intended as an offering for my mother, but her great heart gave out before it was done. It is now dedicated to her memory.

Parts of the Prologue were published in "From Penitence to Charity: The Practice of Piety in Counter-Reformation France," *Vincentian Heritage* 14 (1993): 37–56. Chapter 1 contains some material previously published in "An Age of Gold? Parisian Women, the Holy League, and the Roots of Catholic Renewal," in *Changing Identities in Early Modern France*, edited by Michael Wolfe, 169–90 (Durham, NC: Duke University Press, 1996). Chapter 5 contains some material from "Discerning Spirits: Women and Spiritual Authority in Counter-Reformation France," in *Culture and Change: Attending to Early Modern Women*, edited by Adele Seeff and Margaret Mikesell, 241–65 (Newark, DE: University of Delaware Press, 2003). An earlier version of Table 5.1 and some material in chapter 6 appeared in "Contradictions of the Century of Saints: Aristocratic Patronage and the Convents of Counter-Reformation Paris," *French Historical Studies* 24 (2001): 471–500. Permission to reproduce that material here is gratefully acknowledged.

Contents

From Penitence to Charity

Prologue

The First Dévote

On 11 September 1590, Marie Du Drac died, happy in the knowledge that Henri de Navarre's brutal siege of Paris had been lifted just twelve days earlier. As Du Drac had foreseen in her frequent revelations, God had "delivered the inhabitants of the city by extraordinary means and protected them from the rage and fury of the sworn enemies of the Catholic faith."[1] Or so we are told by her spiritual director, a friar of the Minim order named Antoine Estienne, who seized on the occasion of her funeral to deliver a lengthy oration lauding her piety, enumerating her devotional practices, and recounting her many "illuminations, ecstasies, and raptures."[2]

Born into a distinguished Parisian family in 1544, Marie Du Drac was married at the age of seventeen to one of her father's colleagues in the Parlement of Paris. Bearing her husband seven children in twelve years of marriage, she vowed after his death in 1572 not to remarry but rather to devote her life to God alone. Even during her marriage, Du Drac began to leave aside the "vanities of this world." Moved by a strong fear of the Last Judgment, she abandoned her jewelry and worldly attire, covered her hair, and donned garments so severe that friends and relatives expressed their shock. Beneath these somber robes, she wore a rough hair shirt. Often she fastened a four-inch horsehair strap tightly around her loins as well. She mortified her already frail body with fasts so extreme that they injured her health. When she fell ill shortly after her husband's death, the doctors informed her that she needed a cook more than a physician, so debilitated was her stomach.[3]

Although she prized above all else the contemplative life, she only briefly considered entering a convent.[4] Instead, she made of her well-ordered home a "little monastery" (the phrase was to become a cliché in the spiritual biographies of devout women), raising her children in the fear and love of God and emphasizing from their youngest age the virtue of humble obedience. She devoted the time not absolutely required for household tasks to solitary retreat in her study and to active engagement in works of Christian charity. Not content with distributing alms, she went into hospitals and the homes of the poor to help feed and tend the invalids there. She personally concocted medicines to bring to the indigent and, contrary to the social mores of her time, did not hesitate to help dress their wounds with her own hands. She also visited prisons to bring hope to the inmates and worked to secure their release, paying their debts herself if this was what was required to free them.[5]

Marie Du Drac set about reforming her interior life with the same vigor that she applied to her exterior, or so Estienne tells us. Initially at least, she examined her conscience so scrupulously that she spent long hours in confession, returning to her confessor day after day to add some new little sin she had just remembered. She ceased this practice when she came to believe that her scruples were themselves the product of obstinate pride. In 1570 she began to experience a form of mystical trance that both she and Estienne describe as being "drunk with God." Initially untutored in mystical theology, Du Drac soon acquired spiritual advisers who instructed her in meditative prayer and deepened her theological understanding of the experiences she was having. These experiences were highly somatic, and her raptures were so powerful that she sometimes thought she would die of them. Sometimes in her ecstasies, she had visions, and Estienne attributes to her several prophecies as well.[6]

Du Drac's faith was humble in the extreme. When asked to write an account of the special blessings God had given her, she wrote instead of her excess of sin. Her faith was focused on Christ's passion and, above all, on his cross. Estienne describes a vision she had of Christ, wrapped in a purple robe and crowned with thorns, "holding a reed in each hand and bleeding in all the parts of his sacred body," while "a very soft and lamentable voice" murmured "O my daughter, see how much I have suffered for you." In keeping with her Christocentrism, Du Drac had a deep hunger for the Eucharist and took communion as often as possible—at least three times a week and daily during Advent and Lent. Her consciousness of Christ's real presence in the Eucharist was such that she often remarked that "if the misguided heretics . . . had only tasted the unmistakable delights with which her soul had been divinely nourished, this would have been more than sufficient to convert them from their heresy and bring them back into the bosom of our holy mother church."[7]

Marie Du Drac did not experience Christ's body in the sacraments of the church alone. It was quite literally her meat and drink, and she advised her "spiritual children"—the men and women who sought out her spiritual counsel—likewise to find Christ in their daily bread. In common with other female mystics, she frequently employed images of Christ as food and dwelt on the act of consuming his body.[8] She counselled those who sought her advice to pray before meals that Christ mortify their sensuality and fill them with the "spiritual meat" of his love, not allowing the "corporeal meat" they were about to partake of to impede this spiritual union. They should try while eating and drinking to envision the bites they took as being "sauced from the flow of his grievous wounds" and ask that "he unite you with him perfectly, just as this corporeal food is to your body." "In drinking," she added, "pray that he cause his precious blood to sustain, clean, and wash over the interior of your soul." Each meal thus became an act of Communion, as Christ's body and blood, consumed with and as food, continually cleansed and nurtured the believer.[9]

If Du Drac provided spiritual counsel to devout Catholics, she also undertook a more daring ministry in confronting Protestant friends and kinsmen, admonishing them for their lapse into heresy and persistently attempting to convince them of the error of their ways. Fervently devoted to the ultra-Catholic cause in the French Wars of Religion, she spared "neither gold, nor silver, nor any of the means that God had given her to aid in its affairs." After learning that the son of a friend served as an officer in the Huguenot army, she commented that she would rather "not have any children than to have them turn out like that and not be supporters of the League." To the end of her days, she avidly followed the fortunes of the Holy League, the ultra-Catholic faction that rebelled against the Crown in the name of Catholic truth and seized power in Paris and other French cities. Although she was on her deathbed when Henri de Navarre lifted the siege of Paris in August 1590, she rejoiced to learn that grain was again flowing into the starving city and demanded that visitors describe how Navarre's followers reacted to their failure to subdue the rebellious capital. "I'll bet they are thoroughly ashamed and embarrassed among themselves," she remarked with satisfaction shortly before she died.[10]

In her spirituality, if not her politics, Marie Du Drac was ahead of her time. Contemporaries judged her behavior bizarre, even unseemly for a woman of her station, and took to calling her la Dévote, a nickname that, depending on the speaker, could carry overtones of either admiration or jest.[11] Half a century later, the ascetic practices and penitential spirituality that characterized Du Drac's religious conversion had been broadly adopted by pious adepts of the Catholic revival. Like Du Drac, these women were called dévotes, and the term was still used in both derision and respect.

Marie Du Drac's life, as recounted and shortly thereafter published by Antoine Estienne, offers us, as it offered her peers, a model of devout spirituality. Shocking to her contemporaries, her penitential and ascetic piety had a much greater appeal to succeeding generations of elite women, and many of her life experiences were common to later pious women. At the same time, Du Drac's spiritual biography illustrates a profound tension within French

Catholicism, a contest over the nature and practice of the true faith. While many French Catholics saw her as an enviable model of feminine piety, others identified in her behavior the excesses of a faith gone wrong.[12]

This book seeks to explore the growing popularity of this contested spirituality, to explain its special appeal to women born to lives of wealth and comfort, and to trace its public and private consequences. It begins with the dramatic events that enlivened Marie Du Drac's final days, the rebellion of the Holy League. The explosive religious emotions touched off by these events indelibly altered French Catholicism. No longer an oddity, Marie Du Drac's penitential piety became the order of the day.

Introduction

Between 1604 and 1650, at least forty-eight new religious houses for women—more than one a year—were established in the city of Paris and its suburbs. This book tells the story of the revival of Catholic institutions and spirituality that produced such a stunning burst of religious construction and, more particularly, of the lay and religious women who built, supported, and inhabited these houses. It is a book about women (and men) who lived their lives on a plane of spiritual involvement that, extreme even in their own time, is in many respects shocking today. Tracing the rise of a newly ascetic and penitential religious fervor to the last, tumultuous stages of the civil and religious wars that reduced France to near anarchy in the late sixteenth century, the book explores the impact of this ascetic spirituality on the Catholic renewal that followed. I argue that the spiritual imperatives of self-mortification and renunciation of will that lay at the heart of this penitential piety profoundly influenced not just seventeenth-century religious life but also the values and behavior of devout lay people.

The wars of the Holy League ignited the ideal of a Catholic crusade. A crusading mentality found expression in communal rites of penitence and an ecstatic and apocalyptic spirituality. With the collapse of the League, collective gestures of atonement were no longer sanctioned, but for many devout Catholics a penetrating desire for expiation of both personal and collective guilt remained. Turned inward, this penitential piety found expression in extremes of asceticism modeled on the heroic acts of self-mortification attributed to saints of the early church. Men claimed this path for themselves, but women insisted that they too had (as members of one newly founded order put it) "bodies capable of suffering, and wills as generous as those of men to undertake the sacrifice of their bodies."[1] Heroic asceticism, although consistently gendered as male, was one spiritual path that was *not* barred to women, and the women who pursued this path gained a respect and admiration not otherwise accorded their sex. Their deeds, and the publicity given these deeds, had important consequences for the spiritual and material propagation of the Catholic Reformation in France. Well-publicized acts of renunciation generated a sympathetic and imitative response. They led to a rash of new vocations and spurred generous donations for the founding and expansion of monastic houses.

This process was, however, a self-limiting one. Heroic vocations inevitably declined, and the superiors of contemplative convents had to adjust to a new reality. By the 1630s social, economic, and political stresses worked to change both the internal structures of the new religious communities and their relationship to lay society. The same stresses caused pious women to readjust their religious values, and a preference for charitable service came to supplant penitential asceticism as the dominant spiritual mode. Without abandoning the goals of religious enlightenment and personal holiness, devout women increasingly looked to edify less favored members of their own sex. Moved by a sense of apostolic mission, they incorporated schools and programs for religious retreat into their convents and carried the same mission outside the cloister in lay congregations dedicated to educating and serving the poor. Although traditionally forbidden to preach or publicly teach doctrine, pious women capitalized on the Council of Trent's call to catechize an ignorant laity to take up new religious roles. Even lay women, in joining newly formed charitable confraternities, were moved by an apostolic desire to save souls and not just a compassionate wish to help supply the material needs of society's outcasts and the poor.

In sum, the practice of—and admiration for—heroic asceticism set in motion the Catholic renewal in France. Women played a key role in this process, by their leadership and by the example they set, but also by the fact that they appeared to triumph over the limitations of their sex at the same time that they paradoxically submitted unreservedly to gendered ideals of humility and obedience. Pious women were also instrumental in directing the Catholic revival toward new ends as the penitential impulse waned. They did not simply respond to the appeals of male reformers but worked actively alongside, and sometimes in advance of, these men. And yet, because the women maintained a rhetoric of female submission to male authority and wisdom, the active character and scope of their role have tended to be lost from view.

Examining the part played by elite lay women as patrons of reformed convents and by prioresses as spiritual leaders of these communities, this book reassesses women's contributions to the movement commonly known as the

Catholic Reformation.[2] At the same time, I explore the assumptions about gender and gender roles that have served to obscure these contributions. In doing so, I illuminate the symbiotic ties that linked even the most reclusive contemplative nuns to lay elites. I also offer a new perspective on the active congregations and uncloistered communities that emerged during this period by allowing them to be seen not as the product of a long-thwarted apostolic vocation but as the expression of broadly evolving spiritual values and ideals.

The book emerged from my frustration with discussions of women's role in the Catholic Reformation in recent literature on early modern religion and gender history. In both areas, the Catholic Reformation is most commonly depicted as a period particularly hostile to the female sex, a time when misogynistic male clerics reinforced their domination of church institutions by shutting women who longed to serve actively in schools, hospitals, and missions into strictly enclosed, reclusive convents to control their dangerous sexuality. To be sure, post-Tridentine clergy were charged with enforcing strict rules for monastic enclosure, but portraying women as hapless victims of repressive clerics, church dogmas, and family strategies deflects attention from investigation of their own religious values and choices. Some women enthusiastically supported the call for spiritual and institutional renewal that issued from the Council of Trent; others felt sufficiently well served by traditional institutions and resisted dramatic change. Advocates and opponents of Catholic renewal did not divide along simple gender lines.[3]

Interpretations of the Catholic Reformation's impact on women have also tended to be drawn very largely from research on Italy and Spain, ignoring significant regional differences in the social and cultural factors that shaped women's experience. Although church prelates wanted the Catholic Reformation to be a homogeneous, centrally directed movement across Catholic Europe, it was in fact a diverse and uneven process. The Catholic Reformation came later to France than to Italy or Spain, and the preoccupations of French bishops and the control they exerted over religious foundations in their dioceses cannot be inferred from foreign models. Moreover, French property laws and inheritance customs gave women significantly different rights and a different place in family strategies compared to their Italian and Spanish sisters. This inevitably affected the decisions individuals made regarding religious life and the relationship between convents and lay society.

Given regional differences in custom and law and disparities in bishops' attitudes toward reform and change, even France proved too broad a canvas for a fine-grained study of women's religious choices. I narrowed my field of vision to Paris when, drawing up a list of monastic foundations, I first sensed the magnitude of the revival that occurred in that city alone. Why, I wondered, were there so many new houses? Who sponsored these foundations? Who paid for them? And why were two-thirds of the new houses traditional, contemplative convents when all of the historical literature emphasized the powerful attraction that new active, uncloistered religious congregations held for seventeenth-century women?

Clearly, the answers to these questions would need to be sought not just in the religious history of Catholic reform but in the broader social and political contexts peculiar to the Parisian experience. Paris's Catholic revival came hard on the heels of bitterly divisive civil war, and antagonisms rooted in these wars shaped the religious politics of the seventeenth century in important ways, at the level of the Crown but also at the level of the individual believer. It may be helpful to readers unfamiliar with this turbulent period in French history to briefly survey the key events that determined the character of French Catholicism between the mid-sixteenth and mid-seventeenth centuries.

The religious wars that broke out in France in 1562 initially pitted French Protestants, often called Huguenots, against a Catholic majority that viewed the new religion as heretical and refused to allow its adherents the right to worship publicly in their traditionally Catholic state. Political rivalries deepened religious antagonisms and made it hard to secure a lasting peace. In August 1572 rumors of a Huguenot plot to seize the Crown led Parisian Catholics abruptly to murder several thousand Protestants in the infamous Saint Bartholomew's Day Massacre.[4] The unprecedented violence of the killings prompted the Catholic majority itself to divide, as a moderate faction, favoring peace even at the expense of compromise, emerged to oppose a more radical, ultra-Catholic party intent on putting an end to heresy at any cost. As king, Henri III tried to maneuver between the two factions but ultimately failed. When the death of his younger brother and apparent successor in 1584 left a distant cousin, Huguenot leader Henri de Navarre, as heir to the throne, the ultra-Catholics united in a Holy League. Increasing their pressure on Henri III, they demanded a decisive defeat of the heretics and the annulment of Navarre's right to the throne. The war that began in 1585 with a forced alliance between Henri III and the ultra-Catholic leader Henri de Guise soon dissolved into a three-way quarrel. Radical Catholics drove Henri III from his capital in May 1588. The revenge he exacted six months later in ordering the assassination of Henri de Guise touched off a violent rebellion, as cities and governments withdrew their obedience and prepared to make war against the king.

Paris was one of the first cities to throw its allegiance wholeheartedly behind the League. A chiliastic atmosphere overcame the city, as preachers drummed up support for the rebellion by invoking the Last Days. God is angered, they cried, by our failure to defend the true religion and by our ungodly ways. They called for a war to exterminate heresy and also a moral crusade. Paris must become a "New Jerusalem," a site of repentance and moral reform, to save the city from ruin and appease God's wrath. The emotional intensity of the League's seizure of power was reinforced when Henri III was murdered by a Catholic fanatic in July 1589 and the Protestant Navarre claimed the throne as Henri IV and then besieged Paris in an attempt to make good his claim.

With time, however, the ardor of some of the Leaguers faded. Tired of war, they accepted Navarre as king after he converted to Catholicism in July 1593 and allowed him to enter the capital in March 1594.

Generous in victory, Henri IV exiled only the most radical League leaders and attempted to win over the rest. Publicly demonstrating his new Catholic allegiance, he ostentatiously patronized Catholic causes and made a policy of ignoring past divisions. It took him until 1598 to win over the last of the rebellious princes, and he had to force his high court of Parlement to accept the compromise peace negotiated with the Huguenots that same year. Henri's policies of reconciliation were nevertheless sufficiently successful that his assassination in 1610 by an ultra-Catholic fanatic took many by surprise. Suspicion of a radical plot immediately welled up; the Jesuits in particular were accused of preaching tyrannicide and inspiring the assassin, François Ravaillac, to kill the king. Although Ravaillac insisted even under torture that he had acted alone, the assassination revealed the tense undercurrents still dividing French Catholics. At the same time, Henri IV's unexpected death brought a new uncertainty to the course of French politics by allowing power to fall into the hands of a queen regent ruling on behalf of a child king.

These dramatic events had a powerful impact on the character of French Catholicism and on the Catholic revival that had begun with Henri IV's consent as a platform for the consolidation of his rule. Many prominent members of the devout circles associated with the Catholic renewal—the dévots, as they were known—had actively supported the League. However quick or slow to reconcile themselves to their newly Catholic king, they had experienced first-hand the emotionally charged atmosphere of Leaguer Paris, and their spirituality reflected its penitential and apocalyptic strains. Profiting from the king's desire to conciliate his former enemies, they gained his cautious support for the foundation of new, reformed convents and lobbied for official acceptance of the decrees issued half a century earlier by the Council of Trent.

The latter issue was yet another source of tension among French Catholics. Many magistrates and clerics were Gallicans who favored a relatively independent, albeit Catholic, church and opposed the ultramontanism of the dévots, who looked to Rome for leadership and reform. The tensions carried over into foreign policy, as the ultramontanes tended to favor Catholic unity and policies that worked toward this end, while Gallican Catholics were more open to policies based on strategic considerations and reason of state. Expressions of Catholic religiosity were inevitably freighted with political implications. This became particularly apparent when Henri IV's death brought about the regency of Marie de Medici, a devoutly Catholic and foreign queen.

Henri IV tolerated the dévots and even subsidized their religious foundations and charities, but the support he extended them was cautious and strategic. He knew how much opposition they could still muster. Marie de Medici, by contrast, supported them out of personal inclination, because she shared their religious values and priorities, and they quickly gained a prominent place at court. A political satire published in 1614 made this point well. Purporting to advise women on the new fashions and modes of discourse that would gain them favor at court, the piece catalogued the attitudes and behaviors characteristic of the dévots. Advising women above all to learn to speak eloquently of God, it recommended that they attend services at newly introduced religious orders, adopt the leaders of these orders as their personal spiritual directors, and confer with them an hour or two each day. They should also cultivate connections to new women's orders, visiting the Ursulines and having aunts or cousins among the Carmelites, so as to regularly visit there as well. The piece named names and was obviously written by a close but not sympathetic observer of devout circles, for it went on to satirize the credulity of the dévots and demeaned their beliefs by depicting them as strategies for gaining altogether worldly ends.[5] It underscored the influence the dévots had gained at court but also revealed the suspicion with which they were viewed by those who did not share their religious values.

The lack of unanimity in Catholic opinion made Marie de Medici's patronage of reformed religious orders all the more important to the success of the Catholic renewal. Elite women imitated her in visiting newly established convents and competed to sponsor additional houses where they might enjoy the special privileges accorded founders. The aristocratic revolts that troubled the regency did not interrupt the new foundations and may even have helped spur the movement along by encouraging the wives and widows of rebellious princes to stake out their own circles of influence with conspicuous gifts to new convents. By contrast, the queen mother's tumultuous relationship with her son, Louis XIII, had a negative impact on the dévots and on the policies they promoted at court.

The young bishop of Luçon, Armand du Plessis de Richelieu, who first caught Marie de Medici's eye in 1614 and rose to power through her favor, disagreed with the pro-Catholic foreign policy advocated by the dévots. Bishop, later Cardinal, Richelieu worked to convince Louis XIII not only to avoid entering the Thirty Years War on the Catholic side but also to covertly support the Protestant princes battling against the Holy Roman emperor and king of Spain, both Habsburgs, on the ground that Habsburg supremacy posed more of a threat to French security than did neighboring Protestant states. At the same time, he encouraged Louis to put an end to the independent political and military power the Protestants enjoyed in France by right of the Edict of Nantes. The issues were contentious ones, and policy debates became the object of public polemics. Advocates of a neutral or pro-Protestant foreign policy depicted themselves as "good Frenchmen," while portraying the dévots as "bigots" engaged in a falsely pious cabal and as deliberate or unwitting tools of Spain. Some polemicists even resurrected the history of the League to recall an earlier occasion on which naïve clerics and ultra-Catholic lay men had allowed religious enthusiasm to triumph over political wisdom.[6]

The Catholic revival continued to spread in this polemicized atmosphere. Even Richelieu's ultimate triumph over Marie de Medici and the dévot party in 1630 did not bring the movement to a halt. The queen mother's forced exile was financially disastrous for several convents to which she had promised gifts she could no longer pay, and the arrest of Keeper of the Seals Michel de Marillac was profoundly unsettling to the Carmelites, whom he had helped to establish in France. But patronage of the new orders had long since expanded beyond the original circle of dévots. A generation of women who had not experienced the wars of the League had come of age and begun to impose a new religious sensibility on the Catholic revival. Although they admired the ascetic prioresses who led the reformed houses founded during the initial stages of the postwar expansion, their spirituality was not fundamentally penitential but rather charitable in orientation. It also reflected François de Sales's gentler spirit and more optimistic love of God. The change was a natural and perhaps inevitable one. All intense enthusiasms eventually wane; the institutions they spawn stagnate and become irrelevant unless able to evolve in new directions. In the case of the Catholic revival, this natural fading was in some quarters accelerated by theological quarrels over the nature of true penitence and the virtue of contemplative retreat. At the same time, increasing sensitivity to the growing misery of the peasantry and the dreadful conditions of the urban poor provided a fresh direction for pious women who desired to live out their faith.

Charitable visits to hospitals, prisons, and even the houses of the poor had always been viewed as a praiseworthy part of a devout lay woman's routine. Only gradually, however, did pious elites come to see serving society's less favored members as an admirable and sufficient end for religious life. Before this could happen, women needed to change their orientation toward the poverty that surrounded them. They needed to see the poor not just as objects of compassion but as lost souls who needed to be saved. They also needed to believe that this redemption could be best effected through direct intervention and not merely through prayer. They needed to internalize their devout faith so thoroughly that they were overcome by pity and a determination to help those who remained ignorant of the truths they considered essential to salvation. Where the generation of women who helped initiate the Catholic revival hoped to save the lost souls of the heretic Protestants by their prayers, their daughters sought to shoulder a still broader mission in becoming apostles to the poor.

To do so required at least the tacit consent of the ecclesiastical officials charged with supervising female religious life. The Council of Trent had ordered the strict enclosure of all religious women, and reform-minded bishops needed very good reasons if they were to ignore this rule. Women's expansion into active religious vocations proceeded cautiously on this account. Profiting from the greater freedom allowed secular women, the leaders of the new charitable communities initially remained in worldly dress, refused to take vows, and called their groups simple "societies" or "confraternities" to evade the requirement for religious cloistering. Gaining official approval for these communities only years (sometimes decades) after their humble start, they invented a new form of semireligious life.

Paris's bishops granted official recognition to the new congregations of *filles séculaires* (secular nuns) in large measure because they recognized the important work that the Ursulines and other reformed orders were doing in catechizing and educating young girls, and they wanted to extend this instruction to the urban poor and rural communities outside the reach of the cloister. They were also prompted by the sense of impending social crisis that grew up in Paris during the second quarter of the seventeenth century. Although people had a poor understanding of the reasons for the growing misery they saw about them, they could not help noticing the ever larger numbers of beggars they encountered in city streets. They were very aware of the repeated waves of famine and pestilence that caused sharp rises in mortality in the Parisian countryside in the late 1620s and early 1630s, though they would have had no clear understanding that these crises were symptoms of a long-term decline in the peasants' standard of living, which had made them increasingly vulnerable to famine and disease, as well as prompting many to immigrate to the city in hopes of food and work. Nor would Parisian elites have understood their own role in the pauperization of the regional peasantry. They would not have recognized that, in rushing to purchase the lands of debt-ridden peasants, they were effecting an enormous transfer of wealth from the countryside to the city; nor would they have understood that, in directing the revenues derived from their country estates to urban consumption, they were further increasing the distance between rich and poor. And if they did recognize the extent to which the tax exemptions they enjoyed on account of their bourgeois or noble status had shifted the state's fiscal burden onto the shoulders of the peasantry, this was not a situation they were willing to change. The hefty tax increases that had resulted from the renewal of war against the Huguenots and then war against the Empire and Spain fell on precisely the persons least able to pay.[7]

Without understanding the full measure of the problem, much less comprehending its underlying causes, urban elites were nevertheless aware that poverty was increasing and prepared to respond positively when Vincent de Paul and other popular preachers made charity to one's neighbor the frequent theme of their eloquent sermons. The same charitable impulse that gave birth to the new congregations of filles séculaires prompted lay women to found confraternities that aided the poor directly with nursing care, warm clothes, and food and also raised funds for orphanages, hospitals, and asylums for endangered girls. Efforts to assist the populations of Champagne and Picardy left destitute by invading armies in 1636 and 1637 served as the model for larger-scale fund-raising activities in the early 1650s, when the midcentury wars of the Fronde brought the economic crisis to its peak. Competing armies again laid waste to France's northeastern provinces and, for more than five months in 1652, devastated the Paris region as well.

The Fronde had begun in 1648 as a tax revolt by Parisian magistrates angered by the imprudent policies of Anne of Austria, serving as regent for the boy king, Louis XIV. Although the judges and their allies in the popular classes were quick to make peace, the impetuous princes who joined the rebellion continued to battle the queen regent and her detested minister and favorite, Cardinal Jules Mazarin, in hope of gaining a greater voice in affairs of state. Unable to articulate any broader goals than their own personal and selfish ones, the princes soon lost what popular support they had at the start. They nevertheless fought on erratically, shifting alliances opportunistically, until their rebellion at last fizzled out. The declaration of Louis XIV's majority in 1651 put an end to their claim to act on the king's behalf and in his best interests, and the revolt made no fundamental changes in the politics of state. Its economic legacy was more enduring. The destructive campaigns of 1652 reduced the already impoverished Paris region to famine. Disease spread among the weakened population, mortality rates climbed, and still more peasants were dispossessed. Recovery was slow. For nearly another decade, ruined buildings, ravaged vineyards, and abandoned fields were common sights in the Parisian hinterland. Only after about 1664 did prices and production return to something approaching their prewar rates.[8]

The Fronde also had negative consequences for the dévots, many of whom had been at least temporarily drawn to the party of the rebels, whose cries for reform appealed to their rigorist morality. Most quickly became disillusioned with the princes and reconciled with the king before the end. They nevertheless lost credit with Louis XIV and never enjoyed his full confidence or favor. Moreover, a number of the rebel princes and their wives had been generous patrons of the reformed religious houses. The debts they incurred on account of the Fronde put an abrupt halt to this patronage. Just as Marie de Medici had done several decades earlier when forced into exile after her quarrels with Louis XIII, Frondeur aristocrats defaulted on promises to newly founded convents.

Although it by no means brought an end to the Catholic Reformation, the Fronde did mark a watershed in it. As such, it makes an appropriate termination point for this book. By the Fronde's end, the high ideals, rapid expansion, and innovative new forms of religious life that characterized the initial phase of the Catholic revival had given way to a new era of consolidation but also internal dissension and stress. The accommodations that Catholic reformers made to the new circumstances that prevailed during the personal rule of

Louis XIV deserve a separate study. The present work focuses rather on the period of innovation and rapid growth bounded by the wars of the League and the Fronde.

Beyond the drama of the civil wars with which this period began and ended, it is unified by Paris's emerging role as a social, cultural, and political capital under the first Bourbon kings. With a population that grew from roughly 250,000 residents to 450,000 during the first half of the seventeenth century, Paris was the largest city in northern Europe until overtaken by London in about 1650.[9] Its vast population reflected its complex social and political role. The preferred place of residence of Henri IV and Louis XIII, Paris housed a great many aristocrats who made up the royal court. It was home to the Parlement of Paris (a high court of justice with sovereign jurisdiction over more than half of France), several other sovereign courts that dealt with taxes and finances, and a good share of the kingdom's growing administrative bureaucracy, along with the families of the high magistrates and royal officials who staffed these institutions. It also was home to a bourgeoisie consisting largely of merchants (or ex-merchants) who had grown wealthy in luxury and wholesale trades, along with the middling-level officials, bureaucrats, and lawyers who supported the city's administrative and judicial functions. Paris also contained thousands more retail merchants and artisans, a vast population of workers, a large number of students, and a growing number of poor, but the dévotes instrumental in the city's Catholic revival came from the top levels of Parisian society. Although a few came from families that might be considered part of the old aristocracy, proportionately more were wives or daughters of men who had acquired noble status by serving as presidents of sovereign courts or through other royal offices that conveyed the privileges of nobility. Still others were daughters or wives of men who, as counselors in the sovereign courts, enjoyed the personal prerogatives of noble status but not the privilege of passing hereditary nobility to their children. The remainder came from the upper reaches of the bourgeoisie. Their fathers and husbands were not engaged in trade but lived from investments and property while often also exercising non-noble offices in the royal bureaucracy or the households of great aristocrats.

Contemporaries would have been acutely conscious of the gradations in rank and hierarchy that distinguished various members of this group, and it is important to be attentive to these differences when discussing, for example, the influence that an aristocratic donor's family standing might have given her at court or in communications with church prelates. When taken as a group, however, the fine gradations in social rank that distinguished one pious woman from another are for the most part irrelevant. They shared a common piety, and the nature and magnitude of their acts of charity differed more according to wealth than to status. Moreover, whether aristocrats or technically still bourgeois, all of these women, by comparison with the vast majority of the population, stood very near the top of the social scale, and I have adopted the rather amorphous term "elites" as a kind of shorthand to signal the collectively high level of social distinction enjoyed by the group when further precision is not necessary.

The fact that virtually all of the women who led the renewal of religious life in Paris came from elite families and enjoyed the patronage of women even higher up the social ladder may have insulated them from some of the negative presumptions experienced by women in other cultural milieus. Indeed, it is likely that circumstances in Paris were more favorable to female achievement than they were elsewhere in Europe. Two women, Marie de Medici and Anne of Austria, served as queen regent during the first half of the seventeenth century, and aristocratic women had a prominent place in their courts. Proximity to literary salons where women played an important part made it easier for Parisian women to take on other leadership roles, as did the mores of elite society, which allowed women a relatively large role in family strategies and domestic affairs. Sovereign court magistrates and other royal officers, for example, commonly expected their wives to manage not just their urban household but also their rural estates, so that the men could devote their own energies to their professional tasks. This meant the women hired and fired estate managers and supervised their work; they oversaw the harvest and storage of crops, ensured that rents were collected and peasants fairly treated, contracted for building repairs, and assumed a number of other responsibilities that required the skillful handling of both money and personnel. Parisian men also not uncommonly named their wife, instead of a male kinsman, as executor of their estates and administrator of the properties inherited by their children.[10] The experience—and the confidence—Parisian women gained from administering what were often extensive properties stood them in good stead when they went on to found religious communities, build convents, and invent new forms of semireligious life.

The laws and customs of the Paris region also served women relatively well by giving them a stronger claim to family properties than they enjoyed in many other parts of Europe. Customary law in the region was fundamentally egalitarian. With the exception of the special advantage the eldest son had with regard to noble properties, siblings shared equally in their parents' estate, regardless of sex. Daughters played an important part in their family's social and economic strategies. They were not simply "dowered off" at marriage and excluded from the parental inheritance; rather, their marriage portion was considered an advance on the parental succession and deducted from their share of the estate.[11] And because the special claims of the eldest son applied only to noble properties, even in aristocratic families, daughters might inherit significant wealth. Women also frequently inherited property from brothers who died childless, as the laws of collateral inheritance favored siblings over more distant kin, regardless of sex. These legal traditions, along with the hazards of war, which gave aristocratic males an abnormally high death rate, allowed for the emergence of the rich heiresses whose benevolence built the new convents and funded the new communities of the Catholic reform.

Customary law and practice also help explain why so many of the key donors were widows. A woman's property remained under her husband's control throughout their marriage. The law was equipped with a number of checks intended to prevent a spendthrift husband from dissipating his wife's estate, but she could not dispose of any property herself without his permission. Only in widowhood did she gain full control of her inherited properties, along with half of the community property acquired over the course of the marriage and a portion of the husband's estate known as a "dower." She could not spend all of this money freely; the same laws that had protected her property rights also worked to protect the claims of children, siblings, and even more distant kin to certain forms of inherited property.[12] As we shall see, the property rights women enjoyed under Parisian law allowed them to become important patrons of new religious institutions, but they also permitted family members to challenge and sometimes interfere with promised donations. More than one community launched an ambitious building project only to be caught up short when the anticipated funds failed to materialize.

Even in Paris, women's activities were constrained by age-old assumptions about the innate inferiority of their physical, intellectual, and moral capacities, and yet elite women did enjoy certain advantages over the majority of their sex in this regard. Class bias was at least as powerful as gender bias in the hierarchical society of early modern times, and women who came from elite families were often tacitly—and sometimes explicitly—viewed as exceptional and credited with capacities superior to those of others of their sex. Elite status also potentially influenced women's practice of piety in several ways. Taught from earliest childhood to subordinate their own wishes to their parents' command, girls from upwardly mobile or socially prominent families knew that their future marriage or placement in a convent would be dictated more by family strategy than by personal desire. And although they were raised to accept this lack of personal autonomy as natural, some girls inevitably had a hard time accommodating themselves to the choices made for them. Religious devotion served a dual role here. It helped young women trapped in loveless marriages to accept the life their parents had chosen, but it also offered them a small arena of personal liberty, for however much law and custom subjected a woman to her husband's authority, her soul remained her own. The Catholic Reformation enlarged this limited sphere of autonomy by encouraging devout women to develop their interior life. It also permitted unhappy wives and widows oppressed by the disadvantages they suffered in a male-dominated society to occasionally escape from their secular concerns into the female-centered world of reformed convents. Wives and widows alike sought spiritual guidance at parlor grilles from prioresses who, despite their reclusive vocation, were widely respected for their wise counsel. Under certain circumstances, lay women were even admitted to the seclusion of the cloister.

This book stresses the religious impulses that brought lay women and reformed nuns together in these ways, but the social benefits elite women may have sought in patronizing reformed convents should be acknowledged as well. However piously motivated, gifts that resulted in the founding of convents, building of chapels, and erection of altars were a form of conspicuous consumption. The women who offered these gifts not only acquired for their family the intercessory prayers of whole convents of nuns, but they also publicized their family's wealth and, implicitly at least, allowed them to bask in a reflected godliness. Paradoxically, reformed convents served as refuges where elite women might escape from secular concerns at the same time that their patronage of these institutions helped establish their family's worldly honor.

Beginning with one civil war and ending with another, this book chronicles the rise of two distinct but related spiritual impulses. The mystical and penitential piety with which devout women responded to the wars of the League began to wane by the 1630s, just as the new surge of compassionate charity that peaked with the Fronde began. Although the book's title, *From Penitence to Charity*, implies a simple evolution from one dominant spirituality to the other, the relationship between the two was necessarily more complex. The penitential asceticism these women practiced was intensely permeated with the desire to emulate the *caritas*, or self-sacrificial love, displayed by Christ. The impulse to charity thus inhabited their penitential piety from the start. And if the intensity of the ascetic impulse waned by the 1630s, the transition from penitence to charity was neither thoroughgoing nor complete. Although the ascetic practices I describe bear strong resemblance to those of medieval holy women, I by no means wish to suggest that the Catholic Reformation was characterized by the definitive abandonment of antiquated, or "medieval," forms of piety in favor of a more comfortably familiar and "modern" spirituality.[13] Even at midcentury, many devout women engaged in bodily mortifications quite alien, and even disturbing, to modern sensibilities. Even women who had abandoned hair shirts, flagellation, and other forms of corporal discipline practiced internalized forms of deliberate self-humiliation and denial of will. Seventeenth-century women avidly devoured the published lives of Catherine of Siena, Catherine of Genoa, and other late medieval holy women, and they often quite consciously modeled their own behavior on these lives. Moreover, late medieval and early modern women drew on a common repertory of earlier saints' lives and spiritual writings praising ascetic renunciation as a path to godliness. The tendency toward penitential mysticism that emerged so powerfully in devout circles in late sixteenth- and seventeenth-century France should not be considered just a stale remnant or last bizarre revival of outdated practices and vanishing beliefs. Rather, it was a response to historically specific events and attitudes and, as such, developed its own distinctive logic, character, and momentum.

Penitential asceticism has a long history in Christianity, as it does in many other religions. It is part of a large repertory of characteristic forms of spiritual expression and modes of living out one's faith. Just as Christian spirituality can be warmly emotional under certain circumstances and cooly rational under others, so too can it encompass a wide range of attitudes toward the bodily expression of true piety. It can focus heavily on the necessary cultivation of certain behaviors, or it can ignore adherents' behavior with an almost antinomian disregard. The central preoccupation of the historian of religious practice is not to trace a characteristic form of spiritual expression back to its most distant theological and historical roots, but to explain why, among many possibilities, this particular set of ideas and behaviors came to the fore at a given time and place.

The tendency of seventeenth-century women to model their behavior on that of earlier holy women nevertheless complicates the historian's task. The pious biographies that were written in surprising numbers in the seventeenth century have been an extremely important, but never unproblematic, source for this study. Sometimes written by nuns but most often authored by the subject's spiritual director or another male cleric, the biographies are closely patterned on earlier saints' lives. Didactic in purpose, they were crafted to offer models of piety to admire and emulate. As such, they are a complex blend of literary trope, observed behavior, and documented accomplishment.[14] It is not always easy to distinguish one from the other. For example, the biographer of Barbe Acarie, founder of the Discalced Carmelite Order in France, relates how, visiting hospitalized soldiers during the wars of the League, she overcame her repulsion for the soldiers' festering sores by lowering her face to them so as to inhale more deeply their putrefaction. Barbe Acarie may have deliberately modeled the gesture on an incident recounted in the life of Saint Catherine of Genoa (who almost certainly modeled her own gesture on that of Saint Catherine of Siena or another, earlier saint), or her biographer may merely have attributed the act to her because it was part of his own repertory of the behaviors of saints.[15] In the end, whether or not Acarie actually inhaled the putrid wounds of hospitalized soldiers is less important than the model of devout charity she offered in mingling freely with injured men, offering spiritual counsel but also abandoning class expectations by tending the wounded with her own hands, which was testified to by witnesses at her beatification proceedings. The literary trope of breathing in putrefaction is nevertheless instructive, signaling the humble submission and trust in divine providence the biographer wished his readers to admire and potentially imitate.

It is significant too that these lives were nearly always written by contemporaries with extensive firsthand knowledge of their subjects. Male biographers were often the confessors and spiritual directors of the dévotes whose lives they recorded and therefore privy to their most intimate revelations. Female biographers were invariably sisters in religion. The few authors who did not know their subject personally were careful to point out that they relied on both written and oral testimony from men and women who did. The biographies thus appear to be largely reliable when it comes to describing the basic events of their subjects' lives and the general tenor of their spirituality, even if we must allow for the exaggeration and distortions that inevitably ensue from the dictates of the genre to which they conform.

The biographies serve not only as sources of information about the lives of pious seventeenth-century women; when taken as literary sources, they also reveal a wealth of information about the assumptions and attitudes of devout Catholics toward gender differences and gender roles. Biographers inevitably shaped their subject's life to fit an idealized pattern of female behavior intended to serve as a model for contemporary women. While selectively emphasizing those aspects of a woman's behavior that reinforced traditional gender roles, most authors tended to pass quickly over aspects of their subject's life that deviated from or contradicted traditional norms. Beginning with the 1621 biography of Barbe Acarie by her spiritual director, André Duval, women's active role in shaping Catholic institutions and values in seventeenth-century France began to be obscured by a literature that emphasized submissive obedience.

This de-emphasis on the active part pious women played in shaping institutions was related to the sex of the authors as well as to the biographies' intended readership. Male authors most often addressed their books to a lay audience, whereas female authors tended to write for their sisters in religion. Both had didactic purposes in writing pious lives and sought to inspire their readers to moral rectitude and spiritual advancement. Intending even biographies of religious women to teach their female audience how to live in the world, male authors were more likely to bring in gendered examples of submissive behavior than were women writing for an all-female audience. They also tended to view chastity in more sexualized terms than did female authors, who described a more all-encompassing need to reserve oneself uniquely for God. On the whole, however, differences in both substance and style between male-authored and female-authored or autobiographical accounts proved less significant than I originally anticipated. Male authors may have been more learned in theology, but the literary sources on which they drew most heavily were saints' lives and not theological treatises. Ranging from the vitae of desert fathers to Teresa of Avila's autobiographical *Life*, first published in a French edition in 1601, these writings were the common property of pious women and men, as was the rich literature of mystical and affective spirituality that influenced the way authors of pious biography interpreted the religious experiences of their subject. Neither male nor female authors wrote with the intention of subverting the gendered value system of their time. Close analysis of some passages in these biographies nevertheless reveals that their subjects

Frontispiece for *Modèle de la Perfection Religieuse*, by Abraham Bosse. Typifying the new genre of edifying spiritual biographies, Jean Auvray, spiritual director of the Benedictine nuns of Hautes-Bruyères, depicted Jeanne Absolu, a Parisian dévote who took religious vows at Hautes-Bruyères at the age of sixty, as the very "model of religious perfection." Bibliothèque nationale de France.

were not so narrowly bound to traditional values and behaviors as their authors made them out to be.

I should explain one convention adopted in this book. It concerns the names used for the women who figure in the work. Although a French woman did not legally adopt her husband's family name when she married, it was customary to address her by her husband's name in polite society and, by extension, in seventeenth-century biographies and historical writing. For example, contemporaries referred to Louise de Marillac, the wife of Antoine Le Gras, a secretary to queen mother Marie de Medici, as Mademoiselle Le Gras, even though she continued to sign her correspondence and contracts with her birth name. In the seventeenth century, the honorific "Madame" was reserved for noble women; "Mademoiselle" was used for the upper reaches of the bourgeoisie, whether married or not. Legal documents conventionally identified a woman by her birth name but also her marital status, husband's name, and very often his professional status and titles. To avoid the confusion of calling women by more than one name, I have chosen to use their birth name except when they are titled nobles, in which case I use the title by which they were most commonly known. It would depart too radically from accepted usage to call Jeanne Frémyot, baronne de Chantal, just Jeanne Frémyot, and so I have retained the more standard Jeanne de Chantal (alternatively, the baronne de Chantal, or just Chantal). I have made one exception to these conventions. Barbe Acarie is too well-known by that name to adopt instead her birth name of Aurillot. Following seventeenth-century usage, however, she is referred to as Mademoiselle Acarie rather than the honorific title of Madame adopted by later biographers.

The narrative argument of this book—its story of change over time— imposes a roughly chronological structure on the chapters that follow. Chapter 1 tells the story of women's participation in the Holy League and the impact of this experience on their spirituality. It examines both ardent supporters of the League and their royalist opponents, many of whose husbands left them behind in Paris to defend the family properties while they served in the king's army or courts, and concludes that the trauma of civil war awakened in women affiliated with both political factions a powerful desire for the expiation of sin. Convinced that the wars were signs of God's impending judgment, they sought to appease his wrath through acts of rigorous asceticism and humble penitence. The women introduced in this chapter went on to play key roles in founding the first reformed religious order established in Paris after the wars, the Discalced Carmelites of Teresa of Avila's reform.[16] The ascetic practices in which they engaged as lay dévotes during the decade that intervened between the League's defeat in Paris and the founding of the Carmelites in 1604 are the subject of chapter 2. This chapter also establishes a context for understanding the demand for new reformed religious orders by examining the state of female monastic life in Paris at the end of the sixteenth century. It explains why existing convents held no attraction for women inspired by the ideal of rigorous austerity and why they instead took their models from the new reformed orders already created for men.

Chapter 3 examines the nucleus of dévots that formed around Barbe Acarie in the last years of the sixteenth century, as these and other pious lay people and clerics began to seek concrete ways to put into practice their plans for the reform and renewal of Catholic institutions. Examining the activities of this circle, including their attempts to aid in the reform of two distinguished but much decayed convents, the chapter also explores the intellectual origins of the active mysticism that characterized the group's piety. Contrary to the common understanding of France's early seventeenth-century Catholic reformers as mired in a passive, "abstract" mysticism, I argue that the fusion of Franciscan affective traditions and late medieval mysticism that animated this group's spirituality provided a powerful spur to action. The dévots in Barbe Acarie's circle imagined the highest possible spiritual state as one in which the soul remained entirely occupied with God even when the body was engaged in secular tasks. Mystical absorption into God was not an end in itself but a means of activating oneself to serve as God's tool or agent. The piety of the dévots in Acarie's circle was, moreover, intensely Christocentric and very frequently focused on the imitation of Christ's suffering on the cross. This, along with a broader emphasis on self-abnegation as a means of conforming one's life to God's will, explains the appeal that penitential asceticism held for them.

It also explains the energy they devoted to establishing reformed religious orders in France. Chapter 4 examines the foundation of three key orders in Paris: the Discalced Carmelites, Capuchin nuns (commonly called Capucines), and Ursulines. In each case, the lay patrons who funded the foundation are shown to have played an important role in shaping the new creation, a role underestimated in traditional historical accounts. The Carmelites and Capucines represent slightly different responses to the desire for intensely ascetic contemplative convents where pious women could retreat from the world. An entirely home-grown institution, the Capucines grew out of the desire to adapt the penitential piety practiced by the male order of strictly reformed Franciscans known as the Capuchins to suit women's needs. The Carmelites, by contrast, were intended as a direct importation of Teresa of Avila's reformed order from Spain. To guarantee the order's fidelity to Teresa's guiding principles, its French founders brought in Spanish nuns who had known and worked with Teresa. Despite this emphasis on authenticity, the founders adapted the order to suit local needs in subtle but important ways. The same was true of the Ursulines. Although originally founded in Italy as an open congregation of women who went out into the community to catechize young girls, they were erected as an enclosed order in Paris in keeping with the wishes of the community's lay founder but also the religious sensibilities of the order's first members.

The founding of these three convents was just the beginning of the fruitful collaboration between lay dévots and religious that characterized Paris's Catholic renewal. Another twenty-four contemplative convents had been founded by 1640. This wave of contemplative foundations is the subject of chapter 5, which asks what motivated the rapid multiplication of austere new houses, how they were financed, and how they differed from traditional, nonreformed convents. The chapter attempts to explain why the nuns in these convents embraced religious enclosure, why they felt empowered rather than constrained by strict adherence to their vows of poverty and chastity, and how they used mortification and ritual humiliation to spiritual ends. Observing that prioresses and mistresses of novices in these convents played a far greater role in the spiritual development and guidance of their nuns and acted more independently of the convents' male superiors and confessors than is usually assumed, the chapter further argues that the spiritual authority enjoyed by distinguished prioresses and nuns radiated beyond the convent walls and drew to them the elite patronage that was financially necessary for the convents' survival.

Chapter 6 examines several innovative foundations that, like the Ursulines, combined some form of active religious vocation with a more traditional contemplative life. Departing from the usual view of the Filles de la Visitation, or Visitandines, as an order whose initial purpose of charitable service in the community was frustrated by the enclosure forced on the nuns when they expanded from their first Savoyard convent into France, it emphasizes rather the founders' intention of providing a place where lay women could engage in religious retreats. The other convents examined in this chapter, including the Filles de la Madeleine for repentant prostitutes and several nursing and teaching orders, were also created to serve women's special needs without abandoning the rules of enclosure. Even at the height of the Catholic Reformation, there was more flexibility than is usually assumed in traditional monastic rules. In these, but also in many strictly contemplative convents, cloistered nuns were not entirely isolated from lay members of their sex but found opportunities to aid and edify them.

By the 1630s, the flow of private patronage that had made possible the rapid multiplication of new religious institutions had begun to dry up. Many of the new convents founded during this period were financially insecure from the start, and established houses tended to overexpand and consequently also found themselves vulnerable financially. One common response to the situation was to take in paying boarders, usually girls needing instruction or widows looking for a respectable retreat. Although separate quarters were built for the lay boarders, convent life inevitably changed in response to their presence. The nuns had to feed, house, and provide some companionship to adult boarders and to supervise and educate boarding girls. Chapter 6 concludes by attempting to assess the impact of these changes on the character of cloistered religious life.

Chapter 7 looks at the expansion of women's religious initiatives beyond the cloister. Focusing on the powerful impulse to charity that welled up with the increasingly difficult financial conditions of the 1630s, it examines the creation of new semireligious communities to nurse the sick poor, build asylums for orphans and endangered girls, and catechize children from the laboring classes. It also looks at the lay confraternity of the Dames de la Charité, which provided important services to the poor and also raised huge sums of money to help orphans and the victims of war. The institutions discussed here—the Filles de la Charité, Filles de la Croix, and Filles de la Providence, along with the Dames de la Charité—are closely associated with the work of Vincent de Paul. Indeed, he is frequently credited with their foundation, obscuring the work of the lay women who actually initiated, funded, organized, and directed the new institutions. This chapter attempts to bring these women out of Monsieur Vincent's long shadow and to illuminate the charitable impulse that animated their foundations, along with the social, economic, and institutional factors that determined the shape these institutions would ultimately take. As in earlier chapters, my focus is on the choices women made and the impact these choices had on their own lives and those around them. The story ends with the extraordinary efforts the elite members of the Dames de la Charité made to aid destitute victims of the Fronde, after which women's key role in the provision of charity declined in favor of repressive new public institutions directed by men.

I

Women in the New Jerusalem

In later life, Barbe Acarie was wont to reminisce about her experience in Paris during the six-year period when the city, having rebelled against its king, was dominated by the ultra-Catholic coalition of the Holy League. Referring specifically to the spring and summer of 1590, when the royal army of Henri de Navarre held Paris under siege, she called this period "a golden age, when people didn't think about eating or drinking but only about turning to God." "She had never been happier," she recalled, "or felt more contentment."[1]

Most people recalled the siege in very different terms. Memoirist Pierre de L'Estoile described a horrifying descent into famine and fear, a time when bones from the city's cemeteries were ground into flour to stretch the insufficient grain, when the poor ate the raw flesh of dead dogs they found in the streets or chewed on the hides of mules that had been sold for meat. L'Estoile even claimed that, two or three days before the siege was lifted, soldiers in the city, crazy with hunger, began to chase after little children in the streets and slaughtered and ate three of them. "This cruel and barbarous act was committed within the walls of Paris," he added; "such was the wrath of God that had descended upon us."[2]

If we listen to L'Estoile, as the siege progressed, people could think of little *except* food: How might they appease their starving bellies? In contrast to Barbe Acarie, who saw the mortification of the flesh induced by the conditions of scarcity as a spiritually rewarding by-product of the city's isolation, L'Estoile saw the deprivations produced by the siege as brutalizing and profane. He strongly condemned the "preachers of famine, as if religion consisted of dying of hunger," and memorably captured the twisted value system he attributed to the League's leaders in one soldier's blunt assertion that he would eat his only child rather than give in out of sheer necessity.[3]

One place where Pierre de L'Estoile and Barbe Acarie agreed was in interpreting the brutal wars as the sign of God's wrath. And yet L'Estoile and those who shared his royalist political sympathies and moderately Catholic religious views assumed that, with peace and the reconciliation of opposing factions, God's vengeance would cease. By contrast, for Acarie and those who shared her ultra-Catholic political and religious sensibilities, peace alone would not suffice. Rather, God required the ardent defense of the Roman Catholic Church, in which his unique truth resided. He further required that those who loved him humble themselves in abject repentance and work for their own moral reform and that of others. Those who heeded this call to penitence, thundered down from the pulpits of the League, came to be known as dévots. Long after the surrender of the League's political leaders in 1594, the dévots fought to make Catholic unity the keystone of French foreign and domestic policy. At the same time, they engaged more broadly in the project of Catholic renewal that is the subject of this book. If we are to understand the role that women played in the revival of Catholic institutions and spirituality that followed in the wake of the religious wars, we must begin by examining the impact of these wars on the devout women who took to heart the preachers' call to repent and, like Barbe Acarie, began to remake their inner and outer lives in keeping with their new understanding of spiritual truth.

This chapter attempts first to sketch out the new religiosity that pervaded Paris when the League held sway. I look briefly at the political authority commanded by the female members of the aristocratic Guise family that placed itself at the head of the League, then focus on the women who were to be intimately associated with the founding of the first new religious order for women in Paris, the Discalced Carmelites of Teresa of Avila's reform, in order to examine more concretely the impact of the League on women who helped initiate Paris's Catholic renewal. In doing so, I look not just at women who became nuns when the order was founded in 1604—the youngest of these were just girls when the League was vanquished from Paris ten years earlier—but also at the aristocratic women who lent financial and political support to the order's foundation. Several of these women can be shown to have played an unexpectedly important role in League affairs.

Other early supporters of the Carmelites were on the opposing side in the quarrels of the League. They were members of families loyal to the Crown and, as such, suffered persecution if they remained in Paris during the troubles. These women did not see the League as a golden age, any more than did Pierre de L'Estoile. The connection between League spirituality and Catholic renewal was thus not a simple and unilinear one. The processions of the League were not the only path to the cloisters of reformed Catholicism. We must look instead for more subtle commonalities of behavior and belief shared by women who sided with the League and those who opposed it.

The Holy City

The wars of the League were the climactic stage of more than thirty years of civil and religious war. Although France's kings remained loyal to the Catholic Church and actively tried to suppress the teachings of Martin Luther, which spread into the kingdom as early as 1518, an underground Protestant movement had escaped the control of king and courts to emerge in the 1550s as organized churches on the model of those established by Jean Calvin in Geneva.[4] As the Reformed churches grew, their members became increasingly militant, largely in response to the popular opposition they faced from Catholics, who, stirred up by preachers who condemned the Calvinists as heretics, heckled and even attacked suspected Protestants when they spotted them coming and going from their places of worship. The growing religious tensions fed into a political crisis when the unexpected death of King Henri II in 1559 allowed competing aristocratic factions to attempt to seize more power. Members of the house of Bourbon, who as the nearest cousins to the kings were considered the first princes of the blood, had been drawn to the new religion and styled themselves as protectors of the new Reformed churches. Their chief competitors, members of the house of Guise, took the opposite position and insisted on the need to suppress the Protestant heresy. A younger branch of the family that ruled the independent duchy of Lorraine, the Guises had won a privileged position at court through royal favor. Unable to demand a share of royal power on account of birth alone, they nevertheless had built a strong following among nobles who benefited from the patronage they commanded.

Caught between the opposing pressures of the Bourbons and the Guises, Henri II's widow, Catherine de Medici, sought to maintain royal authority for her three young sons, who came to the throne successively between 1559 and 1574. Catherine's initial impulse was to seek a middle ground, in the hope that religious authorities might work out terms of compromise that would allow France to return to a unified faith. To this end, she authorized limited freedom of worship for members of the Reformed church. The strategy proved disastrous. Protestants seized the opportunity to preach more openly, and church membership mushroomed. At the same time, ardent Catholics became more violent in their persecution of suspected heretics. The situation dissolved into civil war in March 1562, when soldiers of the duc de Guise attacked a group of Huguenots (as French Protestants had come to be called) gathered for worship in a barn adjacent to a Guise estate. Catherine was unwilling to take the risk of vigorously defending the Huguenots, who remained a small minority of the population despite their recent growth and whose escalating demands for toleration and the punishment of their enemies she found importunate. Reluctantly and still hoping to negotiate a peace, she brought the royal family into the war on the Catholic side.

The eight Wars of Religion that took place before peace was finally made with the Edict of Nantes in 1598 are complex, with an awkward, three-sided nature. Faced with the Huguenots' demand for recognition and the right to worship, French Catholics divided. The royal family, although Catholic, found itself consistently outflanked by more ardently Catholic leaders, foremost among them members of the house of Guise, who enjoyed the support of a large noble clientele and also of Catholic commoners from the middle and popular classes. While Catherine and her sons, although sincerely believing that the Reformed faith was erroneous and even heretical, continued to think that allowing Huguenots some measure of religious toleration was a necessary expedient to bring the country peace, more radical Catholic leaders insisted that the Huguenots should be brought to utter defeat and those who refused to recant their heresy forced to flee the kingdom.

This was the predicament Catherine's third son faced when he ascended the throne as King Henri III in 1574. The most pious of the sons, Henri III had been made nominal head of the Catholic armies during the third and fourth civil wars and was credited with several key victories. Militant Catholics, who hoped that his accession would lead to more vigorous prosecution of the campaign to end Protestantism in France, were disappointed when he adopted his mother's moderate policies. Popular as a prince, he came to be scorned as an effeminate weakling of a king. In 1576 an ultra-Catholic League took shape among discontented nobles who promised to destroy the Huguenots themselves if the monarch would not or could not effect the destruction of heresy in his kingdom.[5] Henri III attempted to ward off this challenge to his authority by declaring that he shared the aims of the League and placing himself at the head of the association. He succeeded only in gaining time.

Temporarily muted, the organization sprang back to life in 1584, when the king's younger brother and heir died, leaving the Protestant prince Henri de Bourbon, king of Navarre, as the legitimate heir to the French throne. The prospect of a Protestant king was totally unacceptable to ardent Catholics, who insisted that Navarre's religion made him ineligible to rule. The fact that Henri de Navarre had become the Protestants' chief military leader made the ultra-Catholics' anger more volatile still. When Henri III refused to exclude Navarre from the succession and instead sent an envoy to try to convince him to convert to the Catholic faith, the Guises began to organize a new Catholic League, the Holy Union. They even gained financial support for their cause from Philip II, the ardently Catholic king of Spain.

While the Guises raised an army and rallied aristocrats to the Holy League, urban leagues formed in a number of French cities, Paris foremost among them. The social and political program that emerged from the urban leagues came to differ from, and even conflict with, the aims of the aristocrats. In 1585, however, the League's lack of unity was less evident than the danger that an ultra-Catholic alliance posed for the king, whose authority was simultaneously threatened from the other direction by the growing number of moderate Catholics willing to ally with the Huguenots and accept religious toleration as a necessary price for peace. Bowing to necessity, Henri III signed a treaty with the League's leaders promising to lead a war for the extermination of heresy and, revoking previous concessions, ordered Protestants to return to the Catholic faith. Once again war broke out, with the king uncomfortably allied with more radical Catholics.

At the outset of the war, Henri III secretly strategized to cripple the League at the same time that he defeated the Huguenots. He sent the duc de Guise's Leaguer army to fight the German mercenaries arriving to aid the Huguenot cause and used the royal army to take on the presumably weaker Huguenot force. His calculations proved wrong. The duc de Guise triumphed against the German mercenaries, but the royal army lost to Henri de Navarre. Guise's victory only added to the favor he enjoyed with Catholic Parisians. Fearing the duke's growing popularity and the enthusiasm for the Holy League in Paris, Henri III forbade him to come to the city. When he learned that Guise planned to come anyway, the king brought in troops to maintain order. The move only served to prompt a revolt among angry Parisians. Unable to regain order, Henri III fled his capital in May 1588. In July, he capitulated to the power of the Guises and signed an edict reconfirming his alliance with the Holy Union and his determination to extirpate heresy. At the same time, he rewarded the duke and his allies with titles and offices and other favors. Secretly, he must have been seething. In December 1588, he sought revenge, ordering the duc de Guise and his brother, the cardinal de Guise, seized and summarily executed at the royal palace of Blois.

If Henri III thought that ridding himself of the duc and cardinal de Guise would solve his problems, he was badly mistaken. Guise kinsmen took over leadership of the Holy Union, while news of the deaths sent Leaguer cities into open and violent revolt. In Paris, ultra-Catholic preachers denounced the king as a tyrant, and the urban League's radical leaders raised troops to wage war against him. The Leaguers used their new authority to imprison and extort money from anyone who did not appear sufficiently supportive of their cause. Their revolt soon took on a religious dimension as well. A wave of penitential and apocalyptic piety swept over the city, and for several months, the rituals of daily life gave way to an endless round of religious services, sermons, and processions to invoke God's aid and implore his mercy. Parisians simultaneously lived out their fear of God's judgment and their conviction that they had entered into a new age, where redemption might still be possible for those who humbled themselves in accordance with God's plan.

Mourning for the "martyred" duke and cardinal took on overtones of a popular religious cult, as church after church commemorated their passing with prayer vigils and requiem masses.[6] Tolling bells drew mourning Parisians to the commemorative chapels and black-draped churches from whose pulpits ultra-Catholic preachers denounced the king's iniquity and declared him to be the agent of Satan. On more than one occasion, funeral rites for the Guises spilled out of the churches and into the streets in candlelight processions. When the duc de Guise's widow delivered a son, the infant's baptism was celebrated with an elaborate ceremony that included a formal procession through streets lined with mourning crowds. The city's highest officers stood as godfather to the child. Afterward, they hosted a reception at the Hôtel de Ville, while cannons and guns arrayed in the square outside pierced the joyous din of trumpets and drums with their salutes. After the festivities, the proud godfathers carried the child back to his mother, who had remained at home, still unchurched after giving birth. In the days that followed, Parisian ladies and bourgeoises lined up to pay Madame de Guise the ritual calls that followed childbirth, further cementing the bond between the city and its chosen family.[7]

The public baptismal rites helped fill the emotional need for dynastic continuity normally experienced after the death of a king but now, with the repudiation of Henri III, displaced onto the Guises. The joyous welcome Parisians extended to other members of the Guise family arriving in Paris served the same function. Two days after the baptism, the city sent a delegation some three hundred strong to greet Madame de Montpensier and Madame de Mayenne, the sister and sister-in-law, respectively, of the deceased duke and cardinal of Guise, on their entry into Paris. The arrival two days later of Madame de Nemours, the mother of the deceased, was greeted with special joy, as she had been imprisoned at the time of her sons' deaths.[8] The women of the Guise family, especially Madame de Montpensier and Madame de Nemours, were to assume important political roles in Paris during the League. A warm welcome was also given Charles, duc de Mayenne, the younger brother of the slain duc de Guise and the leader of the Catholic princes on his death, when he arrived in Paris several weeks later. Marks of the city's affection for the Guises, these ceremonies must also be seen as public occasions that provided reassurance and stimulated the loyalties of Parisians faced with the daunting prospect of making war against their king.

Mourning for the princes slain at Blois was closely tied up with other, even more explicitly religious dimensions of Parisian behavior during the first months of the League's revolt. A wave of penitential piety manifested itself both in endless processions to appeal to God's mercy and in serious, if inconsistent, attempts to reform social conduct and morality. The role of the Guises' murders in awakening these new emotions and patterns of behavior is explicitly stated in one pamphlet, which clearly identifies the many processions that took place in the city, the abandonment of luxury and reform of behavior, and the multiple funerals that were held for the Guises as three manifestations of one and the same anguish.[9] On 10 January 1589, boys and girls from all over the city assembled at the cemetery of the Saints-Innocents to parade, candles in hand, to the church of Sainte-Geneviève-du-Mont, where, according to one chronicler, they knelt in groups before the altar and cried out three times for mercy. Another chronicler describes how, outside the church, the children threw down their candles and stomped them out as a sign of the king's excommunication.[10] Toward the end of the month these events became frequent and adults joined in.

Beginning on 24 January and continuing for the next three months, the chronicler known only as François makes almost daily mention of processions orchestrated by various Parisian parishes. Instead of being celebrated with the usual masquerades and partying, the Carnival season that preceded Lent was marked by an intensification of the processional activity. Participants in one procession are said to have carried "all of the instruments and implements with which our Lord was afflicted in his passion."[11] The penitential nature of these processions was further emphasized by the fact that the processions were often held at night and participants were frequently described as being barefoot and dressed only in light penitential shifts, despite the damp chill of the Parisian winter. Indeed, one chronicler recorded that participants had to wade through as much as a foot of snow. The parish processions clearly had a spontaneity that welled up from the powerful emotions provoked by the assassination of the Guises.[12]

The attempt to reform morality also had a popular base or, at the very least, resonated with popular emotions; it was not simply imposed from above. Even before the penitential processions and funeral services for the Guises began, people interpreted the calamity at Blois as a sign of divine judgment that required moral rearmament: repentance and a return to true devotion. The chronicler François noted that, from the moment the news of the murders at Blois arrived, "everyone turned to prayer to appease the wrath of God, and some fasted two, three, or four times a week and others all week long—including one or two days on bread and water alone—by order of their preachers and curates, who at the same time forbade feasts and banqueting of any sort, so that the money they would have spent could be used instead for the defense of the Catholic faith."[13] People also conformed to a new moral code by dramatically altering their mode of dress. Established and aspiring elites set aside their rich fabrics and elaborate fashions, believing that they reeked of the sin of pride, in favor of more modest and self-effacing garb. One pamphlet, noting that Parisian women had banished superfluous luxury from their dress and traded silk and cloth of gold for simple woollen fabrics, even suggested that women were censuring their peers by ripping off frills that violated the new standard of sober simplicity.[14]

Appeals to women to abandon "excessive vanity" and "dissolute" dress for more modest apparel predate the League. Minim Antoine Estienne first published his *Remonstrance charitable aux dames et demoyselles de France sur leurs ornemens dissolus* in 1570. The tract was ahead of its time in that it specifically connected women's immodesty to religious schism, dangerous times, and the wrath of God. Estienne warned Christian women against inciting God's fury through their search for novelty in their clothing and ornaments. Pointing to the recent civil wars, he reminded his readers that the times remained perilous; rebels and heretics continued to plot against the king. And he assigned to women a traditional, biblical role in urging them to lead a movement of national repentance. Streak your face with ashes instead of painting it with cosmetics, he advised; wear sackcloth and hair shirts instead of fine linen and silk; and prostrate yourselves in repentance to appease an angry God.[15] When Estienne first published his *Remonstrance*, it fell largely on deaf ears. We know that Marie Du Drac listened and even followed the advice, and yet the shocked reaction of her relatives when she ceased to wear clothing they considered appropriate to her status suggests that most people were not yet receptive to this call for moral reform.[16] That the *Remonstrance* went through three more editions by 1585 suggests that a willingness to listen became a will to action only under the emotional pressures of the League.

The processions of white-robed penitents that had become an almost daily occurrence during the first three months of 1589 faded from the scene after Easter was celebrated on 2 April. The emotions of the previous months were too intense to be maintained.[17] A mood of heightened religious sensibility nevertheless persisted through the entire period of League domination. When a Dominican monk avenged the death of the Guises by assassinating Henri III in August 1589, joy in Paris was unrestrained. League preachers celebrated the assassin, who was quickly killed by the king's guard, as a holy martyr. They compared him to Judith, who had crept into the enemy camp to deliver her kingdom from tyranny, and interpreted the king's murder as a mark of God's providence and sign of his favor.[18] In doing so, they helped muster resistance to Henri de Navarre, who claimed the throne as Henri IV and sought to induce the rebel League to surrender.

Waves of particularly intense devotion continued to recur at moments of crisis in the city's defense. Not surprisingly, the six-month period in 1590 when Navarre's army held Paris under siege saw a dramatic upsurge in processional activity. The siege began in March, after Navarre defeated the Leaguer forces outside Paris, but it became truly alarming two months later, when Navarre's army tightened its hold on the capital by occupying the suburbs that lay outside the city walls. Crowded with refugees—many of whom turned to begging, having lost all other means of livelihood—and denied access to the daily provisioning that was its lifeline, Paris began to feel the pinch of famine.

The most famous procession of the League, one depicted in several paintings that show helmeted friars awkwardly hoisting muskets as they parade through city streets, took place on 14 May 1590 and was clearly intended to reassure the populace. Two weeks later, on Ascension Day, a general procession involving all of the city's parishes and religious houses was made to the cathedral of Notre-Dame. The procession climaxed with the League's leaders kneeling at the cathedral's high altar to renew their oath to give all they possessed, including their lives, to protect the Catholic Church, Paris, and other cities of the Holy Union. Reiterating that they would rather die than give their allegiance to the king of Navarre, the League's leaders administered the same oath to the attending crowd.[19]

While Parisians waited day after day for rescue, officials took increasingly desperate steps to feed the poor and the soldiers charged with the city's defense. The great belly of Paris had to be kept at least minimally fed to prevent internal unrest from sapping the will to resist Henri de Navarre's army.[20] Bread was adulterated with the by-products of tallow candle making and of rapeseed pressed for oil.[21] When the bread gave out, a weak gruel was made of bran and water to serve to the poor. As crops ripened in the fields outside the city walls, people risked their lives in desperate sorties to gather food. Church treasures were melted down to buy food to keep the soldiers from deserting, but the real problem was the scarcity of food at any price. Even wealthy elites suffered from the shortages. In late July, people were asked to sacrifice their pet cats and dogs, which were boiled with a few pot herbs in the soup served to the poor.[22] No one would have believed that the city could hold out yet another month.

The less there was to eat, the more the authorities relied on sermons and religious observances to keep up morale. Forty-hour prayers were begun in several parishes simultaneously and picked up in relays by other churches, so as to continue around the clock for a week. A papal legate visiting the city announced a jubilee with plenary remission of sins for those who would make a round of specified churches to pray for God's aid and deliverance from the siege. On 17 July, a children's procession from the Saints-Innocents to Sainte-Geneviève mirrored the first penitential procession of January 1589. As on that earlier occasion, after mass at the abbey church of Sainte-Geneviève and a sermon at the neighboring church of Saint-Étienne-du-Mont, the ceremony climaxed with the children prostrating themselves and crying out loudly for God's mercy.[23]

The processions continued into the final month of the siege. L'Estoile mentions a "great procession" held on 1 August and another on the thirtieth of that month, the day the siege was raised. Certain they could not have held out for another day, Parisians thanked God for their deliverance. Processional activity naturally died down after the end of the siege but resumed in February 1591, when the city of Chartres was similarly threatened. In 1592 the siege of Rouen inspired processions, as did the general gravity of the war effort. In 1593 processions and forty-hour prayers were organized on behalf of a solemn meeting of the Estates General called by the League. And in each of the years of League power, the day when Henri III had been driven from his capital was commemorated with a general procession.[24]

It is tempting to regard the increased pace of devotional activities in moments of crisis as a deliberate ploy on the part of city authorities to distract people from their misery—to offer circuses when they could not offer bread. But the religious activities of the League cannot be reduced to artificially induced, propagandistic attempts at social control. Contemporary observers uniformly interpreted the heightened religiosity as a direct and natural consequence of fear and suffering. For many people, the acts of piety gave meaning to, and thereby made bearable, what seemed otherwise unbearable catastrophe. The religious activities of the League brought together disparate social groups. One chronicler wrote admiringly of the "continual processions in which one might see the children of noble families and rich houses, as well as a crowd of other people, who, barefoot, took part while singing litanies."[25] This was a result of shared trauma and not of a strategy deliberately adopted by city authorities.

The same chronicler who admired the social unity the processions produced calls attention to the way the new forms of Counter-Reformation piety were incorporated into the religiosity of the League. He noted in particular the use of forty-hour prayers popularized in France by a new order of reformed Franciscans called the Capuchins and commented that they were continued "not just for forty hours, but for an entire week, during which the Blessed Sacrament was paraded around the church, when it was not being adored on the altar; these prayers and supplications continued night and day, which was greatly encouraging for everyone." From this perspective, the piety of the League was characterized not, as it has often been portrayed, by hysterically ranting preachers stirring their listeners to a fevered pitch, but by sincere demonstrations of penitence in which an entire community took part. That is what the same commentator had in mind when he concluded that "all of these demonstrations denoted a singularly true piety, which certainly did more for the defense of the city than the inhabitants' armaments, such as they were."[26]

Certainly Catholic preaching played a key role in spreading news, keeping up morale, and enforcing certain codes of behavior during the wars of the League. The religious enthusiasm—the vision of a Holy Jerusalem—that pervaded Leaguer Paris cannot, however, be reduced to a transitory hallucination induced by propagandistic ravings of fanatical preachers. Popular response to the preachers had deep roots in a traditional spirituality resonant with the immanence of a judgmental God. Paris's religious leaders built on an old, communal economy of salvation when they brought people into the streets to parade their penitence and beg for divine mercy. At the same time, they intensified the personal and individual dimensions of repentance by focusing worship on Christ's sacrifice—on his passion and presence in the Eucharist. In doing so, they introduced or popularized practices usually associated with the Catholic Reformation, thereby blurring the lines between old and new, between Counter-Reformation and Catholic Reformation, and between a postwar Catholic revival and more continuous, progressive change. In doing so, they imparted to French Catholicism a character that marked it for half a century to come.

For many people, the forms of worship practiced during the League, although sincerely embraced, were too intense to endure for long. We must imagine that, however enthusiastically they participated at the time, they returned with a sigh of relief to less emotionally charged religious practices when the League had passed. For others, however, the emotional intensity of Leaguer worship had a more lasting attraction. It is in this sense that we must understand Barbe Acarie's nostalgic recollection of the League as a "golden age," a time when spiritual preoccupations triumphed over the mundane realities of daily life. And yet Acarie's comment that "she had never been happier or felt more contentment" than during the League may have had other roots as well. In moments of crisis, gender boundaries tend to become more fluid, widening the gap that inevitably exists between prescribed roles and actual behavior. Wartime conditions in particular offer women opportunities for independent action and initiative they seldom enjoy during more settled times. If the experience of the League ignited a passion for moral reform and spiritual regeneration in some pious women, it also fostered the administrative skills and capacity for independent judgment that allowed them to take a leading role in the postwar religious revival.

Women and the Holy League

In even the most traditional histories of the Paris League, the women of the Guise family play an important role. Catherine de Clèves, the widow of Henri, duc de Guise, spent most of the period of the League in Paris, where she served as a symbol and rallying point for the rebellion.[27] Her mother-in-law, Anne d'Este, duchesse de Nemours (the widow by a previous marriage of François, duc de Guise, and mother of the murdered Henri, duc de Guise, and his brother the cardinal), played an even more prominent role in League politics. Arrested in December 1588 when her sons were assassinated by order of the king, she was released the following month and moved into Paris for the duration of the troubles.[28] While her second son, Charles, duc de Mayenne, officially assumed leadership of the ultra-Catholic faction on his brother's death, the duchesse de Nemours played an important part in financing the League, popularizing its policies within Paris, and transmitting information about the situation in Paris to Mayenne when, as was often the case, his military operations required him to leave the capital. Judging from the frequency with which she was consulted by the radical leaders of the Paris League, she also had considerable authority to make policy decisions in Mayenne's absence.[29]

But it was Catherine de Guise, duchesse de Montpensier, the daughter of Anne d'Este and sister of the duke and cardinal assassinated at Blois, who was the most audacious supporter of the Holy Union among the Guise women. Known to be secretly sending funds to the most radical preachers in Paris, she encouraged inflammatory preaching and malicious pamphleteering against both Henri III and his successor, Henri de Navarre.[30] According to L'Estoile, just four days before he was killed on 1 August 1589, Henri III sent an envoy to Madame de Montpensier to tell her that he was well aware that she was the one "who was sustaining and supporting the people of Paris in their rebellion; but that, if he ever succeeded in retaking the city, as he hoped shortly to do, he would have her burned alive." "Fire is for sodomites like [you], and not for the likes of me," she boldly retorted, further fueling rumors about Henri's sexual proclivities. "In any event, he could be sure that she would do her best to prevent him from entering the city."[31] On learning of the king's death, she and her mother climbed into their carriage and paraded through the streets of Paris crying out, "Good news, my friends! Good news! The tyrant is dead!" By L'Estoile's report, Madame de Nemours even climbed the steps to the high altar at the Cordeliers' church and "harangued the people about the death of the tyrant."[32]

In L'Estoile's opinion, this act displayed "a great immodesty and female impotence, that she should continue to gnaw on one who was dead." L'Estoile's disapproval reflects not only his anti-League sentiments but also the misogyny typical of his age. For Madame de Nemours to speak publicly, and from the altar of a church, was to his mind both unseemly and pointless. He criticized her for displaying in public a satisfaction that, as a woman, she should have kept private. At the same time, unwilling to admit that this public harangue might have stirred a popular response, he dismissed it—because it came from a woman—as a display of powerlessness. The sexual slurs evident in anti-League pamphlets and graffiti directed against Guise women, in particular Madame de Montpensier, also show a strongly misogynistic strain. Whether caricatured on a wall as a naked woman being mounted by a mule bearing the name of the papal legate or satirized in a mock confession as having "thought to make a great sacrifice to God by offering up her private parts to advance the affairs of the League," Madame de Montpensier was belittled by the League's opponents.[33]

If the contributions of these important noblewomen were disparaged by sexual innuendo and accusations of an unfeminine meddling in the public realm, the contributions of less prominent women to the League were most often ignored entirely, making it difficult to reconstruct the role they played. Take Madeleine Luillier, dame de Sainte-Beuve, who was later to found the

Ursuline order in Paris along with her cousin Barbe Acarie. Referring to her as "la Sainte Veuve," L'Estoile suggests that she took part in the processions of the League more out of coquetry than piety. He describes her "covered only in a fine linen shift cut low at the neck," allowing herself to be flirted with and led by the elbow through the church of Saint-Jean-en-Grève by the chevalier d'Aumale, one of the more rakish members of the Guise clan, "to the great scandal of the truly devout people who took part in good faith in these processions." L'Estoile also contrasts Madeleine Luillier unfavorably with the well-bred wives of magistrates imprisoned in the Bastille for their suspected royalist sympathies during the spring of 1589. While the latter fasted during the Lenten season, he notes, la Sainte Veuve gave banquets and magnificent parties for the League aristocracy and openly mocked the royalist wives (many of whom must have been her kinswomen) by saying that she took "a singular pleasure in seeing these mud-encrusted ladies go to the Bastille to mend the breeches of their husbands."[34]

Only a copy of a letter written by Madeleine Luillier's stepbrother, Antoine Hennequin d'Assy, a president in Parlement and a committed Leaguer, shows the more serious role that this rich young widow played in helping to raise money to finance the League. Writing to the duc de Mayenne in March 1589, the day after League forces suffered a crushing defeat at Senlis, Hennequin appealed to Mayenne to return to Paris to reassure the populace by his presence. He warned him that the propaganda efforts of the duchesse de Montpensier had lost credibility with the new defeat and that it was becoming more and more difficult to raise money for the cause. "My sister, Madame de Sainte-Beuve, is seeking to borrow money everywhere for this most pressing affair," he wrote, "but she cannot find any, because they say that she is already sufficiently and even too greatly indebted for your sake."[35]

Madeleine Luillier was not the only wealthy Parisian woman who helped raise money for the League. Her cousin Barbe Acarie appears to have been deeply involved in her husband Pierre Acarie's attempts to provide funds for the wars of the League. Both husband and wife mortgaged their properties heavily to contribute to the cause.[36] Moreover, Barbe Acarie seems to have assisted her husband in the financial arrangements he negotiated with the Paris Carthusians, who lent their name to cover large sums of money borrowed for the wars of League.[37] Because early modern legal conventions obscure married women's participation in financial affairs by putting all transactions under the name and authority of the husband, it is impossible to exactly determine Barbe Acarie's fund-raising role, but whatever part she played can be viewed as an extension of her domestic role and responsibilities.[38] The same is true of her role after the League, when she acted to repair the family's finances and secure the return of properties confiscated because of her husband's involvement with the radical faction in the League. In both cases, she acted on her husband's behalf and as his agent. There can be no question, however, that she wholeheartedly supported the League, and her other activities on behalf of the Catholic Union give us a better view of her temperament and initiative.

The testimony for her beatification proceedings gives ample evidence of the enthusiasm with which Barbe Acarie took part in the public displays of piety encouraged by the League, aided poorer neighbors in surviving the deprivations brought on by the siege, and nursed wounded soldiers brought in from the League's battles. She experienced—or at least remembered—the five months during which Paris was held captive by the army of Henri IV as a period of spiritual exaltation. Along with other women from her parish, she was an ardent participant in the era's many religious processions and fervently prayed that these marks of popular devotion might "appease the wrath of God and avert the great misfortunes with which the state was menaced."[39] She did more than most women of her station to help the poor survive the famine caused by the siege. Learning that, like most wealthy people, her mother-in-law, Marguerite Lottin, was hiding the family's store of grain so that it would not be confiscated and redistributed to aid the poor, Acarie is reported to have threatened to give the secret away if Lottin did not give up a generous portion to send to those who were dying of starvation. Wishing to share in the common suffering, she also set aside as much as possible of her own bread and traded it for the inferior, adulterated loaves that were being distributed to the poor.[40]

Most important was her service caring for wounded soldiers and the poor. After the defeat of the League army at Senlis in May 1589, thousands of injured soldiers were brought into Paris, even though the city's hospitals were poorly equipped to care for them. Acarie was one of the first to volunteer to help. She is said to have gone daily to the nearby hospital of Saint-Gervais to bring the patients nourishing broths and healing unguents that she made herself. She also helped clean their wounds and change bandages. In addition to assisting the soldiers with their physical ailments, she had a spiritual mission to those who were dying. Crucifix in hand, she brought them words of comfort, urged them to make final confessions, and helped them through the terrors of death, developing such a reputation that a great many soldiers asked to have her at their side when they died.[41]

Several witnesses pointed out that it was not easy for this good bourgeoise to conquer the repugnance she initially experienced on entering the dirty and chaotic hospital, where the sick and wounded were crowded several to a bed. She had to force herself to remove the soldiers' filthy bandages and clean their putrid sores, and yet she continued after this crisis to help tend poor patients in the Hôtel-Dieu.[42] One witness credited Acarie with having been the first woman of her station to undertake the sort of charitable work later systematized and extended by Louise de Marillac and Vincent de Paul with the organization of the Dames de Charité. This may be an exaggeration, but if Acarie was not the first well-born Parisian woman to volunteer her time and service in Paris hospitals, she nevertheless served as a model for others who followed her in this work.[43]

The most important thing in Acarie's charitable work is its connection with the particular spiritual and emotional climate engendered by the League. What became a classic form of charitable service for upper-middle-class women began as both a religious exercise and a way of helping during a time of serious crisis. The extreme circumstances of the League, and particularly of the siege of 1590, provided unusual opportunities for women to play a public role in religion and politics, which in this case were identical. It is thus not a surprise that women like Barbe Acarie should have found the period liberating—a golden age—much as do participants in revolutions or great social movements, even if they fail to achieve their objectives in the end. At the same time, such events generate enormous physical and psychic tensions. With League preachers calling out daily the need for atonement, might not these tensions have found one outlet in mystical raptures?

In the case of Barbe Acarie, the charitable and managerial activities in which she took part during the League clearly were accompanied by a deepening and interiorizing of her spirituality. Her first mystical trance, in which she lost consciousness for hours while praying in the family's chapel in her parish church of Saint-Gervais, appears to have taken place in the summer of 1590, just about the time that the siege of Paris was lifted. During the next two years, such mystical experiences occurred with increasing frequency. She is said to have experienced at least one trance while taking part in a procession with women of her parish, and in 1593 she received invisible stigmata.[44] An even more explicit connection between the emotional anguish provoked by the League and a religious awakening is evident in the spiritual autobiography of Marie Sévin, one of the first French Carmelites. Although written years later at the command of her confessor, Sévin's autobiography nevertheless conveys the heady atmosphere of apocalyptic piety that dominated in Paris during the initial stages of the League. The daughter of a president of France's highest tax court, Marie Sévin was just nineteen when the radical League tightened its control over Paris in 1589. Swept up in the common enthusiasm, she modified her behavior dramatically in response to the demand for penitence that thundered down from the pulpits of the League. This is how she described her sentiments in 1589:

> Along with most of the Catholics then in Paris, I tried to do what I could to appease heaven's wrath, which appeared openly in the disorders of the war that began in 1589. In a dream I saw France all in flames, and then I saw that fire put out. . . . During this time, I abandoned all that was worldly; I sold some jewels that I had in order to give the money to the poor; I dressed very modestly. I resolved to become a nun, but circumstances didn't allow me to put

this into execution as yet. I did all the penitential acts that I could, and in these exercises the Lord gave me more strength than nature could possibly have done. I didn't find anything difficult. The example of a God who had endured so much for me gave me a continual and very fervent desire to suffer for his glory, even though I believed that I was infinitely unworthy. It seemed to me that I didn't want to ask to suffer, but rather that I offered myself entirely. My heart, penetrated with a pure love for Jesus Christ, seemed to yearn for martyrdom.[45]

The exaltation that Sévin experienced at this time comes through with particular force in her repeated insistence on this wish to suffer with and for Christ. Transfixed by the apparent threat that the war posed to the Catholic faith and detesting the very notion of a heretic king, she felt within herself a powerful urge "to appear before the kings, magistrates, and people, and to speak out in their presence for the defense of Jesus Christ and his church." Recklessly confident that even the harshest measures could not dissuade her from making her stand, she was convinced that "God would make [her] worthy of dying to attest to his glory, because he formed in [her] this vehement desire for martyrdom."[46]

Marie Sévin did not speak out publicly on behalf of the League. Had she done so, she would likely have been taunted for an unfeminine lack of decorum. She did, however, defy the usual limits on female behavior by insisting that her family, which did not share her enthusiasm for the League, leave her behind in Paris when they took refuge in the royalist city of Tours. Like many other families from the Parisian magistracy, they had become alarmed by the growing persecution of individuals perceived to be insufficiently supportive of the League and decided to flee to safer ground. Refusing to accompany them, Sévin insisted that if forced to leave she would speak out so loudly against heresy that she would soon be martyred for her faith. "My resolution surprised them," she recounts, "and, fearing that it would cause me to speak out too freely on this subject, they decided to leave me alone with some servants in the house."[47]

By Sévin's account, the powerful desire to devote herself to God alone lasted for "the four or five years that the troubles of war lasted in France." Regarding as providential the unexpected liberty provided by her family's absence, she gave herself over entirely to devotional exercises and interrupted her newfound solitude only to go to church for mass or sermons or to take part in religious processions. She took communion frequently—daily when possible, but at least four or five times a week—and felt a particular bond with the "sacred humanity of Jesus Christ." She recounts that, in receiving the Eucharist, she had no sensation of the accidents of the bread but rather experienced an inexplicable pulse of joy and spiritual satisfaction. Elsewhere she compares the force of the divine love that embraced her to "an impetuous wind and a devouring fire." "I was entirely occupied with God," she recorded, "and belonged more to him than to myself. Nothing touched me so much as his glory and the salvation of souls."[48]

In time, however, Sévin's spiritual satisfaction began to fade. Although she provides few indications of a parallel dissatisfaction with the politics of the League, it is clear that the two phenomena were not unrelated. The period of spiritual aridity that she experienced as a growing distance from God—a cooling of his love and privation of his grace—is linked to the winding down of the political crisis as Henri de Navarre began to speak of conversion. When her mother and sister came to Paris to urge her once again to join them in Tours, she accompanied them without fuss. Once at Tours, she discovered that the royalists, "those who followed the court," were indeed good Catholics, and she was consoled to learn that there was "much piety and devotion" among these people whom she previously had scorned.[49]

Marie Sévin recorded these experiences years later, when she was ending a long career distinguished by both her admirable personal piety and the administrative skills she displayed as the founding prioress of nine Carmelite convents. There can be little doubt, however, that the spiritual awakening she experienced at the time of the League contributed in no small measure to her determination several years later to escape from the worldly pleasures of Parisian society to the quiet cloisters of a reformed religious order where, through penitence and prayer, she might once again seek the inexplicable joys of total union with God.

On first consideration, the lives of devoutly Catholic women who opposed the League appear very different from the lives of women who supported it.[50] Yet there was a commonality: their experience of extreme conditions. To the extent that the sources reveal them at all, female opponents of the League in Paris endured constant worry, privation, and harassment, sometimes outright persecution, at the hands of the League leaders and their enthusiastic supporters. Often left behind to protect the family's property from confiscation or pillage while their husband sought refuge in royalist cities, they not only had to endure the same privations as other Parisians, but they also had to cope with public animosity that was vented in the streets and in shops, at city hall, and even in their parish churches. They were subjected to punitive taxation, summary confiscations, and even being arrested and held for ransom on trumped up charges.[51]

Among the women later associated with France's Catholic revival, the one most dramatically persecuted by the League is Catherine d'Orléans de Longueville, the princess in whose name and by whose generosity the Carmelite order was officially founded in France. Along with her mother, the dowager duchesse de Longueville, her sister-in-law, Catherine de Gonzague de Nevers (the young duchesse de Longueville), and her sisters Eléonore and Marguerite, Catherine d'Orléans was held prisoner in the town of Amiens for more than three years beginning in December 1588. Having traveled to Amiens for the formal entry of the young duc de Longueville, recently named governor of the province of Picardy, the women and the duke's younger brother, the comte de Saint-Paul, stayed on to celebrate the Christmas holidays, while the duke went off to visit his new province. Word of the deaths of the duke and cardinal of Guise and the arrest of their nearest allies reached Amiens on the day after Christmas, and the townspeople, inflamed by a sermon preached on behalf of the Guises, insisted on holding the Longueville women and the comte de Saint-Paul as hostages to exchange against the liberty of those arrested at Blois. City officials and members of the bourgeoisie invited to attend the city's deliberations decided that they would swap their hostages for no less a person than Charles de Guise, the young son of the martyred duke and a new figurehead of the Guisard movement, and they clung to this decision in the face of every attempt on the part of League leaders to arrange other exchanges.[52]

Because of their high station, the Longueville women were imprisoned in a private house and not the city jail. For several months they were allowed to go outside during the daytime, but they were increasingly restricted for fear they would escape. The comte de Saint-Paul was separated from them, but the others were allowed to remain together, at least until October 1589, when, following an attempted escape on the part of the dowager duchess, they were separated and prevented from seeing one another. It is not clear why the duchess's daughters and daughter-in-law, all in their teens or early twenties and apparently in good health, did not try to escape along with her. Perhaps they thought it was too risky for all to attempt to leave at once. Whatever their reasons for staying behind, surely they were crushed to learn of the humiliating conditions under which the duchess was returned to Amiens after her capture in a nearby town. People came from near and far to scream insults, throw filth, and dance around the cart in which she was carried. One of the men who had helped her to escape was beaten to death in the city streets; another was rescued just short of death and imprisoned. The duchess herself was threatened with sword thrusts and forced to take the barrel of a loaded pistol into her mouth before the authorities rescued her from the cart. She fell into a serious illness shortly after her return, but still her daughters and daughter-in-law were kept from her.[53]

The women experienced other difficulties during their imprisonment. City records are filled with discussions of forced loans and ransoms that might be extracted from them. Possible exchanges of prisoners were repeatedly suggested, but after each discussion the city decided simply to guard its prizes still more carefully and swap them only for the young duc de Guise and his cousin, the duc d'Elbeuf. For reasons of security, the duchess's entourage was repeatedly cut back, and communications with the outside world were strictly limited. Guards were replaced often so that the women would not have the opportunity to suborn them. As time passed, freedom appeared no closer. By August 1591, the city's bad faith was evident. Despite a letter from Charles, duc de Guise, announcing his own liberty and asking that the Longueville women be freed in return, no action was taken. Rather, the city insisted that the women be retained until the duc d'Elbeuf was liberated. Several days later the city added a new condition: they were to be traded against *both* Elbeuf and the vicomte de Tavannes and to pay a ransom to aid in freeing Elbeuf. Once again negotiations dragged on. Changes in the political scene made city officials even more reluctant to give up their captives. In November 1591, Henri de Navarre was marching toward Amiens with his army, and possession of these important noblewomen was thought to offer a possible means of dissuading him from an all-out attack. By January 1592, this crisis had passed. The city now proposed holding the women until the siege of Rouen was successfully completed.[54]

By this time even Mayenne, who had come to Amiens with other Catholic leaders, had lost patience. He summoned the mayor to the bishop's palace and told him in no uncertain terms that he intended to take the Longueville women with him when he left Amiens the following morning. The city's attempt at remonstrances was cut off. City representatives were informed that the women had agreed to pay an indemnity against the freedom of Elbeuf and Tavannes, and the matter was—at last—taken out of the city's hands.[55]

Although we have little insight into what Catherine d'Orléans was thinking or doing throughout, there is reason to believe that her isolation and imprisonment contributed to the cultivation of the piety that had already caused her and her sister Marguerite to reject all suitors and insist that they wanted no husband but Jesus Christ. Certainly all of the Longueville women were upset by the fact that Amiens officials repeatedly refused them permission to attend mass. The officials' original motive seems to have been fear of escape, but they also attempted to use the women's desire to hear mass as a means to extort a letter from the duchess begging for the release of the duc de Guise. Then a new reason for denying permission was found. City officials contended that the women, like other royalists, had been excommunicated for belonging to "the party of the tyrant" and told them that they would need the bishop's approval before they could hear mass. An active supporter of the League, the bishop refused to grant this concession. Even a letter from the duc de Mayenne produced no change in the city's policy. In May 1590, Mayenne requested for the second time that the Longueville women be allowed to attend mass, promising in exchange to arrange the same privilege for the duc de Guise. This was a bargain that the city could understand, and for two weeks the Longueville women, under heavy guard, were allowed to attend services. After much pleading, the women were permitted to hear mass again on All Saints Day and on Saint Catherine's Day. There is no indication in city records that they were allowed out after this time, though they remained in captivity for more than a year.[56]

It is hard for us to appreciate how wounding this denial would have been to a pious early modern Catholic like Catherine d'Orléans, who was used to hearing mass on a daily basis. To be denied access to the most familiar and comforting ritual of faith would have been among the greatest hardships of her captivity. Adding insult to injury was the city's insistence that, along with the other women in the family, she was excommunicated—cast out from the holy Catholic Church and from the salvation that it promised. Even if the women refused to accept this judgment, to be classed with the heretics and virulently scorned by their fellow Catholics cannot have been an easy burden to bear.

Certainly it was not easy for Marie de Tudert, another of the women later associated with the Carmelites, for whom the League was demonstrably not an age of gold but rather an age of lead. The wife of Parisian magistrate Jean Séguier d'Autry (and after 1613 the Carmelite Sister Marie de Jésus-Christ), Marie de Tudert was twenty-two when the League seized control of Paris. The family she had married into was piously Catholic but loyal to the Crown. With the exception of one brother-in-law, the men in the family were forced to leave Paris for the duration of the League.[57] Tudert, her widowed mother-in-law, Louise Boudet, and several sisters-in-law remained alone with the family's young children. Like other women from royalist families, they were shunned by old friends, harassed by city officials, and forced to endure a number of indignities. Louise Boudet, for example, appeared before the *prévôt des marchands* (in essence, the mayor of Paris) in April 1589 to complain that the captain of her district had taken a gold chain that belonged to her. She had a more serious quarrel with the city two years later. When her oldest grandson died in her arms of the plague in September 1591, city officials rushed to the house to seize the possessions of the dead boy on the ground that his mother (his nearest relative and consequently his heir) belonged to "the contrary party" and the properties were consequently forfeit.[58]

But worst of all, the women of the Séguier family heard themselves repeatedly denounced from the pulpit of their parish church of Saint-André-des-Arts. According to Pierre de L'Estoile, Christophe Aubry, the Leaguer curé of Saint-André, explicitly denounced Marie de Tudert as a royalist on 7 February 1593. In July, he called down from the pulpit that "there were ladies in Paris, and in his very parish, who pretended to be devout Catholics and yet had children at Saint-Denis and Tours [royalist cities]," deriding the women for shamelessly claiming that, although "their children belonged to the party of that heretic, they yet did not cease to be good Catholics." This was a lie, the priest thundered, and all of them were damned and excommunicated. On another occasion, Aubry warned Tudert's sister-in-law, the wife of President Pierre (II) Séguier, that he would insult her if she dared to show up for mass. In January 1594 he denounced Louise Boudet for advocating that Henri IV should be accepted as king, as he had now converted.[59] Aubry, along with other

Leaguer preachers in Paris, repeatedly claimed that royalists were no better than heretics and attempted to cut them off from the Catholic community. His more virulent sermons seemed to advocate violence against anyone who favored a peaceful settlement to the conflicts, and Marie de Tudert and her kinswomen had good reason to fear local crowds. Yet Tudert defiantly continued to attend mass in her parish church, taking what solace she could from her faith and attempting to show that, contrary to the curé's accusations, she remained a faithful Catholic. Surely the trials of this period, and the loss of respect Tudert must have experienced for this so-called man of God, prodded her to cultivate a more internalized and personal faith.

When Marie de Tudert entered the Carmelite Convent of the Incarnation in 1613, she insisted that her greatest wish since the time of her widowhood in 1596 had been to retire from the world to dedicate herself entirely to God.[60] She claimed she had only been dissuaded from making an immediate religious profession by the opposition of family members, who insisted that she must first raise her children, the youngest of whom was still a baby. Making a vow of perennial chastity, Tudert had devoted the next seventeen years to "good works: prayer, almsgiving, and visits to the poor," the latter often in the company of her cousin Barbe Acarie. Her fear of damnation is evident in a vision she had of the world all covered with traps and snares; God, appearing to her, encouraged her to leave a place surrounded by so many dangers.[61] She became one of the growing number of devout women, ex-Leaguers and ex-royalists alike, for whom the experience of the League only intensified the conviction that the world was mired in sin and the only hope for salvation lay in retreat.

One of the clearest signs of the spiritual impact of the wars of the League was in the tendency of women—especially widows, but also some married women—to adopt a narrowly ascetic style of living in its wake. They continued the kind of charitable work in hospitals and among the poor begun during the crisis of the siege, but they also adopted more reclusive, individualized, and penitential forms of piety. During her husband's exile after the League, Barbe Acarie cut down her meals to one a day, one so scanty that her friends began to fear for her health. She gave herself over to private devotions, and every evening she had her servant administer corporal discipline by scourging her.[62] Marie Sévin, married in response to her parents' wishes but widowed soon thereafter, divided her life between pious retreat and good works. She sought to convert prostitutes to penitential reform, visited prisoners in their jail, and experienced such a great desire to aid the poor that she "wished that [her] body were cut into pieces, and each piece might serve to satisfy their hunger."[63] Her desire for martyrdom had returned in full force but was now transmuted into social rather than political channels. Similar stories could be told about other women from both royalist and Leaguer families.[64]

We might theorize, then, that it was the trauma of the League more than the admonitions pronounced by its preachers that opened the path to the internalized spirituality of reformed Catholicism. When the League began, both supporters of the Holy Union and opponents who remained faithful to the Crown agreed that the disasters from which France was suffering were products of human sinfulness and signs of God's wrath. Despite attempts by their preachers to claim the high ground of Catholic unity, the Leaguers had no monopoly on faith. Marie de Tudert, Catherine d'Orléans, and other victims of the League may in fact have been prompted by the experience of having their Catholic allegiance questioned or denied to turn their faith inward and seek consolation in personal communion with God sooner than those who, like Acarie or Sévin, joined openheartedly in the demonstrative and collective piety of the League. For the latter, the acts of penitential piety advocated by League preachers must have seemed, for a time at least, to offer a means of appeasing God's wrath. For even the most idealistic, however, the vision of the League as a golden age had to fade before the realization that atoning for human sinfulness was not to be accomplished through attendance at sermons and torchlight processions but required more individual penitence, prolonged introspection, and a humble search for union with God. And so both ex-Leaguers and ex-royalists came to see in the ascetic cloisters of the reformed religious orders that utopian place where "people didn't think about eating or drinking but only about turning to God."[65] Such orders did not exist yet in France—at least not for women—but the seed of their creation was planted during the League.

The battles of the League also gave the women who would take a leading role in the postwar Catholic revival an unusual independence. Elite women in early modern France traditionally enjoyed an important and relatively independent role managing family estates, while their husband followed the king as courtier and administered his affairs or, if a magistrate, presided over courts of law.[66] Wartime conditions, which left many women widowed or separated from their husband for prolonged periods of time, enlarged their sphere of independent activity, as they fought to defend their family's property and reputation and, at least in some cases, worked to advance the political faction they favored. The forceful and very public role enjoyed by the Guise women, as they mustered support for the League and served as conduits for communications between the men in their family and leaders of the urban League, was perhaps unique, but had parallels in the efforts of Barbe Acarie, Madeleine Luillier, and other Parisian women to help finance the League and keep up morale among the urban populace. It also had parallels in the defiant stance of the Longueville women, imprisoned and held hostage in Amiens, and Marie de Tudert, publicly scorned by her own parish priest. Inadvertently, the crisis of the League nurtured the administrative skills and capacity for independent judgment, as well as the ascetic piety, that devout women brought to the postwar Catholic revival.

2

The Ascetic Impulse

The penitential asceticism that surged with the League did not quickly abate. During the decade that followed the League's fall, an increasing number of women responded to the continued call from the pulpit to abandon life's vanities in favor of more spiritually rewarding pastimes. None did so more dramatically than Antoinette d'Orléans de Longueville, a sister of the Longueville princesses held captive in Amiens, who shocked all of elite society by running away in October 1599 to join the famously ascetic Feuillantine convent of Sainte-Scholastique in Toulouse.[1] Kissing her young sons good-bye, she told family and friends that she was going on pilgrimage to fulfill a sacred vow, knowing that if they learned her true plans they would spare no effort in foiling them. Wanting only "to embrace God's cross," she traded her silken gowns for a coarse woolen habit, soft beds for bare wooden planks, and rich meals for a meager diet of black bread and bitter greens. If Antoinette d'Orléans's seventeenth-century biographer can be believed, she not only endured but relished the mortifications she experienced as a Feuillantine. She "never had her fill of hair-shirts, scourges, and other corporal penitences" and took special pleasure in serving the other sisters in the refectory because this allowed her to mortify herself more freely without its being noticed.[2]

The flight of Antoinette d'Orléans shocked her contemporaries because of her high social station and the extremes of luxury she willingly sacrificed. However, the story of two contemporary Parisians who became Feuillantines is perhaps more shocking. Madeleine Sublet des Noyers was only fifteen when she talked her parents into taking her to join the convent of Sainte-Scholastique at Toulouse. Meanwhile, Madeleine's twelve-year-old sister, Marie, was so upset at being left behind that Jean Sublet des Noyers and his wife made a second trip the following year so that Marie could join her sister, even though she had to live in the convent without taking vows until she reached the canonical age of sixteen.[3]

What kind of parent would allow such young girls to choose so severe and penitential a life? A wealthy officer of the king, Sublet des Noyers was not trying to save on the cost of his daughters' dowries. He had offered to build a Feuillantine convent outside Paris at his own expense the previous year to keep his young daughters, already enamored of the Feuillantine life, closer to home. Paris's Feuillant monks, still recovering from the trauma of the League and unwilling to take on the cure of female souls, had refused the offer. Sublet's subsequent concession to his daughters' pleas was not, however, simple indulgence. Rather, he and his wife shared the penitential piety that marked their daughters' faith. They had their country home of Noyers built in the form of a convent, filled it with paintings intended to evoke the stages of Christ's passion, and taught their children from an early age to meditate on the relevant station of the cross with each hour that the clock chimed out. Sublet set an example of high respect for religious life by kneeling to wash the mud-encrusted feet of the mendicant friars who arrived at his door and had the girls nurtured in a penitential piety focused on Christ's passion by their maternal uncle, a celebrated Capuchin preacher named Honoré de Champigny.[4]

The sort of piety nurtured in the family of Jean Sublet des Noyers was not common in the 1590s but became more widespread as the collective and highly emotional religiosity of the League gave way to more personal and interiorized religious practices. Examining devout piety in roughly the decade that separated the fall of the League from the founding of the first reformed convents, this chapter delves deeper into the ascetic roots of the seventeenth century's Catholic renewal. I look first at the options available to women who felt a religious vocation at the end of the sixteenth century. Why were there no convents closer to home that satisfied the spiritual cravings of women with serious religious vocations like Antoinette d'Orléans and Madeleine and Marie Sublet? The answer lies in the general decay of late medieval religious life but also in the image pious women formed of religious perfection in observing the reformed monastic orders that had already been founded for men. I also look more closely at the lay dévotes who, responding to the call to reform their lives, attempted to live a religious life in the world. Focusing on the behavioral dimensions of the ascetic impulse that characterized devout piety in this period, I examine the religious and charitable practices of pious women, the principles of conduct they learned from their spiritual directors, and the values they instilled in their children.

The high value dévotes placed on penitential asceticism represented both a reaction against the perceived corruption of late medieval monastic life and a response to the Protestant emphasis on justification by faith alone. Used to good effect by Catholic preachers denouncing Protestantism as heresy, the tendency to equate bodily mortification with sanctity was at first largely the tool of male clerics, who attempted to reinforce the message of their preaching with the perceived holiness of their lives. By the end of the century, however, the strains of civil war and the apocalyptic fears produced by the prolonged religious crisis encouraged women to insist that they too wished to undertake "the sacrifice of their bodies."[5] Denied many of the other paths that men might follow in imitation of Christ, women showed themselves especially eager to seek spiritual fulfillment through the deliberate mortification of their bodies. Behind the lure of asceticism lay a complex tension between obedience and autonomy, abdication of will and self-control.

Monastic Life on the Eve of the Catholic Reformation

Before the opening of new reformed convents, what options did women have for religious life in Paris? The choices were few in number and, for the most part, poor in quality. Four great abbeys lay outside the city walls, one at each point of the compass. To the north lay the royal abbey of Montmartre, a Benedictine house founded in 1134; to the east, the abbey of Saint-Antoine-des-Champs, a Cistercian convent dating from 1198; to the south, the Cordelières of the faubourg Saint-Marcel, a house of Franciscans founded in 1289 and following a moderated (or "Urbanist") rule; and to the west, the abbey of Longchamp, also a Cordelière convent, founded in 1261. All were prestigious houses with long ties to both the great nobility and Parisian elites. All were in dire need of reform by the late sixteenth century.

There were, of course, other convents farther afield in the Paris basin, the most prominent being the Benedictine abbeys of Gif, Yerres, Chelles, and Malnoue, along with the Cistercian abbeys of Maubuisson and Port-Royal. At a somewhat greater distance lay Poissy, Faremoutiers, and Jouarre. These institutions had traditionally found favor with Parisian families giving over daughters to religious life, particularly as most enjoyed clientage ties to the aristocrats who, formally or informally, exercised patronage rights over the chosen abbey. All, however, had suffered from the same vicissitudes as the convents closer to Paris, and all were in need of reform.

Within Paris itself were a handful of hospitals and other specialized foundations. Most had been established later than the great abbeys that lay outside the city walls and, largely because of their service vocations, drew their membership more from the middling classes than from among elites. There were several congregations of nursing sisters, including the Augustinian nuns of the Hôtel-Dieu and the Filles de Sainte-Anastase in the right bank hospital of

Saint-Gervais. The Filles de Sainte-Avoye and the Haudriettes, founded in the late thirteenth and early fourteenth centuries, respectively, served as hospices for poor widows; neither was subjected to a formal rule. The Filles Pénitentes, founded in 1492, served as a refuge for reformed prostitutes. The Filles-Dieu, dating from 1226, had been founded for the same purpose, but, perhaps because of the house's location near the Saint-Denis gate, its nuns had subsequently expanded their mission and opened a temporary shelter for needy women. Reformed and placed under the authority of the Benedictine order of Fontevraud in 1494, the Filles-Dieu turned over the running of the shelter to lay sisters, so that the choir nuns might adopt a purely contemplative life. The only other house of contemplative nuns was the Franciscan convent of the Ave-Maria, which enjoyed a unique reputation as the only city convent not in need of reform.

Among the houses within city walls, only the Filles-Dieu was generally regarded as an acceptable placement for daughters of the lesser nobility and bourgeoisie. Families may have admired the regular lives and ascetic austerity of the Filles de l'Ave-Maria, but most preferred to place their daughters in more comfortable settings. Local elites were even more emphatic in rejecting convents with a social vocation. As Barbe Acarie's mother informed her in no uncertain terms when she proclaimed her desire to become a nursing sister at the Hôtel-Dieu, working with the sick and poor was not a suitable vocation for a young woman of good family.[6] At the Filles-Dieu the choir nuns did not involve themselves in the actual care of the poor women the convent sheltered but rather enjoyed the quiet—and more prestigious—life of Benedictine contemplatives.

It is not surprising that lists of nuns at the Filles-Dieu from the late sixteenth century include members of many prominent families; nor is it surprising that the Filles-Dieu were lax in observance of their Benedictine rule.[7] Living comfortably off private pensions provided by their parents, the nuns enjoyed finely tailored habits and dined in comfortably furnished cells on foodstuffs purchased with personal funds. In 1602 François de Sales scolded them for disregarding their vow of poverty and engaging in pastimes that were less than devout.[8] Although the Filles-Dieu was a better than average convent by the standards of moderate Catholics, it nevertheless fell far short of the more rigorous expectations of seventeenth-century dévots.

The lax conditions for which dévots criticized the Filles-Dieu were magnified in the great abbeys that lay outside Paris's walls. Long traditions of aristocratic dominance had made these convents the object of competing family strategies that centered more on economic and political advantage than on religious devotion. Moreover, their position in the Parisian countryside and dependence on agricultural revenues had made them vulnerable to a decline resulting from the long-term impact of the Hundred Years' War. By the second half of the fifteenth century, falling agricultural prices and uncollected rents had left even formerly wealthy houses with insufficient funds to cover their continuing needs.

Before the Hundred Years' War, the nuns of Saint-Antoine-des-Champs had overseen the direct exploitation of their lands by lay brothers attached to the abbey. Changed economic conditions after the war forced the nuns instead to offer long-term leases that brought in less and less revenue over time. The abbey itself was ruined by the fighting that repeatedly took place around and for the capital. On more than one occasion, the convent was occupied by invading forces and the nuns forced to flee to safety inside the city walls. Internal conflicts added to the abbey's distress. Contests for power among the nuns, who very often came from prominent noble families, made it difficult for the abbesses to command obedience. Under circumstances so deleterious to religious life, it is little wonder that Charles VII stepped in as early as 1440 to demand the abbey's reform.[9]

Montmartre's experience was very similar. The abbey's strategic position on the heights overlooking Paris made it the logical prey of military commanders determined to seize the capital. The nuns were also the victims of peasant revolts, or *jacqueries*. Many of their properties were seized, and they were forced repeatedly to flee their convent. By 1440, the abbey was no longer habitable, its buildings ruined and its revenues diminished to nothing. Still more lands had to be sold to pay for necessary repairs. By the end of the wars, the quality of religious life the abbey afforded its nuns was as impoverished as its material conditions. In 1462 rules for religious enclosure (*clausura*) were so neglected that the nuns took part as a company in the funeral services for Charles VII. Parisian bishop Etienne Poncher attempted to reform the abbey by establishing the recently reformed order of Fontevraud there in 1503. He brought in new nuns to hold key positions in the abbey and completely rewrote the convent's statutes. The most significant changes were the institution of procedures for regular visitations and the imposition of an elected abbess with a limited, three-year term.[10]

The improvements from this period did not long endure, as convents were often successful in resisting outside pressure for reform. Powerful abbesses intent on preserving traditional prerogatives proved adept at foiling orders for change imposed by lay and ecclesiastical authorities. They took advantage of competing ecclesiastical jurisdictions to refuse, or at least delay, attempts at reform and did not hesitate to appeal their claims to secular authorities if they thought it would help their case. Reformers also encountered stubborn resistance on the part of nuns who refused to give up their comforts for the more rigorous standards of behavior required by strict observance of their rule. Many had entered religious life at the behest of their family and without a true religious vocation. They were willing to make the best of a comfortable seclusion as long as life was easy, family visits were frequent, and demands on either body or soul were few. Even where reformers succeeded in reintroducing strict cloistering and respect for monastic poverty through the elimination of private pensions and personal servants, there was, Charmarie Blaisdell found, "little evidence of change in the nuns' spiritual life."[11] Returning a convent to true piety required an effort that late medieval abbesses, themselves often lacking a religious vocation, were seldom prepared to make.

Most of the convents reformed at the start of the sixteenth century needed reform again by midcentury. And yet, when kings or bishops attempted to impose changes, they encountered the same resistance they had half a century earlier. The Wars of Religion and, in particular, the siege of Paris in 1590 only capped a long process of decay. Already in 1547 conditions at Montmartre were so scandalous that Henri II ordered the abbess and several nuns locked up in the Filles-Dieu, while the priors of four major monasteries were charged with undertaking an inquest. The new abbess installed in 1549, Catherine de Clermont, did little to prolong the attempted reform. When Henri de Navarre, having established his camp on the promontory of Montmartre during the siege of Paris, visited the abbey with some of his soldiers, rumors were rife about the nuns' misconduct.[12]

There was substance to these rumors. Marie de Beauvilliers found when she arrived as Montmartre's new abbess in 1598 that her nuns observed neither the rules of clausura nor their vows of poverty. "Love intrigues were very frequent," and "if some of the nuns fasted in conformity with their rule, it was in spite of themselves, because they had neither money nor friends and could not feast like the others." Although the abbey theoretically had an annual revenue of 2,000 écus, its debts were five times that. Angry creditors had seized the barn and all its contents, as well as furniture from the abbess's rooms and kitchen utensils. Even the cross from the church had to be pawned.[13]

A very similar story can be told of Saint-Antoine-des-Champs. Here, too, the nuns resisted the bishop's attempts at reform in the 1540s. They fought off his authority by filing suit in Parlement and yielded to the court's command to allow the abbots of Clairvaux and Fromment to undertake a reform only when threatened with dispersion of the community and confiscation of its properties. To remedy the abuses they found, the abbots sent some of the nuns to other houses and established a new rule. As with Montmartre, however, the attempted reform did not last long. The wars of the League added physical destruction to moral decay. Parisian supporters of the League drove out the royal armies encamped on the abbey's grounds but then celebrated their victory by pillaging the house.[14]

The Cordelière convent in the faubourg Saint-Marcel was also pillaged during the siege of Paris. Royalist troops ransacked the church, destroying its sacred objects. They stayed long enough to feast on foodstuffs discovered in the convent and took whatever else they could carry.[15] Meanwhile, the nuns sought shelter within city walls or in the neighboring abbey of Saint-Médard, until it too was sacked. The abbey of Longchamp, located in the Bois de Boulogne, was as vulnerable to the depredations of war as the other three convents lying outside the city gates. Like Montmartre, Longchamp became a staging point for Henri de Navarre's armies during the siege of Paris. Here too vicious rumors circulated about relations between Navarre and the nuns.[16] Whereas Barbe Acarie, who had spent three years as a boarder at Longchamp in the late 1570s, claimed that the nuns there retained a more pious demeanor than at many contemporaneous convents, Vincent de Paul wrote in 1652 that Long-champ had "been in a state of disorder for two hundred years." The parlors were open to everyone, he added, "even many young men who are not rela-tives," and nuns visited with them alone, in defiance of the abbess's prohibi-tions. He also criticized the nuns' "immodest" habits and lack of religious education.[17]

Vincent de Paul's complaints echo criticisms frequently voiced against convents located in or near major cities. Until the mendicant orders began establishing convents in urban locations in the thirteenth century, the better to gather alms, women's houses had traditionally been established well outside of urban centers so as to isolate the nuns from overly frequent visits and other distractions of city life. Although many convents established in the later Middle Ages were built inside towns, the notion that convents were best placed well away from urban centers persisted into the late sixteenth century. When Henri III, desiring to bring the reformed Cistercian monks known as Feuillants to Paris in 1587, proposed to offer them the convent of Longchamp and transfer the nuns who remained there to the abbey of the Val, more than five leagues outside of Paris, he justified the transfer on the ground that it would be better for the nuns to be farther from the city.[18]

The depredations suffered by convents unprotected by city walls during the wars of the League did much to change opinion on this point. Protestant troops occupied Yerres in 1587 and so threatened Chelles that the nuns were forced to take refuge in Paris in 1589 and remained there through the siege of 1590. They had scarcely returned to Chelles when Henri de Navarre and his troops occupied the convent to bar the route to Paris to the Duke of Parma, who was bringing Spanish troops to help the League hold the city. Parma responded by seizing the convent of Faremoutiers, which was subsequently much damaged by the Spanish occupation.[19] The reforming decrees issued by the Council of Trent in 1563 encouraged convents to move into cities, but they did so because of wartime experiences as much as respect for ecclesiastical authority.[20]

Throughout the Paris basin, even abbeys not directly affected by troop movements were badly in need of repair and reform by the end of the Wars of Religion. Their buildings were dilapidated, if not actually in ruins. Morale was low, obedience was lax, and recruitment had fallen off badly. The abbey of Yerres had sixty-two nuns in 1547 and only sixteen in 1587.[21] The venerable abbey of Notre-Dame du Val de Gif held only a dozen nuns in 1592.[22] Port-

Royal had about the same number when ten-year-old Jacqueline Arnauld arrived there in 1602 to serve as coadjutrice (assistant) to its abbess. The conduct of one of the nuns was so scandalous that Jacqueline's parents had the nun immediately transferred to another convent. It took longer to rid the house of ill-behaved servants, repair buildings damaged by the wars of the League, and restore order to the abbey's temporal affairs, but this was also accomplished within a relatively short time. Bringing in a new prioress to watch over their young daughter and administer the convent's finances, Jacqueline's parents judged their reforms complete. They made no effort to establish strict enclosure or reduce the inequities that allowed some nuns to live richly off their private pensions while others had barely enough to eat, and their only attempt to improve the quality of the nuns' spiritual life consisted of bringing a Cistercian student from Paris to preach a sermon four times a year. Prior to this time, the nuns had very rarely heard sermons, perhaps once every five or six years. They attended offices, but otherwise, Arnauld later recorded, "did nothing but play and stroll about their grounds." None even knew their catechism. The Cistercian students, however, did little to rectify this situation. According to Arnauld, they "preached so pitifully that their sermons became occasions for sin, on account of the mockery the nuns made of them."[23] A very similar picture emerges from descriptions of life in other convents. In nearly all of them, the nuns lived from private income, came and went freely from the parlors, and neglected religious offices in favor of more secular pastimes.[24]

The single exception is the Franciscan convent of the Ave-Maria, housed in an old beguinage in Paris's Marais district. The Filles de l'Ave-Maria had adopted the strict rule of Saint Clare in the late fifteenth century and, by all reports, remained fully observant of this rule a century later. In conformity with Saint Clare's wishes, they lived from alms alone, a privilege usually denied women's houses because the need to beg contradicted the principle that nuns should remain in their cloisters. Charles VIII had resolved the contradiction by authorizing twelve Franciscan friars to reside alongside the Ave-Maria, both to serve the nuns' sacramental needs and to oversee the collection of alms. Known as the Poor Clares, the sisters lived a life of strictest austerity. They abstained entirely from meat, even during illness, fasted every day except Sunday, and further mortified their bodies by going barefoot year-round. They slept in a common dormitory and did all of the convent's work themselves. Keeping a strict silence, they carried out a demanding schedule of religious observances, which included a matins service at midnight that lasted up to three hours.[25] Charlotte de Harlay de Sancy, marquise de Breauté, who considered entering the Ave-Maria, described the nuns' lives in terms that sound unremittingly grim:

> To her mind, their high walls formed a narrow prison. Their terrible
> fasting . . . made her go pale, but especially their manner of sleeping

without being entirely recumbent at night and the obligation to go about entirely barefoot even in winter and on ice astounded her, such that she indeed believed that the day she entered this house would soon be followed by that of her death, and what she considered only a prison for others would in a short time become her tomb.[26]

Why, among Parisian convents, did the Ave-Maria alone emerge unscathed from the disasters of war, economic change, and internal decay? Most obviously, the convent's position within city walls sheltered it from the direct effects of besieging armies. Equally important, the convent's refusal to own property insulated it from fluctuations in prices and rents. Unlike the distinguished abbeys that surrounded Paris, the Poor Clares had no landed estates to lose through mismanagement, recession, or the effects of war. Having never known wealth, the community could not suffer the pernicious effects that almost inevitably followed on the heels of prosperity. It did not attract the attentions of covetous aristocratic families anxious to annex its fortunes to their own. There was little reason to compete to establish one's daughter as superior of the house, and, given the rigorous conditions prevailing in the convent, only a harsh parent would seek to place a daughter there just to save on the expense of her dowry.

Lacking these incentives to relax the rule, it was much easier for the nuns of the Ave-Maria to adhere determinedly to their austere way of life than it was for nuns in once wealthy houses to gather or maintain momentum for reform. It was easier to demand a true religious vocation of girls who sought entry to the convent and to maintain a high standard of behavior once they took their vows. Having been established only late in the fifteenth century, the Poor Clares did not look back to earlier glories but focused instead on the strict vision of Franciscan poverty that was their distinguishing characteristic and purpose for existing. Admiration for their harsh lives was what kept the coins dropping into the almoners' cups. A decline in standards would have quickly led to the institution's demise.

If the life of the Poor Clares was regular and austere, why didn't devout women flock to enter the convent in the wake of the League's defeat? Some did, including Antoinette d'Orléans, who sought to join the Ave-Maria prior to her flight to Toulouse but was denied entry because the Poor Clares interpreted their calling as consecrated virgins so literally that they refused to admit widows. Charlotte de Breauté was rejected for the same reason in 1601. More speculatively, Madeleine and Marie Sublet may have opted for the Feuillantines rather than the Poor Clares because of rivalries among competing branches of Franciscan friars. They may have consciously or unconsciously absorbed from their uncle Honoré de Champigny the Capuchins' belief that the Observantine friars who served as spiritual directors to the Poor Clares were insufficiently faithful to Saint Francis's rule.

The Poor Clares had another handicap. The Parisian elite had favored them with alms but had never sent their daughters to this humble convent in significant numbers. Its self-effacing nuns were respected by the dévotes inspired to religious vocations in the wake of the League, but their quiet lives did not fire the imaginations of a generation that found more engaging models for religious life in recently reformed male orders, particularly the Capuchins and Feuillants. Burning with apostolic mission, young dévotes yearned for more dramatic ways to consecrate their lives to God's service.

Male Models for Female Religious Life

Pious women flocked to the sermons of clerics celebrated for their mortifications as well as their passionate oratory during France's religious wars. They lionized Minim preacher Jean de Hans, one of the Protestants' most outspoken opponents during the years that immediately preceded the outbreak of war in 1562. Whispering that he wore a hair shirt beneath his rough habit, they clearly admired him as much for his saintly life as for his inflammatory sermons. When he died in December 1562, they gathered around his corpse to touch it with their rosary beads and draw some blessing from his saintliness, even though he was rumored to have died of plague.[27] By the later stages of the wars, preachers from two other austere orders, the reformed Franciscans known as Capuchins and the reformed Cistercians known as Feuillants, were drawing the same admiring attention. Members of all three congregations made rigorous asceticism central to their way of life and used the reputation for holiness gained through their mortified lives to good advantage in preaching and teaching Catholic reform.[28] They called on Protestants to renounce their heresy and return to the mother church and also urged Catholics to become more active participants in their faith. Among their most attentive listeners were the pious women who eagerly sought their spiritual guidance and begged to be initiated into the rich interior life they perceived to be the natural counterpart to the brothers' unworldly exteriors. Inspired by both example and precept, the women sought to incorporate the bodily mortifications they admired in their spiritual directors into their own religious practices.

The Minims were the oldest of the three congregations. Founded by the Calabrian hermit Francis of Paola, they were summoned to France in 1483 by Louis XI, who established them near his palace outside Tours. The brothers made a deep impression on the court by their mortified lives and were rewarded with additional friaries in the Touraine and Paris. Their numbers grew rapidly, and by the time their founder died in 1507, the Minims had established thirty houses, thirteen of them in France.[29] Often mistaken for a reformed branch of the Franciscans, with whom they shared the ideal of a return to apostolic poverty, the Minims were in fact independently rooted in Francis of Paola's ascetic vision of religious life. Francis emphasized three principles: humility, penitence, and abstinence, with abstinence serving as the tool of the first two aims. "Fasting purifies the understanding, raises the senses, subjects the flesh to the spirit, [and] renders the heart contrite and humble," he explained. To this end, he added a fourth essential vow: total abstinence from meat and dairy products and rigorous fasting during more than half the year.[30]

With Luther's revolt, criticism of Catholic clergy became tainted with the suspicion of heresy, and attempts at internal reform of the French church petered out. The ascetic ideal embodied by Francis of Paola and his Minims remained exceptional and gave the order added respect. During the early stages of France's Wars of Religion, Minim friars were conspicuous both for their fiery preaching against heresy and for their austerities, which implicitly reproached the self-indulgence of unreformed clergy and lay people alike. The mortifications practiced by the Minims were, moreover, themselves a weapon in the battle against heresy. Silently advertising the importance of good works in response to the Protestants' claims of justification by faith alone, they embodied a theology of the cross in which Christ's sacrifice was to be endlessly repeated and affirmed through the imitation of his suffering, in opposition to the Protestants' claims that this sacrifice was perfect and forever complete.

Minim preaching was intended to stir a Catholic revival as well as to combat Protestant heresy. One effective tactic in this campaign was the development of a Third Order for lay persons who wished to live a more devout life. By the mid-sixteenth century the Minims, by means of their Third Order, had become spiritual directors to important members of the Parisian bourgeoisie, including Marie Du Drac, whom they encouraged in both physical mortifications and internalized prayer. The publication of the funeral sermon commemorating Du Drac's life by her spiritual director, Minim Antoine Estienne, was clearly intended to help propagate the model of the devout life that she embodied.

By the 1570s, a new mendicant group known as Capuchins was overshadowing the Minims as preachers against heresy. The order was founded in Umbria in the mid-1520s by Matteo da Bascio, an Observant Franciscan who sought to return to a more literal observance of the rule of Saint Francis.[31] Legend has it that Catherine de Medici stumbled on a hermitage of would-be Capuchins—that is to say, of men imitating the Capuchin rule but unable to affiliate legally with the order because it was forbidden to expand outside of Italy—in the woods outside the royal palace of Vincennes and was so impressed by their apparent holiness that she intervened with the pope and convinced him to allow the order to expand into France.[32] Whether or not the story is true in all its details, Catherine was a strong and early supporter of the group. It was on her invitation that they took part in the funeral procession for the deceased King Charles IX in July 1574. The following year, she and her son, King Henri III, moved the Capuchins out of their obscure hermitage in the Bois de Vincennes and built them a friary near the royal palace of the Louvre.

Capuchin annals frequently reiterate that their rough habits, mortifications, and evident self-neglect were spiritually edifying for those who came into contact with them. One account describes Pierre de Besson, a tireless preacher against heresy, as presenting "an exterior rendered fleshless by fasting and austerities, hair shirts, and the frequent scourging that he undertook to attract a favorable attention from his auditors."[33] The suggestion of a calculated appeal to public attention is revealing. The result of a sincerely penitential faith, the Capuchins' ascetic appearance was at one and the same time a warning to repent and an advertisement for the order's true holiness, acquired through the rigorous practice of Franciscan poverty.

Public notice of the Capuchins was by no means uniformly favorable, especially during the early years of their French mission. The Parisian populace appears initially to have been more shocked than edified by the strange appearance of the gaunt and ragged friars. Carters and lackeys heaped abuse on them as they passed in the streets; children ran up to tug on their long, pointed hoods. People ignored their outstretched cups, and the Capuchins sometimes found themselves reduced to living on wild greens. The turning point came in 1580, when the friars were seen to give tireless service to the sick and dying during a severe epidemic of plague. Capuchin chroniclers recount how rich and poor alike developed a new respect for the friars on account of their willingness to risk their lives caring for plague victims. They tell how both ecclesiastics and lay people began to imitate their practice of interiorized, or meditative prayer. They take credit also for influencing other religious orders to be more ascetic in their behavior, dress, and church architecture.[34] A sudden leap in Capuchin professions after 1580 does suggest a new appreciation of the order and the spirituality associated with it. When the plague broke out in that year, the Parisian congregation numbered at most twenty men, at least two of whom died as a result of the contagion, but by the end of the year, fifty-two new recruits had entered the Capuchin novitiate.[35] The order continued to grow and also to expand its geographic base. According to Capuchin historians, by 1590 the province of Paris numbered thirteen friaries and the kingdom of France thirty-one.[36]

The new recruits of the 1580s became key leaders not only of the Capuchins' own expansion but also of the Catholic renewal more broadly. Sons of prominent bourgeois families and even aristocrats were moved to join. Their social skills and contacts gave the Capuchins an entrée among the Parisian elite. The twenty-eight men who joined in 1587 went on to particularly distinguished careers and included, among others, Honoré de Champigny, the uncle of Madeleine and Marie Sublet. They also included Ange de Joyeuse, a courtier and favorite of Henri III, whose unexpected religious conversion and adoption of the Capuchin habit following the death of his wife shocked the French aristocracy every bit as much as Antoinette d'Orléans's flight twelve years later. The most distinguished members of this cohort all joined directly out of their experience as Gray Penitents, one of at least four confraternities of flagellants founded in Paris in the 1580s, providing further evidence that the rise of the Capuchin order was part of the broader revival of ascetic spirituality that sprang from the turmoil of religious war.

The same is true of the Feuillants, a congregation of reformed Cistercians who took their name from the Gascon monastery where the reform had its start. Recognized by the pope as an independent congregation in 1587, the Feuillants were brought to Paris by Henri III that same year and established alongside the Capuchins in the faubourg Saint-Honoré. The reform actually began fourteen years earlier when the Feuillants' young abbot, Jean de la Barrière, decided to radically change his own life and that of his monks. In a letter to the pope explaining the principles of his reform, de la Barrière placed himself in the tradition of Saint Benedict, who, in de la Barrière's words, "had deliberately worked to raise the mind above the body, for the glory of God, and in such a way that the body not only did not oppose the mind in its path to perfection but aided it usefully in this career, even if it was as if by force, and by its own destruction." De la Barrière sought to restore the "perfect regularity of Benedict's order" but also to imitate the desert fathers, meditate on the doctors of the church, and practice what he found in scripture. To this end, he prescribed a life of labor and self-denial. Eating and drinking were to be done "with a frugality that mortified the flesh" but also a spirit of charity that made this abstinence a form of alms.[37] Said to have lived initially on wild greens, roots, and what fruit he could gather, de la Barrière denied himself even the simple sustenance of bread and wine. He later added dark bread to his diet but continued to shun not only meat but also fish, eggs, butter, oil, and salt. He went bareheaded and barefoot whatever the weather, slept fully dressed on bare planks, and ate while kneeling on the abbey's bare floor.

For four years he continued these practices alone. His monks variously ignored him, abandoned him, and sought to challenge his authority. Summoned to the Cistercians' general chapter meeting to respond to charges that his innovations were disturbing the abbey's peace, he made such a profound impression of holiness with his humble replies that he gained his first converts. From 1577 men came in increasing numbers to model their own lives on that of Jean de la Barrière and to work together in silent penitence. In 1587, when Sixtus V freed them from the supervision of the Cistercians, who still contested their reforms, 140 men lived under the Feuillants' ascetic rule. With the foundation of a Paris house in 1587, these numbers continued to grow until the crisis of the League divided and nearly destroyed the Paris community. By 1595 the Paris monastery was so reduced in numbers that Henri IV threatened to shut it down. The remaining monks succeeded in convincing the king to give them time to call back the brothers who had been dispersed to other monasteries on account of the extreme poverty suffered in the wake of the siege. By 1597 the community had recovered to the point that Henri IV proclaimed himself the monastery's founder and accorded it all the privileges traditionally given royal foundations.

The Feuillant community that took shape after the League was, quite literally, healthier than that which had preceded this crisis. The ascetic regime adopted by Jean de la Barrière had proved so debilitating that Pope Clement VIII, shocked by the massive death rate exhibited in the Feuillants' Roman convent, intervened in 1592 to impose a less stringent rule on the order, which he feared might otherwise vanish entirely.[38] Even so, the order remained extreme in its austerity, and the new generation of leadership developed in the 1590s continued to display and to preach a penitential and self-sacrificial piety.

Women as well as men took inspiration from the mortified lives of the Capuchins and Feuillants, and they pleaded with the brothers to found sister houses where they could carry out the monks' ascetic practices. French Capuchins resisted for more than a decade, insisting that their rule forbade them to take on the cure of female souls. Jean de la Barrière also initially discouraged the female followers who begged to establish a convent where they could follow the brothers' austere rule. The women couched their plea for a convent in terms that stressed the equality of the sexes before God. "Aspiring to the same salvation [as the men], they should pay the same price and arrive at it by as narrow and rude a road," they insisted, adding "that they too had bodies capable of suffering and . . . wills as generous as men's to undertake the sacrifice of their bodies."[39]

De la Barrière tested the women's resolution by making them wait two or three years before agreeing to establish a convent for them, during which time their numbers and determination grew. A women's house could not be founded until Sixtus V made the Feuillants an independent congregation in 1587, and, because Henri III summoned de la Barrière to Paris, it was established under the direction of one of his disciples and not the abbot himself. The Feuillantines, as they came to be called, were nevertheless resolutely faithful to de la Barrière's principles of work and self-denial. The fifteen nuns who founded the first convent at Montesquieu-Volvestre, south of Toulouse, cleared and worked their lands themselves, living from their labors in the Feuillants' perpetual silence.[40] Ten years later, having outgrown the Montesquieu house, they moved into a larger convent in Toulouse.

It was at this point that Antoinette d'Orléans de Longueville ran away to join the Feuillantines. Her story illustrates well the spreading influence of penitential piety but also the opposition the new asceticism provoked, especially among elites. She departed for Toulouse in the deepest secrecy, to give her powerful family no opportunity to prevent the quiet entry into religious life that she had been planning for more than a year. As a further measure of security, she arranged with the abbess to be given a novice's habit almost immediately, contrary to custom, which would have required her to remain for some time as a postulant in secular dress. The precaution proved useful when, as she had foreseen, her family intervened and demanded that she be sent home. The first sign of their opposition arrived in the form of a letter from Henri IV insisting that, if Antoinette had not yet taken the habit, she be returned to her family at once. Knowing that she had reached the age of majority and was free to dispose of herself in religious life, the king allowed that if she had already adopted the habit, she was to be left in peace.[41]

Her family refused to accept this outcome. When the king declined to take further action, Antoinette's brother, the comte de Saint-Paul, and a brother-in-law, Henri de Gondi, coadjutor to his uncle the archbishop of Paris, rushed to Toulouse to try to induce her to return to Paris with them. Bearing letters from her father-in-law, the duc de Retz, and the cardinal-bishop de Gondi, they also tried to convince the convent's superior to force Antoinette to leave. When all of this failed, they sought action from the pope. They finally succeeded in prying Antoinette out of her retreat by obtaining papal letters in 1605 ordering her to take up the position of coadjutrice to her aunt Eléonore d'Orléans, the aging abbess of the decayed abbey of Fontevraud. She must, Paul V wrote to Antoinette, work for the sanctification of others and not just herself. Despite the pope's claim to her obedience, Antoinette d'Orléans employed canon lawyers to fight the order for two more years and gave in only at the king's command. For four years, she wore the habit of Fontevraud and worked, largely unsuccessfully, for its reform. Freed by the death of Eléonore d'Orléans in 1611, Antoinette promptly renounced her right to continue on as abbess and sought to return to Sainte-Scholastique. When her family continued to oppose her in this, she took some nuns favorable to reform from Fontevraud and, after reforming the nearby convent of Lencloître, went on to found a new convent in Poitiers modeled on the austere life she had known as a Feuillantine.

Antoinette d'Orléans's insistence on leading a mortified life was at least in part motivated by a desire to do penance for the sins that she had seen the court nobility commit out of *délicatesse*, a term she used to denote over-refinement or self-indulgent fastidiousness. It thus represented a conscious rebellion against the ideals of civility in which she had been raised. And yet, despite the sense of collective salvation expressed in this desire to do penance for the sins of others, she was most strongly driven by fears for her own salvation. Her most powerful reason for battling her family, her king, and even the pope for more than a decade was her doubt that salvation was possible outside of the Feuillantines' "harsh and narrow road to God."[42]

For their part, her family, especially her in-laws, resented her defiance of clan solidarity in daring to dispose of her person without their consent. But they also vehemently rejected the ascetic impulse that drew Antoinette to the Feuillantines. At least most of the family felt this way. Antoinette's sisters,

Catherine and Marguerite d'Orléans de Longueville, saw more to admire in her religious vocation and even sought to found a Feuillantine convent in Paris with the idea of bringing Antoinette closer to home. They could not, however, interest the Paris Feuillants in the project and several years later became sponsors of the Carmelites instead.[43] The men in the family did not share the sisters' sympathy for penitential austerity. Their strategy of placing Antoinette at Fontevraud makes it clear that their objection was not to religious life per se but to the particular sort of religious life that she had chosen. Antoinette's brother and brothers-in-law could accept the idea of her serving as coadjutrice and later as abbess of the rich and venerable order of Fontevraud, where she could live in comfort and enjoy a large measure of power and prestige. They could not accept her determination to be the least of poor nuns in the rigorous convent of Sainte-Scholastique.

The aristocratic relatives of Antoinette d'Orléans de Longueville were not alone in their lack of sympathy for the ascetic impulse that characterized the early stages of France's Catholic revival. The Capuchins and Feuillants were repeatedly sued by angry parents who claimed their sons had joined these orders without their permission. The disposition of these cases by the Parlement of Paris makes it clear that a majority of the magistrates were suspicious of these new orders because of their past associations with the ultra-Catholicism of the League but also because of the character of the new, internalized spirituality they taught. The forceful call to a personal vocation was hard to accommodate within accepted traditions of family obligation and patriarchal authority. At the same time, the interiority, emphasis on penitence, and renunciation of worldly satisfactions that marked the new spirituality were hard to reconcile with the worldly aspirations and increasingly secular values of these upwardly mobile elites.[44]

The Catholic revival in France did not take place as a simple flowering of renewed piety, uniformly welcomed and obviously beneficial in all its effects. Rather, it began as a demanding call to sacrifice worldly affections to the single-minded love of God, and if some persons admired those who responded to this call as heroic and even saintly in their self-sacrifice, others were more skeptical. Memoirist Pierre de L'Estoile recorded in his journal in October 1606, two years after the first new reformed religious orders for women had been founded in Paris, that "there was no greater novelty, in Paris and elsewhere, than the sons and daughters of good family, men and women of quality who were betaking themselves to these new religious orders of Capuchins, Feuillants, Recollettes, Carmelites and Capuchin nuns." He went on to complain that most of the young people who flocked to these new orders did so out of "a simple and silly devotion," persuaded that the Last Days had arrived. "Others were brought to it by various sorts of despair, and many by laziness and cowardice, liking to do nothing," he claimed. "All, in general, preferred the inventions and traditions of men to the commandments of God."[45] This scathing critique of the new orders—and of the motives of those who joined them—came not from a Huguenot but from a practicing Catholic who strongly favored ecclesiastical reform. It illustrates well the division of opinion that existed even within the Parisian elite over the means by which Catholic reform should be achieved and the form it should take.

Pious Women on the Eve of the New Foundations

The challenge to accepted customs and values posed by the new spirituality is evident in the behavior of lay dévotes as well as in the sons and (later) daughters of good families who broke more dramatically with secular society in joining the new, reformed religious orders. A good example is Charlotte de Harlay de Sancy, the marquise de Breauté, who underwent a religious conversion after hearing a particularly moving sermon preached by Philippe Cospeau in the jubilee year of 1601. The recently widowed daughter of a close counselor to Henri IV, Breauté was moved by Cospeau's sermon to seek him out to make her confession. He responded by lecturing her in the most severe terms about the "duties of widows" and succeeded in convincing her to take at least two significant steps to change her ways. First, she altered her style of dress, abandoning the daringly low necklines then fashionable with French elites in favor of more modest garments. Second, she began to rise early to make the extensive round of religious services designated for the jubilee. Charlotte de Breauté later claimed that both of these changes in her way of living had "cost her so much" that she thought that God could not ask more of her. As it happened, they were just the first tentative steps on a path of increasing self-mortification. Within a short time, Breauté not only abandoned the fashions considered suitable for a young gentlewoman of twenty-two but also donned a hair shirt, bound her loins with an iron-studded belt, and scourged herself with an instrument known as a "discipline" until it was stained red with her blood.[46]

Her self-inflicted wounds, according to Breauté, cost her far less than the humiliation she suffered at court when her newly pious ways came to be known. She was embarrassed to be seen wearing prudish clothes and a hair style appropriate to an elderly maiden, and she sought to conceal the amount of time she was spending in church and the frequency with which she took communion so that she would not stand out as "singular." Above all, she found it difficult to cut herself off from the entertainments and social pleasures she greatly enjoyed. Breauté adopted the life of a secular dévote out of conviction and not out of personal inclination. Initially at least, she took little pleasure in her new routines of meditation and prayer, religious services and good works. Time hung heavy on her hands, and she persisted only because she believed it was "better to suffer purgatory in this life than hell in the next."[47] It was this conviction that salvation could be accomplished only through the most rigorous of mortifications that led her to try to join the Poor Clares, despite the fact that the convent's strict regime repelled her. She was forbidden entry because she was a widow and, until other religious options presented themselves, had to seek her salvation in a secular state.

Charlotte de Breauté's fear for her soul's salvation appears to have been commonly shared by the women who adopted the life of lay dévotes in the decade following the end of the religious wars, but if some reformed their behavior only with great difficulty, others did so with more enthusiasm. Marie d'Hannivel belongs to the latter group. Inspired by several conversations with a Capuchin father visiting her family's country estate, she punctuated the reform of her appearance and behavior with dramatic gestures borrowed from the lives of medieval saints. Refusing a prestigious offer of marriage, she imitated Saint Catherine of Siena in cutting off her hair to signify her decision to give herself entirely to God. She adopted the predictable forms of self-mortification: sleeping on a plank, fasting on bread and water at a dining table laden with food, and wearing a hair shirt under the elegant clothing that "obedience obliged her to wear." She also sought to exceed these austerities in ways that mimicked earlier ascetics. Lacking traditional instruments of penitence, she is said to have bound nettles and holly to her skin beneath her dresses and deliberately provoked bees to sting her. In the jubilee year of 1601, she cut the soles out of her shoes and stockings before setting out on a pilgrimage from Rouen to Pontoise to mortify herself more thoroughly.[48]

Louise Gallois took a less dramatic route to the devout life. From the beginning, interiorized devotions played a larger role than corporal mortifications in her spiritual development. Left a widow with young children several years short of her thirtieth birthday, Gallois accepted her loss by becoming more and more wrapped up in her interior life. She spent all of the time she could spare from household duties meditating on Christ's passion. Although she took part in charitable activities, crossing Paris on foot to take aid to the poor, she remained "uniquely occupied with her God and with the desire to return promptly to her dear solitude." She engaged a servant to care for her children so as to leave more time for her spiritual life and subsequently moved out of her house altogether to reside with other dévotes similarly engaged in the pursuit of piety. Said to have been an "excessively tender" mother, she now looked on her offspring with "indifference," having been directed by divine insight to forget "the ties of nature so as to see them only as children of God."[49]

Each in her own way, Charlotte de Breauté, Marie d'Hannivel, and Louise Gallois defied convention by refusing to conform to behaviors customarily expected of their sex. Breauté renounced the fashions and pastimes expected of ladies of her rank; Hannivel disobeyed her father by refusing the husband he had chosen for her; Gallois abandoned her motherly duties to devote herself to spiritual pursuits. If the ways devout women modified their lives to reflect their enhanced piety differed with their individual character and stage of life, the patterns of behavior they adopted had much in common, as did their intense conviction that only this radical reform of both internal life and external activities could relieve their pervading fear of damnation. The new dévotes dressed modestly, even prudishly, by the standards of the day and·their social class. Even if they made some concessions in the externals of their dress to appease family members, they mortified their body beneath this apparent luxury by wearing a hair shirt, studded iron bands, or instruments intended to irritate the flesh and provoke discomfort if not actual pain. They changed their eating habits, giving up favorite delicacies in favor of coarse and simple foods and limiting consumption through frequent fasts. Some even went so far as to doctor foods with ashes or bitter herbs to decrease still further any pleasure that might accompany the taking of nourishment. Sleep was another bodily comfort that had to be limited or denied, so they retired to cold rooms, stretched out on stiff planks, and adopted nightly vigils.

Abandoning the social life common to their class, they adopted strict routines of private meditation and prayer and left the house only for religious services and charitable rounds, each of which consumed a large share of their time. They took food, clothes, and other useful commodities to the poor, visited the sick in public hospitals and prisoners in jail, and aided young girls who had been seduced and abandoned. Some dévotes even made a practice of approaching prostitutes in the street and attempting to convince them to change their ways. While increasing their charitable concern for strangers, they loosened their emotional ties to family. Even filial and maternal love had to be transmuted from earthly bonds to purely spiritual ones.

In her autobiographical reminiscences, Marie Sévin portrays her activities while a lay dévote as motivated not by a simple impulse to charity but by a powerful apostolic mission. "The salvation of souls touched me so powerfully that I was utterly convulsed by the thought of the almost infinite number of souls that were lost every day," she recorded. "It seemed to me that I offered God my life, my blood, and all that I could in order to make souls serve him, and I believed that I would have endured the pains of hell for a time, if it helped in the salvation of those around me!" She prayed continually that God would "touch these hearts of bronze" and awaken them to sincere repentance, while regretting that she could not personally do more to bring lost souls to God. Just as during the League she had resented the limitations imposed by her sex, which prevented her from preaching the truth to kings and magistrates, so now she regretted the female nature that prevented her from becoming a missionary priest. "I felt such a pressing desire for the salvation of all of the world," she recalled, "that I wished that my sex did not prevent me from going to preach the Kingdom of God to the most barbarous and abandoned people, so as to announce to them the redemption of all!" Given this powerful sense of apostolic mission, it is not surprising that Sévin reached out to the souls of the fallen women she attempted to help. "I even went into places where people were living lives of ill repute, to rescue some poor abandoned girl," she remembered, and she noted with satisfaction that "several ceased their libertine ways, and one died shortly after having been well confessed and set at ease; the others retired from their abominations and made a general confession."[50]

Like other dévotes, Marie Sévin was willing to risk the censure of family and peers who disapproved of her unconventional behavior. When kinsmen reproached her for risking her reputation by going into unsavory locales, she made light of the risk: "I replied that I would willingly sacrifice my honor, provided that God was not thereby offended, if by my own humiliation I could work for the safeguarding and conservation of a soul, following the example of the Son of God, who exposed his life and his honor for the salvation of greater sinners."[51] Although a woman, Sévin dared to model her behavior directly on Christ's. She also dared to assert her right to independent values and judgments and acted according to her own understanding of godly behavior rather than submitting to social conventions and masculine authority.

This self-reliance was characteristic of dévotes and coexisted paradoxically with a religious rhetoric that stressed submission to authority and abdication of will. Despite the apparent contradiction, dévotes justified their ascetic practices as exercises in the abdication of will at the same time that they cultivated self-control—the deliberate exercise of will—as a means of accomplishing these mortifications. The same paradox lay at the heart of their relationships with spiritual directors. Although they claimed to submit unreservedly to the director's authority, their aim of abdicating self-will so as to accomplish the will of God ultimately authorized independent judgment.

Most dévotes began their practice of piety essentially alone or in isolation. They may have been inspired by a sermon or conversation with a priest, but they did not have a spiritual director or, often, even a worthy confessor when they took up the path to interior reform. Lacking good spiritual advice, they were often troubled by doubts—not about the need to change their lives but about whether they could trust the spiritual graces that seemed to reward their new piety. Brought up to look to priests to explain and validate religious experience, they intensified the practice of confession and actively sought out spiritual directors to whom they might confide the care of their soul. Once they found a spiritual director, they very deliberately abandoned themselves to his superior wisdom and authority. Celebrated spiritual directors such as the Capuchin Honoré de Champigny impressed on their penitents "the despising of oneself" as the central goal of their spiritual exercises, and they prescribed unquestioning obedience as the best means to achieve this goal. For Père Honoré, "to obey exactly all that is prescribed" was the milk of piety; "to abnegate entirely one's own will" was its meat.[52]

Some spiritual directors proved to be strict taskmasters. Louise Gallois's first director, also a Capuchin, subjected her to demanding tests of blind obedience. First, he ordered her to give away the one object of devotion that decorated her private oratory, a handsome crucifix to which he claimed she was too attached. He had her move out of her house to take up residence with a group of dévotes and then told her to change confessors, again depriving her of things she valued in order to school her in obedience. He next ordered her to give up her practice of taking communion daily and go two weeks without receiving the Eucharist. When this proved too easy, he ordered her to stay away from religious services altogether and to send her servants instead, while she did their customary chores. When she accomplished this joyfully, he tried a more painful command, asking her to watch others take communion but not allowing her the satisfaction of taking it herself. This, her biographer reports, was at first so painful that she cried mightily, but she afterward endured it with "peace and submission." The first time she received the Eucharist after these events, she was rewarded by special graces: God specially privileged her with "an experiential knowledge of his divine essence and perfections."[53]

This dialogue of command and obedience appears at first to reinforce traditional gender roles, with an authoritative and dominant male spiritual director and a passive and submissive female penitent. But not all spiritual directors were men. Women could give spiritual counsel and advice, even if they could not serve as confessors because they were denied the sacerdotal functions of priests. Marie Du Drac had "spiritual children," men and women who sought her guidance in the interior life, as did Barbe Acarie, who by the late 1590s not only received and counseled pious women in her home but also came to "direct as to their interior conduct" groups of dévotes. André Duval credits Acarie with advising dévotes on their behavior and the avoidance of temptation and also with teaching them good practices for meditation and prayer. Recognizing their individual natures and weaknesses, she prescribed hair shirts, fasting, and other forms of corporal discipline as each case demanded.[54] Charlotte de Breauté's biographer explicitly credits Acarie with instructing her in the techniques of meditative prayer but also with "taking on the care of her conscience and becoming in some fashion its director."[55] Nuns offered guidance not only to their sisters but also to lay women and men who, learning of their reputation for spiritual acuity, came to seek their counsel and instruction. Certainly it was most common for dévotes to seek direction from a male priest, and participants in many of these relationships adopted traditional gender roles, but this was not the only pattern these relationships could take. The submission was, in principle at least, that of pupil to teacher or beginner to expert in the spiritual life, and not weak woman to powerful man.

Moreover, exercises in obedience and abnegation of will could counter rather than reinforce traditional social hierarchies and roles. Françoise Hurault, the widow of a gentleman in the court of Henri IV and another dévote in Barbe Acarie's circle, insisted that she found obeying her spiritual director too pleasurable to be counted as penitence, and so she convinced him to allow her to take on a more "heroic" exercise to discipline her will. This exercise consisted in having one of her serving girls adopt the role of mistress, whom Hurault was forced to obey. To Hurault's biographer, the "act of sovereign abasement" this pious widow accomplished in submitting voluntarily to the "contrary humors" of a "rather haughty, critical, and enterprising" servant was both heroic and sublime.[56] Indeed, for Hurault, choosing to submit to the whims of a woman she considered her natural inferior must have been far more difficult than submitting to her spiritual director. Hurault clearly initiated this program of deliberate humiliation, and she had to talk her spiritual director into permitting the exercise. Despite the rhetoric of obedience, she was obviously not a passive participant in the relationship and had strong ideas about her spiritual progress and needs. The same is true for Marie Sévin, who worked for many months to convince her spiritual director to allow her to take a vow of chastity.[57]

The aim of all good spiritual direction was not to create dependence on another but to tame—ideally, to destroy—the penitent's self-will, so as to leave her dependent on, and totally submissive to, the will of God. François de Sales explained this clearly in the very popular guide to the devout life, the *Introduction à la vie dévote* (1608). He explains to his model dévote, Philothée, that once she finds her proper spiritual guide she is to submit to him in perfect obedience. "You must not consider him a simple man," de Sales advised, "nor should you place your confidence in him as such, nor in his human knowledge, but rather in God, who will favor you and speak through the medium of this man, putting into his heart and mouth all that will be required for your happiness; thus you must listen to him as an angel who descends from heaven to lead you there."[58]

The goal the dévotes pursued in their cultivation of the interior life was precisely this unmediated experience of God. They pursued it in their ascetic practices and in the spiritual exercises their spiritual directors prescribed for them. The successive deprivations that Louise Gallois's director commanded her to make were done less to school her in unquestioning obedience than to turn her from external forms of religious practice into a deeper and more internalized faith. He took away the handsome crucifix that she used to meditate on the passion of Christ so that she would have to picture more vividly within herself Christ's sufferings. He took away her familiar surroundings and the confessor to whom she was used to confiding her sins, so that she would have to dig deeper into herself, examine her commitment to the spiritual life, and travel its paths with only the company of other seekers. He took away even the comfort she had in frequently receiving Christ's body in the Eucharist, so that, by her intense longing, she would learn to receive this body spiritually. Moreover, Gallois's successive deprivations were repaid when God rewarded her with "an experiential knowledge of his divine essence and perfections." The lesson that we are intended to learn from these passages in Gallois's biography, like those in many other early modern spiritual biographies, is that abdication of will is a powerfully effective tool for achieving spiritual insight. Only by renouncing one's own will could one hope to be filled with God.

Blind obedience and submission to authority, even deliberate humiliation through a reversal of traditional social roles, were but other dimensions of the self-denying practices of penitential asceticism that early modern dévotes employed in their ardent desire to experience God. Within a religious context intensely focused on Christ's suffering humanity, it was entirely natural to associate bodily suffering with divine rewards. Denying one's will was paradoxically empowering, for imitation of Christ's humble submission to his Father's will was, like imitation of his suffering on the cross, a technique not of social discipline but of religious enlightenment.

The same lesson emerges from accounts of the child-rearing practices of devout women and the relationships between married dévotes and their husbands. The emphasis on the obedience of children to their parents and wives to their husbands tended to reinforce patriarchal norms, and yet in practice these relationships maintained a complex tension between dependence and autonomy, between abdication and exercise of will.

The Devout Family: A School for Obedience

The dévote's role as a mother focused much more on her daughters than on her sons. Boys were handed over to tutors and placed in school at an early age, their education considered a masculine affair that should not be subverted by too much maternal coddling. Girls, by contrast, were kept close to their mother, who was expected to personally supervise their education and deportment. Devout mothers carefully limited their daughters' contacts with the secular world. Barbe Acarie's three daughters regularly accompanied her to mass and other religious services. They were left behind, however, when family members attended weddings and other large social gatherings, to keep them innocent of worldly ways. Still, Acarie was not as strict with her daughters as some dévotes were. Her friend Catherine de Montholon, who later founded the Ursuline convent in Dijon, not only did not allow her daughter to leave the house alone, she did not even allow her to leave the room without permission. She obliged her daughter to follow her everywhere to "learn the exercise of piety, and never tolerated her going to those assemblies where, on the pretext of amusement, young girls in society are exposed to intensive flirtation." In contrast to Acarie, who made sure her daughters had opportunity for innocent games and insisted that "youth should not be too constrained," Montholon insisted that her young daughter spend every morning in church, "during which time she was not permitted to say a word to divert herself, nor to sit on a chair to rest."[59]

Although it may appear from the fact that all three daughters later chose religious vocations that they had been deliberately schooled for the cloister,

Acarie insisted—and the daughters agreed—that she had not destined them for religious orders but had allowed their natural vocations to emerge.[60] She considered the virtues that she nurtured in them as equally suited to secular or religious life. Patience, humility, and above all obedience were qualities as desirable in a wife as in a nun.

What is striking in the accounts of Barbe Acarie's child-rearing practices is not the virtues she aimed to cultivate, which were commonplace enough, but the very deliberate and concerted way she went about training her daughters in a submissiveness that both she and they equated with a total abdication of will. As part of the proceedings initiated for Acarie's beatification in 1632, her eldest daughter, Marie, described at length how her mother had always required of her and her two sisters a prompt and unquestioning obedience. When, at about the age of ten, Marie told a serving maid that she could not eat a particular sort of food, her mother saw to it that she was served this same food for several days running, until she learned to consume it without betraying any sign of distaste. When Marie was fourteen or fifteen and preparing to set out on a visit with her mother, she made the mistake of expressing pleasure at the trip they were about to take. Barbe Acarie promptly stopped the carriage and told her to return to the house. When she reached her room, Acarie summoned her and had her climb into the carriage again. The cycle of dismissal and recall was repeated yet again before they set off. The point of the exercise was to teach Marie not merely to betray no sign of personal preference but to have no preferences, no will of her own. "She desired us to be entirely indifferent in all things," recalled Marie, "even in the littlest of things, such as to desire one color rather than another in our clothing." If one of the daughters did indicate a liking for a particular color dress, she was sure to be outfitted in another hue entirely.[61]

Marie's sister Marguerite told a similar story. As a small child she loved fruit, and her mother, to train her early to subdue her will, would give her a piece of fruit and then ask for it back. She always returned it promptly and with no apparent ill feeling, "but the tears that would pop out a few seconds later were marks of the violence she suffered, and of the sacrifice that she made of her will in submitting to that of her mother."[62] Because Marguerite showed precocious spiritual tendencies, she was treated with particular severity. She was given only the coarsest foods; when she nevertheless consumed them with too great a show of appetite, Acarie had her plate taken away and forced her to stand at the family table while the others ate, so as "to habituate her early to mortification."[63]

These incidents were not presented as the practices of an abusive mother; rather, they were offered by Marie and Marguerite, and corroborated by a great many other witnesses, as evidence of Barbe Acarie's great sanctity. The daughters spoke warmly of the love their mother had for them and insisted that her reprimands had always been gently delivered and her methods of correction had never seemed unfair.[64] They saw their mother as repressing her own maternal instinct to coddle them in order to raise them according to such virtuous principles.

Equally disconcerting are the daughters' accounts of their mother's submissive behavior in the face of their father's frequently arbitrary and unreasonable demands. Marguerite's succinct testimony that her mother "practiced a great sweetness and obedience to my father, who often contradicted or opposed her" is amplified by the more detailed descriptions that several friends gave of incidents that occurred while Barbe Acarie was supervising construction of the Carmelite convent of the Incarnation in Paris. She played a key role in this project, going out daily to the building site and conferring at length with masons and other artisans. Witnesses' portrayal of Acarie as a competent and even forceful construction manager, inspecting materials and negotiating costs, contrasts sharply with their depiction of her as a submissive wife, who humbly acquiesced to the most arbitrary and petulant demands her husband made of her. According to this testimony, on more than one occasion and with no real reason Pierre Acarie simply ordered his wife to stop going to the construction site. When he did so at a particularly crucial moment, he forced the whole project to a halt for more than two weeks, leaving over one hundred workers unable to proceed. On each occasion, Barbe simply waited patiently for him to change his mind. When questioned, she explained that "it was necessary to obey; 'when it pleases God for me to work again, He will make my husband will it so.'" Sure enough, after some time had passed, Pierre told her that she should continue her work and strongly urged her to do so. The same witness told how, when Pierre said she must be home at a given time, his wife was so fearful of being late that she "trembled" just like a timid child who feared her father's switch.[65]

Witnesses clearly believed that Barbe Acarie's obedience to Pierre went beyond the normal bounds of wifely duty. One after another refers to the "spirit of contradiction" that seems to have moved Pierre to find excessive fault with his wife and even deliberately to try her patience. According to one witness, Pierre claimed good humoredly that, because his wife was to be a saint, his own role was to mortify her regularly so as to help her to become one, "and he was doing his duty well."[66] Yet they unanimously interpret Acarie's strict obedience to the husband that God put over her as the symbol and measure of her abandonment of her own will to God's. They recognized the extent to which her submission to her husband's authority, like her disciplining of her daughters, was the conscious product of her religious ideals, and they shared these ideals, even if they did not live them quite so fully in their own lives.

Seen in another light, when Barbe Acarie consciously decided to submit to her husband's authority as a form of self-mortification and obedience to God, she changed the psychological meaning of wifely obedience. Instead of a social practice justified by feminine weakness, it became a personal religious choice. The resultant behavior may have been the same and, lavishly praised by her biographer, may even have helped to reinforce the patriarchal value system for later generations of dévotes, but in her own mind, with each act of submission, Barbe Acarie had the satisfaction of having performed a religiously meritorious act. Triumphing over an innate resistance—perhaps even an unconscious resentment of her husband's arbitrary use of his authority—she offered up her own preferences as a voluntary sacrifice pleasing to God. As the product of a deliberate choice, the very act of submission became, paradoxically, a willful act of self-control and a secret assertion of autonomy.[67]

The same is true of the lessons she gave her daughters in denial of will. When she trained them from a young age to renounce any expression of preference or self-will, Acarie was in fact schooling them in a form of self-control that, far from extinguishing the will, effectively heightened it. From these lessons in self-control the daughters derived a sense of empowerment and a subtle independence of spirit. Teaching them to evaluate every potential act in terms of God's will, Acarie effectively taught them to cultivate the powers of discernment they would later employ to make their own judgments of what, in any given situation, God's will might be.

We can see this most clearly in the life of Marguerite Acarie, the most religiously precocious of Barbe Acarie's daughters. Allowed to make her first communion before the age of seven, Marguerite is reported to have begun to "rudely discipline her body" by the age of eight or nine, probably in imitation of the saints' lives that she read. Although Marguerite, along with her sisters, had to give her mother a nightly account of her "least and most secret faults," the girl very quickly took charge of her own spiritual life. By the time she was twelve or thirteen, she regularly sought spiritual advice from the distinguished clerics who frequented her mother's devout circle and even secretly asked Pierre de Bérulle to procure her a hair shirt. She begged her parents so insistently to allow her to enter the newly founded Carmelite convent that they permitted her to enter at the age of fifteen, even though they thought she was too young to have a mature religious vocation or to endure the Carmelites' austere life. Once admitted to the convent, Marguerite did everything possible to mortify herself secretly, because she knew that her superiors would try to moderate her practices if they realized their true extent. Her biographer calls her "ingenious" at finding ways to make herself suffer and says that if she happened to be observed engaging in a pain-inducing act, such as seizing hold of thorny thistles in the convent garden, "she concealed the pain behind such a display of contentment and satisfaction that it was easy for others to conclude that the cross and mortification were in truth her heart's joy." She continued throughout her life to engage in severe fasts, late-night vigils, and other bodily mortifications to the point where they repeatedly threatened her health. When ordered directly to cease a practice she would do so, only to take up another, equally punishing form of mortification as soon as she had sufficiently recovered. Ironically, when she was made prioress of the Carmelite convent at Tours she moderated the excessive practices of the nuns under her care for fear that they would harm themselves. At the same time, she took advantage of "the freedom that her authority as superior gave her to satisfy the powerful inclination she had always had for mortification and penitence." The strict fasts in which she engaged combined with her other penitential practices to permanently damage her health.[68]

Marguerite continued to engage in such practices because she recognized that Christ called on believers to "crucify the flesh with its vices and concupiscence." Her biographer expressed great admiration for the zeal she displayed in her willingness to destroy "the old Adam" even at the price of her body.[69] The desire to make a sacrifice of their bodies was a trope commonly employed by late medieval and early modern ascetics to explain and justify their mortifications. As with abnegation of the will through deliberate acts of obedience, the urge to "crucify the flesh" must be understood in the context of early modern religious ideas. Marguerite undoubtedly believed, as she had been taught, that it was necessary to discipline the body to subdue its sinful urges. And yet the fundamental impulse behind her extreme asceticism was not a dualistic rejection of the body and an attempt to become spirit alone but a more complicated desire to make use of her body in the pursuit of holiness.

Caroline Bynum has convincingly argued that there was a tendency in the late Middle Ages to see "the person as a psychosomatic unity, as body and soul together." As she points out, this is far from surprising "in a religion whose central tenet was the incarnation—the enfleshing—of its God." The tendency continued well into early modern times and was, among other things, both a cause and a result of popular fascination with the dramatic feats recounted in the lives of ascetic saints. Like the late medieval women whose ascetic impulses Bynum has explored, early modern dévotes assumed the person to be a psychosomatic unity and "not only read unusual bodily events as expressions of soul but also expected body itself to offer a means of access to the divine."[70]

The ascetic impulse that drove devout women like Marguerite Acarie to acts of heroic self-mortification during the early stages of the Catholic revival in France was paradoxical. Although consistently gendered as male, heroic asceticism was one spiritual path not barred to women. They could not enjoy the sacerdotal powers of priests, nor could they become missionaries in their own or foreign lands, but they could and did imitate men in the sacrifice of their body. The results of this sacrifice undertaken for personal religious reasons were unexpected; the women who successfully pursued the path of heroic self-mortification emerged as leaders of a powerful spiritual revival. They gained a respect and admiration seldom accorded their sex. Moreover, their ascetic practices prepared them surprisingly well for this new and unexpected role. Intended to destroy self-will so as to allow the mortified subject to be infused with the will of God, ascetic self-discipline produced individuals who were humble and yet confident in their intimate knowledge of the will of God. They may have ardently desired contemplative retreat, but they were also moved by an apostolic desire to serve. They may have wanted to be self-effacing, but they spurred along the religious revival by their reputation for holiness as well as by their direct efforts and service. Just as their own vocations had been encouraged by a desire to imitate the heroic deeds of desert fathers or medieval saints, so they served as models for a new generation of devout women and girls. The publicity given their heroic austerities generated a sympathetic and imitative response, prompting religious vocations and inspiring the generous lay patronage that built the convents of the Catholic revival.

3

Mademoiselle Acarie's Circle

Sometime late in 1601, Barbe Acarie reported a vision in which
Saint Teresa of Avila called on her to bring to France the order of
Discalced Carmelites that the saint had recently founded in Spain. A
group of distinguished clerics close to Acarie met in the chapel of
Paris's Carthusian monastery of Vauvert soon thereafter to discuss
whether the vision might be made a reality. With regret, they decided it could not. However much they wanted to see austere convents on the model of Teresa's reforms founded in France, the time
was not yet ripe for such ventures. Spain, which had intervened in
France's religious wars on behalf of the ultra-Catholic Holy League,
was in the public mind still the enemy. A diplomatic incident in the
summer of 1601 had threatened the peace made at Vervins in 1598,
and mutual animosities remained strong. Henri IV and the French
people would be no more willing to countenance the establishment
of a Spanish religious order in France than Philip III and the Carmelite superiors would countenance establishing daughter houses
in a hostile land.[1]

Barbe Acarie, however, was not willing to give up her dream so
easily. Prompted, it is said, by a second and more pressing vision,
she made contact with the translator of Teresa's works, Jean Quin-
tadueñas de Brétigny, who had long nurtured the ambition of bringing the Carmelites to France. She also found in Catherine d'Orléans
de Longueville an aristocratic patron with the funds to back the project and the social standing to present the case to the king. In July
1602 a second and larger meeting was held at Vauvert. This meeting
resulted in the decision to go forward with the project—to seek nec-

essary permissions from king and pope and bring some of Teresa's daughters from Spain to establish the new order in the proper Teresian spirit. As it was the presence of Spanish monks that, bringing back unpleasant memories of the League, could be expected to arouse the most opposition, the founders for the time being would seek to create only an order of nuns. This nevertheless would require some real persuasion. Would Spanish nuns consent to come without the Carmelite fathers who served as their confessors and directors? Would the Carmelite fathers consent to let them go? And who would serve as their French superiors in the fathers' absence?

A potentially simpler alternative was suggested. They could just get the Carmelites' constitutions from Spain and bring in French nuns from a reformed house of a different order to oversee their spiritual foundation. But Catherine d'Orléans vetoed this suggestion. She insisted on having Spanish nuns to transmit the authentic Teresian tradition, as well as the constitutions. As she was the major benefactor for the project, her objections carried the day.[2] Even so, the need to give the new order French superiors, in the absence of Carmelite fathers from Spain, meant that from the outset France's Discalced Carmelites were not just daughters of Spain. The French houses were not only juridically independent, issuing from special papal letters; they were also, it would later become apparent, imbued from the start with a subtly different spirituality. As the order grew and adapted to its French circumstances, the differences in character grew more pronounced. But before pursuing the Carmelites' French foundation, we need to look more closely at the women and men who brought it to pass. The narrative of the Carmelites' foundation must be set in the broader context of the spiritual revival just beginning in Paris. This chapter introduces the circle of key clerics and lay dévots who helped Barbe Acarie make her vision come true and explores the intellectual and theological foundations of the dévots' piety, so as to provide insight into the meaning of their personal asceticism and their ideals of reformed monastic life.

A Center of Spiritual Action

By the late 1590s, Barbe and Pierre Acarie's home in the rue des Juifs served as a frequent gathering spot for a group of devout lay people and clerics who sought to nurture their own internalized and often mystical piety and at the same time to spark a broader renewal of Catholic institutions and faith. The use of the house as a gathering place seems to have emerged naturally from Barbe Acarie's charitable works, her involvement in the spiritual and material lives of lay dévotes, and her active support of clerical reformers, whatever the projects in which they were engaged. Witnesses for her beatification proceedings described a constant stream of poor people who showed up on her doorstep seeking not just handouts but also help in finding lodging or jobs. On more than one occasion, Acarie took people in herself, until she could provide other solutions to their problems. Most famously, when a poor young woman who had come to her for help disappeared, abandoning six young children, Acarie took responsibility for the children and kept them in her own home until she could place them as apprentices in various trades. She took in Protestant converts to provide them with a solidly Catholic atmosphere in which to develop their faith. She even took in young women who had been seduced and abandoned, until her husband objected on account of her own three young daughters and she began instead to find the women lodgings in the neighborhood.[3]

In the midst of this domestic and charitable bustle, distinguished clerics and lay dévots came to the Acaries' *hôtel* to carry on high-minded discussions about the practice of piety and ecclesiastical reform. Sometimes as many as five or six masses a day were said in the Acaries' private chapel by priests waiting to speak with Barbe Acarie about the various projects in which they were mutually engaged, while she conversed with other members of her circle in an adjoining room. The names most frequently associated with the group read like a *Who's Who* of Counter-Reformation Paris. They include celebrated preachers Jacques Gallement and Philippe Cospeau; Sorbonne theologians André Duval and Philippe de Gamache; Capuchins Pacifique de Souzy, Benoît de Canfield, Honoré de Champigny, and Archange de Pembroke; Feuillants Sans de Saint-Catherine and Eustache de Saint-Paul; the future founder of the Oratoire, Pierre de Bérulle; and the Minim Antoine Estienne. Jean Quintana-dueñas de Brétigny joined forces with the group in 1602, when he learned that they shared his dream of bringing the Spanish Carmelites to France. François de Sales also frequented the circle when he was in Paris in 1602 and corresponded with some of its members after he left. The Jesuits were exiled from Paris until 1603, but Pierre Coton had close connections to the group after their return. Serving as a conduit to the king, Coton helped them obtain the royal authorization needed for their projects of monastic reform. He also frequently brought them a share of Henri's gambling winnings to distribute as alms.[4]

Among the lay dévots who frequented Mademoiselle Acarie's circle were René Gaultier, a high court lawyer and translator of writings by Spanish mystics; Jean Sublet des Noyers (whom we have already encountered taking his daughters to the Feuillantine convent of Toulouse); and Michel de Marillac, a superintendant of the king's finances and later keeper of the seals. Marillac recalled that, from his first acquaintance with Barbe Acarie in 1602, scarcely a day went by that he did not meet with her for one reason or another. By no means did the circle consist entirely of men. Marguerite de Gondi, marquise de Maignelay, Charlotte de Harlay de Sancy, marquise de Breauté, and Marie de Tudert, the widow of Jean Séguier d'Autry, are just three of the distinguished dévotes who frequented the Acarie house. Claire d'Abra de Raconis, whom

Bérulle converted from Protestantism in 1598 or 1599, came to reside with the Acaries and helped to educate their daughters. Along with other dévotes, she accompanied Acarie on her charitable rounds and visits to convents and churches. Louise Gallois also took an active part in Acarie's devotional and charitable endeavors.

Richard Beaucousin, master of novices and vicar of the Carthusian monastery of Vauvert from 1593 until 1602, must also be mentioned in relation to Mademoiselle Acarie's circle. The Carthusians' rigorous rule did not permit Dom Beaucousin to leave his monastery to join in the conversations held at the Acaries' hôtel. He nevertheless welcomed select seekers of the interior life to Vauvert, outside Paris's southern gate. Bending the Carthusians' rules of silence and solitude, he became, in the words of one historian, "the spiritual master of all of Paris's devout elite."[5] He also bent the rule that forbade Carthusians to accept women as their penitents and served as Barbe Acarie's spiritual director from 1594 until his departure from Paris in 1602.[6] On her recommendation, he accepted Marie Sévin and Charlotte de Breauté as his penitents as well.[7] André Duval, Jacques Gallement, Philippe de Gamache, Pierre de Bérulle, Benoît de Canfield, and Ange de Joyeuse are said to have also confided their inner lives to Dom Beaucousin and, in turn, received his direction. Beaucousin must thus be considered an integral part of Barbe Acarie's circle, even if he never set foot in her hôtel, and even if his role among Paris's dévots was abruptly cut off in 1602, when his superiors reassigned him to their monastery at Cahors. Some of the other monks are said to have complained that the dévots flocking to meet with Dom Beaucousin were disturbing their peace and solitude.[8]

As one historian has noted, we should not see the hôtel Acarie as a sort of devout salon, however distinguished the company: "It was in effect much less a place for meetings and conversations than a center of spiritual action."[9] Visiting convents where reforms were being contemplated or undertaken, Barbe Acarie attempted to reinforce the resolve of superiors struggling against internal resistance. At the same time, she used information gained from these visits to help clerics in her circle convert recalcitrant nuns to the cause of reform. André Duval credits her with knowing the nuns at the Filles-Dieu so well that she was able to coach the preachers she sent to them on just what to say in their sermons to have the greatest impact on their listeners.[10]

In many respects, the group forms a link between the ultra-Catholic politics of the Holy League and the dévot political faction defeated but not vanquished when Richelieu triumphed over Michel de Marillac with the "Day of Dupes" in 1630. We should not take this to mean that the group consisted entirely of ex-Leaguers embittered by the failure of the Holy Union. Marie de Tudert and Charlotte de Breauté, among others, were never associated with the League. Michel de Marillac abandoned his early enthusiasm for the cause by at least 1592 and instead advanced Henri de Navarre's claims to the throne according to the Salic Law.[11] But whether they had been diehard Leaguers ready to place a Spanish princess on the French throne or reluctant *politiques* accepting a Protestant convert as legitimate claimant to the throne, members of Barbe Acarie's circle shared a political outlook that can only be defined as ultra-Catholic. They continued to oppose the concession of civil or religious rights to Protestants and consistently supported activities intended to put an end to the Protestant "heresy." When repression was outlawed, they threw their energy into conversion. Not surprisingly, in 1598 and 1599, members of the group figured among the most vocal opponents to the Edict of Nantes. They also played a prominent role in the controversial exorcisms of alleged demoniac Marthe Brossier, the theological debates with Protestants that commenced with the Fontainebleau conference of 1600, and the campaign to readmit the Jesuits to France.

The role that individual members of the circle played in these activities depended, of course, on both clerical status and sex. André Duval and Ange de Joyeuse took advantage of invitations to preach in various Parisian parishes to denounce the Edict of Nantes; Benoît de Canfield publicly exorcised Marthe Brossier; and Pierre de Bérulle, ordained a priest in 1599, wrote a defense of the controversial exorcisms and proved himself adept in debates with Protestant ministers. By contrast, the women in the circle were limited to behind-the-scenes roles. These roles were not, however, negligible ones. Barbe Acarie prevented considerable embarrassment for the dévots when she revealed that a young woman whose spiritual visions and insights had won the admiration of such distinguished clerics as Beaucousin, Duval, and Bérulle was in fact a fraud.[12] Many of those who testified in favor of Acarie's beatification cited this incident as evidence of her remarkable talent for the discernment of spirits. The principal means she employed to reveal the fraud, however, had nothing marvelous about it. Handing the young woman a letter that was closed but not sealed, she asked her to hold it without reading it until someone came to pick it up. Returning several hours later, Acarie opened the letter, in which she had secretly placed tiny flecks of paper, to see if they were still there. They were not; the girl had obviously opened the letter to read it. This proved only curiosity, but it confirmed Acarie's doubts about her honesty and encouraged her to find other evidence to convince the gullible clerics in her milieu that the spirit possessing the girl was evil and not divine. The incident may appear trivial, but the emphasis all of the witnesses place on it suggests that, by revealing the young woman's bad intentions, Acarie saved her friends from a very public mistake and one that would no doubt have been used to embarrass the ultra-Catholic cause.

On more than one occasion she also helped spirit away young Protestant women converted by priests in her circle so that their families could not put pressure on them to recant. Making use of her broad contacts among Parisian dévotes, she hid the young women with Catholic aristocrats until she could convince the converts' families to accept their change of religious allegiance. Michel de Marillac credits her with being a gifted strategist in her ability to foresee and forestall opposition that would be made by the parents of these young women. Carefully hiding them with women of the very highest social status—he names the countess of Soissons and the duchesses of Guise and Longueville as among the devout women who cooperated in the scheme—she would selectively reveal the plan to either the queen or key members of Parlement, depending on where she expected the protest to be lodged. Then she would arrange for a Catholic relative of the girl to step forward as her protector, ward off the parents' anger, and ensure that the girl was allowed to remain securely in the Catholic household where she might nurture her new faith.[13]

The group's efforts to revive and reform monastic life also inevitably had political dimensions in the charged atmosphere that persisted despite the Edict of Nantes's ostensible resolution of France's religious quarrels. At the same time, the attempt to reform decadent convents and introduce vigorous new religious orders was rooted in a profoundly spiritual impulse, a fusion of mystical and affective piety that moved its adepts to dedicate their lives to Christian service.

An Active Mysticism

Some historians have credited Carthusian Richard Beaucousin and others Capuchin Benoît de Canfield with the dominant role in shaping the piety of other members of Barbe Acarie's circle.[14] The particular blend of Franciscan affective traditions with late medieval mysticism that formed their common heritage was, however, more important than any uniquely personal theological insights these men might have brought to Acarie's circle. Beaucousin and Benoît did not introduce new theological principles to members of the circle so much as guide them in applying already accepted principles to their own lives. In doing so, they helped forge an effective practical divinity from the affective and mystical piety of the later Middle Ages. Their true contribution lies in the spark to action that they, and other members of the circle, drew from the seemingly contradictory principles of self-abnegation and abandonment to God that dominated the literature of late medieval mysticism. Even here, it is the conviction and coherence of their pastoral guidance that is striking and not the originality of their thought.

Called by his biographer "the contemplatives' eye," Beaucousin helped transmit the heritage of northern mysticism to Paris's dévots. The Carthusians had long been engaged in the translation and publication of spiritual works. They brought out French editions of the writings of Louis de Blois, Henry Suso, and other late medieval Rhenish and Flemish mystics. They also helped make available vernacular editions of the lives of Catherine of Genoa and Te-

resa of Avila, along with works by other Italian and Spanish authors.[15] Beaucousin contributed to this project with translations of *The Evangelical Pearl*, the
work of a Flemish mystic (a woman whose identity remains unknown), in 1602
and Jan van Ruysbroeck's *Spiritual Marriage* in 1606. Steeped in traditions of
mystical and affective theology by his formation as a Carthusian, Dom Beaucousin nurtured Paris's devout elite in their pursuit of an internalized piety
whose ultimate aim was a mystical fusion with God.[16] Prized as a spiritual
director, Beaucousin also played an important role in initiating the movement
for monastic revival and reform. The initial plans to bring the Discalced Carmelites to France were worked out in the Carthusians' chapel at Vauvert, and
some historians have suggested that the reforms of Montmartre and the order
of Fontevraud were meditated there as well.[17] Because of the limits imposed
by his monastic vows, Dom Beaucousin's initiatives were carried to fruition by
others. Barbe Acarie was one of those through whom he chose to act: "He
charged her with carrying out the good works that his life of seclusion did not
permit him to accomplish himself."[18]

Although Richard Beaucousin clearly played an important role in the spiritual development of Barbe Acarie and others of her circle, there is nothing to
suggest that he left a distinctive stamp on the dévots' spirituality. In the case
of Acarie, there is evidence that, although she discussed with him every aspect
of her interior life, the relationship that developed between them was a recip-
rocal one; it was not simply a case of a learned male cleric edifying and directing
a passive female penitent. Beaucousin's role as Acarie's spiritual director began
in the early 1590s, when he was called on to advise her about her raptures,
whose frequency and power made her worry that the visions were demonic
and not divine in origin, and yet within months of his first meetings with
Acarie, Dom Beaucousin had confided to André Duval that he found in his
penitent "a hidden treasure," adding that "however well versed he was in spiritual things, he was learning more from her than she was from him."[19]

Unlike Beaucousin, who left no original writings, Benoît de Canfield was
the author of one of the early seventeenth century's most influential treatises
on the devout life, the *Règle de perfection réduite au seul point de la volonté de
Dieu*. Benoît's *Rule of Perfection* was not published until 1609, but it circulated
in manuscript as early as 1592 and, at least in the opinion of some historians,
began almost immediately to leave its mark.[20] Optat de Veghel, Benoît's Capuchin biographer, explains that the *Rule of Perfection* focuses all piety on "the
intention of conforming oneself to the will of God alone":

> This insistence on pure intention centers all of spiritual life on inte-
> rior attitude, which attitude must be that of a soul open, in all its
> human actions, to the pure love of God. It demands an indefatigable
> and continual effort to attain this purity of intention, on which de-
> pends all of the progress of spiritual life, which is ascetic as well as

mystical. In following this road of pure love, the soul will rise, thanks to an active life that is supereminently contemplative, to the most intimate experience of God, the contemplation of Christ crucified in his state of man-God united hypostatically to the Father. In union with the "not my will but Thy will" of Christ in agony at Gethsemane, the Christian sanctifies and makes divine all of life, down to the most profane daily material tasks.[21]

Identifying three successive stages of experiential unity between the penitent's soul and the will of God, the *Rule of Perfection* outlines a progress from conformity to "God's exterior will," as manifest in natural, civil, and ecclesiastical law, through conformity to "God's interior will," as experienced through the illuminations and inspirations of contemplative life, to an ultimate conformity to "God's essential will," in which God himself is joined in his essence through a total annihilation of self-will. This three-part schema builds on the traditional division of mystical experience into purgative, illuminative, and unitive stages. More than his predecessors, however, Benoît identified purgation as a process required of mind and soul, and not just senses. It thus remains central to higher as well as lower stages of spiritual ascent. What is most distinctive in Benoît's *Rule of Perfection* is the requirement that every action, exterior and interior, be performed with the unique intention of conforming to God's will.[22] Both beginners and persons more advanced in their spiritual lives were urged to judge each action by this sole criterion. All but the most gifted souls were advised against even attempting to pursue the last and highest stage of perfection—immediate union with God—though surely reading about such lofty pursuits was a large part of the book's appeal. Even if one ignored the third, or unitive stage of the search for perfection, however, Benoît de Canfield's *Rule of Perfection* offered the prospect of an intense and rewarding spirituality without at the same time requiring retreat from the world.

Herein lies its principal appeal. As one historian observes, "As high as the book rises, it rests on the idea that the exercise of the will of God does not require a cloistered life. One discovers this will in the duties of the worldly estate as well as in religious life, in all of life's occurrences. One discovers it finally, and most profoundly, in one's own soul."[23] The whole idea was to eliminate the distinction between contemplative and worldly states, to bring them together so that even when engaged in secular tasks the soul remained thoroughly engaged with God. The *Rule of Perfection* thus led not to an abstract mysticism or to quietism but to an active and engaged, yet still mystical spirituality, which found both its starting and end points in the essential union of man and God on the cross.[24]

Benoît identified the source of the *Rule of Perfection* as his own interior practices. These practices in turn derived from both his Capuchin training and authors in vogue at the time he wrote. Earlier spiritual writers might have had other ways of expressing what Benoît calls conformity to the will of God, but the idea of the soul rising through "pure love" to God and the principle of the "allness of God and nothingness of humankind" were central to later sixteenth-century spirituality and pervasive in the writings of both northern mystics and Italian and Spanish authors on the devout life. The fact that these ideas were common currency among Benoît's late medieval predecessors and his contemporaries makes it difficult to identify his influence with any certainty. His characteristic terminology and emphases are seldom identifiable outside of the writings of his fellow Capuchins, and the works that have been identified as the most probable direct sources for the *Rule of Perfection* were well-known in devout circles. The works of Henry Herp (Harphius), John Tauler, and Catherine of Genoa, the *Spiritual Combat* by Lorenzo Scupoli, the *Brief Discourse on Interior Perfection* (the anonymously published work of an Italian dévote named Isabella Bellinzaga), and *The Art of Serving God* by Benoît's fellow Franciscan Alonso of Madrid were all readily available in French editions in the 1590s.[25] This makes it difficult if not impossible to separate ideas gleaned from the *Rule of Perfection* from those derived from common sources.

Historians trying to study the origin of Pierre de Bérulle's ideas inevitably encounter the same difficulty. Bérulle's first published work, his *Bref discours de l'abnégation intérieure*, which appeared anonymously in 1599, shares with the *Rule of Perfection* the belief that self-abnegation, or a rooting out of self-love, is a necessary first step toward progress in the spiritual life. On the other hand, Catherine of Genoa, Harphius, Tauler, and the *Brief Discourse on Interior Perfection* all taught self-annihilation (or "spiritual poverty" or "nothingness") as the necessary path to union with God. It is impossible to know whether Bérulle was influenced here by Benoît or merely had absorbed the same spiritual literature.[26]

The problem of common readings similarly complicates any attempt to evaluate Barbe Acarie's spirituality in terms of Benoît's ideas.[27] There is evidence that she was strongly influenced by Tauler's *Institutions divines* even before she met Benoît, and Scupoli's *Spiritual Combat* was, at least in later life, one of her favorite books.[28] Catherine of Genoa and other writers who influenced Benoît were undoubtedly familiar to her as well. It is thus not surprising that Acarie's only preserved spiritual writings, her *Vrays exercices*, employ the same rhetoric of "all and nothing" that Benoît shares with his sources. She may sound like Benoît when she prays "Make my spirit conform to your human and blessed spirit . . . enlighten my interior with the light of your divinity, inasmuch as I believe that you are in me totally," but the *Vrays exercices* have been shown to be largely an expansion of and embroidery on a variety of late medieval spiritual writings, most particularly a treatise by Louis de Blois, a Flemish mystic whose work Benoît undoubtedly knew as well.[29]

In the end, it matters little if we cannot separate the lessons that Acarie, Bérulle, and other dévots learned from Richard Beaucousin and Benoît de

Canfield from those absorbed more broadly from spiritual works circulating in late sixteenth-century Paris.[30] The important thing is that all drew on a common intellectual heritage dominated by the concepts of conformity to God's will, pure love, and the allness of God and nothingness of humankind. Whatever personal emphases they subsequently developed, the dévots shared a belief that spiritual progress depended on emptying oneself of all that was human and therefore base so as to effect union with the divine by the unique power of God's pure love as manifest in Christ's sacrifice on the cross. The spirituality that emerged was mystical but also active; it emphasized purgation more than illumination and envisioned the state of union with God as a spur to action and not retreat. It was Christocentric, focusing most often on the suffering humanity of Christ on the cross, although sometimes, as with Benoît, the fusion of man and God on the cross became a particular focus of meditation.

If Benoît offered a distinctive synthesis of these ideas, they were nevertheless already available in the writings by late medieval mystics that were the favorite readings of late sixteenth-century dévots. Their influence can be readily detected, for example, in the spiritual exercise that Marie Du Drac set down for one of her spiritual children some years before her death in 1590, which was premised on the need to empty oneself entirely of self-will so as to become a vehicle for the will of God. In language that closely resembles that later flowing from the pens of Benoît de Canfield, Pierre de Bérulle, and Barbe Acarie, Du Drac wrote that "human perfection consists of an entire mortification of all evil passions and all self-love and sensual love, with regard both to ourselves and to all other creatures of this world." It was necessary to remove from the heart anything that might separate it from God, so that our love would be pure and we would seek him and not ourselves. Pray, she wrote, that "you be crucified to the world, and the world be crucified in you." The tool for accomplishing this purgation was meditation on Christ's life, death, and most especially his passion. "Picture to yourself Christ on the cross, the agony of death," she advised, "and then ask for the entire mortification of your imperfections." At bedtime, she recommended, after recollecting your sins and asking God's pardon for them, offer to him "all of the pains, sorrows, and sadness" that Christ endured in this world. She recommended reciting afterward a little prayer by Saint Gertrude, in which she asks to rest in the breast of Christ in the same union in which he has rested for all eternity in the breast of his heavenly Father, in which he rested for nine months in the Virgin's womb, and in which he rests with all of the elect, united to them by perfect love. Then go to sleep, she added, meditating on the cross.[31]

I dwell on Marie Du Drac's Christocentrism because historians of seventeenth-century French religion, intent on demonstrating the originality of their chosen period, have tended to depict the late sixteenth century as mired in an "abstract mysticism" that aimed at direct absorption into the Godhead, unmediated by contemplation of Christ.[32] Identifying a new "French school of devotion" in the works of Pierre de Bérulle and François de Sales, historians see as the key innovation of this "school" a Christocentrism that owes much to Teresa of Avila. They cite as evidence a letter that Ana de Jesús, the Spanish prioress of the first French Carmelite monastery, sent back to Spain in 1605, in which she wrote: "I take care that they [the Carmelite novices] consider and imitate our Lord Jesus Christ because here people pay little attention to him; everything takes place in a simple looking at God. I don't know how this is done. Since the time of the glorious Saint Denis who wrote mystical theology everyone has continued to apply himself to God by suspension rather than imitation. It is a very strange manner of proceeding."[33]

Ana de Jesús is not, however, a reliable guide to contemporary French spirituality. She arrived in Paris in 1604 speaking no French and believing herself embarked on dangerous missionary work in a country destroyed by heresy. Her correspondence reflects her presuppositions and biases more than it does any true understanding of French spirituality.[34] As we have observed, Parisian piety was clearly Christocentric at the time of the League, and there is no reason to assume that this was new. When Marie Sévin's mother instructed her as a child that "we were not made for the world but rather for God, who put us into the world to have us imitate Christ," she was repeating a lesson commonly taught in pious Catholic families in late sixteenth-century Paris.[35] The imitation of Christ was as central to the piety of lay dévots as it was to members of the new religious orders, and only a willful exclusion of the many manifestations of eucharistic devotion in the later sixteenth century can produce the impression that God was sought in any way exclusive of Christ.

The northern mystics were, moreover, far from being the only spiritual writers favored by sixteenth-century dévots. The writings of Saint Bonaventura, the "Seraphic Doctor" considered after Francis himself as the font of the Franciscan affective tradition, were available in French translation at least by 1580, when his *Contemplations on the Passion* appeared. These teachings reached the dévots directly and not just through the medium of northern mystics and later Franciscans, as is sometimes assumed. Marie d'Hannivel's religious conversion, for example, is reported to have been sparked by Bonaventura's *Arrow of Divine Love*: "While reading the passage where he discusses pure love, her mind, illuminated by a celestial light, conceived instantaneously the greatness of God, the vanity of the world, and the nothingness of its creatures; this supernatural light touched her heart and imprinted upon it divine love in all of its ardor and the disdain for oneself that Jesus Christ requires of those who would follow him." One can hardly imagine a more precise summary of the premises that formed the solid kernel of spiritual truth for the dévots than this single lapidary sentence in which these truths are attributed at one and the same time to Saint Bonaventura and divine illumination. Marie d'Hannivel's biographer impresses on the reader the impact of this illuminating moment by directly connecting it to the changes she made in her behavior so as "no longer to follow her own inclinations in anything but rather to combat them in even the most indifferent things." It was at this point that she began to fast rigorously and discipline her body with thistles and holly, lacking proper scourges and whips, and a short time later that she undertook her barefoot pilgrimage from Rouen to Pontoise, a distance of more than fifty miles, thereby obliging her body "to subject itself to the fervor of her soul."[36] Hannivel's asceticism thus derived directly from her understanding of Bonaventura's doctrine of pure love, which, far from encouraging an abstract mysticism, urged her to take up her cross and follow Christ.

The most popular spiritual writer in late sixteenth-century Paris, moreover, was not a northern mystic but the Spanish Dominican Luis de Granada. More than twenty works by this prolific teacher of the devout life were published in Paris between 1572 and 1600, many in multiple editions.[37] Granada is one of only two authors that Marie Sévin singles out by name in recalling the devotional literature that gave her great pleasure from childhood.[38] François de Sales recommends him above all other writers on prayer and meditation in a letter to a Dijonnaise dévote, and he places his name first among the guides to confessing well in his *Introduction à la vie dévote*.[39] Granada's appeal, moreover, extended beyond the dévots. Even Pierre de L'Estoile, who dismissed most writings with mystical overtones as superstitious claptrap (he called the *Life of Saint Teresa* "the Bible of Bigots"), had complimentary things to say about Luis de Granada. Although he sold his fine calf-bound edition of Granada's works to "the community of dévotes" living in his parish in 1607, he appears to have parted with the books with some regret. "There are lovely things contained there," he noted, "and great consolation and edification."[40]

What was in Granada's works that appealed simultaneously to ultra-Catholic dévots and a very moderate Catholic like L'Estoile, whose unusually ecumenical taste in spiritual literature caused him to read as many Protestant as Catholic devotional works? L'Estoile's key criterion in judging a devotional work was whether it reinforced the message of the New Testament. His evangelical tendencies are evident in the comment he made on purchasing Benoît de Canfield's *Rule of Perfection* hot off the press in December 1608. He bought the book only on the insistence of a cousin who had joined the Capuchins and clearly doubted that he would like it. "I have no other rule of perfection than that which is contained in my New Testament," he remarked, "where I seek it and not elsewhere, not approving either a Capuchin [rule of perfection] or any other except insofar as it agrees with it."[41] The dévots would have disagreed with L'Estoile's judgment of many of the devotional works they prized, but they would nevertheless have agreed that conformity to the Gospels was the touchstone of religious truth and prized the lessons they found in Granada's writings on the imitation of Christ.

Historians who attempt to build a case for the prevalence of abstract mysticism not only ignore the clear evidence of traditional religious practice and popular trends in spiritual reading, they also distort the message of the spiritual works read and written by those whom they accuse of this practice. German mysticism was strongly rooted in the affective piety of Bonaventura and other Franciscan writers. Modeling one's own abnegation on Christ's surrender of will was everywhere recommended, and, as both Marie d'Hannivel's lessons from Bonaventura and Marie Du Drac's prayer by Saint Gertrude demonstrate, the idea of the "pure love of God" encompassed rather than bypassed Christ.[42] It is particularly ironic to see the Capuchin Benoît de Canfield, heir to the Franciscan affective tradition, accused of abstract mysticism. It is also unjust. The *Rule of Perfection* teaches clearly that even the highest form of mystical union with God is to be reached through contemplation of Christ crucified. Benoît is quite explicit, moreover, in rejecting "speculation" in favor of "abnegation" as a path to God. "The former is more pleasant, the latter more useful," he writes. "The one prevails through joy, the other through solidity and security; the former is not within the grasp of all, even if they wish to follow it, [but] no one is excluded from the latter, if he be of good will."[43]

It is equally unjust to accuse Barbe Acarie of indoctrinating would-be Carmelites in "a method of prayer that encouraged suspension of the faculties and bypassing the humanity of Christ."[44] That Acarie's piety was intensely focused on Christ—and in particular on his passion—long before she encountered Teresa of Avila cannot be in doubt. This is strikingly demonstrated in the lines "O sweet Jesus! I take all the sins that are in me and plunge them into your very dear wounds to be lost and annihilated; I throw them, my beloved, into the admirable fire of your divine love, in order that you may annihilate and consume them entirely" in her *Vrays exercices*, but the exercises as a whole display the same passionate confidence in the redemptive power of the suffering Christ.[45] The *Vrays exercices* have sometimes been dismissed as unoriginal and therefore of little value because they consist largely of a reworking of and embroidery on writings by Louis de Blois. It is true that the image of plunging one's sins into Christ's wounds is among the identifiable borrowings, and yet it is wrong to dismiss the deep emotions expressed here as inauthentic just because the central image was taken from another work. Originality was not valued by Acarie (or others of her generation), particularly where spiritual writings were concerned. The *Vrays exercices* demonstrate well a technique for prayer commonly adopted by Acarie and other dévots in which passages from a favorite author became explicit objects of meditation, so that through both repetition and imaginative contemplation they were personalized and interiorized.[46] The deep yearning and repeated calls to Christ's love in Acarie's *Vrays exercices* are clearly heartfelt and not mere mechanical borrowings.

Far from engaging in abstract mysticism, Barbe Acarie warned against precisely this sort of practice: "She strongly condemned the devotion of those who practiced an objectless prayer . . . and strongly advised always taking some point for meditation, whether the Passion or another mystery." At the same time, "she was a great enemy of palpable [*sensible*], or rather sensual devotions, which she believed subject to grave illusions and called fodder for self-love." She opposed excessive religious fervor for the same reason. Condemning it as sensual and therefore transient and even bestial, she taught that it lowered those who practiced it rather than raising them closer to God.[47] Her advice on this point shows how thoroughly she had assimilated the all/nothing dialectic central to late medieval theology, with its Neoplatonic premise that only by emptying oneself of everything that acted on the senses and even the emotions could one make progress toward virtue and ultimately rise to the pure spirit that was God.

Equally important, she opposed any form of devotion or prayer that did not result in "the practice of virtues."[48] This is the crux of the matter. For Acarie, and for others in her circle, even the highest state of mystical absorption into God was not envisioned as an end in itself but as a means of activating oneself to serve as God's tool or agent. As Feuillant Dom Sans de Sainte-Catherine explained it, Acarie had learned that "although occupying oneself with God is a more divine and noble action and sweeter to the soul than to occupy oneself for God, nevertheless, when it is necessary to descend from God to the things of this [worldly] life for the service of this same God, this is called leaving God for God."[49] On the other hand, as Jesuit Pierre Coton saw it, Acarie did not in fact have to "leave God for God" when she occupied herself with mundane tasks. He explained by analogy with Christ that Acarie

> was ordinarily united to God by a very eminent elevation of the su-
> perior part of her soul, which would have caused in someone else
> an almost continual state of ecstasy, without anything, or with very
> little, spilling over to the senses, or even to the lower portion of the
> soul. And just as the soul of Our Lord was never distracted, even
> though it was occupied with some exterior action, preaching, work-
> ing of miracles, verbal discussions, travels, taking of nourishment,
> or other [activity]; similarly . . . [Mademoiselle] Acarie's soul, even
> when she was engaged in worldly activities, the care of her house-
> hold, the service of the poor, and spiritual matters of those who vis-
> ited her, or whom she visited, did not ordinarily lose God from
> sight.[50]

According to Anne de Saint-Laurent, a Carmelite lay sister at Pontoise, this ability to remain entirely engaged with God regardless of what was occurring around her was not just characteristic of Acarie's own piety but was also a behavior she encouraged in others: "She strongly incited us . . . to unite all of our actions to those of Our Lord Jesus Christ and [taught] that a soul outside of the presence of God was like a fish out of water."[51]

This quality of carrying out secular tasks while remaining in the highest part of one's soul united with God, which we might call an "active mysticism," is something Acarie had to learn. When her first mystical raptures occurred, they were so powerful that they interfered with all other occupations. This was disruptive to her family life, as a wife and the mother of small children, as well as profoundly embarrassing to her. Identifying her abandonment to ecstasy as a form of self-indulgence and therefore a hindrance to true spiritual progress, she sought to control her raptures through "suffocation of her appetites and mortification of her [human] nature." Observing in Paris "certain devout souls wasting their time in elevations while others were making swift progress through mortifications," she realized that the latter path was the more certain one and that it was necessary to proceed through "a long purgation and penitence" if one hoped to achieve spiritual heights.[52] Acarie's spirituality was thoroughly permeated with the belief that it was necessary to empty oneself of all that was human, or sensual, so as to create a void that might be filled with God. The late medieval fusion of mystical and affective spirituality was not a superficial or intellectualized religious outlook adopted because of a particular fashion in spiritual readings or pastoral guidance. Rather, it shaped devout behavior on a far more fundamental level.

It is important to recognize this if we are to understand the extreme ascetic practices of the dévots as an intrinsic part of their spirituality instead of dismissing them as bizarre behaviors symptomatic of psychic imbalance. For Barbe Acarie, as for others of her generation, penitential practices like flagellation and other mortifications of the flesh were not simply forms of self-discipline intended to aid in controlling unruly sexual or sensual appetites or to modify behavior into more "godly" channels. Rather, they were fundamental to the process of abnegation that lay at the heart of the pursuit of holiness.

"Souls Have No Sex"

Historians of late medieval religious practice have called attention to the "bodily" nature of this spirituality and, in particular, to the role of the body in women's pursuit of holiness.[53] The asceticism practiced by members of Barbe Acarie's circle was, however, common to both men and women, as it was common to both lay people and clerics and, in the latter category, to both secular and regular ecclesiastics. Michel de Marillac's penitential practices were as harsh as those of most of the women discussed in the previous chapter. He fasted regularly, scourged himself frequently, wore a sharply studded belt against his skin, and slept on the cold tiles of his household chapel until the practice began to ruin his health.[54] Jacques Gallement, although a secular priest, practiced mortifications as extreme as those of the early Capuchins or Feuillants. He fasted on greens doused with salt and vinegar, slept fully clothed on bare boards, wore a hair shirt, and flagellated himself often, doing rude penitence for even the slightest of faults. His biographer is explicit, moreover, in saying that he practiced these austerities not only "to more easily sap the foundations of sensuality," but also out of a desire to follow Christ's example.[55]

Male as well as female members of the group had visions and experienced ecstasies that, in some cases, deprived them of the use of their senses for hours at a time. Jacques Gallement's adolescence was marked by a prolonged ecstatic vision that, when he came to his senses again, left him shaking with fear. Seeking reassurance, he told his confessor that he had "entered into the chamber of God's vengeance and there seen Hell and the strange sulphurous fire in which the damned will forever burn. He heard the shuddering and desperate cries of devils and even recognized some people who had recently died, and he saw there a place that he learned was to be his if he were ever unfaithful to the grace God had given him." Although Gallement's confessor assured him that his fear was "filial," even if violent, and perfectly consonant with God's love, the experience left Gallement shaken. It loomed so large in his mind that through most of his life he was subject to bouts of prostrating terror. Gallement's ecstasies, however, were by no means always accompanied by terrifying visions. One Christmas he held up midnight mass for two full hours staring entranced at the host he had just consecrated. The assisting priests were unable to bring him to himself, and both they and Gallement's parishioners just watched in astonishment. As with Barbe Acarie, however, Gallement eventually moved on to a higher stage of mystical rapture. By the time of his association with the Carmelites his raptures are said to have affected only his "higher spirit," leaving his exterior behavior unaffected, so that he could carry out his functions as a preacher "thus ravished and yet with full liberty." He highly recommended to his penitents that they ask God for this gift.[56]

It comes as no surprise to find ecstatics among the Capuchins associated with Acarie's circle. While still a novice, Honoré de Champigny "was overtaken by the mystical sleep during which the brides of Christ rest in the midst of their outpourings of prayer and transported in spirit to the stable in Bethlehem where our Savior chose to be born in time. There he contemplated the mystery of a God bedded in a manger."[57] This vision is unusual for its time only in that it focused on the infant Jesus, to whom devotion became much more pronounced only in the mid-seventeenth century. The gender reversal implicit in the image of a Capuchin novice as a "bride of Christ" should not, however, surprise and serves as a reminder that, at least as metaphors, certain gender categories remained fluid. The medieval mystics whose works were commonly read by late sixteenth-century dévots frequently employed such reversals in the spousal imagery they used to express God's love.[58] Early modern writers borrowed this imagery, which was all the more effective on account of the asymmetry expected of the relationship of husband to wife.

Even by Capuchin standards, Benoît de Canfield's tendency to raptures was extreme. His vocation declared itself in an ecstatic union with God that transported him "entirely outside of himself" in a great fire of divine love. While a novice, his ecstasies were frequent, powerful, and often prolonged. He is said on one occasion to have spent two entire days in so deep a state of rapture that he gave not the slightest sign of life. Even poking him with pins provoked no response. His raptures, moreover, were so filled with frightful visions and anguishing temptations that Benoît and his spiritual directors feared that the devil was playing a part. As both Benoît's and Gallement's experiences show, it was not just women whose mystical excesses might be greeted by suspicion and even alarm. Benoît seems later to have gained somewhat greater control over his ecstasies. His penitent Marie de Beauvilliers nevertheless recalled that, while conferring with her, he sometimes fell into raptures that left him without speech or movement for indeterminate periods of time.[59]

The emotional and affective character of the spirituality of women in the group was also a quality shared by the men. Jacques Gallement again provides a useful example. His biographer describes his having a heart so filled with contrition and devotion every time he approached the altar that his masses were punctuated with tears, sighs, and even sobs. In his later years, the tears flowed so profusely that he preferred to celebrate mass only behind closed doors, so as to be able more freely to yield to his emotions.[60]

My point in summarizing some of the spiritual characteristics shared by women and men in Barbe Acarie's circle is not to assert that gender made no difference in the spiritual practices or religious roles played by members of the circle. Of course it did. Gender roles were clearly defined and their boundaries firmly fixed in this hierarchical and patriarchal society. No one questioned the notion that women were the weaker sex and intended by God to remain subject to the guidance and control of men. Subordinated to their father and husband within the family, they were subordinated to their confessor and director of conscience where spiritual matters were concerned. It is this latter context that is pertinent here. André Duval, Richard Beaucousin, Jacques Gallement, Pierre de Bérulle, Benoît de Canfield, Jean de Brétigny, and other clerics in Barbe Acarie's circle served as spiritual directors to the women in the circle but also more broadly to several generations of dévotes. They counseled lay women but also, in dedicating themselves to the reform and renewal of monastic life, became intensely involved in the spiritual direction of religious women.[61] Indeed, all of those just named except perhaps Beaucousin gained the reputation of being especially gifted in the cure of female souls, and even Beaucousin showed more inclination for directing women than his strict order normally allowed. It is extremely important, then, that the spiritual direction the clerics in Acarie's circle gave devout women reflected their personal understanding and experience of the ascetic, mystical, and affective tendencies they witnessed in their female penitents. They did not look on the spiritual states these women described to them as alien. Nor did they view them as inferior, "female" ways of relating to a God whom men might approach in different, more intellectualized, or superior ways. Recognizing, as André Duval's nephew and biographer wrote of him, that "souls have no sex," they treated their female penitents as their equals—and sometimes superiors—on a spiritual plane.[62]

This was exceptional at a time when suspicion of the female sex still caused many religious orders to forbid their priests to hear confessions from women, much less to establish the greater intimacy that spiritual direction implied. It is significant, for example, that Antoine Estienne decided to preface his *Oraison funebre* for Marie Du Drac with the "apology against those who imprecated against and despised the revelations Our Lord made to certain devout women and girls" that John Landsperg composed for his edition of Saint Gertrude's writings.[63] Clearly, Estienne felt somewhat defensive about the high claims he was making about Du Drac's spiritual capacities and hoped to silence potential critics through this appeal to Landsperg's authority. Landsperg's "apology" serves this purpose well. Noting that God "makes no distinction or difference between one sex and the other, having created them both," he singles out Old Testament examples of women to whom God gave a gift of prophecy, remarks on the fond attention Jesus paid to "devout women," and even offers the opinion that the feminine sex seems to be "more devout" and more apt "for loving God and contemplation" than the masculine. He concludes by expressing regret that so many priests shy away from demonstrations of this "inflamed desire for God" on the part of women, thereby depriving them of much needed consolations and leaving them "starving of hunger."[64] Subtly reaffirming the traditional gender order in suggesting that even visionary women required affirmation from their male spiritual directors, Landsperg (and, by extension, Estienne) nevertheless defends their value as witnesses to the marvelous graces of a loving God.

Antoine Estienne's citation of Landsperg's preface to the writings of Saint Gertrude is also a reminder that the authors favored in devout circles included a significant number of women, a fact that must certainly have contributed to the higher than usual regard in which the clerics in Acarie's circle held devout women, as well as to the opinion these women may have unconsciously formed of the validity of their own spiritual vocations. The female saints whose lives are most often cited among the readings of the dévots are those who inspired not just by their lives but also by their teachings and writings. The names of Catherine of Siena, Catherine of Genoa, and Teresa of Avila occur most frequently, but Angela of Foligno and Saint Gertrude are commonly cited as well. Two of the most widely read guides to the devout life, *The Evangelical Pearl* and *Brief Discourse on Interior Perfection*, were also written by women, though early readers of these anonymously published works may not have known this. Devout men as well as women savored these texts and sought to imitate the penitential asceticism, humility, and intense love for Christ's humanity that they displayed. Men too sought to learn from the visionary experiences of these late medieval women and to follow their ardent pursuit of union with Christ. But the authority these female writers gained from their visionary experiences—particularly, as Elizabeth Petroff observes, "the conviction of divine approval that comes to them with the experience of union with Christ"—would have conveyed an additional message to readers of their own sex, authorizing them to probe their own inner lives and validating their desire to share their spiritual insights with others.[65]

Among the women writers favored by Parisian dévots, Teresa of Avila was doubtless the most influential, because she spoke to their fear of heresy and desire to reform religious life, as well as to their search for models of the devout life. Teresa's critique of the relaxed standards of monastic life that she experienced for more than twenty-five years before beginning her reform and her reasons for premising this reform on strict observance of a rigorous rule directly inspired the founding of the Discalced Carmelite Order in France, but they also inspired attempts to reform Montmartre and other convents that had fallen away from their rule. The thirty-second chapter of Teresa's *Life*, in which she describes the terrifying vision of hell that precipitated her religious conversion, must have had a special impact on her French readers on account of the firm link that it establishes between hatred of heresy and religious reform.

The chapter tells how Teresa emerged from her horrifying vision of the place the devil had reserved in hell for her with an immense gratitude for God's mercy in delivering her from such a harrowing fate. At the same time, she explains, the vision inspired a powerful impulse to apostolic service: "From this experience also flow the great impulses to help souls and the extraordinary pain that is caused me by the many that are condemned (especially the Lutherans, for they were through baptism members of the Church). It seems certain to me that in order to free one alone from such appalling torments I would suffer many deaths very willingly." Resolving to do all that was in her power to serve God, Teresa sought the means to do penance for her sins, which, she firmly believed, merited even worse punishment than the tortures she had seen. But she also wanted to become "in some degree worthy of winning this great blessing," and this resolve caused her to look with a newly critical eye at the religious life enjoyed in the traditional, unreformed convent where she had long resided. "I was thinking about what I could do for God," she recalled, "and I thought that the first thing was to follow the call to the religious life, which His Majesty had given me, by keeping my rule as perfectly as I could." Instead of following the relaxed, or mitigated rule adopted by the Carmelites in 1432, she resolved to return to their original strict rule, which, among other things, forbade the visits to family and friends commonly undertaken by nuns in Teresa's convent.[66]

In the first chapter of her *Book Called the Way of Perfection*, Teresa explains to her daughters "the reason which moved me to found this convent in such strict observance" in words very similar to those used in her *Life*. At the same time, she expresses still more explicitly her belief that her prayers and conformity to a strict way of life might help overcome the evil of heresy:

> At about this time there came to my notice the harm and havoc that were being wrought in France by those Lutherans and the way in which their unhappy sect was increasing. This troubled me very much, and . . . I wept before the Lord and entreated Him to remedy this great evil. I felt that I would have laid down a thousand lives to save a single one of all the souls that were being lost there. And, seeing that I was a woman, and a sinner, and incapable of doing all I should like in the Lord's service . . . I determined to do the little that was in me—namely, to follow the evangelical counsels as perfectly as I could, and to see that these few nuns who are here should do the same, confiding in the great goodness of God, Who never fails to help those who resolve to forsake everything for His sake.[67]

Jean de Brétigny's translation of Teresa's *Life* appeared from the Parisian press of Guillaume de la Noue on 31 January 1601. His translation of the *Way of Perfection* appeared just a month later. Teresa's French readers would thus have had access to the works almost simultaneously, with the straightforward lessons Teresa offered her nuns on their practice of the rule and pursuit of religious perfection in the latter work reinforcing the account she gave of her own spiritual journey in the former.[68] It is no surprise that the dévots in Barbe Acarie's circle, sharing Teresa's hatred of heresy and eager to see French convents adopt a higher standard of religious life, should have welcomed her writings as offering concrete advice for the reform of old religious orders, at the same time that they awakened the desire to partake more directly of Teresa's way of perfection by bringing her order to France.

The Reforms of Montmartre and Montivilliers

Even before they read Teresa's *Life* or launched their plan to bring the Discalced Carmelites to France, members of Barbe Acarie's circle were actively engaged in trying to bring about the reform of convents in the Paris area. Efforts to reform the Benedictine abbeys of Montmartre, begun in 1598, and Montivilliers, in 1601, commenced with an intense focus on the spiritual development of already pious abbesses to awaken their desire for change but also to fortify their spirit against the opposition they would inevitably encounter to any attempt to impose new rigor where laxness had ruled. Port-Royal and other convents would later follow a very similar pattern of reform.

Marie de Beauvilliers arrived at Montmartre in February 1598 to take up the position of abbess that her brother-in-law, Pierre Forget du Fresne, had acquired for her. Raised in the well-regulated Loire valley abbey of Beaumont, she found herself at the age of twenty-four totally unprepared for the difficulties she was to face in ruling over this ancient but thoroughly impoverished and unruly house, all but two of whose thirty-three nuns were to prove resolutely opposed to any change in their way of life. A visit from her cousin Cardinal François d'Escoubleau de Sourdis, archbishop of Bordeaux, helped encourage Beauvilliers to undertake the reforms that her experience at Beaumont convinced her were necessary. Equally important, Sourdis, through his contacts with Barbe Acarie's circle, convinced Benoît de Canfield to act as Beauvilliers's spiritual director to fortify her for the battles to come. Benoît left to missionize in England in 1599, but his fellow Capuchins Pacifique de Souzy and Ange de Joyeuse took over the cure of Beauvilliers's soul on his departure. André Duval and other members of Acarie's circle also lent active support.[69] Acarie herself frequently visited Beauvilliers at Montmartre to "console and fortify" her, and she sometimes brought other dévotes along as well.[70] Dom Beaucousin encouraged her with letters, as did François de Sales, who visited the abbey during his 1602 trip to Paris and continued to correspond with Beauvilliers after his return to Annecy.[71]

Benoît de Canfield's direction aimed primarily at developing Marie de Beauvilliers's spiritual resources. In the words of the Benedictine historian Jacqueline de Blémur, "Benoît's work aimed less to remedy exterior disorders than to form [Beauvilliers's] interior to support submissively the crosses that God gave her to bear; he composed an exercise of divine will that was very useful to Madame de Montmartre, because she undertook its practice with a marvelous fervor, recounting to that father [Benoît] the least little sins that she committed; which caused her to advance with great strides in the paths of grace."[72]

Benoît's characteristic emphasis on conformity to God's will can be clearly seen in the *Conférences spirituelles* that Marie de Beauvilliers later set down for her nuns. We can, moreover, identify in these conferences the same key tendencies that marked the piety of Barbe Acarie and other dévots of her generation. For Marie de Beauvilliers, as for Barbe Acarie, emptying oneself of one's own will so as to accomplish the will of God led not to abstract and speculative mysticism but to positive action and, in particular, to church reform. The need to abandon one's own natural desires to live out those of Jesus is the central message of the *Conférences*. "This spirit of Jesus Christ, does it consist of doing great and heroic actions?" asks Beauvilliers. "No, rather it resides in a very common and ordinary life, a general deprivation of everything, a continual abandonment to the will of this good heavenly Father." For Beauvilliers, as for other early seventeenth-century dévots drawing on the same traditions of late medieval mysticism, progress in spiritual life was to be achieved through purgation. It was necessary to empty oneself out, to become a hollow vessel, so that Christ could enter. Again following late medieval traditions, she distinguished between the "spirit of mortification" necessary to purge the sensual passions and pleasures and the "spirit of death" necessary to purge the higher mind of self-love. But if mortification and the death of one's own will were necessary preludes to union with Christ, the means to this union for Beauvilliers—as for Benoît, Acarie, and other dévots of their generation—was the contemplation of Christ's sufferings on the cross:

> If the ignominious sufferings of our divine master are excessive, his heart is consumed with an entirely different martyrdom which continually makes him aspire to the state of host and victim, makes him desire infinite sufferings, and, finally, makes him die in a disposition of total annihilation and complete adoration with regard to the majesty of his Father: give homage to this victim God in allowing yourself to be penetrated by these sentiments.[73]

Marie de Beauvilliers's reform of Montmartre thus shares the spiritual foundations common to members of Barbe Acarie's circle. It is easy to imagine the pleasure that she and Acarie would have taken in their discussions in the abbess's parlor and the encouragement that each might have offered the other, sharing as they did the same understanding of the means of spiritual perfection. Outside encouragement did not, however, moderate opposition to change within the abbey, and Beauvilliers was able only gradually to put into practice a concrete program for reform. Ange de Joyeuse, with a special talent for gentle persuasion, helped her win over many of the younger nuns to the cause of reform. Within a year she had successfully reestablished strict cloistering and a common refectory, but further change took place only slowly. The recalcitrant older nuns put up great resistance at every stage of the way. Convent tradition even has it that they plotted against Beauvilliers's life and on two occasions attempted to poison her.[74] Only in 1608 was it possible finally to publish a new rule for the abbey, and even then the rule prescribed was a very moderate one. Still later, with an influx of new vocations, Beauvilliers was at last able to move the abbey toward the more ascetic life she herself had practiced from the start.[75]

One reason the process of reform at Montmartre was so slow was that Marie de Beauvilliers insisted on trying to win over the recalcitrant members of the community rather than expelling older nuns from their offices and using forceful disciplinary tactics. Benoît de Canfield's spiritual direction, which lauded the patient suffering of adversity, would have encouraged this approach. It was also counseled quite explicitly by François de Sales in a letter written in January 1603 in which he reminded Beauvilliers that "the gate is narrow and difficult to pass." She needed to patiently lead the sisters one by one. The older ones especially required care; "they cannot accommodate themselves so easily [to change], for the nerves of their spirits, like those of their hearts, have already contracted." Her own youth, de Sales added, also dictated a gentle and gracious approach, "for rigor is not becoming to the young."[76]

Louise de L'Hôpital was thirty when her well-connected family acquired the Norman abbey of Montivilliers for her in 1596 and thirty-five when she began to undertake the abbey's reform, but she too had her patience tried by internal opposition to her reforms. Located near Le Havre, the abbey lies outside the geographic limits of this study. The active role that members of Barbe Acarie's circle played in its reform nevertheless brings it within our purview, and we can benefit from the fact that evidence about the contributions made by Acarie's friends is in many respects richer than in the case of Montmartre. We are also better informed about the key role that Saint Teresa's writings played in inspiring Louise de L'Hôpital's program for reform.

Jacqueline de Blémur insists that, raised in the well-regulated Dominican convent of Poissy, Louise de L'Hôpital was shocked by the disorders she found among the Benedictines of Montivilliers when she arrived to take up the position of abbess in 1596. The nuns had not only abandoned their rule and constitutions, but they no longer even "frequented the Blessed Sacraments."[77] Despite Blémur's assurances that L'Hôpital knew from the start that she needed to restore order in the house and even admitted five novices only on the promise that they would accept the reforms she intended to make, the evidence suggests that L'Hôpital's own conduct at this time, though certainly not scandalous, remained more worldly than truly religious. Like most other abbesses who owed their position to family wealth and influence, she surrounded herself with the pomp and luxury more suited to her family's aristocratic status than to her own religious state.[78] She employed private servants, dined off silver plate, and wore a habit specially tailored from fine cloth. If the nuns of Poissy had raised her to respect the canonical offices and ceremonies of her rule, she had learned very little about the interior life of prayer.

Ironically, it was her casual disregard for the rules of strict cloistering that permitted her introduction into Barbe Acarie's circle. Visiting Paris in 1601, she encountered an old acquaintance from her time at Poissy, Théophraste de Bonjeu, sieur de Beaulieu and an almoner of the king, while making a social call on Henri IV's Protestant finance minister, Maximilien de Béthune (later duc de Sully).[79] Beaulieu, apparently recognizing some potential in the young abbess, subsequently introduced her both to the recently published *Life* of Teresa of Avila, which was already the rage in devout circles, and to the circle of dévots gathered around Acarie. Her personal conversion occurred very soon thereafter and, along with it, her intention of reforming the abbey entrusted to her care. On 24 February, she made a general confession to Philippe de Gamache in the chapel of the Acaries' home. Gamache subsequently confessed her several more times, including once in the queen's chapel, and celebrated a mass at which he gave her communion with the specific intention of "further confirming her in her holy resolution."[80]

Louise de L'Hôpital returned to Montivilliers in mid-April, but members of Acarie's circle continued to encourage her deepening piety. They also offered both spiritual and material assistance in the abbey's reform. Jacques Galle-ment, whose own parish of Aumale was located in Normandy, came to preach the Advent and Lenten sermon cycles and made good use of the opportunity to urge the nuns of Montivilliers to reform their lax ways. On his advice, L'Hôpital replaced all of the abbey's officers with nuns favorable to reform.[81] In June 1602 she established community for the nuns, requiring them to eat together in the common refectory instead of having meals prepared in their private quarters. At the same time, she reestablished strict cloistering. This meant, among other things, dismissing all of the private servants employed in the abbey to empty the convent of all nonreligious personnel. Acarie's associate Louise Gallois tried to assist with this stage of the reform by sending a widow and seven girls from Paris to become lay sisters at Montivilliers and take over the work formerly done by the private servants. Regrettably, we lack further information about who these women were and how they were chosen. It is evident, however, that the plan misfired. All but two of the women subse-quently abandoned Montivilliers.[82] The gesture nevertheless demonstrates a continuing effort on the part of Parisian dévots to further the Montivilliers reform.

The failure of this particular endeavor did not bring reform efforts to a halt. On Louise de L'Hôpital's request, the archbishop of Rouen appointed Jacques Gallement to draw up new constitutions for Montivilliers in 1603. The bishop also assigned two local clerics to the task. Gallement joined to them his young associate Jean de Brétigny and also the Capuchin Archange de Pem-broke, whom he knew from Acarie's circle. The constitutions they drew up were relatively moderate. As with Montmartre, they initially aimed largely at restoring the forms and essential substance of religious life by enforcing the rules of community and claustration and improving attendance at offices. Only much later did L'Hôpital try to inculcate in her nuns the ascetic practices con-sistent with her own very austere spirituality.[83]

Jean de Brétigny helped write the new constitutions for Montivilliers at the same moment that negotiations with the Spanish Carmelites over the plan to found a French sister order were coming to a head, and it is easy to imagine how the frustrations encountered on the slow path to reform in both this abbey and Montmartre lent a special urgency to the plan to bring the Discalced Car-melites to France. Witnessing the difficulty that abbesses such as Marie de Beauvilliers and Louise de L'Hôpital encountered in reforming old monasteries that had fallen away from their rule must surely have made the idea of estab-lishing entirely new reformed communities seem particularly appealing to the members of Barbe Acarie's circle. At the same time, the growing number of devout women who claimed to want nothing more than retreat to a well-regulated convent life must also have encouraged the desire to make a fresh start and establish new orders that ultimately might serve as models to the old.

4

First Foundations

On 15 October 1604, Catherine d'Orléans, princesse de Longueville, her sister Marguerite d'Orléans d'Estoutville, Charlotte de Harlay, marquise de Breauté, and Barbe Acarie and her daughters gathered at Paris's southern gate to welcome the Spanish Carmelites to Paris. Proceeding first to Montmartre, they prayed before the tomb of Saint Denis and commended to him the success of the order they were about to begin. The Carmelites remained for two days as guests of the Benedictine abbey before being escorted by their French patrons to their new convent in the faubourg Saint-Jacques, where a "great crowd of distinguished persons" gathered to witness their arrival. The anonymous chronicler who recorded the Carmelites' reception boasts of the "cries of joy" emitted by the gathered crowd, as "each thanked God for the treasure that his mercy accorded the capital and the great advantages that the faith would thereby gain."[1] The account is clearly partisan; anti-Spanish feeling still ran high, and not everyone was so welcoming. For the dévots who had labored for years to see reformed convents established in Paris, the entry must nevertheless have been a triumphant occasion, and it is not immaterial that the triumph was a very public one. The crowds whose witness solemnized the nuns' entry conferred public recognition on the pious donors whose money and effort had brought the day about. The nuns were deeply veiled, their faces invisible to the public eye, but their lay escorts deliberately placed themselves on view, associating themselves publicly with the newly founded order and the spiritual benefits they hoped would thereby accrue to themselves and their city. Such ceremonial entries assumed an important ritual role in the founding of new religious houses. Affording urban populations a rare glimpse of the holy recluses whose daily lives were shielded by their convents' high walls, they rooted the new communities in their neighborhoods by allowing the neighbors to participate vicariously in their piety. There was a curiosity factor here, but one that superiors of the new orders learned to turn to good advantage, just as they used the elaborate ceremonies for the vesture of novices and their subsequent vows to gain favorable notice from more elite groups—including both potential benefactors and recruits.

This chapter examines the foundation of the first reformed convents in Paris. It begins with the founding of the Carmelites' convent of the Incarnation and how a Spanish order was adapted to its new French home, and then looks at the almost simultaneous creation of a house of Capuchin nuns, or "Capucines," under the sponsorship of Marie de Luxembourg, widow of the powerful duc de Mercœur. The story of the Capucines is less known than that of the Carmelites because the former order ultimately radiated less broadly than the latter. Unlike the Carmelites' male directors, the Capuchins actively discouraged the Capucines from founding new houses, thereby stunting the order's growth and perhaps also inadvertently denying them the tradition of chronicling the progress of their foundations and recording the lives of their nuns to send to sisters in other convents. At the outset, however, these differences were impossible to predict. The two foundations proceeded from the same spiritual impulses and even involved many of the same individuals. Looking at the two orders in tandem can help us to understand the appeal they had for devout women seeking retreat from the world. The third section of the chapter examines the creation of a French order of Ursuline nuns out of women who had initially offered themselves as potential Carmelites. As with the Carmelite foundation, analysis focuses on the adaptation of a foreign order—the Ursulines were founded in sixteenth-century Brescia—to local conditions. In each section, I ask how elite patronage helped shape both the institutional structures of the new religious order and the social and spiritual roles it was to play.

Barbe Acarie's Circle and the Carmelite Foundation

Most of the key decisions affecting the shape of the new French order of Carmelites were worked out in July 1602 in the course of several days of meetings held by Barbe Acarie, André Duval, Jacques Gallement, Pierre de Bérulle, Jean de Brétigny, François de Sales, and Dom Beaucousin in the Lady's Chapel of the Carthusian monastery of Vauvert.[2] Although initial discussions focused on Rouen as the site of a Carmelite house, the group decided instead on Paris, which, as "the capital of the kingdom and gathering place of all the best people," would be advantageous for the order's later spread. At the same time, they decided to seek nuns from Spain to establish the proper Teresian spirit, instead of just adopting Teresa's constitutions, and to seek papal approval for the establishment, even though this was not really necessary, as the order already existed elsewhere in Europe.[3]

They also debated whether to found an endowed or mendicant order. According to André Duval, who has left one of two firsthand accounts of this meeting, Barbe Acarie "battled firmly . . . for mendicity"; she held out "for the greatest poverty, for she prized above all else blind abandonment into the arms of divine providence, even where the most necessary and essential things were concerned."[4] Others in the group were more realistic. They pointed out that Teresa, although as zealous as Acarie in her love of poverty, had not made this a condition for the founding of the order in Spain. The issue was left unresolved and is not mentioned in the letters patent authorizing the Paris foundation that the princesse de Longueville obtained from Henri IV later that month. Parlement, however, insisted on an endowment when registering the letters in October 1602. Catherine d'Orléans de Longueville agreed to supply the endowment, and in January 1603, she signed a notarial contract in the Acaries' parlor that provided the Carmelites an annual income of 2,400 livres per year. Michel de Marillac, who had assumed responsibility for getting the letters patent approved by Parlement, accepted the funds on behalf of the Carmelites.[5]

Equally important, members of Acarie's circle meeting at Vauvert in July 1602 settled key questions concerning governance of the new order. Recognizing that the current political situation made it impossible to bring Carmelite friars from Spain, they decided to give the new order French superiors. François de Sales, delegated by the group to seek papal permission for the new foundation, pointed out in his letter of November 1602 to Clement VIII that there was a precedent for this decision in that the Carmelite convent recently founded in Rome had been given a member of the Oratory for its superior.[6] Despite opposition from Spanish and Italian Carmelite friars, Clement VIII accepted the plan and inscribed it in the bull authorizing establishment of the order in November 1603.[7] The three men chosen to serve as the French order's superiors were core members of Acarie's circle: Jacques Gallement, André Duval, and Pierre de Bérulle.

While papal bulls for the order's founding were procured from Rome, Jean de Brétigny and René Gaultier set off for Spain to negotiate for the Spanish nuns considered essential to the new order's Teresian spirit. Louise Gallois, a Spanish-speaking cousin of Jean de Brétigny named Marie Le Prévost du Pucheuil, and a serving woman named Rose Legru, who aspired to be a Carmelite lay sister, accompanied the negotiators so that the Spanish nuns might have appropriate female companionship on their voyage to France. They were later joined in Spain by Pierre de Bérulle. Meanwhile, back in Paris, Barbe Acarie devoted herself to two important tasks. Having already begun to assemble in her own home the women who would be the first Carmelite novices, she moved the growing group into a house on the montagne Sainte-Geneviève, where she visited them almost daily. She also supervised the remodeling of the old priory of Notre-Dame des Champs, which had been acquired from the Benedictines of Marmoutiers to house the Carmelites, and oversaw the construction of their new quarters. Although Bérulle, Brétigny, and Marillac were all involved in one stage or another of negotiations with the abbot and monks of Marmoutiers for cession of the decrepit and underutilized priory, witnesses agree in attributing to Barbe Acarie a major role in planning and supervising construction of the new convent. Showing an instinctive understanding of building techniques and architectural principles, she dealt personally with the construction crews and their bosses. Visiting the site daily, she stayed away only when her husband, out of concern for her health or his own comfort, demanded that she spend more time at home.[8]

Along with Michel de Marillac, Barbe Acarie also assumed major respon-

The Carmelite church in the faubourg Saint-Jacques, by Israel Silvestre. Acquiring the decayed priory of Notre-Dame des Champs from the abbey of Marmoutiers, Barbe Acarie and Michel de Marillac extensively remodeled and rebuilt the priory to serve the Carmelites' needs. Bibliothèque nationale de France.

sibility for finding funds for the new convent. Catherine d'Orléans's promised endowment was intended to support the convent once founded. It did not cover the initial costs of sending to Rome, transporting the Spanish nuns to France, supporting the potential novices in their "little seminary" on the montagne Sainte-Geneviève, or, most significant, remodeling the aged priory of Notre-Dame des Champs and transforming it into a suitable convent for the nuns. Remodeling costs in particular exceeded initial expectations and required constant fund-raising efforts. Witnesses for Barbe Acarie's beatification testified to the supreme confidence she showed that God would provide, even though at one point the convent's debts totaled more than 80,000 livres.[9] Marie de Tudert, for example, cited Acarie's ability to get up in the morning knowing that 1,800 écus needed to be found to pay the workers by day's end as evidence of her saintliness. The Carmelites did succeed in paying off their debts, so perhaps Acarie's great confidence was justified, but the strategy was a risky one. Later convents made similar plunges into deficit spending without enjoying such providential rewards. More important than the relative prudence or recklessness of the financial arrangements, however, is the fact that so much responsibility for the project remained in the hands of a woman. According to Acarie's closest collaborator, Michel de Marillac, beginning with the meetings at Vauvert, "she was the one at the helm [cestoit elle qui congduisoit la barque]."[10]

Even more remarkable than her responsibility for the temporal side of the Carmelite foundation is the role Acarie played in selecting the women who would be the Carmelites' first French novices and guiding their spiritual development. As Marie de Saint-Joseph Fournier later testified, even more than she worried about securing funds for the convent's buildings, Barbe Acarie worried about selecting the "living stones [les pierres vives]" on which the foundation would rest.[11] As a lay woman, Acarie could not have been solely responsible for the spiritual guidance of the dozen or more women gathered at the house on the montagne Sainte-Geneviève. André Duval and Jacques Gallement came to the house frequently to celebrate mass, preach sermons, and hear confessions. Nevertheless, by all accounts, Barbe Acarie assumed a semi-sacerdotal role with regard to the postulants. She quizzed them on their inner lives and affirmed the vocations of some, at the same time that she selected out others as unsuited to the Carmelite profession.[12] Her assumption of functions usually reserved for the priesthood shows how much spiritual authority could be wielded by a woman—even a lay woman—with a reputation for personal sanctity.

A French Order of Carmelites

When members of Mademoiselle Acarie's circle debated whether bringing nuns from Spain was the best way to convey to their new order the true spirit of Saint Teresa's reform, they focused on institutional and logistical issues: Would the Spanish fathers allow the nuns to come without them? But at least one member of the group also raised questions about cultural compatibility. Unfortunately, the Carmelites' chronicles conceal the speaker or speakers' identity by using the passive voice, but the point of the objections is clear:

> Another difficulty was raised: the spirit [génie] of the two nations, which seemed to render them incompatible—the Spanish, of a grave and circumspect character, given to ostentation and exterior display; the French, by contrast, lively and frank, loving liberty . . . [ellipsis in the original] "Never," it was said, "could such a contrast be overcome. And the difference of languages? Another stumbling-block. How could the girls learn from others who didn't understand them? To count on miracles was to tempt God."

Despite these strongly expressed reservations, the group decided to proceed with the foundation. In narrating the decision, the Carmelite chronicles abruptly shift from a cautious fear of depending on miracles to a forceful assertion of divine intervention: "The moment marked out through all eternity for transplanting the Carmelites to French soil had arrived; divine power suddenly changed the apprehensions of these enlightened men into an entire confidence. They henceforth saw only the advantages of the foundation. It was decided."[13] The narrative strategy adopted here—the shifting of agency from the human participants in the enterprise to God's will—continues through the story of the French foundation, with the result that subsequent changes made to adapt Teresa's Spanish order to French ways are depicted as natural and inevitable: in short, as divinely ordained. A close reading of the sources makes it clear, however, that the interplay of human personalities powerfully influenced the adaptation process.

The fact that the Spanish nuns knew no French gave Barbe Acarie the opportunity to play a more direct role in shaping the new order than would otherwise have been the case. Ana de Jesús de Lobera, the companion of Saint Teresa chosen to head the new foundation, could not interview the postulants herself and left selection of the first French novices to the order's male superiors, who in turn relied heavily on Acarie's judgment. They chose as the first novices Acarie's maidservant and confidante Andrée Levoix, her assistant Louise Gallois, and the young Rouennaise Marie d'Hannivel. Within the next six weeks, four more young women were admitted as novices, among them Marie Sévin and Charlotte de Breauté. Of the seven, only Hannivel was fluent in Spanish. It was natural, then, for Acarie to continue to speak with the French novices about their inner lives, as she was accustomed to doing in the little seminary of Sainte-Geneviève (and as she had done for an even longer time with Andrée Levoix and lay dévotes Louise Gallois, Marie Sévin, and Charlotte de Breauté). Accompanying the princesse de Longueville, whose role as founder gave her the privilege of entering the cloister, Acarie spent a great deal of time in the convent instructing the French novices and "fortifying them against spiritual difficulties." The chronicles insist that she acted with the consent of the Spanish nuns in this and add that "this useful assistance, necessary in these beginnings, did not in any way diminish the activity, zeal, and application of the Spanish mothers to perfect their pupils in all ways possible to them. Overseeing their comportment at meals and during daily periods of recreation as well as during religious services, they observed the behavior of the novices in their least detail."[14] There is an important difference, however, between observing behavior and discoursing at length about the innermost movements of one's soul. It was Barbe Acarie who had privileged access to the thoughts of the new novices, she who helped them interpret and act on their spiritual insights, longings, and fears.

The Spanish nuns' power to shape the new order was, moreover, limited even before their arrival in France by certain decisions made by the members of Acarie's circle. The decision to entrust the order to secular clerics by appointing Messieurs Duval, Gallement, and Bérulle as the first French superiors was perhaps in the long run the most significant of these choices. Bérulle in particular was to mark the French order with his characteristic devotional style through the powerful influence he had on the first French novices, many of whom went on to become founding prioresses of other houses across France. But also important—and more immediately apparent—was the decision to build the Paris convent on a scale far greater than Teresa, who wanted her houses small and poor, had ordained. Although Jean de Brétigny was careful to obtain descriptions of just how Teresa had laid out the convents of her reform, the French departed from the dimensions set out in these plans so that the Paris convent "might contain the number of nuns necessary to prompt development of the order."[15] Envisioning the Paris convent as a hub from which a whole order might grow, the founders built the dormitory wing to contain not twenty-one cells, as in Spanish houses, but forty-eight. They proudly presented their work to a dismayed Ana de Jesús, who wrote back to a friend in Spain that it was not at all in keeping with Teresa's ideas but resembled just the sort of convent she hated. Teresa would have accepted it, she added, only because "it was built by secular persons who were as pious as they were ignorant."[16]

Although accustomed to worshiping in Baroque churches heavy with incense and crowded with images and shrines, Ana de Jesús found the newly remodeled convent church of Notre-Dame des Champs too rich as well as too large. She described it as having "ten chapels, each of which resembles the most sumptuous of temples down there [i.e., in Spain]."[17] Most of the many art treasures known to have belonged to the convent of the Incarnation— paintings by Philippe de Champaigne and Charles Le Brun, among others— were later gifts, marks of favor from the royal family and other distinguished

donors. Even from the beginning, however, the church interior was architec-
turally imposing, its grandeur more consistent with the French founders' vision of a great order that would spread through all of France than with Teresa's
idea of humble poverty.[18] From the start, there was thus a tension between the
French and Spanish understandings of the poor and humble life Teresa intended her daughters to live.

The importance of the language barrier in limiting the ability of Ana de
Jesús and the other Spanish nuns to impose their understanding of the true
spirit of Teresa's reforms on the French novices is evident in the reputation
that Spanish speakers like Marie de la Trinité d'Hannivel gained as not just
favorite daughters of the Spanish nuns but their most faithful imitators as well.
Hannivel's biographer pointedly remarks, for example, that she imitated Spanish and not French convents in the two foundations she supervised at Troyes.
Insisting that convent buildings clearly reflect the order's poverty, she kept
them small, with cells for only twenty nuns, and unadorned. Her biographer
further presents the disciplined work habits and rigorous poverty she instilled
in the nuns at Troyes as direct reflections of her training in the "holy school"
of the Spanish mothers. A simple anecdote illustrates the point. When Mère
Marie discovered that the pious founder of the convent in Troyes had been
given feather pillows to ease the pain of her final illness, she took them away
and substituted wool-stuffed ones on the ground that the constitutions' prohibition against wearing fur-trimmed robes was "more extensive in the spirit
of the Spanish text than in the French translation." Marie d'Hannivel's insistence on adhering to the spirit as well as the letter of the constitutions is
significant here, but it is equally significant that she modeled her behavior
directly on that of Ana de Jesús, whom she remembered having ordered a
feather pillow she found in the attic of the Dijon convent taken away and given
to the poor. "If the French find it here," Mother Ana told Marie, "they will make
use of it, and our blessed mother not wanting this, we should not have it."[19]

As the words attributed to Ana de Jesús suggest, the Spanish prioress
believed that French nuns "were not as hard on themselves as the Spanish
were." The greater self-discipline of the Spanish nuns was, however, at least
partly a matter of cultural style. The Spanish sisters, for example, were used
to carrying their handwork everywhere. They spun and embroidered without
pause through the evening's recreation and chided the French novices if, while
speaking, they allowed their handwork to cease. The Spanish nuns even
brought their distaffs into the church and continued to spin during religious
offices and prayers. They thought it perfectly natural that their hands should
be occupied while their minds were given over to adoration of the Blessed
Sacrament. They enjoyed singing while they worked and, "by a thousand demonstrations and exclamations of joy, testified to our divine Savior the ardor of
their love." The French had a very different idea of what constituted a pious
demeanor. They preferred a greater solemnity in their worship and thought it

disrespectful to offer God less than one's full attention, even if the repetitive manual task of spinning occupied only the hands and not the mind. They also appear to have regarded as unseemly the joyous cries with which the Spanish punctuated their prayers. This style of worship was, in the words of the chronicles, "very foreign to the French taste."[20]

Tensions caused by the cultural differences could emerge in unexpected ways. A festive occasion was nearly spoiled for everyone when the French novices found themselves struggling to swallow a highly spiced dish of cod with prunes that Spanish lay sister Ana de San Bartolomé García had taken great pains to prepare. Their evident distaste for the dish prompted a rebuke from prioress Ana de Jesús: "We have to eat your way every day, my sisters, and you can't accommodate yourselves even once to ours!"[21] The words reveal a broader undercurrent of tension than the specific occasion would seem to warrant.

Despite such occasional outbursts, the sources agree that for the first year or two after the Carmelites' founding, feelings of goodwill and mutual respect engendered by the high hopes that everyone entertained for the new order gave rise to a spirit of harmony that triumphed over differences of language and culture.[22] The new order grew quickly, which encouraged but also required everyone to pull together. A second house was founded at Pontoise in January 1605 and a third at Dijon in September of that year. The fact that a novice and two postulants were sent with the founding nuns to Dijon because the convent of the Incarnation was already full is a good indication of the Carmelites' initial popularity. Within two years of its beginnings in France, the order had sixty members.[23]

When the foundation was made at Pontoise, the French superiors decided that Ana de San Bartolomé, whom some regarded as an even closer companion to Saint Teresa than Ana de Jesús, should be given the black veil and raised from her status as lay sister so that she could serve as prioress of the new convent.[24] Ana de San Bartolomé and Ana de Jesús both opposed the plan, but the French superiors were insistent and overcame their objections. Clearly, they thought it important not just to have a Spanish superior for the new convent (which was necessary in any event, as the French were all still novices) but to have one who had personally known and worked with Teresa. When Ana de Jesús went off to Dijon to make the third foundation, the superiors brought Ana de San Bartolomé back to Paris, which had a special importance as the hub of the order even though by Carmelite tradition each convent functioned autonomously and the convent of the Incarnation had no superior authority as motherhouse.

During the first year of Ana de San Bartolomé's term as prioress in Paris, harmony still reigned between the French and Spanish nuns. In 1606, however, serious conflicts arose. The principal source of these conflicts was the Spanish mothers' unhappiness at learning that Messieurs Gallement, Duval, and Bérulle, whom they believed were to be spiritual governors of the order only until Discalced Carmelite monks of Saint Teresa's reform could be established in France, had sought and obtained a papal bull that prevented this shift in jurisdiction so as to perpetuate their own rule over the order's spiritual affairs. The quarrels between the Spanish mothers and the French superiors, especially Pierre de Bérulle, over government of the order have received considerable attention from historians of the Carmelites.[25] Most accounts of the quarrels, however, focus so narrowly on the conflict over the order's superiors that they neglect the broader clash of cultures embroiled in the affair. There are big differences between French and Spanish sources here. Ana de San Bartolomé's autobiographical memoirs in particular disclose a very high level of tension between the Spanish nuns and French participants in the new foundation. The memoirs were written fifteen or twenty years after the events they relate, at a time when battles over who was to serve as the Carmelites' superiors were raging in the Spanish Netherlands as well as in France, and Ana de San Bartolomé's fervent partisanship of the Carmelite fathers' cause inevitably influenced her writings. A number of historians have consequently assumed that the memoirs more accurately reflect her later frame of mind than the events they purport to recount. But Ana de San Bartolomé also left several contemporaneous accounts of the spiritual anguish she experienced during these years.[26] These writings, which have only recently been published, largely substantiate the story told in the memoirs, at least insofar as the question of Ana de San Bartholomé's state of mind is concerned. Whether she misread the intentions and actions of Bérulle and the French Carmelites is more problematic. The profound tensions her writings reveal nevertheless deserve a closer look.

The memoirs tell how, during her first year as prioress in Paris, Ana de San Bartolomé got along very well with the French nuns, who were "open and affable toward [her], as if [she] had raised them." But then the nuns became very distant and guarded. She blames the French superiors for this and claims that they feared that if the Carmelite fathers came to France all of the sisters would follow her in accepting the Carmelites as their superiors. As she saw it, the French sisters admired her actions as holy and wanted to imitate her, but "little by little they [the French superiors] won over the nuns. And as soon as they had them on their side, they told them, 'Don't disclose your souls to the Mother; her spirit does not suit you. She is a foreigner and, what is more, Spanish. Don't trust her. If she wants those friars, [be aware that] they will make life very hard for you. They are severe; their way of acting is not for you.' "[27]

Ana de San Bartolomé goes on to tell how, when she informed one of the superiors, presumably Bérulle, that the attitude of the French nuns had changed markedly and they did not tell her anything anymore, he replied curtly, "It is not necessary for them to speak with you, nor you with them. Your spirit is bad; we do not want you to contaminate them; you are possessed and you hate us." Accepting the pain this situation caused her as a cross she had to bear, Mother Ana was nevertheless distressed to see the French sisters "lose the simplicity and fervor with which they had begun." She also suffered greatly from having to make her confessions to the superior "who persecuted her most actively." When she asked him for another confessor, he refused, saying that "God showed him her sins." The situation got worse. She even claims that if she had not been so absorbed in her own agony, she would actually have feared for her safety. She tells us that the princesse de Longueville begged Ana de Jesús to take the beleaguered prioress with her when she left to establish Saint Teresa's reform in the Spanish Netherlands.[28] However, Ana de San Bartolomé refused to leave. She was convinced that God still had plans for her in France and spent three years establishing a convent in Tours before finally departing in 1611 for Flanders, where she hoped to return to obedience to the Discalced Carmelite fathers, whose direction she still considered essential to the order's rule.

How much of Ana de San Bartolomé's colorful account of her trials in Paris can be taken as true? Surely not all of it. However strained relations might have become, it is hard to imagine that her very life might have been in danger. Moreover, her correspondence from this period suggests that relations with Bérulle and the French nuns remained rather more cordial on both sides than the autobiography and private notes indicate.[29] Her conviction that the French superiors deliberately alienated the French nuns from her and that they played on cultural differences to diminish her influence nevertheless remains troubling.

The autobiography makes it clear that, although the choice of superiors lay at the heart of the issue, Ana de San Bartolomé saw the constitutions handed down by Saint Teresa as being under broader attack. She tells how one day Bérulle spent more than an hour talking with her about things he wished to change in the constitutions and the rule, insisting all the time that "he understood these things as well as [she] did." "He told me that Spain was one thing and France another," she relates; "I said that the Rule and the Constitutions should be one and the same thing here and there, and that I would not consent [to the changes he proposed]." This was not an isolated discussion: "These battles went on every day. They continually wanted to change things and to do them in their own manner."[30]

Moreover, it was not just the French superiors with whom Ana de San Bartolomé quarreled. Although she remained prioress, Mother Ana claims to have found her role reduced to that of "the least members of the house," and she blamed the French nuns as well as their superiors for this:

They had taken the government of the house into their own hands, as if they were prioresses, and they acted in the same way with regard to the novices. They had that lay woman [Barbe Acarie] and that lay man [Michel de Marillac] come to speak to them and inquire into how they were progressing. I suffered on this account, not for myself but for the order, for I saw that they introduced things very foreign to the religious observances for which they had brought us here. When I told them this, they told me to leave them alone, that they knew very well what the constitutions said.[31]

Even more than Ana of Jésus, Ana de San Bartolomé regarded herself as the protector of Saint Teresa's heritage.[32] When Bérulle insisted that he understood the constitutions as well as she did, she replied that he knew them "in a bookish way" but did not, as she did, have "experience in the way the order worked."[33] She was frustrated that, having been brought to France for the specific purpose of instructing the French nuns in "the way the order worked," her directions should be so frequently overruled.

Whether the French founders were right or wrong in repeatedly placing their own understanding of the spirit of Teresa's constitutions above the interpretation articulated by the Spanish nuns is not the issue here. Despite the claim to authenticity based on the importation of Spanish nuns, the founders of the French order consciously and deliberately adapted the order to fit their perception of local mores and needs. The quarrel over superiors was in its essence a battle for control of the new order. The French superiors needed to secure and perpetuate their authority if they were to continue to move the order in the direction they thought it should take. The Spanish mothers, by contrast, hoped to replace the French superiors with Discalced Carmelites because that was how Teresa set up the order but also because they expected this change to restore their own authority among the French nuns. Both sides believed that the order's future was at stake.

The choice of superiors was not the only point where the Spanish nuns believed the French founders had departed from Teresa's rule. The implications of the decision to build the first convent on a grand scale remained worrisome to them. Teresa had wanted her convents small to prevent the sort of factionalism she had experienced in Avila's unreformed convent of the Incarnation, but she also believed that small convents could best maintain the quiet isolation she believed essential to the cultivation of a deeply interiorized spirituality. Poverty was another means to this end. Reacting against the aristocratic values that had made Avila's convent of the Incarnation a microcosm of secular society, Teresa wanted her nuns free from the social conventions and liturgical obligations she had observed to be the products of aristocratic patronage and control. She wanted her nuns completely cut off from worldly preoccupations and affections, and she sought to achieve this end by building convents so poor, simple, and humble that they would elude the distracting attentions of secular society. There was, however, an inevitable contradiction here. Convents depended on the secular world for their material subsistence and could not simply disappear from view. Whether living from alms, as Teresa had originally planned, or funded by the income-providing donations she later accepted as necessary (at least for convents in rural areas, where the population was too sparse or poor to support them), the Carmelites needed to maintain a delicate balance between the contemplative retreat they desired and the cultivation of lay sponsorship necessary to their survival. The Spanish nuns brought to make the Paris foundation had experienced this tension both in Teresa's lifetime and after her death, when there was a perhaps inevitable resurgence of the aristocratic influences that Teresa had sought to eliminate from monastic life.[34] Although applauding the French founders' ambition to spread the Carmelite order across the kingdom, Ana de Jesús and Ana de San Bartolomé recognized the dangers inherent in the founders' plan to use the social connections afforded by Paris's role as a capital to help facilitate this spread. Mother Ana de Jesús, for example, objected to the princesse de Longueville's frequent visits to the convent's cloister, even though the privilege of entering the cloister was specifically granted the princess by the papal bull for the convent's foundation.[35] Like Teresa, Mother Ana believed in a firm separation of the sacred and the profane. Visits to the cloister by secular persons, however pious, inevitably risked corrupting the purity of the nuns' sacred reclusion by relaxing high standards and reintroducing worldly concerns.[36]

Within a few decades, the expectation pious benefactors had of entering the cloisters of convents they patronized would profoundly influence the character of Parisian convent life. From the beginning of the Catholic revival, however, there existed a tension between the desire to accommodate rich benefactors by giving them privileged access to the foundations they patronized and the competing desire to limit any intrusion by seculars into the convent's sacred space. Although the Carmelites' French superiors agreed in principle with restrictions intended to enforce a strict separation between the convent and the world, in practice, their desire to cultivate the elite patronage that would help the order spread caused them repeatedly to undermine the letter and, to some minds, also the spirit of the constitutions in this regard.

It was impossible to say no when Marie de Medici and the royal princesses chose to honor the new convent with a visit three days after the Spanish nuns were settled in. Arriving *en grand cortège*, the queen and her suite must have caused quite a stir in the quiet neighborhood bordering the convent, as well as by their visit within. The visit had immediate tangible rewards—the queen "left the nuns generous marks of her passage"—and was the first of many that Marie de Medici was to pay the Carmelites. According to the Carmelite chronicles, "she took great pleasure in coming once or twice a week to edify herself in this sanctuary" and brought or sent her daughters just as often, so that they were "from the cradle, so to speak," nurtured in affection for the order. By 1610, the queen's visits were sufficiently frequent and her desire to spend an occasional night in the convent sufficiently strong that she decided to build a special apartment for herself within the convent walls. Although the chronicles carefully specify that, when Marie de Medici came to stay in the apartment, she brought "only three of her women" and was careful not to disturb the solitude and silence of the nuns, it is impossible to imagine that the convent's routine was truly undisturbed. The rewards of the queen's patronage, however, were great. She continued to distinguish the convent with gifts of art and liturgical objects for the church.[37] The interest she took in the convent also brought other aristocrats to favor the Carmelites with their visits and gifts, thereby providing the support necessary to the order's expansion.

Ceremonial events also helped focus the attention of potential benefactors on the new order. Each of the first novices was accompanied to the convent by family members and friends, who stayed to watch the vesture ceremonies. During the first six weeks of the convent's existence, these ceremonies took place on four different occasions. The fact that the last of these took place at four in the morning "to avoid the tumult" suggests that the local populace found the ritual processions of elites to surrender their daughters and kinswomen to the Carmelites a compelling sight.[38] Pierre de L'Estoile's description of the Carmelites' move into their permanent quarters ten months later suggests that popular interest in the new convent was not always admiring. Telling how a great crowd gathered, "as if to gain pardons," to observe the solemn parade of nuns into their new quarters, he adopts a satirical tone in describing André Duval as looking for all the world "like a werewolf" as he accompanied the nuns. He goes on to say that "this beautiful and holy mystery was disturbed and interrupted by two violins, which began to play a rustic tune, scattering the poor geese and causing them hastily to return in fright, along with the werewolf, their conductor, into their church, where, having arrived, as it were, in a place of delivery and security, they began to sing the *Te Deum laudamus*."[39] Probably the pranksters just wanted to disturb the solemn occasion with a little levity, but whatever the popular reaction—or the skeptical view of moderate Catholics like L'Estoile—ceremonial occasions that brought pious elites to the convent of the Incarnation garnered both financial patronage and potential recruits. Several of Marie de Medici's ladies in waiting are said to have left court to join the Carmelites as a result of their visits in the company of the queen. One in particular left her mark on the records. When she entered the Carmelites as Sœur Gratienne de Saint-Michel in March 1606, Henri IV joined his wife and "all of the court" in attending the vesture ceremonies. Charlotte-Marguerite de Montmorency, soon to be married to Henri de Bourbon de Condé, the first prince of the blood, dated the long attachment that later made her a great benefactress of the convent to the powerful impression this ceremony made on her.[40]

If the inauguration of new convents and admission of novices in Paris attracted attention primarily from neighbors and pious elites, in provincial towns they became occasions for citywide festivities. The Carmelite convent founded in Pontoise in 1605 is a case in point. The nuns arrived from Paris in a splendid company that included the princesse de Longueville and other court ladies, as well as Barbe Acarie, her daughters, and other members of the Acarie circle. The magistrates of Pontoise paraded out to meet the nuns en route and formally accompanied them to the city gates, where they were greeted by the archbishop's grand vicar and a huge procession of city residents. The press of the crowd is said to have been so great that the nuns were forced to descend from their carriages and continue to their new house on foot. A great many people returned the following day to witness the entry of the first four novices, all of whom came from local families. Public ceremonies occurred again in 1607, when the foundation stones were laid for a new and larger convent, and twice in 1610, first when the new convent's bells were christened and again when the nuns formally entered their new home. The latter occasion in particular was festive, with processions of clergy and lay people from all of the local parishes accompanying the nuns from the old convent to the new. As had become the custom for ceremonies that took the nuns outside of their cloister, each Carmelite sister was escorted by a distinguished dévote, with the pious gentlemen who attended the ceremonies forming a kind of honor guard around them to protect the women from the press of the crowd. After the ceremonies, the accompanying dévotes enjoyed the special privilege of dining in the refectory with the nuns. The chronicle of these events underscores the emotional resonance of the inaugural ceremonies by concluding the narrative of these events with the pleas of one of the pious visitors, Marie de Tudert's daughter Jeanne Séguier, to be allowed to stay on in the convent and try out religious life as a Carmelite postulant.[41]

Pontoise was entirely welcoming of the Carmelites and became so attached to prioress Ana de San Bartolomé that when it came time for her to return to Paris her escorts draped her in a man's cloak and hat and ushered her out under cover of darkness for fear that local residents would oppose her departure.[42] By contrast, residents of Dijon, where the third Carmelite convent was founded, were actively hostile to the nuns on their arrival. Dijon's proximity to the border of the Spanish-governed Franche-Comté kept alive an anti-Spanish sentiment that was gradually dying down elsewhere in the kingdom, and the hostility was most particularly directed against prioress Ana de Jesús and the two other Spanish nuns sent to make the new foundation. Accusing local elites of having kept the project secret until the last minute, rioting members of the populace sought to prevent the new foundation and drive out the Spanish nuns. Unrest flared up again when people learned that Ana de Jesús had broken a fleur-de-lys off the grille that surrounded the church choir. Primed by xenophobia, they took the gesture as a mark of disrespect for the French Crown, when it was in fact prompted by the austere prioress's objection to the church's ornate decor.[43] The hostility died down, however, and the new convent's parlor soon became a gathering place for local dévotes. Among them was the young baroness Jeanne de Chantal, who later founded the order of the Visitation with François de Sales.[44]

The anti-Spanish sentiments of the Dijonnaise populace can only have reinforced the desire of Ana de Jesús and the two Spanish nuns who accompanied her to Dijon to leave France as soon as possible. Their departure in January 1607 made it necessary to promote a French nun to the position of prioress in the Dijon convent. Louise de Jésus Gallois was chosen to assume this position. One of the first novices, she had taken her vows just fifteen months earlier. When Mother Isabella de San Pablo, who was serving as prioress in Pontoise, decided later that year also to leave France, she was replaced by Marie de la Trinité d'Hannivel. And when Ana de San Bartolomé moved on to found a new house at Tours in 1608, Madeleine de Saint-Joseph de Fontaines was named prioress in Paris. Within four years of their beginnings, the Carmelites had founded five French convents, three of which were already headed by French nuns.

The young order continued to expand at a rapid rate. By 1615 ten convents had been founded in France; by 1620, twenty-seven; and by 1625, thirty-seven.[45] This expansion placed a considerable strain on the order's financial and human resources. Pious women who became Carmelites with the expectation of devoting themselves entirely to contemplation of God instead found much of their time devoted to the more worldly tasks involved in negotiating and administering the new foundations. Louise Gallois served as founding prioress of three convents over the course of her career, Marie d'Hannivel of five, and Marie Sévin of nine. The rapid spread of Carmelite convents is indicative of the widespread appeal of the new spirituality the order represented, but it also affirms the wisdom of the initial plan to locate the first house in Paris so as to profit from the city's role as the social nexus of the kingdom. Three of the first four Carmelite convents were funded largely or entirely by Parisian benefactors. Many of the later foundations were also made by benefactors closely connected to the capital through circles of kinship, royal office, or both.[46] Hearing about the Carmelites from family members and visiting their convent while in Paris, provincial elites with close ties to the capital sought to bring the benefits of the new order back to their home towns.

In the provinces, as in Paris, Carmelite prioresses struggled to accommodate the legitimate expectations of elite benefactors without compromising the Carmelites' strict rule. This attempt to throw light on some of the cultural differences that gave rise to tensions between the Spanish and French founders of the new order should not be taken to imply that the French order was inauthentic or unfaithful to the Carmelite rule, or that the French Carmelites truly did scorn the teachings of the Spanish mothers, as Ana de San Bartolomé was later to charge. Differences in interpretation of the constitutions did not always break down on national lines. Ana de San Bartolomé, for example, thought Ana de Jesús too lax on certain points of behavior and tried to correct these lapses when she became prioress in Paris.[47] The French nuns too differed among themselves on how strictly to adhere to the letter of the rule. Whatever differences of opinion the Spanish mothers might have had with the French superiors, and even French nuns, they did instill in them a strong respect for the Teresian heritage and the principles on which Saint Teresa had founded her order. The French permitted certain convents to be larger than Teresa had prescribed but insisted that they be silent, orderly, and unperturbed by factional division. They allowed benefactors and sometimes other elites more ready entrance to the convents than Teresa would have approved but at least tried to insist that all except for one or two nuns specially delegated to converse with the visitors maintain their usual routines undisturbed. As pressure to admit lay visitors to the cloister increased, Carmelite prioresses found Teresa's strict rule a useful tool against the intrusive demands of pious elites.

One particular way the Spanish mothers instilled a great respect for Teresa's principles was to have important consequences for the authority that French Carmelite prioresses ultimately wielded. When Mother Ana de Jesús came to France in 1604, she had been battling for more than ten years against certain changes that the Discalced Carmelite fathers, who were the nuns' superiors in Spain, had imposed on the constitutions. She considered the constitutions published at Alcalá in 1581 (and republished with minor revisions in 1588) the authentic Teresian constitutions—the rules Teresa herself had laid down for her order—and objected strongly when Carmelite provincial Nicolás Doria modified these constitutions in a way that increased the power of the order's male superiors at the expense of the prioresses. The Dorian constitutions deprived prioresses of the right to choose their convent's confessors and in other ways sought to limit their role in guiding the spiritual development of their nuns.[48] In 1590 Ana de Jesús, who at that point was head of the Madrid convent, with other prioresses obtained a papal brief reaffirming the constitutions of Alcalá. This success was only momentary. Doria obtained his own brief ordering use of the revised constitutions in 1592, and these constitutions remained in effect in 1604, when Ana de Jesús and her companions came to France. Ana de Jésus never stopped believing, however, that the constitutions of 1588 represented the authentic Teresian vision, and she impressed this belief on her French daughters and on the French superiors as well. When Messieurs Duval, Gallement, and Bérulle obtained a papal brief in 1606 confirming their exclusive right to govern the French Carmelites, they promptly adopted the constitutions of Alcalá in place of the Dorian constitutions.

Ana de Jesús, who should have been delighted by this change, had already left for the Spanish Netherlands, where she waged an ultimately losing battle to see the same change instituted. It is ironic that, despite her quarrels with the French superiors, Ana de Jesús succeeded in bequeathing to French prioresses a level of institutionalized authority and autonomy that she herself had long ago lost and would never regain. She succeeded so well, in fact, in convincing French Carmelites of the superiority of the constitutions of Alcalá that distaste for the Dorian constitutions was a principal reason that Mother Ana's French daughters ultimately disagreed with her over the issue of the order's superiors. In the opinion of the French nuns, the Dorian constitutions violated Teresa's central principles by depriving the nuns of their "freedom to disclose to the prioress the depths of their soul." The very voice of the prioress was lost, they claimed; she was now always placed beneath the superiors' authority. Blaming these changes on the Carmelite fathers' desire to gather all power to themselves, Marie de Jésus de Breauté's biographer offers them as the principal reason that Marie and her companions rejected the fathers' claims to authority in France.[49]

Daughters of the Passion

While members of Barbe Acarie's circle were making plans and obtaining permission to establish the Discalced Carmelites in Paris, one of the richest and most powerful aristocrats in France, Marie de Luxembourg, duchesse de Mercœur, was working to establish an order of Capuchin nuns. The idea had originated with her sister-in-law, Louise de Lorraine, the devout widow of King Henri III, who had hoped to found a Capucine convent in Bourges and left 20,000 écus for this purpose in her will. Making her brother Philippe-Emmanuel de Lorraine, duc de Mercœur, executor of her estate, Louise had charged him with completing the foundation. The duke's own death, however, followed his sister's by just a year. The last Leaguer grandee to surrender to Henri IV, which he did only in 1598, Mercœur had subsequently carried his ultra-Catholic crusade to eastern Europe, where he died fighting the Turks in February 1602.

The duchesse de Mercœur's role in the League has never been studied and deserves a closer look. The properties and titles she inherited as a descendant of the dukes of Brittany provided Mercœur's power base when he was appointed governor of this province in 1582. Together, the couple established a ducal court at Nantes. While the duke built up an army and fought on behalf of the League, the duchess managed the family's estates and was politically active much in the same way that women in the Guise family were active in Paris. In 1589, for example, she had the royalist mayor of Nantes imprisoned because he opposed a tax Mercœur wished to levy to support his army.[50] In 1598 it was the duchess who came to meet the king to negotiate the duke's surrender.[51] In 1609, L'Estoile characterized the duchess as "the most devout lady in France, and the richest," but then added cynically that her devotion was largely an attempt "through the many masses and services she had said, to expiate the brigandage and thefts to which she had subjected her poor people on her lands and duchy of Brittany."[52] L'Estoile's anti-League bias accounts for his cynicism; what is important is that the pious duchess inherited Louise de Lorraine's charge and made it her own. She sought and obtained permission from Henri IV in October 1602 to establish a convent of Capucines.

The king's letters specified that the convent was to be in Paris, rather than in Bourges, as Louise de Lorraine's will had stipulated. It is not clear who was responsible for the change in plans. There is no indication that Marie de Mercœur's thoughts had turned to Paris; just a week before the king's letters were issued, she had sent a representative to Bourges to discuss plans for the convent, which was apparently eagerly awaited by local magistrates, clergy, and townsfolk alike.[53] Regardless of who initiated the change, it was a momentous one. Establishing the convent in the capital instead of a second-tier provincial town radically altered the character of the foundation. Newly widowed with just a daughter to raise, the duchesse de Mercœur threw herself into the project in a way that she would almost certainly not have done had it taken place in distant Bourges, a city to which she had no personal connection.[54] Combining the roles played in the Carmelites' foundation by the princesse de Longueville and Barbe Acarie, she used her influence to get the necessary permissions and employed her personal fortune, in addition to Louise de Lorraine's bequest, to build and endow the convent. She also devoted enormous energy to the project and contributed in the end not just to the temporal aspects of the foundation but to its spiritual character as well. Giving generously of both time and money—her financial contribution is said to have exceeded 100,000 écus, five times Louise de Lorraine's original endowment—she made the Capucines a prominent center of religious life in the capital. She also inadvertently introduced the same tension between wealth and poverty, between secular patronage and religious retreat, that the Carmelites were to know.

Once the king's permission had been obtained for the new foundation, the biggest obstacle was posed by the French Capuchins, who refused to assume responsibility for the spiritual direction of convents of nuns, insisting that their rule forbade them to take on this task. Marie de Mercœur, however, was determined that the nuns could be properly schooled in the Capuchins' ascetic spirituality only by members of this order. She did not want secular priests to serve as the nuns' confessors or the bishop to serve as the convent's superior, as the Capuchins suggested. Faced with the friars' recalcitrance, she appealed to the pope, telling him that "the order could not possibly persevere in the exercise of its rule if it was not entirely governed by the Capuchin fathers, both for confession and for visitation." With the help of French envoys in Rome, she brought Pope Clement VIII around to her view. In July 1603, while conceding that the spiritual direction of convents was contrary to the Franciscan rule, he ordered the Paris Capuchins to take charge of the Capucines' spiritual needs. The order was reaffirmed in the papal bull officially establishing the foundation in September 1603.[55]

Fortunately, not all of the Paris friars were opposed to the project, and the duchesse de Mercœur soon secured the active collaboration of such key members of the Paris friary as Ange de Joyeuse, Archange de Pembroke, and Raphael d'Orléans. Indeed, Ange de Joyeuse played such an important role in the Capucines' foundation that when he died in 1608 the Capuchins acceded to the nuns' pleas to give them his heart, which they placed in a gold reliquary in their church alongside that of the duc de Mercœur.[56] Père Jérôme de Rouen served as spiritual director to the Capucine postulants. His experience as master of novices in Paris and Orléans qualified him well for this position, but so did his experience as spiritual director to such Parisian dévotes as Marguerite de Gondi, marquise de Maignelay.[57]

The marquise, who was to become an important patron of the Capucines, helped the duchesse de Mercœur negotiate the purchase of a property belonging to the Gondi family in the faubourg Saint-Honoré, where the duchess wished to locate the convent. The property lay directly opposite the Capuchin friary, which would make it easy for the nuns' confessors to visit. It also had the advantage of being large, with extensive gardens—an important consideration in that the Capucines intended to grow the vegetables that made up a large part of their restricted diet.[58] To enlarge the property still further, Marie de Mercœur talked owners of several adjoining properties into selling. Construction of the new convent began in June 1604, with Mercœur laying the first stone in the name of Princess Elisabeth, the eldest daughter of Henri IV.[59] In doing so, she showed gratitude for the king's approval of the foundation but also tacitly associated the convent with the Crown, implying sponsorship but also implicitly appealing for continued benevolence.

Building the convent took two years. During this time, Marie de Mercœur made frequent visits to the construction site. Like Barbe Acarie, she spent long days watching the walls go up, keeping a close eye on the quality of the work and encouraging the builders to work quickly but well. Her confessor, Antoine Malet, who published a history of the foundation in 1609, says that she came to the site every working day and often remained there from five or six in the morning until nine at night. He describes her as freely giving directions to the craftsmen and laborers and also suggests that, far from resenting her interference, they enjoyed the generous bonuses with which she encouraged them.[60] It is possible, even probable, that Malet stretches the truth in his depiction of both the long hours that Marie de Mercœur spent on the construction site and her cordial relations with the workers. Even so, it is worth noting that he depicts her presence on the site as admirable but entirely natural; there is no hint that these were unwomanly activities or beneath the dignity of the high aristocrat that she was.

Malet observes that, if Marie de Mercœur paid close attention to the "material walls" of the convent as they went up, she paid even closer attention to building the "spiritual edifice" of the Capucines. As word got out about the

foundation, young women eager to join the new order began to present themselves at the Hôtel de Mercœur. According to Malet, more than three hundred
aspirants appeared. The papal bull for the foundation of the Capucines allowed
Marie de Mercœur to select the girls who would be the Capucines' first novices
with the advice and permission of the Capuchin fathers. Her role in the actual
selection process, however, appears to have been rather less active than that
played by Barbe Acarie with regard to the Carmelites. Although extremely pious, the duchess made no claim to the spiritual discernment commonly attributed to Acarie, and there is no evidence that she took part in the formal
interviews conducted by Père Raphael d'Orléans and his companions to select
the first Capucine postulants in 1604, even though these interviews took place
in the Hôtel de Mercœur.[61] Once the initial decisions were made, however,
Marie de Mercœur took charge again and conducted the chosen candidates to
a secluded house that she owned at La Roquette in the faubourg Saint-Antoine.
There they engaged in religious exercises, tested their vocation, and awaited
the beginning of a formal novitiate. La Roquette thus served much the same
function as the "little seminary" that Barbe Acarie established on the montagne
Sainte-Geneviève.

Although twelve candidates received the habit on 14 July 1604, three
months before the Spanish Carmelites made their arrival in Paris, they were
only officially raised to the status of Capucine novices two years later, when
they were introduced into their permanent home. During this two-year period,
Père Jérôme de Rouen came out daily from the Capuchins' friary in the faubourg Saint-Honoré to instruct the young women in the rituals and practices
they were to follow in religious life. Unlike the Carmelites, Ursulines, and
most other reformed orders, whose first novices were supervised by professed
nuns from other branches of the same order or, if necessary, from other reformed orders, the Capucines were directed by Père Jérôme alone. This is
particularly surprising in that Paris did possess in the Ave-Maria a house of
strict and well-regulated Franciscan nuns who might have been asked to assist
in forming the Capucines. Attached to the Observant branch of the Franciscan
family, the nuns of the Ave-Maria observed the same rule and constitutions as
the Capucines.[62] Their ceremonies and customs were somewhat different from
those of the Capuchins, though these differences may have been less important
than traditional rivalries among mendicant orders in keeping the Capuchins
from soliciting the Poor Clares' assistance with their new house of nuns. It is
also possible, however, that Marie de Mercœur and the Capuchins simply
thought such assistance unnecessary. Whatever the reason, Père Jérôme
worked to form the women alone or with only Capuchin collaborators.

From the very first day he taught the postulants humility by appointing
one among them to serve as superior and insisting that the others obey her
without question. He delegated others to serve in various offices and began to
instruct them in Capuchin customs and introduce them to the austerities of

Capuchin life. From the beginning, their diet was meatless, but they progressed more gradually into the strict fasting and mortifications practiced by the friars. According to Antoine Malet, Père Jérôme "made them do very austere and difficult acts of penitence, along with many other exercises and disciplines to mortify and test them . . . but he proceeded with such gentleness and so encouraged them to admit all their difficulties that they did not find anything too rigorous or hard."[63] The last part of this observation at least is something of an exaggeration. Over the course of two years, six aspiring Capucines dropped out, when either their health or their vocation proved unequal to the rigors of the regimen. They were replaced by other aspirants, so that when the day came for the formal move into the newly completed convent, twelve white-veiled novices left La Roquette, the same number as had originally entered in 1604.[64]

While Père Jérôme oversaw the novices' spiritual development, Marie de Mercœur supervised construction of the convent that was to be their home. Looking ahead to the day of the move, she envisioned a splendid ceremony—a huge procession and elaborate mass with the queen and all of her court in attendance—to mark the long-awaited event. But the duchess was not to get her wish. The Capuchin fathers opposed the costly festivities she proposed on the ground that they ran contrary to the order's traditions of poverty and humility. In addition, the plague was abroad in Paris in the summer of 1606, and large assemblies were unwise. The duchesse de Mercœur's wishes could not be ignored entirely, however; a compromise ceremony was planned. Although scaled down considerably from the duchess's initial vision, it almost certainly remained more elaborate than the Capuchins would have liked.

On 9 August 1606, the twelve novices were brought into Paris at two in the morning to avoid crowds and housed overnight at the duchess's Paris residence, conveniently located in the rue Saint-Honoré, down the street from the new convent. The following morning the entire Capuchin community of approximately eighty friars came in procession to the Hôtel de Mercœur and escorted the future nuns, invisible beneath their white veils, back to the Capuchin church, where Cardinal Pierre de Gondi and his nephew, Henri de Gondi, archbishop of Paris, awaited them. In the ensuing ceremony, the cardinal placed on each novice's head a crown of thorns, signifying their vocation as "Daughters of the Passion." The entire group then proceeded to the new convent with the mass of Capuchins leading the way, followed by the thorn-crowned novices, each accompanied by a distinguished aristocrat. A great crowd of people followed as well, with clergy from other Paris churches and the presiding prelates, Pierre and Henri de Gondi. Pères Raphael d'Orléans and Ange de Joyeuse, newly elected as the Capuchins' provincial and superior of the friary of Saint-Honoré, respectively, brought up the rear. A celebrated preacher, Père Ange delivered a moving sermon, after which the cardinal de Gondi celebrated mass and gave communion to the novices. After receiving the cardinal's benediction, the novices were ushered into their new home by the aristocratic ladies who had accompanied them earlier. Later the same afternoon, Louise de Lorraine's remains and the duc de Mercœur's heart were interred with great ceremony in the convent church.[65] Despite the absence of the queen, who stayed away out of fear of the plague, the duchesse de Mercœur had good reason to be proud of the reception her protegées received from the aristocracy and populace alike.

The favorable notice the Capucines received from Parisian elites was important in several respects. In the first place, it helped the nuns financially by attracting alms. Like their Capuchin brothers, the Capucines were a mendicant order. Because they could not go out themselves to seek alms in the city, the Capuchins established six lay brothers in special quarters adjacent to their convent to collect alms for them and tend to their needs.[66] Why did the king and Parlement allow the Capucines to be established as mendicants within months of denying the same privilege to the Carmelites? The answer may lie in the favor the Capuchins already enjoyed in Paris, so that supporting a sister order was not seen as problematical. More probably, the key point is that, despite the avowed intention of living by charity, the convent enjoyed an endowment of 45,000 livres by the terms of Louise de Lorraine's will. At the interest rate of 6.25 percent established as standard by royal ordinance in 1601, this would have yielded an annual income of 2,815 livres, marginally more than the income of 2,400 livres that Mademoiselle de Longueville had promised the Carmelites.[67] Despite the Capucines' emphasis on Franciscan poverty, the convent was not in fact destitute but enjoyed a comfortable income, one that would grow with the dowries new novices brought. Like the requirement that the nuns wear habits made from coarse cloth and go barefoot except in the kitchen or garden, their dependence on alms was in large measure symbolic and intended to reinforce the nuns' humility. The tension between the Capucines' theoretical poverty and the actual conditions in which they were founded is evident, for example, in Malet's notation that, on the festive day when the Capucine novices first entered their new convent, they were fed entirely by the charity of "people of quality."[68] Just what this charity consisted of is left to the reader's imagination, but it is hard to imagine that the elite donors, though unable to deck the convent's tables with the rich meats and game birds that were traditional gifts among the aristocracy, limited their donations to the true bread of poverty.

The favorable notice that the duchesse de Mercœur orchestrated for the Capucines was also important as it brought the new order more recruits and may have meant that proportionally more came from elite families. According to Malet, lots of girls of "good birth" now wanted to enter the order. The first person admitted after the Capucines' formal entry into their new convent, he tells us, was the daughter of a count.[69] Unfortunately, the register of professions for the Capucines has not survived, and there is no way to systematically analyze the social status of those who joined. The Capuchins' annals say only that, in selecting the initial novices, Pères Ange de Joyeuse and Jérôme de Rouen imitated Christ, who, "when he went to choose disciples, did not name princes or priests or doctors of the Old Law but rather simple fishermen."[70] This would seem to suggest that those who made it through the rigorous initial screening were for the most part of modest origin. It is nevertheless possible that the annals' author intended the passage as praise for the Capuchin fathers' high-minded selection criteria rather than as a commentary on the novices' social status. At least three of the first Capucines—the first abbess, Agnès de Tours Barentin, her sister Claire, and Anne du Jardin—were daughters of magistrates.[71] Moreover, at least three of the first Carmelites—Marie de la Trinité d'Hannivel, Marie de Jésus de Breauté, and Madeleine de Saint-Joseph de Fontaines—seriously considered becoming Capucines before deciding, for a variety of personal reasons to join the Carmelites instead, which suggests that the orders drew on a common pool of eager dévotes.[72]

A French Order of Ursulines

The third new women's order founded in seventeenth-century Paris was dedicated not to contemplative prayer but to the education of young women, and yet Paris's Ursulines too were rooted in the fervent and ascetic piety that characterized the initial stages of the Catholic revival in France. Their close ties to the Carmelites in particular gave shape to an order that would be very different from the Italian Ursulines whose Provençal branch constituted their direct line of descent.

The order was born of the women in the little seminary of the montagne Sainte-Geneviève whom Barbe Acarie and the Carmelite superiors judged better suited to an active than a contemplative religious life. Once the first Carmelites had been selected, the question occurred of what to do with the other women living in the house. The idea of forming them into a teaching order dedicated to instructing young girls in the Catholic faith appears to have come from several directions. While curé of Aumale in Normandy, Jacques Gallement had shaped a household of dévotes into a school for the instruction of young girls; he later did the same in Pontoise. Convinced that the only way to reform Christian morality and behavior was through education, Gallement's experience in Aumale and Pontoise led him to advocate the founding of other schools that would similarly offer "free and charitable" instruction to young girls.[73] Such schools already existed in several towns of Provence and the Franche-Comté and in Dijon, where Ursuline congregations had been founded on the model of Angela de Merici's Italian foundations. Communication among devout milieus was sufficiently intense that members of Mademoiselle Acarie's circle had doubtless heard of these congregations, and the visit to Paris in late 1606 of the principal patron of the Ursulines in Aix helped spark plans for a Parisian foundation. On arriving in Paris, Lucrèce de Sainte-Foi, wife of the Aixois magistrate François de Forbin de la Fare, deliberately sought introduction to Barbe Acarie's circle. Eager to learn about the recent foundation of the Discalced Carmelites, she was equally ready to share her understanding of the work the Ursulines were doing in Aix.[74]

By the time Lucrèce de Sainte-Foi returned to Aix early in 1607, the members of Acarie's circle had agreed not only that they wished to found a school for girls in the house on the montagne Sainte-Geneviève but also that they wished to bring Ursulines from Provence to help shape the new foundation. Sainte-Foi served as a useful intermediary, helping to convince Françoise de Bermond, the founder of the first Ursuline communities in Provence, to come to Paris in 1608 to direct the institution. As it happened, the school opened even before Bermond's arrival. Jacques Gallement brought Nicole Pelletier from Pontoise to instruct in good teaching methods those members of the congregation of Sainte-Geneviève who aspired to be Ursulines. Lucrèce de Sainte-Foi sent copies of the Ursulines' constitutions and the books they used for instructing girls in their catechism, and various members of Acarie's circle sought pupils for the school among their devout friends. Michel de Marillac showed his confidence in the new foundation by enrolling his own daughter and a niece.[75] Because the religious instruction the Ursulines offered was at this point such a novelty, grown women are said to have asked to sit in on the lessons to profit from the explications of Christian doctrine.[76] These visitors spread the word about the new school as well.

The transformation of the little school into a full-fledged religious order was in large measure the work of Madeleine Luillier (Madame de Sainte-Beuve), whom Barbe Acarie had convinced to serve as founder and patron of the new congregation. The "Sainte Veuve" who had raised eyebrows with her exploits during the League had matured into a serious and very devout widow eager to use her great wealth to promote the Catholic revival that she, like other dévots, still believed to be seriously threatened by the persistence of heresy in France. To this end, she had collaborated with Bérulle and other members of Acarie's circle to help convince Henri IV to readmit the Jesuits to France. Along with her kinsman Jean du Tillet de Bussière, she sponsored a Jesuit novitiate, where new recruits could be trained and educated apart from the more senior members of the congregation.[77] Strengthening the Catholic Church by educating young girls in the faith was just the sort of project that would inspire Madeleine Luillier's support, and she responded favorably to Barbe Acarie's appeal for help. As the project was launched, she increasingly stamped it with her own vision of religious perfection.

From the time she agreed to serve as patron for the new foundation, Luillier gave it her time and energy as well as her financial support. Along with Barbe Acarie, she taught classes in the new little school. Enrollments quickly exceeded the capacity of the house on the montagne Sainte-Geneviève, so Luillier arranged to purchase a property adjacent to the Carmelites in the faubourg Saint-Jacques. With Michel de Marillac's help, she planned and supervised construction of a spacious home for the growing congregation. Although wealthy, Luillier had nothing like the fortune possessed by the princesse de Longueville or the duchesse de Mercœur. The daughter of a president of the Chambre des comptes and widow of a counselor in Parlement, she came from the magisterial elite—from a family ennobled by service to the king—and not the landed aristocracy.[78] Serving as founder of the Ursulines thus required a greater sacrifice on her part than it did for the founders of the Carmelites and Capucines. Worried that she might abandon the project part way through if costs rose in the precipitous way they had for the Carmelites, Barbe Acarie sent a reluctant Michel de Marillac to go over a detailed estimate of expenses with Luillier to make sure that she understood just what she was undertaking. Luillier proved determined to carry the project through, even though it meant selling her house in Paris, cutting down on her household staff, and making other financial retrenchments.[79] She further demonstrated her commitment by promising not only to pay the costs of construction for the new foundation but also to leave certain properties and annuities to the Ursulines on her death, on condition that they use the income thereby gained to admit without dowries twelve young women, six of them from noble families.[80]

Plans for the Ursulines' new home changed several times before it was complete and ready for occupancy in October 1610. Each change made it larger and more elaborate, as Luillier's vision for the Ursulines' future became more expansive. Most significant, the buildings were specially designed to serve the dual function of convent and school. In this they reflected the most important change that Madeleine Luillier sought to impose on the new foundation. Unlike the open congregations of teaching sisters, bound by only simple vows, that Françoise de Bermond had created on the Italian model in Provence, the Parisian Ursulines were to be a formal order of cloistered nuns. To this end, Luillier had the complex of buildings that would serve as classrooms and student dormitories separated from an inner cloister reserved for the Ursulines, so they might retreat to silent contemplation when their teaching duties were done. The buildings were designed, moreover, so that the Ursulines could teach their students without violating the rules of clausura. Although separate from the inner cloister, the school areas were enclosed by high walls, and only the pupils were permitted inside. In this way, the Ursulines could instruct their girls without coming into contact with other lay persons. As in contemplative convents, the church effectively isolated the Ursulines from the view of the lay people who attended services there. The nuns remained invisible behind a screen that separated the public space of the nave from their places in the choir, while the pupils took their place in a closed tribune that allowed them to be supervised by their teachers unseen by the broader public. The convent parlors were also designed with the rules of cloistering in mind; covered grilles separated the Ursulines from their visitors.[81]

According to Ursuline tradition, Madeleine Luillier intended from the beginning to make a formal order of the Ursulines but kept her intentions secret until the new buildings were completed.[82] This is not entirely plausible, especially if, as Luillier's biographer Henri de Leymont contends, her chief collaborator in building the new convent, Michel de Marillac, was one of the most vociferous proponents of keeping the Ursulines a simple congregation. The convent's architecture suggests that an enclosed order was envisioned from the beginning. Exactly when the decision was made is, however, less important than the fact that the sources agree in crediting Luillier with taking the initiative here and imposing on the Paris Ursulines a change that radically altered the character of the institution.

The change was a controversial one, provoking debate even among the members of Barbe Acarie's circle. Marillac and others who favored keeping the Ursulines a simple congregation argued that the sisters' teaching duties were incompatible with the reclusive life demanded of contemplative nuns. Those who held the opposing view, Madeleine Luillier foremost among them, countered by insisting that formal incorporation as an order, with irrevocable vows and full observance of the rules of cloistering, would raise the Ursulines to a higher and more perfect form of religious life. The latter view clearly reflects the spiritual values that made the reclusive Carmelite and Capucine foundations so popular from the start. Congregations of women who lived and worked together, bound only by simple vows, had long existed in French cities. Most were transitory households of dévotes, though several venerable congregations existed in Paris as well. The "Bonnes femmes" of Sainte-Avoye and the Haudriettes both dated their origins to the thirteenth century, when they were founded as places of refuge to allow impoverished widows a dignified way to live out their lives.[83] Although respectable, the way of life they represented clearly lacked the prestige of the Catholic Reformation's reformed religious orders, and the Bonnes femmes of Sainte-Avoye sought incorporation into the Ursulines to became Paris's second Ursuline convent in 1622.[84]

As with the Carmelites and Capucines, the ascetic impulse that characterized the early stages of the Catholic revival in France played a powerful role in the Ursulines' spirituality. Madeleine Luillier's piety was shaped by her experience during the League, by the several years she subsequently spent in retreat at the convents of Chelles and Saint-Pierre de Reims, and by her participation in Barbe Acarie's circle on her return to Paris. Although her preferred spiritual director, Jean Gontery, was a Jesuit, Capuchin Benoît de Canfield was, in Gontery's absence, Luillier's confessor of choice.[85] With this combination of influences, it is natural that her vision of religious perfection should have blended social activism with penitential retreat. It is also natural that the first Parisian

Ursulines should have enthusiastically adopted this vision as their own, as a number of these women had initially been drawn to the little seminary of the montagne Sainte-Geneviève by their desire to become Carmelite nuns. Even if it was later decided that they were unsuited to an exclusively contemplative life, they admired and wished to emulate the Carmelites' ascetic virtues, and it should not come as a surprise that they welcomed the opportunity to combine their teaching mission with contemplative retreat—to join Martha's part with Mary's, as Ursuline historians liked to say. There has been a tendency in recent historical writing to portray the movement toward strict enclosure of nuns in the Catholic Reformation as the result of misogynist clerics' determination to lock women firmly behind convent walls.[86] The Paris Ursulines depart significantly from this stereotype in that enclosure was not forced on them—and certainly not by men—but was adopted voluntarily as an expression of their own religious ideals and those of their (female) founder.

The decision to make the Ursulines an enclosed order had immediate consequences for the new congregation. Françoise de Bermond's superiors recalled her to Provence to prevent her from taking vows that would have removed her from their obedience. Deciding that the Ursulines should follow the rule of Saint Augustine, which was less restrictive than either the Benedictine or Franciscan rules, Madeleine Luillier and Barbe Acarie went personally to Soissons to ask the reformed Augustinians of the abbey of Saint-Etienne to direct the new congregation and school its members in obedience to the Augustinian rule until they were able to govern themselves. To their pleasure, abbess Anne de Roussy and her prioress, Marie de Villiers de Saint-Paul, agreed to come themselves to assist with the foundation. On their arrival in Paris in July 1612, they found thirty women provisionally admitted to the new congregation and awaiting their direction. With the advice of Acarie and Luillier, they selected twelve to be the first novices. Two months later the papal bull erecting the new congregation as a religious order, which Luillier had solicited in 1610, arrived from Rome. As she had requested, the Paris Ursulines were to be an entirely new sort of religious order. Bound by the traditional three vows of poverty, chastity, and obedience, they added a fourth vow that encapsulated their originality in dedicating them first and foremost to "the instruction of young girls and their education in Christian piety, virtues, and morality, and in the works and exercises suitable for their sex."[87]

To shape the Ursulines for this novel enterprise, they were given spiritual directors who led them by the same paths of penitential introspection and social activism that characterized Madeleine Luillier's faith. The choice of Jacques Gallement as one of the Paris Ursulines' first superiors guaranteed that the ascetic impulse in their spirituality would continue to be nurtured. Resigning his position as curé of Aumale in 1611 so that he could devote himself more fully to his "dear daughters" the Carmelites, he soon began to extend the same attention to the spiritual development of the neighboring Ursulines. As with the Carmelites, Gallement's penitential faith became the heart of his instruction. "He led them [the Ursulines] in spirit onto Calvary and brought them to the feet of the suffering Christ," writes his nephew and biographer, Placide Gallement, adding that the "transformation" this experience of the "mortified life" worked in the Ursuline novices was visible "in their faces, their mouths, and their hands." But Gallement also impressed them with his "prodigious abnegation and continual practice of self-impoverishment before the eyes of God. He had them enter into this state of abasement through the wounds of a heart made contrite and humbled by the sight of all the sufferings of the Savior, which he made the lengthy focus of their prayers."[88] Ursuline historian Mère Marie de Pommereuse confirms the importance of this ascetic and penitential spirituality among the first Ursulines when she tells us that the new novices "day and night invented a thousand ways to crucify their bodies."[89]

Jacques Gallement did not shape the Ursulines' spirituality alone. Their other two superiors, Guillaume Geslin and Thomas Gallot, theologians attached to the Sorbonne, no doubt played a part. Unfortunately, the sources reveal nothing of their specific contributions. Although preoccupied with founding the Oratory and directing the Carmelites, Pierre de Bérulle interested himself in the Ursulines as well. As a group, however, it was the Jesuits who were most influential. Madeleine Luillier would doubtless have wanted them to serve as superiors of the new congregation, were it not that their constitutions forbade them to take on such a role. Her spiritual director, Jean Gontery, nevertheless came frequently to preach at the new convent and offer guidance to the novices. So did Charles de la Tour, rector of the Jesuits' new novitiate. Pierre Coton brought two nieces to be schooled by the Ursulines, both of whom later joined the order, and continued whenever possible to favor it with his attentions. When Gontery died in 1616, Coton published a work of controversy that he had left in manuscript, the *Instruction du procez de la Religion prétendue réformée*, and dedicated it to Luillier.[90] The book, which summarized the arguments that Gontery had used to counter the Protestant faith in his missions, serves as a reminder of how strongly the Ursulines' teaching mission was imbued with the Counter-Reformation's determination to defeat heresy by strengthening the Catholic faith. But the Jesuits contributed more than a vibrant anti-Protestantism to the Ursulines' spiritual development. Père Barthélemy Jacquinot gave the entire community Ignatius's spiritual exercises in 1613. Repeating the exercises under the direction of Père de la Tour in 1615, the Ursulines judged the experience so fruitful that the Ignatian exercises became a customary part of their preparation for their solemn vows.[91] However disparate these spiritual influences, they appear to have been complementary. The Jesuits' sense of apostolic mission fused with Gallement's lessons in penitential self-abasement to instill in the Ursulines a conviction that both their teach-ing and their humble lives of renunciation and prayer served to advance the cause of the Roman Catholic Church.[92]

Elite Patronage and the New Orders

The arrival in September 1612 of the papal bull erecting the Paris Ursulines as a religious order made it possible at last to consecrate the convent, finished two years earlier, and allow the women selected as the first novices to receive the habit. The vesture ceremonies took place on 11 November, with the arch-bishop of Paris, Henri de Gondi, later cardinal de Retz, presiding. Following the pattern established by the Carmelites and Capucines, each of the women receiving the habit was escorted by an aristocratic lady. Inviting the princesse de Longueville and her sister Marguerite d'Orléans d'Estoutville, and also the duchesse de Mercœur to perform this function, Barbe Acarie and Madeleine Luillier implicitly identified the three new women's convents—the Carmelites, Capucines, and Ursulines—as part of a common project of Catholic revival and reform. These were not competing institutions; they shared common pa-trons, ideals, and ends, but each was to serve the church in a slightly different way.

Although the royal family did not take part in the festivities inaugurating the Ursuline convent, the queen regent and her daughters honored the convent with their visits on a number of other occasions. Already in 1609, Marie de Medici had come to visit Françoise de Bermond, and on two occasions she had the dauphin Louis brought to listen to the aspiring Ursulines catechize their charges.[93] One of the innovations that Bermond introduced was the practice of holding special classes to prepare girls for their first communion, followed by a collective ceremony with all the young communicants dressed in white. These communion classes soon became very popular among both court aris-tocrats and local elites. Anne de Montassié, wife of Charles de Bourbon, comte de Soissons, sent her daughter Louise de Bourbon (later duchesse de Longue-ville) to attend the classes in 1615–16. Marie de Bourbon de Montpensier, the daughter of Henriette-Catherine de Joyeuse, duchesse de Guise, spent two months in the convent preparing for her first communion. Promised in mar-riage from earliest childhood to a younger son of Henri IV, Mademoiselle de Montpensier continued to visit the convent frequently, often in the company of the queen mother and princesses Christine and Henriette de France.[94] The favor thus shown the Ursulines by powerful aristocrats helped guarantee the convent's financial success by attracting daughters of good family to the con-vent as boarders. The fees charged boarding pupils offset the cost of the classes offered free to hundreds of day students from surrounding neighborhoods.

The interest that Parisian elites took in the Ursulines was not confined to their teaching mission. Lay women came to visit the new convent, just as they visited the Carmelites and Capucines, in the hope of deepening their own piety through spiritual conversations with the nuns. As with those other cloistered orders, most visitors spoke to the Ursulines only through the parlor grille, but a select few were allowed to enter the convent itself. As founder, Madeleine Luillier enjoyed by papal prerogative the right to enter the cloister whenever she chose and to bring with her one or two "respectable women of suitable age or modestly dressed girls."[95] She made use of this right frequently, introducing "ladies of quality" into the convent in the expectation that the benefits of these visits would be mutual, with the ladies profiting from their spiritual conversations and the convent profiting in turn from their benevolence. Although in theory Luillier was the only lay person permitted to stay overnight in the convent, there were exceptions to this rule, and other women too got special permission to make religious retreats with the Ursulines. Mère Pommereuse informs us, for example, that Marguerite de Montmorency, widow of Anne de Lévis, duc de Ventadour, "retired to the solitude" of the Ursulines on several occasions by permission of the pope and with the consent of the nuns.[96] Like the Carmelites and Capucines, the Ursulines quickly became a place where pious ladies sought escape from the pressures of lay society.

Madeleine Luillier was clearly sensitive to the potential conflict between the nuns' need for seclusion and the financial benefits to be gained from allowing select lay women some access to the cloister. Although she took advantage of her right to introduce gentlewomen into the convent, she is reported to have been "very jealous" of the "good order" of the house and to have worked hard to maintain it, asking permission before bringing lay women into the convent and carefully keeping them with her during their visits so that they could not wander around and distract the nuns. She also curtailed her own visits out of fear that too much coming and going on her part might prove disruptive. Having sold her Paris townhouse to help pay for the new convent, she initially moved into the cloister with the nuns. Finding that she frequently had to go out to take care of business or visit members of her family, "who were not happy to see her only at the grille," she decided after about a year to move into a house adjoining the convent. She had the house fitted with a special door so that she could enter the cloister when she chose and usually dined with the nuns on feast days and Sundays, took part in the subsequent hour of recreation, and returned in the evening for Vespers.

Mère Pommereuse is careful to point out in her chronicle that Luillier did not meddle in the internal affairs of the convent but understood well "the difference between the secular state and the religious, and that the privileges of a founder were given in order to maintain the monastery and not to trouble it by usurpation of an authority that was not her due."[97] Later founders were not always so scrupulous about remaining aloof from the internal affairs of the convents they patronized. Strict rules governing the admission of visitors to the cloister also proved increasingly difficult to enforce over time. Even very strict convents, like the Capucines, who initially admitted only the duchesse de Mercœur and her daughter to the cloister, became more liberal with their privileges.[98] The marquise de Maignelay eventually gained permission to enter the Capucine convent up to sixty times each year! In the long run, the desire of elite patrons to share in the life of the convents they patronized helped transform the character of the Catholic revival.

In both the short and the long term, this patronage was nevertheless essential to the movement's growth. Just as the news of the Carmelites' Paris foundation resulted in multiple demands for provincial foundations, so the Capucines and Ursulines were quickly deluged by requests to establish houses in other towns. Because of the Capuchin fathers' reluctance to take on direction of more women's houses, the Capucines had to limit their growth. In 1615 the Cordelières of Amiens reformed themselves by adopting the Capucine rule. In addition, daughter houses were founded by nuns from Paris in Tours (1620) and Marseilles (1626).[99] Other requests to found Capucine convents were refused. With secular priests for their superiors, the Ursulines encountered no such limitations and responded favorably to as many as possible of the requests that were made to establish daughter houses. By the time Madeleine Luillier died in 1630, thirty-six Ursuline convents had been founded on the model and with the guidance of the Paris house. With such rapid growth, it was impossible for the Paris Ursulines to supply nuns to head each new convent. Instead, it became the practice for cities wishing to establish Ursuline houses to send several young women to Paris for a two-year novitiate, after which they would return to provide leadership for the convent being founded in their home town. Although in some cases the initiative came from the town council, the foundations were almost invariably sponsored and financed by notables or aristocrats with both local and Parisian connections.[100]

In addition, some Ursuline congregations initially founded on the Italian model without formal vows or enclosure decided to imitate Paris instead. Here too elite patronage was important, as it cost significantly more to found and build a convent than to house an open congregation of dévotes. A good example is Catherine de Montholon's foundation of the Ursuline convent in Dijon. Born into a distinguished Parisian family, Montholon was an intimate friend of Barbe Acarie and participated in many of her charitable projects. After her husband died in 1611, she decided to take religious vows. Inspired to join the Ursulines after witnessing the elaborate procession that celebrated the congregation's move into new and larger quarters in Dijon, she nevertheless hesitated, troubled by the fear that the retreat from the world that she sought in a religious vocation would be impossible in a congregation whose members still went out to care for the poor and do other works of charity, as the Dijonnaise Ursulines did. To resolve the dilemma, she offered a generous endowment to the Ursulines if they would admit her but made her entry conditional on the congregation's acceptance of enclosure and formal vows. Reluctant to abandon their work among the city's poor, Dijon's Ursulines put Montholon off for more than a year before deciding to accept her request. They even consulted François de Sales, who strongly advised them to refuse enclosure as not suited to their congregation's nature. In the end, however, Catherine de Montholon "wore the sisters down by her constancy," and they agreed to allow her to seek papal bulls erecting them as a formal order.[101] The bulls arrived in 1619.

By force of personality—and the offer of a handsome endowment—Catherine de Montholon thus brought the already flourishing Ursulines of Dijon to accept the same fundamental change in nature as Madeleine Luillier imposed on the nascent congregation in Paris. In neither case was the transformation forced by outside religious authorities. And yet, if we ask why the Dijonnaise Ursulines accepted this radical change even against the advice of François de Sales, we can only conclude that there was more to the story than a single woman's money and force of will. The same ascetic impulse—the same desire for retreat into silent communion—was at work in Dijon, where the Carmelite convent had served since 1605 as a focus of devout culture, as in Paris. The idea that a formal and enclosed religious order represented a higher and more perfect form of religious life than an open congregation was part of the mood of the times.

5

The Contemplative Revival

The founding of the Carmelite, Capucine, and Ursuline convents marked the beginnings of a new enthusiasm for religious life that touched off a blaze of construction in Paris. Between 1604 and 1650, at least forty-eight new religious houses for women—more than one a year—were erected.[1] Some began and remained small and poor, particularly among those founded in the late 1630s by nuns fleeing cities endangered by the Thirty Years War, but others were large and prosperous foundations that cost hundreds of thousands of livres. Along with the approximately two dozen religious houses for men established during the same period, these new congregations transformed the urban environment of Paris and its spiritual geography as well. The circumstances surrounding their creation and the new opportunities they offered pious women form the subject of this chapter and the two that follow.

Although the foundation in 1610 of the Ursulines as an order devoted to catechizing and instructing young girls offered an alternative to the reclusive life of prayer of the Carmelites and Capucines, the importance of this new model was not immediately apparent. Recent literature on the Catholic Reformation has tended to stress women's desire for an active religious vocation in congregations dedicated to teaching, nursing, or ministering to the poor.[2] The fact remains that over 60 percent of the female religious houses founded in Paris during the first half of the seventeenth century were traditional, contemplative convents. Mary Magdalene's tears remained a more powerful religious ideal than Martha's humble service.

A growing preference for the active life did make itself felt as the century progressed. Although 80 percent (20 out of 25) of the religious houses founded between 1604 and 1633 were contemplative convents, this proportion declined to less than 45 percent (10 of 23) between 1634 and 1650. (See table 5.1 for a list of convents and their foundation dates.) The number of teaching orders in particular was on the rise. However, a simple division between active and contemplative congregations fails to do justice to the rich variety of female religious institutions available in Paris by the mid-seventeenth century. The ideals of

TABLE 5.1. Religious Houses for Women Built in Paris between 1604 and 1650

Date[1]	Type[2]	Religious House and Affiliation
1604	C	Carmel de l'Incarnation (Discalced Carmelites)
1606	C	Capucines, or Filles de la Passion
1610	A/E	Ursulines du Faubourg Saint-Jacques
1613	C	Bénédictines de la Ville-l'Evêque (Notre-Dame de Grâce)
1614	C	Filles de Sainte-Elisabeth (Third Order Regular Franciscans)
1616	C	Carmel de la Mère de Dieu (Discalced Carmelites)
1618	C	Monastère de la Madeleine (Madelonnettes)
1619	C	Filles de la Visitation de Sainte-Marie
1621	C	Val-de-Grâce (Benedictines)
1621	C	Filles du Calvaire (Benedictine Order of Calvary)
1621	A/E	Ursulines de Sainte-Avoye
1622	C	Notre-Dame-de-Charité (Feuillantines)
1622	C	Filles de l'Assomption (Augustinians)
1622	C	Annonciades Célestes
1623	C	Visitation du Faubourg Saint-Jacques
1625	A/E	La Charité Notre-Dame (Third Order Regular Franciscans, then Augustinians)
1626	C	Couvent des Filles de la Croix (Dominicans of Saint Thomas)
1626	C	Port-Royal (reformed Cistercians)
1627	C	Récollettes (Reformed Franciscans)
1630	A/S	Filles de la Providence de Dieu
1632	C	La Nativité de Jésus (Cordelières)
1632	C	Annonciades du Saint-Esprit
1633	C	Congrégation du Saint-Sacrement
1633	C	Filles du Calvaire du Marais (Benedictines of the Order of Calvary)
1633	A/S	Filles de la Charité
1634	A/S	L'Exaltation de la Sainte Croix (or Nouvelles Catholiques)
1634	A/E	Notre-Dame de Consolation (Couvent du Chasse-Midi; Congrégation de Notre-Dame)
1635	C	La Conception (Third Order Regular Franciscans)
1635	A/E	Prieuré du Saint-Sépulcre de Jésus (Bellechasse)
1636	C	Bernardines réformées de Sainte-Cécile (du Précieux Sang)
1637	C	Couvent de la Sainte-Croix (Dominicans of Saint Thomas)
1637	C	Annonciades du Saint-Esprit (Annonciades des Dix-Vertus)
1638	A/E	Notre-Dame de Liesse (Benedictines)
1639	A/S	Hospitalières de Saint Joseph (Augustinians)
1639	A/S	La Divine-Providence (Filles de Saint-Joseph)

TABLE 5.1. *(continued)*

Date[1]	Type[2]	Religious House and Affiliation
1640	A/E	Sainte-Anne-la-Royale (Augustinians)
1640	C	Notre-Dame de la Victoire et de Saint-Joseph (Augustinian Canonesses)
1640	C	Filles du Saint-Esprit (or d'Hubate)
1640	A/S	Congrégation des Filles de la Croix
1643	A/E	L'Annonciation (Congrégation de Notre-Dame)
1643	A/E	Dames de Charonne (Congrégation de Notre-Dame)
1644	A/E	Filles du Verbe Incarné (Augustinians)
1644	C	La Madeleine-de-Traisnel (Benedictines)
1646	C	Sainte-Perrine de La Villette (Augustinian Canonesses)
1648	A/E	Hospitalières de la Miséricorde de Jésus (Augustinians)
1648	C	Notre-Dame de Bon-Secours (Benedictines; mitigated rule)
1649	A/E	Filles de Notre-Dame de la Miséricorde (Augustinians)
1649	C	La Présentation de Notre-Dame (Benedictines; mitigated rule)

Source: Compiled from information in Biver and Biver, *Couvents de femmes à Paris;* Raunié, *Epitaphier du vieux Paris;* Hélyot, *Dictionnaire des ordres religieux;* and Hillairet, *Connaissance du vieux Paris.*

Notes:

[1]The founding of a house was never a simple process and could take a number of years. I have tried to identify the year that royal *lettres patentes* were granted for the founding of a house, if this was followed relatively swiftly by the accord of the bishop and the pope and construction began a short time afterward. If a foundation was delayed or contested, I have chosen a date that seems to mark a significant step toward actually creating the authorized house. Some dates, however, remain debatable; those given in this table necessarily provide only an approximate chronology of the building process.

[2]The houses are categorized by the nuns' principal vocation. Key: Contemplative (C), Active (A). Active congregations are further divided between those that accepted enclosure (E) and those that rejected it, taking only simple vows (S). Here too, there are some ambiguities. For example, I have categorized Bellechasse, Notre-Dame de Liesse, and the Verbe Incarné as Active/Enclosed because the nuns announced a teaching mission from the beginning, although in practice these convents seem to have operated much like contemplative convents that took in boarding students. They did not give free classes to local children or take a fourth vow dedicating themselves to the education of young girls, as the Ursulines did.

cloistered religious life existed in tension with an apostolic impulse to spread the faith and serve the sick and poor. Some congregations followed the Ursulines in resolving the tension between Mary and Martha by adapting their rule to permit the exercise of an active vocation within the formal constraints of religious enclosure. Other groups of women increasingly sought innovative organizational forms that, eschewing formal and permanent vows, freed them as filles séculaires to serve in the community. At the head of these new institutions, moreover, we often find lay elites who devoted themselves to funding and administering their chosen projects without entirely abandoning their domestic roles. Rather than sharply dividing contemplative and active religious vocations, we might better envision a continuum extending from the most highly reclusive contemplative convents to open congregations in which proportionately less time was given to ritual devotions and meditation and more to Christian charity. The continuum, moreover, extended into secular society, stretching beyond those women bound by only simple vows to encompass those dévotes who, without taking any vows at all, dedicated a significant amount of their time and energy to Christian service.

However useful it is conceptually to recognize the continuities between the religious impulses of the most withdrawn nuns and their lay sisters engaged in teaching and charitable service, coherent analysis of this vocational spectrum requires that lines be drawn. For analytical purposes, this chapter focuses on the founding of traditional contemplative convents, the character of religious life in these convents, and their place in the larger community. Chapter 6 examines some innovative hybrids that brought a measure of the active life inside the cloister, and chapter 7 the new uncloistered forms of religious life and the charitable endeavors of lay dévotes.

The New Spiritual Geography

The Catholic revival in Paris took place quite literally over the ashes of the League. A great many of the new religious institutions sprang up just outside the old city walls on lands that had been laid waste in the Wars of Religion. This was particularly true of the Left Bank, where the twelfth-century wall of Philip Augustus had long ago proved too confining. With no unbuilt land left within the city walls, the faubourgs outside the city gates had experienced significant growth. Many of the buildings outside the walls had been gutted, however, in the course of the religious wars, especially during Henri IV's fight to gain his capital by laying siege to it in 1590. Although the siege began from the north with shelling from the heights of Montmartre, royal armies had quickly encircled the city. Easily overrunning the temporary earthworks thrown up around the southern faubourgs, the attackers had burned fields and sacked houses and churches.[3] The ruined lands subsequently became prime real estate for the Catholic revival. Easily accessible from the city and yet sheltered from its bustle and noise, they were well suited to the needs of the new reformed orders, permitting them to build large and tranquil cloisters to mitigate the sense of confinement due to rules of strict clausura and allowing them to enclose extensive gardens within their high walls where the nuns could grow the fresh produce that played an important part in their austere diet.[4]

The Carmelites and Ursulines led the way in acquiring large parcels of land in the faubourg Saint-Jacques. They were soon joined by a host of other male and female reformed houses. Further to the west, on the other side of the fields belonging to the Carthusian monastery of Vauvert, another cluster of convents and monasteries formed in the rue de Vaugirard and extended westward into the faubourg Saint-Germain. Because the Right Bank's fourteenth-century wall still enclosed some open fields, there was less need for new religious institutions to cluster outside the walls on this side of the river than there was in the more constricted Latin Quarter, and yet here, too, many

Map of Paris in 1649, by Jacques Gomboust. As was traditional at the time, the map has an east/west and not a north/south axis. The largest concentration of new convents occurred outside the old Left Bank walls of the city, that is, in the upper and lower right-hand quadrants of the map. Marquand Library of Art & Archaeology, Princeton University.

of the new foundations took advantage of the lower costs and greater spaces available outside the city walls. Several houses joined the Capucines, Capuchins, and Feuillants in the faubourg Saint-Honoré. Another handful scattered across the northern suburbs; still others settled in the faubourg Saint-Antoine. At the same time, at least a dozen convents were established within the old Right Bank perimeter, some in the relatively undeveloped outskirts of the Marais, others on smaller properties in more densely built central neighborhoods.

Angélique Arnauld, who left the quiet of Port-Royal in 1633 to help establish a new (and ultimately unsuccessful) convent dedicated to the perpetual adoration of the Blessed Sacrament, left a vivid account of the inconveniences of too central a location. The new house, she wrote, had been situated near the Louvre because one of the institute's male superiors believed that this would help attract young women from wealthy and aristocratic families to enter as novices, but its location in the crowded rue Coquillière meant that the building was hemmed in on all sides and could be expanded only at very great expense. Worse, the nuns' tranquil life and even religious services were frequently interrupted by noise from the street. The sisters overheard all kinds of rude jests, Mère Angélique recorded, and sometimes found it impossible to stifle inappropriate laughter when distracting cries competed for attention with the ritual adoration of the Eucharist that was supposed to be their principal occupation.[5] Although the nuns were rigorously cloistered, the constant clamor of the Parisian populace made it impossible truly to forget the world outside the walls. The best-situated convents would prove to be those located outside the bustle of the city center and yet conveniently close to the neighborhoods where their wealthy patrons made their homes.

The Multiplication of Ascetic and Contemplative Orders

Far from satisfying the desire for reclusive new convents in which to retreat into penitential austerity from a dangerous and sinful world, the example of the Carmelites and Capucines appears to have stimulated additional foundations. The rapid growth of the Carmelite order was itself a response to this new demand for the contemplative life. In addition to sponsoring foundations in one after another provincial town, the Carmelites established a second house in Paris in 1616. But other reformed religious orders sought to establish Parisian convents as well. The Benedictines of Montmartre spawned a daughter house at Ville-l'Evêque in 1613. Under the direction of Marguerite de Sainte-Gertrude d'Arbouze, it soon adopted a more stringent rule than the motherhouse. The Franciscan Penitents of the Third Order Regular, strictly reformed by Parisian Vincent Mussart, created a sister house, the Filles de Sainte-Elisabeth, in 1614. In 1620 Capuchin Père Joseph de Paris founded a convent of Filles du Calvaire, whose strict observance of the rule of Saint Benedict had been introduced by Antoinette d'Orléans de Longueville at Lencloître after her departure from Fontevraud. The following year, Marguerite de Sainte-Gertrude d'Arbouze, made abbess of Val-de-Grâce in the Bièvre valley on the initiative of Anne of Austria, reformed this house as she had Ville-l'Evêque and transferred it to the faubourg Saint-Jacques. The Feuillants, who had strongly resisted creating new houses of Feuillantines after the initial foundation at Toulouse, succumbed to the pleas of Anne of Austria and agreed to establish a Parisian convent in 1622. That same year, the Annonciades Célestes, a reclusive order founded in Genoa in 1602, came to Paris from Nancy. They were followed by the reformed Dominican order of the Filles de Saint-Thomas, who arrived from Toulouse in 1626. Angélique Arnauld, the celebrated reformer of the Cistercian convent of Port-Royal in the Chevreuse valley, established a house across from the Val-de-Grâce in the faubourg Saint-Jacques in 1626 as well. The following year, members of yet another branch of reformed Franciscans, the Récollettes, arrived from Verdun to launch a Paris foundation.

This is by no means the end of the list, but it is worth stopping here to ask what lay behind this surge in austere, contemplative convents. Why were so many new houses founded? What distinguished the new foundations from traditional religious orders and from each other? And where did the religious orders that sponsored them find the wealth to build so many new convents?

On the most elementary level, it is evident that other reformed orders sought to gain a base in Paris for the same reason that the founders of the Discalced Carmelites chose that city as their first home. Locating in proximity to the court and an aristocracy that, although residing in or frequently visiting the capital, also maintained close ties to provincial France was a self-evidently useful strategy for religious orders bent on further expansion. Reformed congregations sought to use Parisian houses as a way of publicizing their participation in the Catholic revival and, it was devoutly hoped, gaining both members and aristocratic—or even royal—sponsorship.

Two elements were crucial to a successful foundation. The first was leadership from within; the second, financial patronage from without. In contrast to the Carmelites, Capucines, and Ursulines, which were founded on the initiative of lay donors, most new convents of the Catholic Reformation were daughters of reformed congregations already established in Paris or elsewhere in France or sister branches of reformed male orders. The impulse to build thus often came from within. Because religious orders were seldom wealthy enough simply to spawn daughter houses at will, however, making good on the impulse to expand required the leadership of clerics and nuns whose charismatic authority drew in the wealthy donors who actually paid for the new foundations. Vincent Mussart's reputation as a charismatic preacher and saintly ascetic helped win support for the foundation of a female branch of the Franciscan Third Order Penitents. The celebrity of Sébastien Michaelis, the Dominicans' reformer and author of a widely read treatise on demonic possession, served the Filles de Saint-Thomas in the same way. The Filles du Calvaire benefited from Père Joseph's fame and the Feuillantines from the very active role that Feuillant general Dom Sans de Sainte-Catherine and theologian Dom Eustache de Saint-Paul Asseline played in Paris's dévot community.

It would be wrong, however, to suggest that only men could play this leadership role. Women played the key part in the foundations of Ville-l'Evêque, the Val-de-Grâce, and Port-Royal. It was through their own charismatic and spiritual authority, and not that of associated male clerics, that Marie de Beauvilliers, Marguerite de Sainte-Gertrude d'Arbouze, and Angélique Arnauld commanded the support that made their new foundations possible.

Women played a key role in other foundations as well, even if their names have a smaller place in histories of the Catholic revival. The Feuillantines' first Paris superior and at least two of the nuns who accompanied her from Toulouse came from prominent Parisian families. Many people would have remembered how superior Marguerite de Sainte-Marie de Clausse de Marchaumont, the widow of a Catholic brother of Henri IV's famous minister Sully, fled secretly to the Feuillantines in 1602. They would also have remembered the heroic vocations of sisters Madeleine de Saint-Jean and Marie de Saint-Benoît Sublet, whose parents had taken them to Toulouse to become Feuillantines at the ages of fifteen and twelve, respectively.[6] All three women had extensive kinship networks in Paris, and the Feuillantines undoubtedly counted on the utility of these connections when they chose them to lead the Paris foundation. It is easy to imagine these pious nuns invoking their strict rule to clear the convent parlor of visitors eager to reestablish contact with them on their return, and yet they doubtless cultivated these contacts as well. To take just one example, Feuillantine chronicles credit councillor of state Jean Sublet des Noyers, the brother of Madeleine de Saint-Jean and Marie de Saint-Benoît, with convincing Louis XIII to contribute more than 45,000 livres to the convent in its early years.[7]

Poverty and Community

What did the new convents offer that traditional convents did not? The answer can be approached collectively. Although each new religious congregation had a distinct identity reflecting the monastic traditions of its parent order, all subscribed to a common ideal of strict reform. The differences among them were in many respects superficial. Each congregation identified for itself a particular vocation, combining special devotion to a particular mystery, or religious teaching, with a special object for its prayers. Thus, the Order of Calvary centered its devotion on the Virgin at the foot of the cross and took as its object the conversion of infidels and the deliverance of the Holy Land.[8] Franciscan Third Order Penitents focused their devotion on Christ's passion and took as their object penitence for not only their own sins but also those of their fellow beings.[9] Congregations differed also in the details of their daily lives. They adopted somewhat different institutional structures, ritual practices, and devotional calendars. All of the reformed orders, for example, required their nuns to do at least two hours of work a day, but where the Franciscan Penitents, among others, had a common workroom so the nuns could listen to spiritual readings while they labored, the Carmelites dispersed the nuns to their cells so that they could meditate in silence even while their hands were occupied with their work.

Despite the differences imposed by their specific vocations and constitutions, new congregations had much more in common with one another than with unreformed houses of their parent orders because of their shared commitment to certain principles identified with strict reform. Whether they wore the dark brown of Carmelites, plain gray of Franciscan Penitents, or undyed homespun of Capucines, members of Counter-Reformation congregations demonstrated their love of poverty by fashioning their habits of sparely cut, coarse wool and wearing them over a simple woolen shift, without the comfort of linen undergarments or the luxury of the fine fabrics and tailoring that many unreformed convents permitted their members.[10] Most reformed orders stopped short of the Capucines' practice of going entirely barefoot except in the gardens and kitchen, but congregations in the mendicant tradition limited footwear to sandals as a mark of their identity, even if, like the Franciscan Penitents, they permitted sisters to wear woolen stockings with their sandals in winter.[11]

The reformed orders' embrace of poverty was more than symbolic. It profoundly affected the nuns' common life. Surrendering all individual property, members gave over their dowries as well as any personal effects or gifts to be administered by the convent's officers for the benefit of all. In contrast to the lax practices of unreformed houses, whose nuns had special delicacies purchased and prepared for private consumption in their rooms, reformed nuns took all their meals in a common refectory. The situation that Marie de Beauvilliers discovered on her arrival at Montmartre, where the only nuns who respected the fasts imposed by their rule were those who lacked the money to feast in private like the others, was all too frequent in unreformed convents. Returning to common meals was thus a first step to more regular religious observance but also to greater sisterhood by eliminating the differences in wealth that allowed some nuns to go hungry while others feasted.

For the same reason, reformed houses forsook the custom of having novices' families provide the furniture for their cells. The Filles de Sainte-Elisabeth were typical in forbidding nuns not only curtained beds, tapestries, and other luxuries but even private images or paintings in their cells. Sleeping on straw pallets under a simple woolen blanket and taking their meals on rough pottery at bare wooden tables, nuns in reformed houses deliberately employed a common poverty to erase the social distinctions that were perennial sources of discord in unreformed houses. The saintly nun who insisted on wearing the poorest, most ragged habit, despite her sisters' efforts to give her a new one, is a common topos in the biographies of Counter-Reformation nuns for the reason that it encapsulates so well the reformed ideal of charitable self-sacrifice. The saintly prioress whose first act on arriving in an unreformed convent was to order the rich hangings, tapestries, and other luxurious furnishings removed from her personal quarters is another topos that speaks to this ideal, as does the common depiction of the reforming prioress as being the first to lend a hand when there was wood to be carried, manure to be spread, or linens to be washed. Poverty and community were inseparably joined in the Counter-Reformation ideal.[12]

Chastity and Spiritual Retreat

Alongside poverty, a vigorous embrace of chastity was central to the vision of a reformed religious life. This was most obviously reflected in the elaborate regulations that specified the physical character of the grilles through which reformed nuns communicated in their convent parlors and the nature of the communications that were allowed to take place. The Catholic Reformation's emphasis on the strict cloistering of nuns was expressed not only in restrictions on entry to and exit from convent cloisters but also in attempts to limit communication with the outside world. None of these restrictions, it must be emphasized, were new. The novelty lay, rather, in the determination to revive practices that had been allowed to lapse in the lax convents of the later Middle Ages.

Many reformed orders explicitly cited the Council of Trent's rulings on clausura in their constitutions. The Filles de Sainte-Elisabeth were typical in specifying that the nuns' chapel was to be closed off by a grille with two-inch-square openings to protect the nuns' enclosure and still let them hear mass and see the host. A barred window in the grille, normally locked, could be opened for vestures and professions, and several banks of black curtains allowed the nuns' voices to be heard in the outer church while their persons remained invisible. The upper tier of curtains could be opened to allow them to witness the elevation of the consecrated host, while the fixed lower tier hid them from view. The nuns' parlors were also equipped with heavily shrouded iron grilles whose black curtains might be opened only when a nun met with members of her most immediate family, with high church dignitaries, or with persons of such high rank that it would insult them to leave the curtain closed. Even if the curtains were open, however, the nun was normally expected to keep her veil lowered over her face. Exceptions were few and closely monitored. The Filles de Sainte-Elisabeth, for example, were permitted to speak to princesses with their faces uncovered if they had the permission of their superior, if the conversation was brief, and if there were no men present in the parlor. They were permitted face-to-face visits with their brothers and sisters only once a year and might raise their veil to speak with their mother and father two or three times each year at most.[13] None of these conversations, moreover, took place alone; a second nun was assigned to listen in on every conversation.

So central was the principle of strict claustration to the Counter-Reformation ethic that the Annonciades Célestes made it a defining characteristic of their order and even took a fourth vow to this effect. They prided themselves on being even more reclusive than other Counter-Reformation orders and refused to lift their veils even for princesses and queens. Even family members were allowed only the most rare and abbreviated visits.[14] Historians have shown little sympathy for—and less understanding of—the Catholic Reformation's strong emphasis on reclusive claustration, which they take to epitomize the Counter-Reformation's drive to control and discipline women's unruly sexuality. As much as the high walls that surrounded the cloister, the thick grilles of convent parlors symbolize the imprisonment of cloistered nuns.[15] This interpretation misreads the nuns' own understanding of their cloistered state in important ways. A fear of sexual contact was far from the only, or even the predominant reason for locking nuns away from the perceived dangers of the outside world. One clue is that most of the rules for conversations in the parlors concerned not meetings with unattached men, who would not in any case have been allowed to speak to a young nun without very good reason, but rather with parents and other members of the nuns' close family.

Convent superiors knew they could not shut the world out entirely. Parents retained a natural love and concern for daughters who took religious vows; they and other family members wanted to continue to see them and to reassure themselves that their offspring were healthy and at least relatively content with their lives. Equally naturally, parents wanted to continue to share the family's news, its trials and joys, even with daughters who had renounced the world. Reformed convents knew they had to permit these conversations and yet at the same time to prevent them from turning into gossip sessions that would distract vulnerable nuns from their spiritual occupation by turning their thoughts to worldly matters, whether the courtship, marriage, and motherhood they had forsaken, the health problems of aging parents, or crises that would cause them to worry about loved ones outside.[16] Nuns in reformed orders were expected to pray for family members and to offer spiritual consolation, but at the same time they were required to detach themselves emotionally from even the closest of kin. That is why the stoic curtailment of family visits and, for nuns who entered as widows, the willing abandonment of their own children because of a higher spiritual calling are common topoi in nuns' biographies. Thus, for example, Jean Macé tells how Marie de Saint-Charles de Veuilly struggled to master her emotions when confronted with her crying baby, which family members had brought to the parlor of the Filles de Sainte-Elisabeth to convince her to renounce her decision to enter the order. Depicting Veuilly as tormented by "the memory of an infant," "an only child still at the breast" whose cries she heard night and day, Macé celebrates the heroic virtue of her triumph over natural, maternal emotions by emphasizing the difficulty with which this triumph was won.[17]

Strict claustration was both a symbol and a tool of worldly renunciation. As the Annonciades Célestes defined it, their special fourth vow of strict clausura was "their defensive wall, their sure asylum, and the cause of their greatest happiness." The Annonciades' founder, Victoria Fornari, wanted them to live "as angelic a life as mortals could," and to this end had determined that they should be "inaccessible and invisible to all creatures," so as ceaselessly to adore God. Only by removing themselves entirely from secular life and destroying every worldly thought could they hope to achieve this end.[18] But shutting out every least thought of the world could never be easy. More than ten years after she began the reform of Port-Royal by forbidding her visiting father to enter the cloister, Angélique Arnauld confessed to Jeanne de Chantal that she still seized on the opening of the choir curtains during mass to study what was happening in the outer part of the church, instead of focusing her attention on the consecrated host as the opening of the curtains was intended to permit her to do. She sometimes lost track of the sermon for the same reason, she admitted with chagrin.[19] The rules of strict cloistering were thus, among other things, a defensive wall intended to help the nuns avoid temptations to sin. The concept of monastic chastity encompassed a broad renunciation of worldliness and did not refer to sexual continence alone.[20] Even prohibitions against nuns touching one another or forming particular friendships were first and foremost warnings against the tugs of human affection and not signs of a fear of lesbian relationships.[21] Special friendships threatened the bonds of community through favoritism and factionalism; they also reintroduced the distraction of emotions the nuns had promised to leave aside.

Mortification of Body and Spirit

The desire to separate themselves from worldly thoughts and emotions was responsible also for the emphasis on mortification of both body and spirit in reformed orders. The same penitential spirituality penetrated these orders as earlier Counter-Reformation foundations. The Filles de Sainte-Elisabeth, for example, scourged themselves three times a week during Advent and Lent and twice a week at other times of the year. To further their central purpose of doing penitence "not only for themselves but also for their fellow beings," they built a secluded chapel dedicated to Christ's passion where the nuns might retire for private rituals of penitence. Decorated with art depicting stations of the cross and penitential saints, the chapel was arranged in such a way that several sisters simultaneously might find a secluded place to pray, meditate, and, with the superior's permission, make use of the scourges and other instruments of discipline that were kept in the chapel.[22]

Not surprisingly, stories of self-mortification find an important place in biographies of the Filles de Sainte-Elisabeth and other ascetic orders. Predictably, Anne de la Passion de Rabot made frequent use of hair shirts and scourges even before her entry into religion, and Madeleine du Sauveur d'O de Baillet engaged in friendly competition with a fellow novice to see who could "perform the most mortifications in the course of the day."[23] Jean Macé's account of how

Marie de Saint-Charles de Veuilly scourged herself so vigorously that she fell ill is also commonplace in pious biographies. However stereotypical, such stories should not be overlooked. Macé gives a good insight into Marie de Saint-Charles's spirituality when he paraphrases a letter she wrote to a sister in an equally austere convent in which she describes how, overtaken by "a cruel insomnia, with violent headaches, and a constant fever" and "reduced to the last extremity" by the frequent purges her doctors prescribed, she "is no longer in the active life but rather is suffused with the suffering life and entirely annihilated with her crucified Jesus. She finds it impossible to say how much joy she finds in this deplorable state, seeing herself intimately united to the will of God."[24]

Other reformed nuns also welcomed illness as a path to union with Christ through the imitation of his suffering.[25] Carmelite Madeleine de Saint-Joseph de Fontaines's biography of Sœur Catherine de Jésus Nicolas repeatedly emphasizes the way God graced the latter nun's illnesses with revelations of Christ's sufferings that served to unite her soul to his. She depicts Sœur Catherine's five-month final illness in particular as a period of martyrdom in which the nun not only suffered indescribable pains but also was literally consumed by the divine spirit, so that "when she died, there appeared to be nothing human left of either body or soul; no flesh whatsoever remained, only skin and bones." Those who prepared her body for burial were shocked at her skeletal appearance and marveled that she had survived as long as she had, and they reported that one of her last visions was of God telling her that she would be received as a martyr in heaven.[26]

Catherine de Jésus's martyrdom was not by any means limited to the passive process of submitting to illness without complaint. She invented imaginative mortifications through which to experience Christ's sufferings. This comes across most clearly in the startlingly original variation she imposed on the cult of the infant Jesus, which was just beginning to take hold in Carmelite and other reformed convents in the second and third decades of the seventeenth century. Although many convents celebrated the infant Jesus with the affective language of a mother's love for her child, the Carmelites, under Pierre de Bérulle's influence, developed a more reserved cult and viewed Christ's infancy largely as a period of humiliation in which God consented to take on all of the weaknesses of a child.[27] Catherine de Jésus carried this line of reasoning still further and, focusing her worship on the unborn baby Jesus, marveled that the Son of God, timelessly perfect in his reason and senses, would consent to a voluntary captivity—deprived of sight, sound, and the use of his other senses—for nine long months in the dark prison of Mary's womb. Desiring to imitate Christ's sacrifice, Sœur Catherine begged Mère Madeleine, as her prioress, and Bérulle, as her spiritual director, to allow her to celebrate Advent with a retreat during which she would each day spend nine hours in prayer and do nine acts of obedience and nine mortifications of the senses to honor and imitate Christ. Because of her fragile health, Sœur Catherine's superiors allowed her to accomplish only a part of the mortifications she proposed. According to Mère Madeleine, she was nevertheless so taken with the idea of Christ's captivity that, immersing herself in contemplation of this state, she lost all use of her own capacities and was unable to move or act of her own accord, although she remained perfectly obedient to her superiors' command.[28] Admiration for this behavior—and the humility and innocence they read into it—caused Madeleine de Saint-Joseph to record Sœur Catherine's biography and Pierre de Bérulle to dedicate its publication in 1628 to the queen mother, Marie de Medici.

As has been shown, this idea of redemptive suffering as a path to union with Christ was one of the themes of late medieval spiritual writing that found an important place in Catholic Reformation piety. Teresa of Avila's announced desire to suffer, and even to die, so as no longer to be separated from God resonated with nuns in a variety of religious orders, just as Teresa's life served more broadly as both model and conduit for the affective and mystical spirituality that pervaded early seventeenth-century convents.[29] But even as Teresa herself came to emphasize mortifications of the spirit over those of the body, so at least some Counter-Reformation orders chose to limit bodily mortifications that might endanger the health in favor of acts of self-abnegation that tested the will in other ways. The Annonciades Célestes, for example, believed that "austerities of the body" should be carefully measured against an individual's strength so as to test but not exceed her powers of endurance. Annonciades were to be "limitless," however, in "mortification of the spirit and self-abnegation" so as to "extinguish worldly desires and thoughts, and subject the senses to reason and reason to God."[30]

Prizing humility, the reformed orders often adopted the tactic of deliberate humiliation as its tool. Prioresses ordered penitent nuns to eat on the refectory floor instead of at the table, to confess their imperfections out loud to the assembled community, or to parade through the convent wearing a noose around their neck and crying out for mercy in imitation of the *amende honorable* (public reparation) commonly employed by early modern justice systems. At Sainte-Elisabeth, Marie de Saint-Charles de Veuilly used carefully staged humiliation to evoke communal repentance and not just to punish individual nuns. Jean Macé offers a vivid description of an emotional encounter that she deliberately engineered to induce an outpouring of tearful penitence among the Filles. First speaking of the virtues of Saint Francis, whose feast day was being celebrated, she next began to berate the assembled nuns, telling them that they should fear that their patron would disavow them as his daughters because "we are so opposed in our imperfections to his holiness." She went on to say that she knew one person among them to be especially at fault, and she asked them to pray for this person, imploring God to touch her heart, while they "confounded her by telling her her faults." She then handed each of the nearly fifty nuns an individual letter and ordered them to do the penance that it contained. The letters were harsh. One said, "Miserable nun, you are a sepulcher whitened on the outside by a handsome exterior, while on the inside filled with sins, passions, and all sorts of imperfections." Another said, "You are but a shadow and a semblance of virtue in religious life. You need to hide yourself away from the community, which you infect with the foul odor of your sins." The other letters, we are told, said roughly the same thing and in the same forceful language. Having handed the nuns these powerful missives and, we may assume, convinced each that she was the sinner whose imperfections would now be revealed, Marie de Saint-Charles startled them all by falling to her knees and proclaiming herself to be the "wicked nun, so infinitely opposed by the innumerable number of her sins and imperfections to the holiness and virtues of Saint Francis." She begged her daughters to come do their penance, as she had ordered, and confront her with her sins, but the nuns were in tears and incapable of the confrontation she demanded, on account of both their ingrained respect for their superior and their acute consciousness of their own imperfections. In the end, she relented, changing their penance to ones they found more acceptable and leaving everyone emotionally drained but, the biography implies, spiritually edified.[31]

Marie de Saint-Charles's emotive style—the harsh language she used to force her daughters to contemplate their sins—and her dramatic gesture of self-mortification probably owe as much to preaching traditions in her order of Franciscan Third Order Penitents as to her personal character and spirituality. It is hard to imagine Jeanne de Chantal, steeped as she was in the gentler tradition of François de Sales, or Madeleine de Saint-Joseph de Fontaines, who also cultivated a gentle approach to the conduct of souls, engineering such a scene.[32] And yet the evidence suggests that, each in her own way but also in keeping with the traditions of her order, the superiors of reformed convents played a very important role in shaping the piety of their daughters. To a perhaps surprising extent, the spiritual guidance that prompted nuns in Counter-Reformation convents to cultivate a deep and personal religious vocation came from inside the cloister's walls.

Spiritual Guidance of Contemplative Nuns

Counter-Reformation convents offered at least four distinct settings in which nuns could offer spiritual advice and direction to their sisters.[33] These were the weekly chapter meeting, the daily hour of "recreation" that occurred after the principal meal, the private conversations that superiors and mistresses of novices had with the nuns entrusted to their care, and the letters of advice that prioresses often exchanged among themselves. The chapter meeting was an occasion for discussion of the convent's business and the disciplining of faults disruptive of convent life, but it could also provide an occasion for the superior formally to address the collected community. At least some superiors used these meetings to deliver "exhortations" that would surely merit the word "sermon" if the latter term were not reserved so strictly for men. The constitutions of the Filles de Sainte-Elisabeth specify that the mother superior should give her daughters spiritual instruction "two or three times a week or more," with each lesson lasting thirty to forty-five minutes—a not insignificant preaching responsibility, in view of the fact that nuns did not regularly hear sermons from other sources, as even in reformed convents outside (male) preachers were brought in only on holidays and special occasions.[34]

Jean Macé is just one of many pious biographers who included examples of these exhortations in his work. In common with other biographers, he regretted that he could not include more samples of his subject's wisdom because, in her humility, she had burned most of her writings. What he says about Marie de Saint-Charles's delivery of these exhortations is nevertheless more important than their contents. He praises them in remarkably strong terms as a form of "public eloquence" entirely appropriate, even necessary, for a woman in her position. "If silence is one of the handsomest ornaments of the female sex," he avers, "eloquence is no less so when a superior is obliged to speak in public. It is for this purpose that chapter meetings are held in convents every week, and that a holy custom obliges superiors to make exhortations on the eve of principal holy days." Calling Marie de Saint-Charles the "channel through which the Father of rain poured his grace onto the Filles de Sainte-Elisabeth," he goes on to say that she prepared herself by taking communion, "so that Jesus Christ himself put on her lips what she would say to her daughters."[35]

Macé adopts a technique that women themselves often used to authorize their public speech in making Marie de Saint-Charles the channel through which a divine message flowed.[36] As the medium through which God speaks, she has an honorable role but one that denies her personal agency. The words she speaks are not her own. Elsewhere, however, Macé describes Mère Marie's lessons in far more vigorous terms, belying the image of female passivity and establishing her leadership qualities with a rhetoric that subverts traditional gender boundaries. Borrowing his metaphors from the masculine sphere of battle, he tells how she draws on the lessons of her own spiritual combats to inspire in her daughters "a male devotion and benevolent courage." Like Teresa, he says, she makes "Amazons"—female warriors—of her nuns. Then he blurs gender boundaries still further by shifting abruptly from martial to nuptial imagery. In one short sentence he describes the sisters as both Amazons and "true brides of Christ crucified." Metaphors of spiritual combat were commonly employed in Counter-Reformation writings, as was the nuptial imagery of brides of Christ, which, in the spiritual language of the time, connoted a mystical union with Christ and a sharing of his suffering and passion. Macé's use of this language is not original, but it is striking in this close conjunction of oppositely gendered images. Obliterating traditional distinctions between male action and female receptivity, Macé attributes to Marie de Saint-Charles an uncommon ability to lead her daughters to transformative spiritual achievements.

It is not just Macé's rhetoric that transgresses expected gender roles. In the spiritual lessons that she addressed to the sisters of Sainte-Elisabeth, Marie de Saint-Charles explicitly rejected traditional notions of womanly weakness. She would accept no excuses; the women she led were fully capable of scaling spiritual heights. "Let us in no way allege or fear the weaknesses of our sex," she taught her daughters; "the Word of God was made incarnate to take upon himself all of the weaknesses of our poor nature, and by a precious exchange, to give us all his force and virtue."[37] Although Mère Marie begins with a gendered reference to womanly weakness, the "precious exchange" to which she refers is not a gendered one. Rather, it is the essential Christian mystery: Christ taking on the sins of humanity and conveying his divinity in exchange. By focusing on this fundamental Christian transaction, Marie de Saint-Charles abolishes gender differences. She not only rejects traditional limits on women's roles, but she also blurs the line between male and female, active and passive, speech. The "precious exchange" operates identically for women and men. By implication, both men and women need to make themselves hollow vessels for the reception of Christ, and all godly teaching and preaching serves to give voice to divinity. Men's speech is as passive as women's, but the converse is also true: women's speech is as active as men's.

Other spiritual biographies also sometimes describe a woman's eloquence in terms that make her sound like a receptive vessel or mere channel for divine speech.[38] Jacques Ferraige's biography of Marguerite de Sainte-Gertrude d'Arbouze, founding abbess of Paris's great Benedictine abbey of Val-de-Grâce, tells how several priests, "hearing her discourse on spiritual subjects one day in the convent's parlor commented on departing that this young woman speaks the words of Heaven." And yet here too, the suggestion of passivity is largely illusory. Certainly Ferraige has no intention of belittling Marguerite de Sainte-Gertrude's ability to reason and speak in her own clear voice. He devotes an entire chapter to praising Mère Marguerite's "gift of explaining thoughts and scripture, which Saint Paul calls the *donum sermonis*." Although remarking that she thought it even more important to guide her daughters through "visible examples" than "eloquent discourses," Ferraige praises her subtle penetration of the scriptural passages she chose for her lessons and attributes to these talks a gripping affective style. He does not hesitate to compare her to the greatest medieval preachers: "Her heart aflame and her mouth speaking from the abundance of her heart, her words were so many sparks of fire, which burned the hearts of her listeners and ravished them by their sweetness, transporting their souls, as that great preacher Saint Anthony of Padua was wont to do."[39]

Marguerite de Sainte-Gertrude's ability to articulate spiritual matters found recognition after her death in the publication of a book, the *Exercice journalier pour les religieuses bénédictines de Nostre-Dame du Val-de-Grâce*, which included a treatise on silent, or meditative, prayer. She was not, however, the only seventeenth-century Parisian superior whose spiritual advice to her nuns was deemed to merit publication. The *Conférences spirituelles* of Marie de Beauvilliers, abbess of Montmartre, were published, as was the *Avis de la venerable mere Madeleine de S. Joseph pour la conduite des novices*, begun by the Carmelite nun to whom the advice is attributed but completed by her fellow Carmelite and close friend Marie de Jésus de Breauté.[40] The exhortations that Mère Françoise des Séraphins Saline delivered to the novices of Paris's reformed Dominican convent of Saint-Thomas were not published, but they were copied down and circulated to other convents of the order.[41] Along with other writings, enough were preserved to allow her biographer to quote extensively from them in his account of her life and teachings.[42] It was common for spiritual writings to circulate in this way.

Private letters also served to convey spiritual advice. Jeanne de Chantal and Madeleine de Saint-Joseph wrote an enormous number of letters to prioresses in their orders in response to both general and specific queries about the conduct of souls.[43] Other distinguished prioresses doubtless did the same, even if all or most of their letters have since been lost. Newly elected prioresses in particular required reassurance and encouragement in the challenging task of spiritual guidance, but even more experienced superiors frequently confided quandaries they faced, for example, with novices who claimed special spiritual gifts, seemed rather too fond of extraordinary mortifications, or displayed other hard to interpret behaviors. The private nature of some of these communications is obvious from Mère Madeleine's occasional closing reminder to "burn this letter," but the more general letters discoursing on a particular virtue, religious practice, or saint quite likely were read aloud and shared with the entire convent to whose prioress they were addressed.

Clearly, the superiors of Parisian convents were engaged on a very personal and individual level with the spiritual development of their nuns. As Madeleine de Saint-Joseph reminded one prioress who sought her advice, the need to oversee the convent's temporal affairs should never be allowed to get in the way of "the interior conduct and perfection of souls, which are the principal obligations of our office."[44] In the words of Marguerite de Sainte-Gertrude d'Arbouze, the abbess was "accountable for the souls as well as the bodies" of the nuns entrusted to her care. As a consequence, she encouraged her daughters, in particular novices, to "communicate their souls" to her as well as to their confessor. The confessor in turn was to urge the girls to recount their innermost thoughts to the mistress of novices. The abbess, confessor, and mistress of novices were secretly to share this intimate knowledge, so that all

Vray Portrait de la V. Mere Madeleine de St. Joseph Religieuse Carmelite deschaussée.

Portrait of Mère Madeleine de Saint-Joseph, by Grégoire Huret. The first French prioress of the newly founded Order of Discalced Carmelites, Madeleine de Saint-Joseph de Fontaines offered spiritual counsel to several generations of Carmelite nuns, as well as to numerous lay men and women who frequented the convent's parlor. This illustration from her biography dramatizes the importance of eucharistic devotion for the new reformed orders. Bibliothèque Nationale de France.

three might gain credit for their perceptive understanding of the nuns' souls, thereby further encouraging them to confide in all three.[45]

The mistress of novices was by no means the junior partner in this threesome. The importance of her role in forming new generations of nuns was clearly recognized. Marguerite de Sainte-Gertrude d'Arbouze served as mistress of novices during at least part of her tenure as abbess of Val-de-Grâce and did not hesitate to take on this office again after stepping down from her position as abbess. Her lessons for the novices are reported to have been so popular that the new superior gave permission for the professed nuns to attend as well. But perhaps most remarkable here is the implicit equality of the sacramentally ordained confessor, the abbess, and the mistress of novices when it came to offering spiritual direction. Ferraige even suggests that the abbess's role as spiritual counselor was more important than the confessor's. It is only in unreformed houses that the nuns seem to want always to have a confessor around, he comments; in well-regulated houses, they are "content to communicate their souls to their Mother."[46]

Nor was the Val-de-Grâce unique in this regard. Jean Macé describes how the Filles de Sainte-Elisabeth looked on Marie de Saint-Charles de Veuilly as "their true spiritual mother" and showed her "the depths of their soul" with "the candor of true children."[47] The mother-child metaphor is also explicit in the constitutions of the order of the Visitation, which provided that all sisters were to "lay bare their heart" to their mother superior. They were to do this with total openness, "with the same sincerity and candor that a child would have in showing its mother its scratches, boils, or bee stings," and to relate their spiritual "advancement and progress but also their backsliding and failures ... so as to receive consolation but also to fortify and humble themselves."[48] Recognizing that some women would resist opening their hearts in this way, Jeanne de Chantal cautioned Visitandine superiors never to force their daughters to confess the sins they withheld. At the same time she urged them to try discreetly to aid those they knew were troubled by unconfessed faults, and she praised the benefits that openness might bring.[49]

Madeleine de Saint-Joseph de Fontaines was even more emphatic in her *Avis pour la conduite des novices* about the need to make novices understand that they must "tell everything in them, whether temptations, or feelings of excessive guilt, consolation, profligacy, or imperfections. In short, there should be nothing that they conceal voluntarily. A soul must be entirely open to she who guides it," she concluded; "a Carmelite carries her soul in her hand." Mère Madeleine was explicit about the need to allow each novice to proceed at her own pace and in keeping with her special gifts and talents. What was good for one soul was not necessarily good for another. But she was also explicit about the need for the mistress of novices to cultivate in her charges feelings of closeness and love for their prioress. Warning that it was easy for novices to make their primary attachment to the nun specially charged to work most

Frontispiece for Jacques Ferraige's biography of Marguerite de Sainte-Gertrude d'Arbouze. Christ's real presence in the Eucharist is also the focus of attention in this frontispiece depicting Marguerite d'Arbouze with her patron, Anne of Austria. The image presents the abbess, kneeling on an open Bible and crosier, as the equal of the queen, who has set down the symbols of her worldly power. At the same time, Marguerite d'Arbouze's crossed arms suggest obeisance and respect. Bibliothèque nationale de France.

closely with them, she advised mistresses of novices that it was good to make themselves loved, "because one accomplishes more by love than by fear." They must nevertheless be careful to make the novices' primary attachment to the prioress, "whom God has principally charged with their care."[50]

Madeleine de Saint-Joseph presents this notion that the Carmelite's soul must be completely open, or transparent, to her female superiors as so natural and expected that it is easy to forget that prioresses of the Spanish convents of Saint Teresa's reform by the end of the sixteenth century had lost this crucial role as spiritual guides of their daughters' souls.[51] As the previous chapter established, the Carmelites' French superiors had accorded the nuns the right to live under Teresa of Avila's original constitutions and not the revised constitutions the Carmelite fathers had imposed on them in Spain, which increased the male superior's authority at the expense of the prioress's. When the Carmelite fathers subsequently established themselves in France and sought to displace the French superiors, the French nuns resisted their claims on the ground that this would deprive them of their "freedom to disclose to the prioress the very depths of their soul."[52] Considering the guidance they received from their prioress a precious commodity, the nuns were willing to fight to preserve the spiritual authority the prioress enjoyed in France.

Why were the French superiors more willing than the Spanish fathers to allow a large measure of spiritual authority to their prioresses? To all appearances, their long experience with spiritually gifted women gave them a high level of respect for the women they envisioned as the French Carmelites' leaders. All three of the first French superiors were close advisers and confidants to the order's founder, Barbe Acarie, and had such a high opinion of her spiritual acuity that they not only entrusted her with helping to select and form the first French Carmelite novices but also, even after the arrival of the Spanish nuns intended to direct the foundation, encouraged her regularly to enter the cloister, where she "instructed" the French novices and "fortified them against spiritual difficulties."[53] The superiors also served as spiritual directors to other women in Acarie's circle, including those who became the first Carmelite novices (and subsequently their first French prioresses), and they had worked closely with Marie de Beauvilliers, Louise de L'Hôpital, and other abbesses who undertook major religious reforms. This experience probably gave the superiors confidence in the ability of spiritually gifted women to offer the attentive guidance necessary to their sisters' pursuit of an intense spiritual life without usurping or subverting the sacramental role of the convent's confessor.

There was a second reason for allowing the women this authority. The high spiritual ideal that was at the very heart of the Catholic Reformation's project for the renewal of religious life would have been unattainable if the convents had to depend for spiritual guidance on the rare visits of their male superiors and guest preachers, or even the sporadic attentions of their regular confessors. To the credit of the religious reformers—both male and female, secular and lay—responsible for founding the Catholic Reformation's new convents in Paris, they recognized that key leadership roles would have to come from the women within. They encouraged these roles, nurtured them, and even celebrated them in their writings.

Spiritual Guidance of Lay Women and Men

Nuns were not the only beneficiaries of religious women's spiritual counsel. In visits to the convent grille, as in lengthier retreats, lay women sought private counsel and guidance from prioresses and other nuns with a reputation for spiritual discernment. The beatification proceedings of Carmelite Madeleine de Saint-Joseph de Fontaines give ample evidence of this. Anne-Geneviève de Bourbon, duchesse de Longueville, for example, testified that she confided to Mère de Saint-Joseph "her most secret thoughts" and received in return "very holy advice and a great deal of assistance." Crediting her with "penetrating God's secrets of the soul," Madame de Longueville describes the tactful spiritual direction Mère Madeleine gave one young woman (quite possibly Longueville herself) who mistakenly believed that she had a religious vocation. She also recalls how the prioress addressed the queen and royal princesses with such authority "that it seemed that she had the right to teach and reprimand them, as she very appropriately did on occasion."[54]

In her letters to other prioresses, Madeleine de Saint-Joseph cautioned them not to take on the regular spiritual direction of lay women. The prioress's cloistered existence made it impossible to observe how the lay women who sought her advice actually conducted themselves in the world. More important, the prioress's first obligation lay with her own household and the spiritual development of her nuns. This should give her enough to do, and if time remained, she should spend it in solitary prayer and not at the parlor grille.[55] But even if prioresses declined to take responsibility for directing the consciences of lay women, as Mère Madeleine advised, they found it hard to avoid the requests for advice from women who frequented their parlors, particularly when the women were actual or potential patrons. The Carmelites' chronicles recount, for example, how Richelieu's favorite niece, Marie de Vignerot, marquise de Combalet (later duchesse d'Aiguillon), entrusted Anne du Saint-Sacrement Viole with "the secrets of her soul and the direction of her conduct." It was impossible to say no to such an influential dévote. The chronicles further recount how, on Madame de Combalet's advice, her brother-in-law and his wife brought a niece of theirs to meet Mère Anne, "trusting to her lights for the choice of estate that [the niece] was to embrace." From their first meeting, Anne du Saint-Sacrement "penetrated the depths of the soul of her young protegée," who shortly afterward experienced a sudden conversion and recognized, as Anne du Saint-Sacrement had foreseen, a profound religious vocation.[56] Such stories are common in Carmelite biographies. Virtually all of the order's distinguished prioresses are credited with the spiritual direction of prominent lay women, who confided their secrets and sought their advice. Discerning spiritual vocations was a natural part of this role, and the narratives inevitably unfold in such a way that the prioress is credited with penetrating God's will and perceiving the disposition he wished to make of the supplicant's soul. Without prematurely betraying this knowledge, she would then help arrange favorable circumstances for this divine will to manifest itself.

The Carmelites were not alone in crediting their superiors with such talents. Similar stories appear in a great many spiritual biographies of the time. Agnès Dauvaine, for example, is credited with the conversion of a Lutheran countess, who subsequently brought her husband to convert and after his death entered the Annonciade convent of which Dauvaine was superior.[57] The stories are not limited to the spiritual direction of women. Men too found their way to the parlor grille and sought advice from nuns with a reputation for spiritual discernment. Dispatched to found a new convent in Troyes, Carmelite Marie de la Trinité d'Hannivel became a close confidante of the local bishop, who is said to have "communicated to her his most important business" and "sought out her advice in the most delicate of affairs." A brother of Chancellor Nicolas Brûlart de Sillery is also reported to have had "the greatest confidence in her." He "did nothing important without her advice" and "recounted to her all that took place in his soul, in person or through letters." Even Vincent de Paul had "so particular an esteem for her virtue and capacity" that he consulted her about his growing congregation and told members who were in Troyes "to do nothing without her advice."[58]

Madeleine de Saint-Joseph's surviving correspondence includes eight letters of spiritual direction addressed to male clerics who wrote asking her advice on the conduct of souls. Unlike comparable missives to fellow Carmelites, several of the letters to male ecclesiastics open with apologetic statements about her incapacity when confronted with such difficult and important questions. They also include assurances that, far from needing this advice, the correspondent already knows these things. Revealing Mère Madeleine's discomfort at the gender reversal implicit in a woman's offering advice to a man, these rhetorical devices were clearly intended to set things right. Once past the obligatory demurrals, however, she plunged ahead and gave her male correspondents the same clear-headed guidance she offered her sisters in religion. Moreover, if her correspondent continued the dialogue by posing further questions, she dispensed with the self-effacing rhetoric and responded in the unapologetic and straightforward manner she used with fellow prioresses.[59]

In addition to establishing close and mutually supportive relationships with distinguished prelates and other clerics, women with a reputation for spiritual acuity used their authority to offer guidance to devout lay men and to urge repentance on those enmeshed in the snares of worldliness. They are credited with bringing men leading dissolute lives to see the errors of their ways, with taking a special pleasure in convincing heretics to return to the mother church, and with awakening religious vocations in men who subsequently joined the priesthood or entered reformed orders. Marguerite du Saint-Sacrement Acarie is said to have urged Count Philippe-Emmanuel de Gondi, commander of the king's galleys, "in the strongest possible terms and without regard to the rank he held at court" to reform his worldly ways, separate himself from the court's pleasures, and begin to lead a pious life. Failing to convince him by reason alone, she adopted a different tactic and revealed that God had a special plan for him. "Do not be so obstinate," she chided him; "God is still the master. What you refuse to do to please him, he will do himself as sovereign. He won't force you but rather will sweetly charm you by the appeal of his mercy." As she went on to predict, Gondi's wife died a short time later, and he joined the Oratoire, a new company of secular priests dedicated to raising the educational level and standards of parish clergy.[60] Such stories form an important motif in pious women's biographies, establishing their subjects as possessing a spiritual authority that brought men, as well as women, in search of their wise direction.

If some accounts of the techniques that spiritual women used to lead men out of the error of their ways emphasize forceful argumentation and emotional remonstrances, others initially at least suggest that the woman effecting this conversion played a more passive role, serving merely as the conduit of divine grace. This is well illustrated by the role that Anne du Saint-Sacrement Viole played in convincing a Protestant minister to return to the Catholic fold. Although the convert later marveled that it was this meeting and not consultation with learned men that had "put him back onto the path of salvation," the narrative makes it clear that his whole reason in seeking out Mère Anne, then serving as the Carmelite prioress in Amiens, was her spiritual reputation. Tortured by doubts, the minister had asked on arriving in Amiens who had the greatest reputation for spiritual direction. The name of Anne du Saint-Sacrement was one of several suggested, but he first sought help from others. Described as "the most learned persons in the city," these presumably were men. Finding no satisfaction from his conversations with them, he turned up at the Carmelite house and asked to see Mère Anne. According to her Carmelite biographer, she had scarcely begun to speak when the man felt compelled to reveal to her "the most secret recesses of his soul." Her response is conveyed only in a brief and mixed metaphor. She is reported to have allowed "several drops of the celestial dew" of her own "interior illumination" to fall into his heart and "provoke there the tears of sincere repentance."[61] The narrative nevertheless emphasizes how the Carmelite prioress triumphed where the most learned men in the city had failed. And if the boundaries between personal agency and divine will here are blurred, that is because Anne du Saint-

Sacrement's spiritual authority lay precisely in her ability to deliver a message that the recipient believed came from God.

Given the gender biases that existed in early modern times, it may be surprising that learned men should seek out the counsel and follow advice of women, even women known for their sanctity, and yet the evidence suggests that the qualities attributed to holy women included a wisdom that was all the more respected in that its origins were seen to lie in direct communion with the divine and not the mere study of books. Cloistered women had less opportunity to offer guidance to men than to women, because men were never admitted to a convent's private spaces and were probably also less likely than women to make visits in the parlor. And yet, time and again, the Parisian lives tell of men seeking the spiritual counsel of noted prioresses, reforming their lives on the women's insistence, and even positioning themselves as their "spiritual sons."[62] These men served as important protectors and benefactors of the convents they visited. So did elite women, whose generosity was further stimulated by the knowledge that, if their gifts gained them the title of founder of a convent, they might enter the cloister and share in the life of the nuns they admired.

Aristocratic Patronage of Counter-Reformation Convents

Historians have suggested that male religious orders received more generous patronage than female ones for the simple reason that nuns could not say masses for the souls of the dead but could offer only their prayers. This was doubtless true; one has only to look at the records of male houses to see how many of the donations were made on the condition that masses be said. And yet gifts to convents were also calculated in terms of spiritual benefits. Pious donors expected spiritual rewards from the prayers of nuns in the convents they founded, and they often required these prayers in their contracts of donation. They also looked on the foundations themselves as good works with redemptive value. This is clearly expressed in the contract by which Anne Gobelin, dame de Plainville, gave the Feuillantines 27,000 livres and an additional annuity of 2,000 livres for the privilege of serving as founder of their new Paris convent. The contract states explicitly that Gobelin's motive in founding the convent was "the remission of her sins and the repose of the souls of the aforesaid seigneur de Plainville, her husband, and her mother and father and other deceased family and kin."[63] But Gobelin, like the founders of the Carmelites, Capucines, and other reformed convents, also expected to get spiritual benefit from her gift during her lifetime. She expected to enjoy a special intimacy with the reformed religious community that she endowed. Specially exempted from the rules that prohibited lay people from entering the sacred space of the cloister, founders expected that their devotional life would be enriched by time spent in the secluded company of devout nuns. Hoping to profit from the wisdom of the mother superior and the pious example of the community, they anticipated edification but also a quiet space for retreat from the world. These expectations were spelled out in a detailed way in contracts for the foundation of Counter-Reformation convents, and there is no mistaking the importance that donors attached to these privileges.

Anne Gobelin's contract with the Feuillantines is typical in its insistence on establishing her unique relationship to the convent. It specified, for example, that, even if other generous donors came along later, she was to be the only recognized founder and, most particularly, the only one to enjoy the right to sleep in the convent. If, moreover, the nuns agreed "for some consideration regarding the glory of God or utility of the convent" to permit another benefactress to enter during the daytime, this donor was nevertheless to be forbidden to visit on days when Gobelin was in the convent. Gobelin wanted the exclusive right to the nuns' company, but she also wanted to share this privileged status with her friends. To this end, she further negotiated the right to bring two women or girls of her choosing into the convent with her and to have her guests stay overnight whenever she pleased.[64] These privileges violated the Council of Trent's decrees on clausura and also several subsequent papal bulls that voided any claims lay women might make to the privilege of entering convent cloisters. It nevertheless remained an accepted tradition in France for founders to enter the cloister.[65] The papacy itself had so frequently contradicted its stated policy by granting permissions for entry that local clerics found it hard to take the prohibition seriously.

In the end, it boiled down to a simple question of supply and demand. Financial realities encouraged donors to demand generous privileges of entry in exchange for their funds, while the convents, desperate for money, compromised their ideals of strict seclusion and prayed that the donors' piety would keep them from abusing the privileges thus gained. The archbishop of Paris, who had to approve all religious foundations, only rarely intervened. He made only minor modifications, for example, in the rights accorded Anne Gobelin. Limiting her freedom to select the guests who accompanied her and specifying that she might bring only one servant when she stayed overnight, he otherwise left intact the privileges she had negotiated.[66] While these changes do suggest a desire to ensure that the nuns not be subject to a continual parade of secular visitors, the archbishop's failure to curb Gobelin's right of unlimited access to the convent shows how loudly money spoke.

The High Price of Success

Because the agreements between donors and the convents they funded were individually negotiated, each convent's story is unique. Few convents enjoyed the benefits of a single, very rich donor in the way the Capucines did. The most financially secure were, in general, those like the Val-de-Grâce that enjoyed not just private patronage but generous gifts from Queens Marie de Medici and Anne of Austria. On the other hand, even royal patronage could abruptly cease, leaving a convent with unexpected debts, as the Filles du Calvaire learned to their dismay when Marie de Medici was forced into exile by her quarrels with her son Louis XIII.[67] Many, if not most, convents encountered serious financial difficulties soon after their founding or, most commonly, when they decided to expand. It was easy to underestimate both the day-to-day expenditures a community required and the costs of constructing the more comfortable quarters that every group of nuns began to dream about as soon as their congregation tasted its first signs of success.

The Feuillantines were in many respects typical. The convent could not have been founded without the intervention of Anne of Austria, who succeeded in convincing the Feuillants to permit the establishment of a Parisian convent in 1622. It was not the queen, however, who supplied the money for the foundation but a wealthy widow from an old and upwardly mobile Parisian family. The widow of Charles Destournel, seigneur de Plainville and governor of the town of Corbie, Anne Gobelin gave the Feuillantines 27,000 livres to purchase a house and garden in the faubourg Saint-Jacques. She also gave them a 2,000 livre annuity (representing capital of 32,000 livres) that was earmarked for ongoing expenses and, more specifically, for supporting the six nuns who came from Toulouse to make the foundation. Apparently the motherhouse either was not asked or refused to transfer to Paris the dowries the six nuns had paid to the convent at Toulouse. Of the 2,000 livres, however, only 1,200 was promised up front. The Feuillantines were to receive the remainder only after Gobelin's death.[68]

The community thus began with an income of 200 livres per year per nun. This is precisely the amount that came to be required of new foundations as a guarantee of financial solvency, and it might thus be considered a realistic amount necessary for the day-to-day operations of the convent.[69] There would have been little or nothing left over to pay for further additions to or expansion of the convent. And yet the nuns very quickly decided that such expansion was necessary and also that they should build anew rather than attempt to remodel their current quarters. The Feuillant fathers, who had initially purchased the convent's lands with the intention of establishing their novitiate there, had promised to take care of basic repairs and those renovations required to make the buildings habitable by cloistered nuns. Any additional construction would have to be at the Feuillantines' expense.

The entry of six postulants during the very first months the convent was established undoubtedly encouraged the Feuillantines to look ahead optimistically and plan to replace their improvised quarters in several small buildings with a spacious new convent. No record exists of the dowries these novices brought, but it appears highly unlikely that any of the women made unusually large contributions to the convent's funds, as surviving records would almost certainly mention novices whose gifts qualified them as benefactresses. The records indicate, moreover, that construction costs mounted precipitously and with them the convent's debt. Expenses for the new house, begun in 1625 and inhabited though not yet complete as of 1631, eventually totaled more than 309,000 livres. This did not include the church completed in 1672 at the price of 211,000 livres.[70]

Many Parisian convents fell into debt on account of the same sort of premature and overly ambitious building projects. The Feuillantines' high building costs however, were, unusual in one respect. The nuns had the extreme misfortune of having been given a property that, although well located and spacious, was tunneled with limestone quarries from which great quantities of Paris's handsome building stone had been extracted. When workers began to lay the foundations for the new convent in 1625, the fragile soil, badly undermined by centuries of quarrying, caved in. Great yawning pits opened up, and the newly laid stones tumbled down. Work ceased immediately because of the danger, and a great deal of money had to be spent reinforcing existing buildings, filling in holes, and attempting to ensure that construction could safely proceed. Despite the precautions, another collapse occurred the following year, completely burying scaffolds, hoists, ladders, and a host of other tools but, very fortunately, costing no lives. Because of these delays and added expenses, masonry alone for the new convent, always the biggest construction cost, came to more than 176,000 livres.[71]

Despite gifts from Louis XIII that totaled over 45,000 livres at the time of his death, the Feuillantines' new buildings left them deeply in debt. Finding that they could not pay off these debts from the nuns' dowries and gifts alone, the Feuillantines, like nuns in other convents, began to allow lay donors to furnish rooms for themselves and reside in the convent for a fee. Feuillantine chronicles suggest that the marquise de Mirebeau became the convent's first *pensionnaire en chambre* in 1636. By the time the Fronde was over, with its additionally crippling financial consequences, the Feuillantines were also accepting young girls as boarders. Mademoiselle de Crussol, the daughter of the duke of Uzès, is reported to have been their first boarding pupil in 1652.[72] With Marguerite de Sainte-Marie de Clausse, who ran away to join the Feuillantines in 1602, serving as their first superior and Madeleine de Saint-Jean Sublet, who had been a member of the Toulouse congregation since 1599, as mistress of novices, we can be sure that the Paris Feuillantines inherited a strong allegiance to the ascetic traditions that constituted the distinctive identity of their order. And yet, it is hard to imagine that the presence of lay boarders in the cloister did not impose significant changes on their way of life. Caring for the schoolgirls they took in after 1652 must have imposed greater changes still on the lives of these contemplative nuns.

The same deviation from initial principles of strict cloistering and monastic seclusion occurred in most of the austere contemplative convents founded during the Catholic revival. The case of the Filles de Sainte-Elisabeth is instructive. The convent's perennial financial worries stemmed from its economically precarious origins and not just its strict observance of the rule of Saint Francis. Founded as a sister house for the reformed Franciscan Penitents of the Third Order Regular established at Picpus shortly after the turn of the century, the convent dated its origins to 1613, when the Penitents' syndic acquired a large house in the parish of Saint-Nicolas-des-Champs with the explicit intention of establishing there a convent of daughters of Saint Elisabeth "on the model already established in the city of Toulouse." Vincent Mussart, the reformer of the male branch of Franciscan Penitents, is usually credited with the decision to establish a female branch of the order in Paris.[73] He recruited his sister and stepmother for the new house, lined up another ten potential recruits, and brought in nuns from a Burgundian convent of Third Order Penitents, who had spontaneously reformed themselves along the lines of his teachings, to direct the new foundation.[74] Père Vincent was probably also responsible for recruiting the convent's first patron, Jeanne de La Grange. Her donation of half a house (and sale of the other half) gave the group its first home.[75]

But if Vincent Mussart had the ambition and charismatic appeal necessary to establish a reformed religious order, he did not, as a Penitent friar, have the financial means to ensure the foundation's success. Nor did his stepmother and sister, the widow and daughter of a Parisian merchant of modest standing. They were able to contribute an income of 600 livres to the new convent. The funds were important, as they served to purchase the other half of Jeanne de La Grange's house. They did not, however, qualify the women as benefactresses. At 300 livres each, they provided an income only marginally larger than the pensions brought by several other new recruits. On the other hand, some recruits entered with pensions as little as 100 livres per year. All told, and subtracting the funds applied toward purchase of the house, the institution commenced with an annual income of approximately 1,840 livres.[76] The sum fell far short of the amounts advanced for the founding of the Carmelites or Ursulines, much less the Capucines. It was, however, sufficient to convince the Crown to issue letters patent authorizing the convent's foundation in January 1614.[77] Parlement, always fearful that new religious houses would be a burden on the city, expressed its hesitation by delaying registration of the king's letters patent for a full year.

The bishop's letter of authorization also hints at reservations. Limiting the new convent to twelve nuns—exactly the number of aspirants—he further specified that any over that number must guarantee the convent an annual income of at least 150 livres. Only three-quarters of the 200 livres per nun required at most other convents, 150 livres per year must, in the bishop's eyes, have represented the absolute minimum amount needed to feed and house a single nun. The 1,840 livres promised for a house of twelve nuns just barely met this minimum; indeed, it fell short if the two nuns brought from Burgundy did not bring endowment monies with them. Nor did the sum leave any margin for remodeling the private residence purchased for the convent to suit the nuns' needs or paying the priest who conducted the religious services the convent required. The Filles de Sainte-Elisabeth thus started life with an extremely small endowment. Undoubtedly they assured themselves that beginnings were the hardest and, God willing, conditions would get better as time went on.

Financially secure or not, the founders allowed the twelve novices to take the habit in May 1616. The nine who survived their novitiate made their profession the following year. The bishop dedicated the temporary chapel erected in the donor's house just a week before the novices took their final vows.[78] And yet, despite their strained financial situation, the sisters were already planning to build a new and larger convent on the other side of the rue Neuve Saint-Laurent. In August 1616 Jeanne de La Grange made a second and larger gift to the Filles de Sainte-Elisabeth for the specific purpose of allowing the congregation to build bigger quarters "so as to be able to receive and nourish a larger number of women." Although the nuns may have had some justification for believing that their financial conditions would improve if they could only admit more nuns, they discovered, as did many other orders, that expansion was both risky and costly. The new donation—which included the large house where La Grange resided directly across from the convent, along with 110 *arpents* (roughly 100 acres) of farmland in the Parisian hinterlands and 650 livres in annuities—had some expensive conditions attached. Jeanne de La Grange was giving her own residence to the nuns and received in return the right to enter the convent whenever she chose, even to live there full time, without taking religious vows.[79] She nevertheless retained the income from the promised farmlands and annuities throughout her life. What is more, she required the nuns on her death to pay off a debt she owed of 8,000 livres and to disburse a further 6,000 livres in charitable bequests. In addition, they were to pay 300 livres annually to the monks of Picpus in order that daily masses should be said for her soul. They further promised to accept a young woman in La Grange's household as a novice without a dowry and, should she decide to leave the convent, to pay her an income of 200 livres annually.

Welcome as the gift of additional property undoubtedly was, the terms of the donation imposed important burdens on the convent. The nuns would receive no income from the gift until after the donor's death, and yet when this death occurred they would need to pay out 14,000 livres. If they could not supply the amount from their treasury, they would have to borrow it at interest. It is impossible to estimate just what revenue the convent might have anticipated from the 110 arpents of farmland promised in the donation. Contemporary farm revenues in the region suggest, however, that income from the promised fields and rentes would very likely have proved insufficient to cover the payments promised on La Grange's death.[80] Though providing the lands needed for a more spacious convent, the gift threatened to deplete rather than augment the convent's liquid resources.

The gift, moreover, encouraged still greater expenses. Deciding that they required still more space for the larger convent and gardens they envisioned, the nuns began quietly to buy up additional parcels of adjacent land.[81] The money for these purchases came from the dowries of newly admitted novices. Dowry records for this period are incomplete, but it is clear that at least a few of the new novices came from more socially distinguished and wealthier families than the first novices. The turning point appears to have come with the entry early in 1617 of Madeleine d'O, daughter of Jacques d'O, seigneur de Baillet and Franconville and founder of the Penitents' Franconville friary. Descended on her mother's side from the Luillier de Boulancourt clan, Madeleine could claim kinship ties to many of the most prestigious robe families in Paris. She is said to have fled the world shortly after attending the court ballet that celebrated the arrival of Anne of Austria in Paris.[82]

Madeleine's vocation helped prompt that of Marie de Veuilly, who, as a relative, had been invited to attend her vesture ceremony.[83] Perhaps it was the same ceremony, reported to have been attended by "a great number of persons of the first rank," that prompted Françoise de Mauleon, a *fille d'honneur* of the duchesse de Vendôme, to enter as well in 1618. The fact that François de Sales gave the veil to Françoise de Mauleon and delivered a sermon for the occasion suggests that, however simple its origins, the convent of Sainte-Elisabeth had established a very respectable place for itself in just a few short years.[84] And yet, despite the entry of these—and perhaps other—women of high social station, the financial position of the Filles de Sainte-Elisabeth remained precarious on account of their extensive property purchases. The nuns complained in 1626 that they had been forced to pay considerably more than market value for the properties and, in doing so, had liquidated the better part of their revenues.[85] Although the convent acquired a new benefactress that same year in the person of Anne de Rabot, widow of Christophe de Harlay de Beaumont, financial difficulties made it necessary to proceed slowly with construction of the new convent.[86] The church was not completed for another twenty years.[87]

The financial worries brought about by this construction had two important consequences. First, the Filles de Sainte-Elisabeth relaxed the rules of clausura to allow other lay benefactresses the privilege of entering the cloister and even residing there when they chose, just as their initial founder had been allowed to do.[88] Second, after some debate, they decided to accept young girls as paying boarders and pupils. Although some sisters argued that this would interfere with the solitude and prayer to which they were consecrated, others countered with financial necessity. They further argued that, if they took only girls who thought they wanted someday to be nuns, they could solve not one but two potential problems, acquiring a supply of willing postulants at the same time that they earned needed funds by their labors. This argument won the day.

There is no way of knowing whether the Filles de Sainte-Elisabeth lived up to their intention of accepting only girls who thought they had a religious vocation. The biographer of Marie de Saint-Charles de Veuilly, who was the convent's superior at the point this decision was reached, assures his readers that "the novitiate was soon filled with nuns who proved worthy of their vocation," but he does not say how many girls went back into the world to be married. Perhaps more important, he suggests that, although the Filles de Sainte-Elisabeth went into the teaching business only reluctantly, they took their new vocation very seriously. Even Marie de Saint-Charles, despite her occupations as superior, joined actively in "the instruction and entertainment of these young people," for whom she "invented innocent games" as lessons in virtue and piety.[89] The Filles de Sainte-Elisabeth became teachers, then, not because they aspired to an active religious vocation, but as a pragmatic way both to earn money and to recruit worthy novices. Many other contemplative convents were to take the same path.

The Ascetic Impulse at Midcentury

The ideal of contemplative retreat in a perfectly regulated and strictly reformed convent persisted through midcentury. Contemplative convents continued to be founded in the 1630s and 1640s at only a bit slower pace than during the previous decade. Some of these convents were born of the success of earlier Parisian foundations. The Filles du Calvaire founded a second house in the Marais in 1633 and the Dominicans of Saint-Thomas a house at Charonne in 1637. Other new convents were daughters of reformed orders that did not yet exist in the capital. Melun's Annonciades des Dix-Vertus, Grenoble's Bernardines de Sainte-Cécile, and Rheims's Augustinian canonesses of Saint-Etienne established Paris houses in 1632, 1636, and 1640, respectively.[90] Still other foundations were made with little regard for convents already existent in the city. Annonciades from the motherhouse in Bourges founded a Paris house in 1637 despite the presence of Annonciades from Melun; Franciscan Third Order Penitents from Toulouse established a Paris house in 1635 over the objections of the Filles de Sainte-Elisabeth.[91]

The latter were not the only nuns who, already worried about their financial security, feared the competition for patronage and novices that additional new foundations would bring. When Sébastien Zamet, bishop of Langres and spiritual director of Port-Royal, decided to found a new convent dedicated to the perpetual adoration of the Blessed Sacrament, he encountered opposition at every step of the way from authorities said to have been moved by the Carmelites' fear of the competition the new convent would provide.[92] With the support of Angélique Arnauld, Zamet received papal bulls for the new foundation in 1627, but he could not get the necessary letters patent registered until 1633, delaying the congregation's beginning for a full six years.[93] When the convent at last opened, moreover, it was not the extremely austere and reclusive institution Zamet had originally intended but a much more worldly and fashionable place. According to Angélique Arnauld, Zamet abandoned his original plans because he became convinced that the congregation "could not grow without making many friends and having girls from wealthy and elite families." The way to do this, he decided, was to locate the convent close to the royal palace of the Louvre. Appealing to the vanity of potential recruits, he outfitted the nuns in fine white habits with scarlet scapulars and he moderated the austerities of convent life so as not to frighten away comfort-loving daughters of the court nobility and rich bourgeoisie. Although she remained enthusiastic about the congregation's spiritual purpose, Arnauld strongly disapproved of the way Zamet sacrificed the ascetic foundations of the Catholic revival in pursuit of financial success.[94]

Arnauld was equally disapproving of the changes introduced at Port-Royal after she stepped down as abbess in 1629. Here too, Zamet had persuaded the nuns to introduce more worldly practices. The kitchen served up a more highly spiced and varied cuisine, splendid linens and bouquets of flowers garnished the church, and a continuous stream of fashionable clergymen arrived to preach and celebrate mass. Attributing the new practices to the desire to cultivate elite patronage, Arnauld observed that those now in charge at Port-Royal "no longer wished to received boarders if they were not the daughters of marquis or counts." She was even more disturbed to witness new recruits engaging in "extraordinary austerities—fasts on bread and water, terrible scourging, and the most humiliating penances in the world"—when, a short time later, the same girls might be seen "laughing as hard as they had cried in the morning." In short, "they made a game of everything," even the humiliations that should have been intended to form their character as nuns.[95] To Arnauld, this was the greatest blow of all, to see the behaviors she associated with true Christian piety trivialized by being made into a game.

By the time she recorded these observations in 1654, Angélique Arnauld had long since returned Port-Royal to the austere practices of its initial reform. She had also become a recognized leader of the controversial movement known as Jansenism, a rigorist Augustinian theology that emphasized human sinfulness, the need for penitence, and dependence on God's grace. That she should have been critical of any compromise with worldly morality is thus predictable. Already in 1635, she had abandoned Zamet's spiritual direction to become the penitent of Jansenism's spiritual founder, Jean Duvergier de Hauranne, abbé de Saint-Cyran. Her critique of the changes Zamet imposed on the nuns of the Saint-Sacrement and Port-Royal is thus not impartial.[96] It is nevertheless revealing, because it illuminates an incipient division among the dévots even before the Jansenist movement took shape. Equally important, a debate over the penitential impulse lay at the heart of the quarrel.

A popular spiritual director recognized by many as the dévots' leader following the death of Pierre de Bérulle in 1629, Saint-Cyran encouraged his penitents to withdraw from the world, which could only distract them from the introspection necessary to experience genuine contrition and so to benefit from God's saving grace—teachings later associated with Jansenism.[97] Taking his advice literally, several bright young men in Saint-Cyran's circle resigned their royal offices to devote themselves to lives of solitary penitence. This only confirmed Cardinal Richelieu, already troubled by the political implications of Saint-Cyran's teachings, in his view that the abbé's theological principles were detrimental to the public good, which depended on worldly service and not contemplative retreat. When Richelieu had Saint-Cyran arrested on charges of heresy and thrown into prison in 1638, the dévot community initially came to his defense, viewing his teachings as but an extension of the penitential spirituality that had sparked the Catholic revival. In time, however, the dévots divided. Some enthusiastically embraced Saint-Cyran's rigorous position and hailed him as a martyr when he died shortly after release from prison in 1643. These included Angélique Arnauld and most of the nuns at Port-Royal, along with her brother Antoine Arnauld d'Andilly and other leaders of the Jansenist movement. Others, including Vincent de Paul, moved away from their earlier support of Saint-Cyran and joined the growing chorus of anti-Jansenists. Although a definitive break did not come until 1653, when the pope condemned five propositions allegedly taught by the Jansenists as heretical, Richelieu's condemnation of excessive introspection inevitably undermined a penitential impulse that was already fading of its own accord.[98]

Sébastien Zamet was not alone in perceiving that the young women who aspired to a contemplative religious life in the 1630s did not share the enthusiasm for penitential practices that had characterized the first generation of reformed nuns. In keeping with the spirit of the Catholic revival, most of the contemplative convents founded after 1630 adopted a strict monastic rule, but the Benedictine houses of Notre-Dame de Bon-Secours and La Présentation de Notre-Dame, founded in 1648 and 1649, respectively, reverted to the less stringent mitigated rule, surely a sign of changing times.[99] Even in strictly observant convents, moreover, internal mortifications had largely replaced corporal austerities as means of cultivating humility and obedience to superiors. Madeleine de Saint-Joseph de Fontaines, for example, was troubled to observe that, not only did few of the younger Carmelites seem drawn to penitential practices, but some actually seemed greatly to fear corporal mortifications. As a member of the founding generation of French Carmelites and the admiring biographer of the extremely ascetic Catherine de Jésus, Mère Madeleine could not help but think that the younger nuns' apprehension reflected some weakness, or lack of love for God, "for where love is great, fear has no place; nothing is difficult to one who loves." She accepted, however, that times had changed and advised her fellow prioresses not to demand other acts of penitence than those prescribed by the rule, while nevertheless allowing the rare girls who felt called to penitential austerities to test themselves, if this seemed God's will.[100]

The change in sentiment was primarily a generational one. Born in 1578, Madeleine de Saint-Joseph had come of age amid the turmoil of the League. The girls who entered contemplative convents in the 1630s and 1640s were too young to have shared this experience. They heard stories of the heroic mortifications in which the first generation of reformed nuns had engaged but did not feel the same powerful need to atone for their own sins and those of the world through acts of bodily suffering. The fact that young nuns at Port-Royal could make games of penitential practices that an earlier generation had identified as effective paths to union with God is a good indication of the distance that separated the religious imagination of the newer nuns from that of their elders. The economic circumstances prevailing in Parisian convents by the 1630s also contributed to the change. To finance their elaborate building programs, contemplative convents necessarily sacrificed some of their reclusion and accepted living in closer collaboration with the secular world. Zamet compromised more than most religious superiors were willing to do in his attempt to draw wealthy girls to the convent of the Saint-Sacrement by tailoring the nuns' habits to fashionable standards and replacing the rules of strict observance with politesse, but all of the convents relaxed their rule in at least minor ways to please the patrons whose funding they eagerly sought.

However careful superiors tried to be, opening contemplative convents to schoolgirls and widows or unhappily married women seeking escape from worldly society inevitably changed the institutions' character. Even if lay sisters did most of the domestic work needed to lodge and feed the boarders, the choir nuns had to take charge of the girls' religious and secular education. They also had to supervise their recreation and visits to the parlor, to speak with the girls' parents about their progress and potential religious vocation, and otherwise to take time from their routines of prayer and worship to deal with their boarders' needs. In theory at least, adult boarders provided fewer distractions, but this was not always the case. They often accommodated themselves poorly to the fixed routines of convent life and, despite a professed desire to retreat from the world, continued to maintain secular relations, entertaining visitors in specially constructed "exterior" parlors and even leaving the convent for family visits and other social occasions. Serving as a conduit for worldly news and rumors, lay boarders could pose a distinct threat to the tranquility of the cloister, as Angélique Arnauld discovered in the midst of her quarrels with Sébastien Zamet. Madame de Pontcarré, a lay patron who occupied an apartment in Port-Royal, was smuggling out letters from discontented nuns and even allowing Zamet secretly to visit them in her exterior parlor.[101]

The Carmelites of Paris's second, and poorer, convent faced a different sort of problem with a benefactress determined to bend the rules. In 1639, Marie Vignerot, the duchesse d'Aiguillon, forced the nuns to take in two of her nieces as founders. The girls were two and three years old, respectively. The Carmelite rule forbade the presence of small children in the convent, but the duchess had taken the precaution of having her uncle, Cardinal Richelieu, secure a letter from the king himself. The girls resided in the convent for fifteen years. As they matured, the nuns tested their religious vocation and, at their request, even gave them the habit in 1653. The duchess, however, continued to use every excuse possible to take them out on excursions "for a change of air," even after they had accepted the habit. This was another violation of convent rules, but Marguerite du Saint-Sacrement Acarie, the convent's superior, did not dare to intervene and settled instead for trying to help the girls in their struggle to decide between religious and secular life. Both ultimately returned to the world.[102]

By the mid-seventeenth century, changes in the social, political, and economic climate thus combined to undermine the ascetic and penitential piety from which Paris's Catholic revival had sprung. Generational change, coupled with a strong desire on the part of lay elites to enter the cloister for visits, take up residence there in widowhood, and send their daughters to be educated by the nuns, made it hard to keep Counter-Reformation convents as isolated from the secular world as their founders had intended. New spiritual currents, including the more optimistic love of God preached by François de Sales, also diminished the prestige of rigorous austerity. Cardinal Richelieu's disapproval of contemplative retreat was addressed largely to young men whose labors he wanted to employ on behalf of the state. The debate over Saint-Cyran's rigorist theology nevertheless had repercussions for women as well because it raised questions about the value of ascetic unworldliness as a path to God. These changes were reinforced by the economic disruptions brought on by the Thirty Years War, which further aggravated financial problems caused by convents' premature expansion and their superiors' tendency to underestimate the continuing costs of religious life. The influx of nuns fleeing war-torn areas augmented competition for the patronage of wealthy elites.[103] At the same time, widespread misery and pauperization caused many of these elites to redirect their alms to the suffering poor instead of presumably comfortable cloistered nuns. At the very least, they sought to fund convents that combined a social purpose with the contemplative life.

6

Both Mary and Martha

However powerful the contemplative model of religious life remained, it was not a life that suited all women with religious vocations. Some women, because of age or poor health, were too frail to endure the austerities imposed on nuns in such reformed orders as the Carmelites and Capucines. Others, although desiring to devote themselves in the future entirely to God, could not claim the stainless past traditionally required of brides of Christ. Still others lacked the dowry that, despite a theoretical insistence in reformed houses on considering only vocation, in practice remained necessary for women entering convents. Perhaps most important, many pious women wanted to combine Martha's part with Mary's. Aspiring to the sanctity of the cloistered life, they nevertheless wanted to serve with more than their prayers and to imitate Jesus in his acts of charity as much or more than in his suffering on the cross.

This chapter looks at those new convents that, while still accepting the principle of strict clausura, found ways of bringing some measure of the active life into their cloisters. It begins with the Filles de la Visitation Sainte-Marie, usually known as the Visitandines, an immensely successful new order that established a first Paris convent in 1619 and a second in 1626. Previous historians have tended to focus on the founders' intention of creating a community that might welcome women whose age or health did not permit them the rigorous mortifications that typified the Counter-Reformation's austere contemplative convents. The focus here is on a different, but equally innovative, purpose of the Visitandines, which is their aim of providing a place where lay women could engage in religious retreats. I then examine several other convents that aimed in one or another way to serve women's special needs, among them the Filles de la Madeleine, which offered a place of retreat for repentant prostitutes; the Hôpital de la Charité Notre-Dame, which provided nursing care for women too proud to go to the Hôtel-Dieu; and the convent of Notre-Dame de la Miséricorde, which served well-born women unable to pay the dowry that traditional convents required. I also look at several cloistered teaching communities founded on the model of the Ursulines. The urge to help other members of their sex emerged most commonly in the desire to found schools where girls could be instructed in the fundamentals of the faith and also in skills that would help them get along in the world.

Like the contemplative convents that were the subject of the previous chapter, but to an even greater extent, these new institutions were often inadequately financed. Here too, the turning point occurred in the mid-1630s, as the political and economic crisis brought on by the Thirty Years War began to affect religious patronage. Nuns fleeing the war-torn cities of Champagne, Lorraine, and Picardy sought refuge in Paris, often with the assistance of Parisian dévots. Competing with older houses for resources that were, in any event, both diminishing and being turned to other charitable uses, the new houses were often built on shaky foundations. Their economic vulnerability inevitably had a direct impact on the quality and character of religious life.

The Filles de la Visitation

In April 1619, Baronne Jeanne-Françoise Fremyot de Chantal, who, in collaboration with François de Sales, bishop of Geneva-Annecy, had founded a new religious order called the Filles de la Visitation Sainte-Marie in the Savoyard town of Annecy, came to Paris to establish the order in the French capital. She came in haste, in response to a summons from de Sales, who, visiting Paris in the suite of the prince-cardinal Maurice de Savoie, was enjoying tremendous popularity as a guest preacher in the city's churches. Some dévots remembered the inspiring sermons de Sales had preached on his previous visit to Paris in 1602; others knew him strictly through his writings. His *Introduction à la vie dévote*, first published in late 1608 and very often reprinted, was an essential text in devout circles. The warm reception he received among pious elites gave de Sales reason to believe that the time was right to bring the Order of the Visitation to Paris. The foundation nevertheless remained a risky proposition. Although de Sales had promises of help from several elite women, one of whom offered the loan of a house while the Visitandines established themselves in Paris, he had not yet found a major donor willing to foot the bill for the purchase of property and construction of a convent. For two years, Jeanne de Chantal and the handful of associates she brought to help make the foundation struggled along in abject poverty.

Visitandine chronicles later romanticized this period of dire necessity as a time of perfect happiness. The topos was a common one, a foundational myth evoking the triumph of faith over adversity. The adversity, however, was very real. During much of this period, Paris was beset by plague. Although daily reminded of the epidemic's heavy toll by the clamorous bell and clanking wheels of the cart that circled the city to pick up the dead, the nuns appear to have escaped contagion largely on account of their isolation from the plague-stricken houses that surrounded them. They received no alms; the elite women who might otherwise have come to visit bearing gifts had all fled to their country estates, but at least no one brought plague through the convent's doors.[1]

The Visitandines' financial circumstances took a dramatic turn for the better in February 1621, when Hélène-Angélique Luillier entered the convent with a dowry of 45,000 livres. As with many other convents, the Visitandines soon discovered that the gift that at first seemed so enormous did not suffice to buy the desired property for their new home, much less to renovate its buildings to suit the convent's needs. The Visitandines were fortunate, however. Once the plague had receded and Parisian life returned to normal, a growing number of woman sought entry to the new convent. When Jeanne de Chantal returned to Annecy in February 1622, she left behind a community of nineteen professed nuns and fifteen novices or postulants. During the next few years the community grew at a remarkable rate. Twenty-five nuns took their vows between 1622 and 1625 alone. By 1623 the original convent on the rue Saint-Antoine was so crowded that the Visitandines began to talk of founding a second house. In 1626 they purchased a property in the faubourg Saint-Jacques and began this second foundation.[2]

The Visitandines were doubly fortunate in that their convents not only proved very popular, but they also had a strong appeal to local elites. More than half of the women who entered Paris's Visitandine convents in the seventeenth century came from noble families. The dowries they brought were hefty ones, averaging over 8,000 livres for the decade 1630–39. Although the Visitandines also benefited from several other large gifts, dowries alone funded much of their initial expansion and gave them not only enough money to build and furnish their convents but also, once these needs were taken care of, to purchase additional properties whose rental provided an important source of continuing income. This proved a valuable hedge against the decline in new professions that inevitably occurred as the houses filled up. By the end of the seventeenth century, the convent of the Visitation in the rue Saint-Antoine drew nearly 60 percent of its ordinary revenue from the rental properties it owned.[3]

How can we account for this success? Certainly François de Sales's fame and the growing reputation for sanctity enjoyed by Jeanne de Chantal helped bring the Visitandines to the public's attention. And, despite the initial setbacks, it appears that de Sales was right on the question of timing. The Visitandines were poised to profit from the new prestige religious life enjoyed after the founding of the first reformed convents. With de Sales's sponsorship, they were closely associated with the new spirituality. At the same time, they reached out to women who, because of their age or fragile health, could not undertake the life of heroic austerity that characterized the first reformed foundations.

The Visitandines' vocation evolved by force of circumstance, but from the beginning François de Sales and Jeanne de Chantal intended for the congregation to serve women whose poor health or continuing family obligations prevented them from joining traditional religious orders. The community began in 1610, when Chantal and three companions first established themselves in a little house on the outskirts of the Savoyard town of Annecy. The women proposed to live a reclusive life of meditation and prayer without being formally bound by rules of enclosure or solemn vows. Taking only simple, annual vows, they might still go into the city to handle urgent business and, at least on a limited basis, visit the sick and needy. As a mark of their deliberate intention of combining the good order and internalized spirituality of the new Counter-Reformation religious orders with continuing service in the world, the young community initially planned to take the name of the Filles de Sainte-Marthe. When they drew up their first constitutions in 1613, they adopted the name of Visitation Sainte-Marie instead. The constitutions explain that the congregation "took as its patron Our Lady of the Visitation because in this mystery the most glorious Virgin made the solemn acts of neighborly charity of visiting and serving Saint Elizabeth in travail with her pregnancy and at the same time also composed the canticle of the 'Magnificat,' the sweetest, most elevated, most spiritual and contemplative [song] ever written."[4] In the minds of the founders, then, the Visitation of the Virgin evoked more perfectly the joining of active and contemplative vocations they envisioned for the community than did the title of Filles de Sainte-Marthe, which privileged the notion of humble service at the expense of meditative prayer.

A letter from François de Sales to Jeanne de Chantal suggests the importance that unifying the Visitandines' dual vocation in a single symbol or person must have had for him. In this letter he described some thoughts that came to him as he meditated on Saint Martha, whom he imagined busily preparing dinner for Jesus, her guest, and somewhat jealous of her sister Mary who, instead of helping with the preparations, remained devotedly at Jesus' feet. Martha may have been justified in wanting some help in caring for her guest, observed de Sales, and yet she would have been wrong to want her sister to cease what she was doing and leave Jesus alone in order to help out. "Do you know how I would have wanted to resolve these differences?" he asked. "I would have wanted Saint Martha, our dear patron, to come to the feet of Our Lord in the place of her sister, and her sister to have gone off to finish preparing supper; in this way they would have shared the work and the repose like good sisters. I think that Our Lord would have approved of this." Apologizing some-what sheepishly for daring to correct a saint, de Sales continued his lesson with the comment that, even if Martha did not behave in the way he might have wanted, he hoped that her daughters now would and that they would divide their time so as to give a part of it to "external works of charity and the better part to the interior [works] of contemplation."[5]

If the change of names was intended to convey a desire to balance charity with prayer, the Filles de la Visitation took a more decisive step toward the "better part" of contemplation in 1616. The move was not, however, a voluntary one. A group of dévotes in Lyons had asked for help in establishing themselves on the Visitandines' model, and François de Sales and Jeanne de Chantal were eager to seize the opportunity to expand into France. They found their plans blocked, however, by the archbishop of Lyons, Denis Simon de Marquemont, who insisted he could establish the new congregation successfully only if the women agreed to accept clausura. He proposed incorporating the Visitandines as a regular religious order on the ground that, without formal vows, they would never be truly nuns and honorable people in his town would never allow their daughters to join.[6] This left de Sales and Chantal with a difficult choice. They knew that Marquemont's decision would have enormous influence among his fellow bishops in France. If they refused to go along with him, they ran a serious risk of cutting off the possibility of further French foundations. Unwilling to abandon dreams of expansion, they yielded to Marquemont's wishes and sought papal bulls to establish the Filles de la Visitation as a formal religious order, even though this meant submitting to clausura and therefore sacrificing the opportunity for Visitandines to leave their convents to attend to personal business or make charitable visits in their towns.

Like the Ursulines, the Visitandines thus changed their form of organi-zation and certain aspects of their life in establishing themselves in France. The importance of this change should not, however, be overstated. Viewing the Visitandines as an early and ill-fated attempt to create an active congregation based on community service, a number of historians have criticized de Sales and Chantal for deviating from their original intentions in submitting to Mar-quemont's demands. One interprets the Visitandines' submission as evidence that the very idea of a female religious order that was *not* subjected to strict claustration was simply inconceivable in seventeenth-century France.[7] Another writes that the Visitandines "could not escape the fate of enclosure in 1618, despite the strenuous objection of Chantal and François de Sales's negotiations with Rome."[8] These historians have missed the point: community service was never the central purpose of the Visitandines' foundation. Rather, it was always intended as a voluntary activity to be undertaken on a limited basis and by only some of the Visitandines. Even before the proposal for a convent in Lyons, de Sales had recognized that what was appropriate for religious women in small towns like Annecy might not be equally suitable in the more turbulent atmosphere of major cities, and his initial rules for the congregation made charitable visits optional and conditional on local circumstances. Nor is it true that Jeanne de Chantal and François de Sales strenuously objected to the principle of religious enclosure. Quite the contrary; like others of their time, they admired cloistered convents as the highest form of religious life. They did not think that solemn vows were necessary to the religious life the Visitandines intended to undertake, but they willingly agreed to Marquemont's insistence on erecting the Visitandines as a formal religious order provided—and this was the key point—that he left intact those distinctive qualities that were, in their opinion, essential to the Visitandines' vocation.

Chantal and de Sales both expressed these sentiments in letters to Mère Marie-Jacqueline Favre, who had been sent to serve as superior of the Visitandines' Lyons foundation.[9] De Sales's letter in particular deserves quoting at length. "I willingly assent," he wrote, "that it should be a religious order, provided that, by the mildness of the Constitutions, frail girls might be received, widows find retreat, and secular women find some refuge [to pursue] their advancement in the service of God." Later in the same letter he again specified as "the principal aim of our congregation: that widows, at least in their widow's garb, might retreat there until, free of impediments, they can take the habit and make their vows; and that secular women might have entry in order to practice and deepen their devotion." He insisted on the very same points in a letter to Cardinal Robert Bellarmine in Rome, in which he solicited the cardinal's aid in getting the new order approved. Here too, de Sales claimed to have "rallied easily" to Archbishop Marquemont's desire to see the Visitandines erected as a formal religious order, on condition that several key principles, or "particularities," were maintained. Among these was that widows should be allowed to live in the convent in secular dress for years if necessary, until they could finally sever the business and family ties that prevented them from taking religious vows. The widows would be permitted to leave the convent once or twice a year, as their domestic affairs required, but they would otherwise observe the rules of clausura. De Sales also argued forcefully for allowing married women who wanted "to undertake a new life in Christ" to enter the convent for short periods during which they might engage in spiritual exercises to prepare for a general confession and meditate in a quiet place shut off from the distracting bustle of the world.[10]

Both purposes required defending because they were violations of the rules of clausura, which not only prohibited members of religious communities from exiting the cloister but also prohibited anyone except the community's members from entering. Insisting that legitimate reasons existed for making occasional exceptions to the strict rules of religious enclosure, de Sales attempted to strengthen his case by pointing out that there was "far less peril" in allowing widows who had not taken vows occasionally to leave the cloister than there was in the common practice in "many of even the most pious convents" of allowing lay sisters to exit in order to attend to the community's affairs. And what was the great difference, he asked, between allowing entry to widows "for the purpose of conserving their chastity" and the common practice of allowing entry to young girls for the purpose of continuing their education?[11] Although he did not name names, clearly François de Sales had in mind here the situation of widows like Jeanne de Chantal, whose own children ranged in age from eleven to fifteen when she moved to Annecy to begin the Visitation in 1610. Chantal overcame her own hesitations and the objections that her father-in-law made to her joining the new congregation only when de Sales repeatedly assured them that nothing in his plans for the community would prevent her from continuing to look out for her children's well-being, even if this meant returning to the family estates in Burgundy from time to time.[12]

In making a strong case for allowing widows to reside in Visitandine convents, François de Sales justified and made explicit a practice that, as we have seen, other convents adopted more tacitly simply by stretching the rules that defined founders and set out their prerogatives. As such, the practice of admitting lay widows to the cloister represented a more modest break with tradition than did the other "particularity" on which de Sales set great store. This was the right of married women to make religious retreats in Visitandine convents in the company and under the guidance of the nuns. For de Sales, the presence of lay women in the convent was not a necessary but regrettable concession to the demands of rich benefactors; it was a positive goal. The Visitandines could and should edify secular society from within their walls. Already in the original constitutions of 1613 we can see that the congregation aimed less to serve society's poor than to serve the poor in spirit: "As no poverty is as great as that of the soul . . . they [lay women] may enter the house not only in cases of necessity but also for the utility, consolation, and edification of their souls."[13] The apostolic vocation that de Sales envisioned for the Filles de la Visitation lay not in nursing the sick or assisting the indigent but in sheltering and offering spiritual counsel to lay women. This was fully in keeping with the Catholic Reformation's drive to educate people in the duties and teachings of their faith, and yet it made use of women's spiritual knowledge and abilities in new and influential ways. The idea of religious women offering spiritual guidance in structured retreats for lay women was to be one of the most imitated aspects of the Visitandine foundation.

François de Sales's insistence that a religious congregation could be well ordered and truly devout without practicing extremes of austerity was also enormously influential, at least in the long run. At the time the Visitandines were founded, the ascetic ideal was so deeply ingrained as a model for religious perfection that de Sales was harshly criticized for daring to moderate it.[14] In fact, those critics who accused him of creating an excessively gentle model of religious practice were poorly informed. He did not eliminate bodily mortifications, but rather urged that each nun regulate her practices according to her abilities. "Dominate your flesh by fasts and abstinence as your health permits," he advised. He did warn against excessive self-mortification, but his real intention was to point out the error of those who believed that sanctity was to be achieved "by depriving their stomachs of food rather than their hearts of self-will."[15] Like the Annonciades Célestes, he emphasized mortification of the will over mortifications of the body.

Jeanne de Chantal's letters of advice to the superiors of other Visitandine convents make it clear that she fully shared these views. She repeatedly urged the superiors not to endanger their health by excessive fasts and vigils and reminded them that, although there were times when it was good to discipline one's body, they needed strength to accomplish God's work and must not weaken themselves by too many austerities.[16] Urging them to keep a close eye on sisters who fasted excessively, she showed a strong preference for mortifications whose impact was psychological, encouraging humility, over those that undermined the body by depriving it of food or sleep. Even those "exterior mortifications" that encouraged humility had to be closely controlled. Superiors should never allow them to be undertaken without prior permission and should consent to them only rarely, as their impact and value were lessened if they were too common. It was more effective, moreover, in Chantal's opinion, for the superior to prescribe a mortification than for the penitent to select her own penitence. As she explained in a letter to Mère Marie-Jacqueline Favre, "When someone comes to ask me permission to do a particular thing, I command something else; for example, when one of our sisters asked me, after having recounted her faults, to kiss the feet of her sisters, I told her 'no, but have them instead kiss your hand,' which [hand] being quite ugly was a true mortification."[17]

Mortifications were thus useful tools for schooling nuns in such virtues as humility. Chantal even suggested to Mère Favre, who was perplexed about how to handle a young nun given to not entirely convincing raptures, that by "gently exercising" the young woman in "humility and mortification of self-will," she might lead her to abandon the exaggerated behavior that both Chantal and Favre believed to be the product of an overheated imagination and not the result of either divine or malign spirits.[18] Under the influence of Chantal and de Sales, mortifications thus had a very different place in Visitandine convents than we have observed in ascetic contemplative convents, where the penitent's suffering body was viewed as a tool, or medium, for attaining holiness.

This is not to say that the Visitandines led the easygoing and comfortable life that their critics charged. Angélique Arnauld, who at one point aspired to leave Port-Royal for the Visitation, defended François de Sales against accusations of creating *une dévotion doucette* by pointing to the order's rule, which, she noted, showed well that he wanted his nuns "as dead to themselves and crucified with Christ as any [other order]." She also cited her personal experience on several visits to the Visitandines' Paris convents, where she claimed to have been "ravished by the devotion, silence, and mortification" she witnessed. "They were in effect more austere than anyone imagined," she reported.[19] Austerity did not, however, receive the same emphasis among the Visitandines as it did in other Counter-Reformation orders. As much as anything, de Sales wanted to change the tone of religious life and make it more appealing by insisting on the joy to be found there and not on the rigors and renunciations it involved. Mortifications had a place in this life but never a dominant one; they were not undertaken for their own sake but only insofar as they served the larger purpose of deepening the interior life of the person who undertook them.

The principle was not a new one; any number of earlier writers, including Teresa of Avila, had warned of the danger of mortifications becoming an end in themselves instead of a means to an end. And yet, in the emotional climate of a France still scarred by the apocalyptic visions of the religious wars, François de Sales's use of a language of love and his consistent emphasis on the joys of the devout life, whether religious or lay, sounded a new and welcome note. Through at least the mid-seventeenth century, biographers of both lay dévotes and nuns continued to recount in emphatic, often painful detail the physical sufferings and emotional deprivations their subjects imposed on themselves, even as they described their joyous union with God. And yet the ascetic model of religious life gradually did become less exclusively dominant. The constitutions that Cardinal François de la Rochefoucauld gave the newly founded convent of the Assumption, for example, specify that the rule should be "almost within the reach of the most weak and sickly [individuals]." A comparison between these constitutions and those of the Visitation indicates that de la Rochefoucauld must certainly have had the Visitandine constitutions before him when he composed those of the Assumption; there are borrowings of language, as well as principle, that cannot be coincidental.[20] The influence of the Visitandines may have been less direct in other cases, but other convents as well moved away from the extreme asceticism dominant in the seventeenth century's first reformed foundations.

François de Sales's innovations in religious life had perhaps their most profound impact, however, on the new, uncloistered institutes of filles séculaires that began to take root in the 1620s. Paris's Visitandines played a key role in communicating de Sales's vision of a female apostolate to the lay women who created these new institutions. In opening the convents of the Visitation to the devout laity, even on a limited basis, de Sales and Chantal made them into centers of devout spiritual action. When he secured the appointment of Vincent de Paul as the Visitandines' new superior before he left Paris in 1619, de Sales assured the success of the apostolic role he envisioned for the Visitandines but also guaranteed its wider spread. Vincent de Paul was to prove as skilled a director of female penitents as de Sales was, and even more skilled in spurring his penitents to put their charitable thoughts into action. It is no coincidence that many of the women whose names are most closely associated with the new charitable institutes founded in seventeenth-century Paris had close ties to de Paul but also to the Visitation.[21]

Marie Luillier de Villeneuve, who was to found the Filles de la Croix on the model of the open congregation that François de Sales and Jeanne de Chantal had originally intended the Visitation to be, was the sister of Hélène-Angélique Luillier, the principal benefactress and long-time superior of the Visitandines' first Paris convent. Because she took the habit in 1621 and could not herself enjoy the founder's privileges, Hélène-Angélique arranged for her sister Marie to enjoy them in her stead. Marie Luillier made extensive use of these privileges, which allowed her to live in the convent and raise her daughters there. She remained in close contact with François de Sales and, when she confided in him her desire to found a congregation of women dedicated to educating and aiding others of their sex, received from him a copy of his original constitutions for the Visitation to assist her in her planning.[22] She used her close contacts with Vincent de Paul to seek his aid when she encountered difficulty establishing the Filles de la Croix, and it was he who arranged for other dévotes in his circle to take charge of the congregation after Marie Luillier's death in 1650.[23] Besides teaching young girls, the Filles de la Croix made conducting religious retreats for lay women a central part of their vocation. In doing so, they took one of the distinctive missions of the Visitandines and expanded it to serve a larger and less elite audience.

A generation later, another pious young widow, Marie Bonneau (Madame de Miramion), placing her young daughter as a boarder in the convent of the Visitation, secured extensive rights to enter the convent herself in return for her gifts. A member of Vincent de Paul's Dames de la Charité, Madame de Miramion also engaged in a wide variety of other charitable works. Founding an orphanage (the Sainte-Enfance) and a congregation of dévotes who taught girls and engaged in charitable works in their parish (the Filles de Sainte-Geneviève), she also established a retreat house where lay women could come for periods of pious meditation and recollection. Monies collected from the elite women who made week-long retreats there allowed the house also to serve women of modest means and even those too poor to contribute anything toward their stay.[24] Here too we see the influence of the Visitandines' retreats.

The Visitandines' dedication to the spiritual growth and education in piety of other members of their sex brought them a new apostolic role in 1629, when they accepted responsibility for supervising a convent and refuge for "fallen women," a term that encompassed girls who had yielded to the seductions of a single lover as well as women actually plying the prostitute's trade.

The archbishop of Paris, Henri de Gondi, cardinal de Retz, had tried to coax the Visitandines to take on this role when they first arrived in Paris, but they succeeded in convincing him that, for the time being at least, they did not have any members capable of taking on such a position.[25] It was hard to make the same claim ten years later, and so the Visitandines agreed to take up what was to prove a difficult and often thankless task.

From 1629 until 1671, the Paris Visitandines delegated four to six nuns at a time to administer the Filles de la Madeleine and instruct them in religious life. During this time, forty-one Visitandines served a term at the convent of the Madeleine. Most stayed only two to four years, but a few stayed much longer. Anne-Marie Bollain spent thirty-two years, Marie-Monique Samier thirty, and Marie-Marthe Alorge twenty-eight helping out with the Filles de la Madeleine.[26] The letter circulated among Visitandine congregations on Marie-Marthe Alorge's death in 1676 praises her great talent "for the conduct of souls" and her zeal for winning these lost souls over to God. Jeanne de Chantal, the letter claims, used to take great pleasure in hearing about how "supple" the Madelonnettes proved in Mère Alorge's hands, and she attributed part of the benedictions with which God graced the Visitandine congregation to "the charity they showed in going to work in this new vineyard of the Lord."[27] Such moments of satisfaction nevertheless alternated with long periods of frustration. Despite the conviction that they were engaged in "an office of charity important to God's glory and the salvation of souls," the Visitandines never forgot that they had taken on this office only reluctantly and, they hoped, only temporarily. They repeatedly sought to withdraw from their supervisory role at the Madeleine, whose internal struggles sorely tested their resolve. However powerful a mission they felt for aiding members of their own sex, they were more comfortable leading retreats for willing and pious elites than mediating conflicts in an institution that inevitably sheltered some women more eager to escape from the streets than to deplore their past and engage in a path of true repentance. The Visitandines breathed a collective sigh of relief when the bishop of Paris allowed them to relinquish the Madeleine to the direction of another religious order in 1671.

Penitent Magdalenes

The desire to create a contemplative convent where repentant prostitutes could expiate their sins in prayer and meditation reflects both the religious idealism and the puritanical moralism of the early Catholic Reformation. Although the convent of the Madeleine soon came to serve a punitive function housing women incarcerated by order of the courts, it was originally intended as a purely voluntary refuge for fallen women. The community had its start in the spring of 1618, when Capuchin preacher Athanase Molé asked a devout wine merchant named Robert de Montry to find shelter for two fallen women who desired to change their ways. These women were soon joined by others, and Montry had to move them several times before he found them a permanent home. With each move, the women's numbers grew, and, at least by Montry's account, they themselves began to ask first for religious instruction and then for the institutional structures of a true convent. Within four months, Montry had about fifteen women installed in a house next to his own residence in the faubourg Saint-Germain. They built a makeshift chapel in an unused stable and began to learn the Little Office of the Virgin Mary and engage in religious exercises. A month or so later, they invited a priest to celebrate their first mass in the little chapel. The priest had to supply all of the ornaments and vessels for the ceremony himself, as the women were too poor to purchase any of their own.[28]

Almost from the beginning, the project attracted interest and aid from the broader community of Parisian dévots. Vincent de Paul began very early to visit the women and encourage their efforts, and it was probably on his recommendation that his patron, Marguerite de Silly (Madame de Gondi), helped furnish the house where the women were living. Until they had their own chapel, they attended mass at the Jesuit novitiate, and it was Madeleine Luillier de Sainte-Beuve, who had founded the novitiate, who paid for the grille installed when the women agreed to cloister themselves and no longer go out into the world. At her solicitation, François de Sales gave the habit to the first Madelonnettes on the feast of Saint Mary Magdalene in 1619. When Henri de Gondi, cardinal de Retz and archbishop of Paris, decided in 1620 to consider giving the informal community a more formal status and rule, the committee he assembled to discuss the matter included Michel de Marillac, Pierre de Bérulle, Etienne Binet (then rector of the Jesuits' Paris house), and Guillaume Gibief (superior of the Oratoire and later of the French Carmelites as well). The cardinal also invited his niece, Marguerite de Gondi, marquise de Maignelay, to the meeting, as she had stepped forward to serve as the Madelonnettes' primary patron and founder. She contributed 26,000 livres toward the purchase of a house in the parish Saint-Nicolas-des-Champs and paid pensions for several of the women whom she had personally rescued from the streets. The marquise de Maignelay also left the convent more than 100,000 livres in her will, though it appears that disputes among the marquise's creditors may have prevented the Madelonnettes from receiving most of this bequest.[29]

Despite the growing involvement of the larger dévot community, during its first two years the rescue mission remained very much the personal project of Robert de Montry and his first associate, an archer in the king's guard, Monsieur de Fresnes. As such, the practices adopted by the community reflect a tension between the founders' optimistic expectations for moral reform and their very traditional understanding of the way repentance should be expressed. Because Montry and his collaborators envisaged a voluntary community consisting only of women who truly wanted to "retire from sin," they thought it important to treat the women who came to them as gently as possible. They sometimes even paid off their debts to free them from the world's remaining claims. Recognizing that a punishing life of penitential asceticism would frighten away many of the women whose repentance he wished to encourage, Montry tried to play down the importance attached to bodily mortifications.[30] He believed it necessary first to provide sanctuary—to free women from the vulnerabilities that followed on their violation of society's rigid moral code— and only then to bring them truly to understand the need to deplore their sins and work toward the salvation of their souls. At the same time, the ascetic model of religious life clearly had a compelling hold on Montry's imagination. The women who came to the Madeleine had their hair shorn as a sign that they were abandoning worldly vanities and were given hair shirts and made to go barefoot, just like nuns in strict, penitential orders. For Montry and his associates, repentance had to be made manifest in ritualized acts of self-mortification.

Inevitably, some women took to this regimen better than others. It quickly became apparent that many of the women who came to the Filles de la Madeleine would never have a true religious vocation. Believing that most were nevertheless capable of reforming their way of life, Montry and his collaborators envisioned a community in which some women might live the life of cloistered nuns while others prepared for an eventual return to secular society as practitioners of an honest trade.[31] When constitutions were drawn up for the Madelonnettes, this division of the community into two distinct groups was formalized with the creation of separate congregations for the women whose solemn vows consecrated them irrevocably to religious life and those who, bound only by simple vows, retained the freedom one day to return to secular society as working women or wives.

Although an innovative solution to the problem of how to take women off the street without forcing those who felt no religious vocation to become nuns, the creation of separate congregations within the framework of a single convent posed problems for the Filles de la Madeleine and their Visitandine superiors. From the beginning, all women who entered the institution, whether they felt a religious calling or merely wanted to escape the prostitute's life, were subjected to the mortifications associated with their status as penitents. They were also subjected to the same rules of strict claustration. Shortly after the first mass was celebrated in the impromptu chapel made from a stable, Montry made a little speech in which, praising the women for their courage and decision to give themselves entirely to God, he urged them to agree to remain enclosed in their house, without going out into the world or even speaking with lay men and women except across a grille, just as nuns did. "In a single voice," he tells us, "the women replied, 'Good brother, give us a grille; give us a grille.'" And yet it is doubtful that the agreement really was so unanimous.

How much choice did the women feel they had in the matter? Clearly, for Montry and other dévots fostering the Filles de la Madeleine, enclosure was a necessary condition for a true religious life. Observing that "it was a marvelous pleasure once the grille was installed, to see these good women imitate [*contrefaire*] nuns," Montry betrays a certain naïveté, for it must already have been apparent that, if some women were imitating nuns in hopes of becoming them, others were only going through the motions so as not to find themselves once again on the street.[32]

Histories of the convent suggest that almost from the beginning tensions ran high between the professed nuns of the congregation of Sainte-Marie-Madeleine and the sœurs de Sainte-Marthe, who took only simple vows and might still leave the convent for a husband or a job. Anne L'Espicier, who was the first to receive the habit from François de Sales and was subsequently made the convent's mother superior, may have been truly pious and penitent, but she was entirely lacking in the experience and strength of character necessary to succeed in the leadership role she was assigned. As early as 1619, it was suggested that the Filles de la Madeleine should be put under the direction of experienced nuns, in particular the Visitandines. De Sales backed away from the suggestion, saying that the time was not yet right for such a move. When the suggestion was made again, the Visitandines' new superior, Vincent de Paul, supported it. Mère Hélène-Angélique Luillier, the mother superior of the Visitandine house in the rue Saint-Antoine, sought advice from Jeanne de Chantal but then consented to take up the task. On 20 July 1629, five Visitandines were conducted to their new home in a formal procession. They were accompanied not only by the usual dévotes—among them the marquise de Maignelay and Anne de Caumont, comtesse de Saint-Paul—but also by the archbishop of Paris and their Visitandine superior, Mère Hélène-Angélique Luillier, who took the extraordinary step of exiting the cloister for the occasion.[33]

Sister Anne-Marie Bollain, who took on the role of prioress, worked closely with Vincent de Paul, Denis Le Blanc (the archbishop's vicar general), and Jean Dupont (curé of Saint-Nicolas-des-Champs and the Madelonnettes' superior) to draw up constitutions for the house.[34] On arrival, women were placed in the second congregation, the one dedicated to Saint Martha, where they spent the next six months in secular garb while deciding whether they wished to stay and become novices. Only after successfully completing a year's novitiate in the second congregation might they be admitted, if they so desired, to the first congregation, at which point they would need to do another year's novitiate before being allowed to make solemn vows.[35] Women in the second congregation were to be taught to read, sew, and do other handwork so that they would be better able to find honorable work or a husband if they left the convent. One of the Visitandines was to serve as "mother mistress" to the congregation and offer religious instruction but also help teach skills useful for either religious or secular life. The nuns of the first congregation were expected to help with the other women but were given a separate chapel and housed in separate quarters so they might have the tranquility necessary to their religious exercises.

By the time the constitutions were drawn up in 1631, however, it was apparent that the Madelonnettes needed to make provision for not just two but three different sorts of women. By all accounts, members of the first group, those admitted to the congregation of Sainte-Marie-Madeleine, were admirable in their practice of piety. It is even claimed that elites sought to make retreats in the convent so to profit from their example, and certainly it does appear that standards were kept high and membership limited to those who could demonstrate a true vocation. On the other hand, the second group, the congrégation de Sainte-Marthe, was far from homogeneous. Some of its members were well-intentioned and docile, though perhaps more interested in the liberty they hoped eventually to gain than in the religious exercises that occupied their days. Others were rebellious and persisted in making trouble in ways the congregation's high-minded founders had not foreseen. Inevitably, there were clashes between this group and members of the first congregation, whose air of moral superiority members of the second congregation inevitably resented. A third congregation was created under the invocation of Saint Lazare to isolate misbehaving members of the second congregation from their more docile sisters.

The third congregation also came to house reprobates sent to the convent by order of the courts. The papal bull officially erecting the convent in 1631 provided that it should house married women who had quarreled with or been abandoned by their husband and adulterous wives sent by the courts to expiate their sins until such time as their husband decided to take them back.[36] It is not clear whether the idea of using the convent for the involuntary incarceration of women who violated the social code came from the bishop of Paris or the dévots associated with the house; certainly it was not part of Robert de Montry's original vision. A letter from Visitandine Marie-Marthe Alorge, who served as superior of the Madelonnettes from 1633 to 1638 and again from 1640 to 1651, suggests that they accepted misbehaving women only to please "certain good families" or when commanded to do so by the queen, and that they accepted only a few such women at a time.[37] The service was nevertheless a remunerative one. It brought in hefty pensions but also goodwill from distinguished families, who found this a convenient way to hush up the potential scandals caused by their black sheep.

As long as they were generally well behaved, adulterous and abandoned wives were housed with the second congregation. The congrégation Saint-Lazare was to be used for the truly rebellious and unrepentant women sentenced there by the courts, but it was also used as a place to punish women who violated the second congregation's rules in serious ways.[38] The constitution's assertion that these women would mend their ways out of a desire to "regain full liberty and the conversation of their sisters" hints at something approaching solitary confinement. Although the third congregation was supposed to house a maximum of six women and was not intended to receive women transferred from prisons like Bicêtre, its presence within the Filles de la Madeleine meant that the convent inevitably assumed a punitive function very much at odds with Montry's original intention of creating a strictly voluntary community of true penitents.[39]

Women's Mission to Women

The same sense of women's special vulnerability that motivated the founding of the convent of the Madeleine lay behind the foundation of other Counter-Reformation convents. Traditional assumptions about women's innate moral weakness played a role here, but so did a pragmatic understanding of the limited options that faced a woman alone and lacking economic security and the protection of kin in the male-dominated culture of the seventeenth century. Just as the Visitandines hoped to keep the women who sought refuge at the Madeleine from returning to the streets by giving them the tools necessary to earn an independent living, so founders of other institutions took the protection of women and improvement of their condition as their special goal. Some of these institutions took the form of open congregations and are discussed in the next chapter. Others, however, were traditional convents where the mission of service to other women was combined with the customary life of contemplation and prayer.

Most of these convents resembled the Ursulines in that they made teaching their principal mission, but there were other ways of serving women as well. The nursing sisters of the Charité Notre-Dame took as their special charge the care of sick women who were too poor to hire private nurses but too proud to enter the public charity wards of the Hôtel-Dieu. As was common with early modern charitable initiatives, the hospital was intended for what were known as the *pauvres honteuses* ("shame-faced poor"), people from respectable families who, through no fault of their own, had fallen on hard times. Reflecting the social biases and ingrained sense of social hierarchy prevalent at the time, the founders and sponsors of these charities believed that the shame-faced poor were the victims of bad luck or misfortune and did not bear the same responsibility for their poverty as those who came from the lower ranks of society, who were generally assumed to be shiftless and prone to immorality. Particularly deserving of charity, the shame-faced poor also deserved to be treated respectfully and not forced to submit to the humiliation of seeking handouts alongside the destitute masses.

If the Charité Notre-Dame reflected social biases, it reflected contemporary gender biases as well. Its founder, Françoise Gaugin (in religion, Françoise de la Croix), felt a special calling to nurse only female patients, and her advisers approved this calling on the ground that serving men was never entirely without danger. The donors sponsoring the foundation shared these sentiments and insisted on the creation of entirely separate institutions for women and men, as opposed to merely separate wards, such as existed in the Hôtel-Dieu.[40]

The constitutions the Charité Notre-Dame received from their superior, the archbishop of Paris, located the spirit of the institution in the commandment to "love God with all thy heart . . . and thy neighbor as thyself" and instructed the nuns to care for their patients as if they were caring for Christ himself. At the same time that they spiritualized the humble work of nursing the sick, the constitutions emphasized that the religious obligations of the Filles de la Charité Notre-Dame as Augustinian nuns must be very exactly kept. The rules of clausura received special emphasis. The presence of lay women in the hospital was in no way to cause a relaxation of standards, and the sisters were cautioned to be models of chastity in both body and mind. They were told to conserve an "interior and exterior purity" by carefully keeping their eyes and voices lowered and walking with a "modest and grave" demeanor. They were especially cautioned never to meet the eyes of the lay people they encountered in their hospital service.[41]

The constitutions emphasized interior rather than corporal mortifications, explicitly preferring "the knowledge of one's nothingness and love of God and neighbor, and the renouncing of one's own will in order to accomplish that of God" to "great macerations of the body, such as the wearing of hair shirts." The sisters observed the fasts prescribed by the church and the Augustinian rule and took discipline on Fridays, but their austerities were largely symbolic ones, such as omitting their linen shifts and wearing only sandals on Holy Thursday and Friday.[42] Like members of other active congregations, the Filles de la Charité Notre-Dame needed strong bodies to accomplish their service mission.

This mission, moreover, extended to the souls as well as the bodies of their sick patients. The Filles de la Charité Notre-Dame were expected to teach the women they nursed "the principal mysteries of the faith, how to confess and take communion well, and the practice of exercises of piety and devotion, to a greater or lesser extent, as the capacity of the patient allowed."[43] Given the poor state of early modern health care, which meant that people sick enough to enter hospitals often did not leave them alive, this mission would have been considered extremely important. The Filles de la Charité Notre-Dame would have been very conscious of the need to bring their patients to understand the religious obligations imposed by their faith, in particular the need to make a good confession, receive absolution, and take communion before they died. If the patient recovered, the teachings might encourage her to continue leading a devout life, but it was the omnipresence of death in early modern hospitals that made the obligation of spiritual instruction a central part of the Filles' vocation.

Like the Hôpital de la Charité Notre-Dame, the convent of Notre-Dame de la Miséricorde aimed at serving the shame-faced poor. Begun in Provence in 1633, the order aimed to provide a refuge for girls from good families (*filles de qualité*) who lacked the dowries needed to enter other religious orders. As was common for new religious houses, it took nearly ten years for the Filles de Notre-Dame de la Miséricorde to secure the episcopal, royal, and papal approvals necessary for the formal erection of the new order. By the early 1640s, however, these formalities had been accomplished, and the congregation had expanded from its original house in Aix to Avignon and Marseilles. Religious reformer Jean-Jacques Olier brought the new order to the attention of Anne of Austria and convinced her of the merits of founding a convent of Filles de Notre-Dame de la Miséricorde in Paris. Unfortunately, by the time Madeleine Martin (in religion, Madeleine de la Trinité), the founder and mother superior of the Filles de la Miséricorde, was free to take up Anne of Austria's summons to found a house in Paris, the revolt of the Fronde had broken out. Mère Madeleine arrived in Paris to find that the queen had fled. Richelieu's devout niece, the duchesse d'Aiguillon, took in Mère Madeleine and her companions and served as their patron. With her donations and the aid solicited from her devout friends, the Filles de Notre-Dame de la Miséricorde purchased an ample house in the faubourg Saint-Germain in 1651 and gave the new community a home. Women who entered the order were nevertheless obliged to work with their hands to supplement the alms and gifts received from pious elites and to make up for the fact that they had entered with only small dowries or none at all. The principle of working with their hands was so important for the Filles that their constitutions specified that any house that produced more revenue than it needed to cover its own expenses was to donate the surplus income to poorer houses of the order, other needy religious congregations, or indigent families. The community also undertook to aid the poor by offering free education to girls in their neighborhood. Although their principal mission was to serve as a refuge for women of good family who lacked the means to establish themselves suitably in other convents, the Filles de Notre-Dame de la Miséricorde thus also aimed more broadly to improve women's lot by providing the instruction in reading, writing, and domestic skills through which poor girls might secure more honorable marriages or better-paying jobs.[44]

In this the Filles were joined by a number of new foundations, including nuns of the Congrégation de Notre-Dame originally founded in Lorraine and several independent houses, among them the priory of Saint-Sépulchre de Jésus (usually known by the house's location as Bellechasse) and the Benedictine convent of Notre-Dame-de-Liesse. All of these communities claimed to take teaching as an important part of their mission. Among them, however, only the Congrégation de Notre-Dame established classes for day students of modest means as well as elite boarding pupils.

Like the Ursulines and Visitandines, the Congrégation de Notre-Dame was originally created as an open community without solemn vows but, pressured to conform to the Tridentine ideal of religious life, became an enclosed religious order instead. The congregation's origins date to 1597, when a young woman named Alix Le Clerc confided to Pierre Fourier, the curé of her rural parish in Lorraine, that she felt a powerful mission to create a new community of women dedicated to serving the public good. Fourier initially tried to discourage Le Clerc by telling her how difficult it would be to find other women who shared this vocation, but when she returned two months later with four other women ready to take up a common life he dropped his opposition and became her closest collaborator. The women announced their intention to live as a community by appearing together at midnight mass on Christmas of 1597 in plain dark dresses and veils. Their principal purpose, as set out in the provisional rule they adopted in 1598, was "to establish public schools and, without charging anything, to teach young girls to read and write and do needlework and instruct them in the faith."[45] The first school proved popular, and they expanded into other localities.

As with other attempts to create new forms of religious life, however, problems arose when they attempted to regularize their status. Religious authorities pressured them to adopt clausura, along with a formal religious rule. The Filles de Notre-Dame had a mixed reaction to this pressure. They admired the retired life of nuns and wanted insofar as possible to imitate this life, but they hoped to moderate the rules of strict enclosure to be able to leave their houses to teach in country schools and do other works of charity. But opposition proved too strong, particularly in Rome, and in the end they sacrificed the ambition of establishing small rural schools to gain the episcopal approval needed to expand broadly across the towns of Lorraine and Champagne.[46] They satisfied their desire to educate girls whose family could not afford to hire private tutors or board them in convents by opening free day classes for city girls and subsidizing this work with the pensions their elite boarding students paid. The Filles de Notre-Dame followed the model of the Ursulines very directly here. Forced to rethink her mission with the acceptance of enclosure, Alix Le Clerc came to Paris for two months to learn how the Ursuline communities functioned. Pierre Fourier furnished her with a long and very precise list of questions about Ursuline practices, and on her return to Lorraine they put in place new constitutions for the Congrégation de Notre-Dame that borrowed freely from the Ursulines but also attempted to maintain a distinctive identity in both their curriculum and practices of worship.[47]

For the most part, the Filles de Notre-Dame established themselves in towns where the Ursulines were not already present. Paris, however, must have appeared to be big enough for both orders. In 1634, nuns from Laon founded a convent in the rue du Chasse-Midi in the faubourg Saint-Germain. This was the first of three attempts to establish the Filles de Notre-Dame in the French capital, only one of which succeeded. Too little is known about two of the convents, including the one that survived, to trace their early years in any detail.[48] The difficulties encountered at the convent of the Chasse-Midi are nevertheless instructive, as are the financial problems that nearly resulted in the collapse of the independent convents of Notre-Dame de Liesse and Belle-chasse. Each convent's story is unique, and yet together they tell us a lot about why it was so difficult for teaching convents founded in the 1630s and 1640s to achieve financial stability.

The Crisis of the 1630s and 1640s

Convents whose nuns had a teaching vocation were vulnerable to the same financial problems as the contemplative convents discussed in the previous chapter. They may, however, have been particularly prone to taking on excessive debt during the initial stages of their foundation because the nuns believed they needed ample and attractive quarters to draw high-paying boarders. At the same time, they anticipated that revenues from boarding pupils would help pay off this debt. Every new convent would have felt the pressure of competing with the Ursulines, who by their success enlarged but also threatened to dominate the market for elite boarding convents. The Filles de Notre-Dame, moreover, had the expense of providing two separate teaching areas. Their constitutions provided that boarders and day girls should follow the same curriculum (though boarders were expected to advance further in their studies and to learn "more exquisite" sorts of needlework), but their classes were to be staffed and run entirely separately. The boarding pupils, who paid a hefty pension, were to have no contact whatsoever with the day pupils, whose schooling was free. The boarders were also to be kept apart from the nuns. They were to have their own courtyard—their own cloister, we might say, for once they entered their school, they were allowed to leave only very rarely, certainly not more than once a year. This meant that, in addition to bedrooms and classrooms, they needed their own refectory, their own parlor for family visits, and their own enclosed space in the church equipped with a confessional and a window opening into the choir where mass was celebrated so that they could see the elevation of the host and hear sermons. In other words, the facilities for boarding pupils essentially duplicated those built for the nuns. This was deemed necessary to respect the nuns' rules of cloistering and the seclusion considered appropriate to boarding students. The constitutions further specified that the school for day pupils was to be built around a closed courtyard, so that the nuns who came to teach the girls might remain isolated from contact with the larger world outside their gates.[49] All of these arrangements would have been costly, and, because they needed to be put into place before the school could open, they were costs that had to be paid up front, even before the revenue that would justify them could be assured. The Ursulines, who also had separate schools for boarders and day students, would have encountered the same costs, but they at least had a generous and devoted patron, along with strong support from the rest of Paris's dévot community. The Filles de Notre-Dame did not enjoy these advantages.

From the very start, the Filles de Notre-Dame who arrived from Laon in 1634 overextended themselves financially. The property they purchased in the rue du Chasse-Midi was an expensive one. Unable to come up with the full purchase price of 80,000 livres, the convent's mother superior, Madeleine des Anges, promised to pay 45,000 livres down and constituted a rente (annuity) of 2,187 livres 17 sous for the remaining 35,000 livres. To round out the property, she purchased a smaller parcel of land two months later at a cost of 5,000 livres. This time Mère Madeleine paid nothing up front, promising to pay the entire cost in two years time. To furnish the buildings and adapt them to the needs of the community, the Filles de Notre-Dame spent more than 32,000 livres over the course of the next decade. Accounts drawn up in 1644, ten years after the convent's foundation, make it clear that the burden of debt the nuns assumed with these purchases and construction costs was too great. Although the convent was successful in recruiting both nuns and boarding pupils and took in over 75,000 livres in dowries and 43,000 livres in student pensions over the course of the first ten years, expenses outweighed income. At first glance, the balance sheet the Filles drew up for their superior, the prior of Saint-Germain, does not look too bad (see Table 6.1). As presented, expenses totaling 139,945 livres only slightly outran the income of 139,698 livres. If we look closer, however, we see that the nuns listed loans of 6,000 livres from Madame Dareyne and 3,700 livres from an unnamed party as income, but did not also list them as debts. If this was money that needed to be repaid, it should

TABLE 6.1. Income and Expenditures for the Convent of the Chasse-Midi, April 1635–September 1644

Source of Income	Amount[1]	Expenses	Amount
Nuns' dowries	75,083£	Property purchase	46,434£
Boarding pupils' pensions	43,296£	Buildings	32,034£
Nuns' pensions	1,725£	Church	2,022£
Alms and gifts	9,894£	Salaries and wages	4,784£
Loan from Madame Dareyne	6,000£	Costs of legal actions	376£
Another loan	3,700£	Food and maintenance	54,295£
Total	139,698£	Total	139,945£

Source: Based on Raunié, Epitaphier du vieux Paris, 3:99, from accounts in AN, L 1044.

[1]Amount in livres tournois.

figure also in the debit column, bringing the shortfall to 9,947 livres.[50] More crucial, in listing the entire 75,083 livres received as the nuns' dowries as income, the accounts reveal that the Filles were living off the principal, rather than just the income, from their endowment. Such a practice could only lead them ever deeper into debt. The accounts also suggest that they had fallen behind on the payments promised for the purchase of their house, as by this time they should have paid more than 70,000 livres and not the 46,434 livres listed in the accounts. Far from breaking even, the Filles de Notre-Dame were on the brink of financial disaster.

They carried on, but only by borrowing ever larger suns. In 1655 the sisters admitted that they had been unable to pay the rentes due on their property for over ten years. In 1663 Parlement ordered the house sold to satisfy the Filles' creditors.[51] The Filles de Notre-Dame were able to avoid the total dispersion of their community only by arranging to sell the convent to the abbess of Malnoue, who transformed it into a Benedictine dependency of the abbey. She allowed the Filles de Notre-Dame living in the convent the choice of shifting to the rule and habit of Saint Benedict or remaining in the house under their former rule. She also maintained the convent's teaching vocation, though it appears that the school for day students, which brought in no revenue, was closed and the buildings converted to the use of the *dames pensionnaires* whose pensions helped keep the Benedictines of the rue du Chasse-Midi from falling into the same debt their predecessors had.[52]

The nuns who came from Charleville in 1635 to establish the priory of Saint-Sépulchre de Jésus also overextended themselves from the beginning by purchasing a very expensive property in the faubourg Saint-Germain. Like the Filles de Notre-Dame, they bought from Louis Le Barbier, the speculator responsible for much of the real estate development that took place in the faubourg Saint-German when Marguerite de Valois's immense holdings were sold off to pay her debts.[53] Le Barbier sold the Charleville nuns a handsome property known as Bellechasse for the price of 90,000 livres. When they made the purchase they confidently expected a gift of 40,000 or 50,000 livres from a widow who, urging them to come to Paris, had promised to retire to the convent and serve as its benefactress. Alas, she died without completing the donation, and the promised money was lost. The nuns found a new patron, the duchesse de Croy, who took the title of founder and promised an annuity of 2,000 livres. On the basis of this promise, Louis XIII approved the convent's foundation in 1637. And yet this money too failed to materialize; the duchesse de Croy died without making good on the rente.[54] Despite these setbacks, the sœurs de Saint-Sépulchre came up with 18,000 livres in cash for Louis Le Barbier and promised to pay 4,000 livres annually for an annuity constituted on the remaining 72,000 livres. Because the nuns' only income at the time of the foundation consisted of a few small pensions, they must have anticipated paying this annual charge out of the dowries of new recruits and the pensions of boarding pupils. As with the Filles de Notre-Dame, however, the revenues they received from these sources did not suffice to cover day-to-day expenses and at the same time pay off the debt.

The first dowries the convent received had to go toward the cost of adapting the newly purchased buildings to suit the needs of an enclosed convent, but it was the day-to-day expenses of maintaining the nuns that made it especially difficult to get ahead. As we have seen, it cost at least 150 livres per year (requiring capital of 2,400 to 3,000 livres, depending on the rate at which the annuity was fixed) just to feed and maintain each nun. The income of 200 livres per year per nun (equal to a capital of 3,200 to 4,000 livres) that the archbishop of Paris generally required of newly founded convents would probably be a more realistic figure. We have only a very partial record of the dowries received by Saint-Sépulchre during its first years, but it appears that most girls who entered brought dowries that barely covered the cost of their maintenance. Even the generous dowry of 5,000 livres that one young noblewoman brought the convent in 1637 would, once maintenance costs were deducted, have left at most 2,600 livres toward construction costs or paying down the convent's debts, and this was an unusually large dowry from one of the few noblewomen who joined during the convent's first years. The typical entrant was the daughter of a merchant with a dowry of between 2,500 and 3,600 livres.[55] Like the Filles de Notre-Dame, the sœurs de Saint-Sépulchre thus spent their first years struggling to overcome the substantial debts incurred with the convent's creation.

The same story plays out with only slight variation in the case of Notre-Dame de Liesse. Here too the sisters who made the foundation had expectations of patronage that failed to materialize. Here too poverty and a relaxation of standards went hand in hand. First established in the Ardennes in the town of Rethel in 1631 with the purpose of educating young girls, the Benedictines of Notre-Dame de Liesse came to Paris in 1636 to escape the wars that had overtaken their homeland. Too poor to purchase a property, they rented a small house in the faubourg Saint-Germain. They still needed a guaranteed income to obtain the necessary royal and ecclesiastical authorizations for the new convent, but they had promises of 2,000 livres a year from Anne de Montassié, comtesse de Soissons, and another 500 livres in rentes from Louise de Bourbon, duchesse de Longueville. On the basis of these promises, the king granted them permission in October 1638 to build a convent in the faubourg Saint-Germain and, in the meantime, to establish religious practices in their rented quarters. Neither aristocrat, however, made good on her promise. The new convent succeeded in attracting some novices, but those who entered were not from wealthy families and their dowries were small. As the nuns later admitted, they received "little temporal advantage" from these dowries.[56]

By 1642, the community consisted of eleven nuns and was in dire straits financially. It was also riven with internal dissent. When the convent's founding

mother, Gertrude de la Trinité, decided to return to Rethel in 1642, none of
the members of the house was deemed qualified to replace her. A new superior,
Mère Hillaire de Sainte-Thérèse de Tillier, was brought in from Montmartre.
The appointment was a serious mistake. However well she might have behaved
in the ancient cloister of Montmartre, Mère Hillaire proved totally lacking in
the skills needed to take charge of a small handful of poor and bickering nuns.
Installing an underling to handle the mother superior's traditional duties, she
ceased to hold chapter meetings and attended offices only rarely. According to
the other nuns, she spent her time playing cards and gossiping in her chamber
with a few favorite nuns, a disreputable priest, and some lay people who visited
all too frequently. This state of affairs continued for two years, at which point
Mère Hillaire gave up any pretense of serving as mother to the other nuns and
abandoned the house, leaving the convent in a state of total poverty. The remaining sisters had no food or firewood, and no money with which to purchase
them. When Benoist Brachet, the prior of Saint-Germain des Prés and the
convent's male superior, inquired of the nuns how they expected to live, they
replied that they would have to depend on charity.[57]

The convent only survived because a dévote named Barbe Descoulx, who
with four other lay dévotes had been running a school for girls in a nearby part
of the faubourg Saint-Germain, offered her house to the nuns of Notre-Dame
de Liesse so that she could finally take the religious vows she had long desired.
Melding the two households was no simple task, as Descoulx's associates were
content with their secular state and had no desire to take religious vows. A
lawsuit eventually confirmed Descoulx's right to dispose of the property,
though she agreed to allow those dévotes not wishing to take vows to remain
in the house.[58] The convent's trials were not finished, however. Forced to leave
their house during the Fronde, most of the sisters took refuge with the nuns
of Port-Royal, in obedience to their prior's orders. When they attempted to
return to their house, they found that two sisters who had abandoned the
convent several years earlier had laid claim to it and disputed their right to
return. The ensuing lawsuit dragged on for years.[59]

It would be easy to blame the problems of Notre-Dame de Liesse on the
misbehavior of individual nuns, especially Mère Hillaire de Sainte-Thérèse,
who ran away in 1644. But clearly the problems were deeper and more sys-
temic. At their root lay both a failure of leadership and a lack of money. The
house never knew the benefit of strong and stable guidance from above. Mère
Gertrude de la Trinité was almost continually ill from the time of the foundation until her decision to return to Rethel in 1642.[60] When she departed, there
was no one who enjoyed the nuns' confidence prepared to replace her. The
house's financial officer, Sœur Marguerite de Saint-Benoît, had ambitions of
succeeding Mère Gertrude as mother superior, but the majority of other nuns
mistrusted her ambition and brought in a total outsider, Hillaire de Sainte-
Thérèse, instead. Angry at the snub, Sœur Marguerite left the convent and

worked from the outside to return as superior. Notre-Dame de Liesse was thus a house divided even before Mère Hillaire's arrival. She did nothing to improve the situation but let things go from bad to worse. When she abandoned the convent after two years, there were still no good internal candidates to take her place. Prior Brachet followed the path of least resistance and appointed the nun who had belonged to the order the longest as interim superior. We know nothing about her conduct in office, but it is clear that none of the internal problems was resolved. In 1649 the nuns succumbed to outside pressure and agreed to give Sœur Marguerite a try. She lasted three months, at which point, at least according to the other nuns, she resigned the position to relieve herself of the superior's obligation to feed and provide for her daughters. Again she left Notre-Dame de Liesse. Again her abandoned sisters sought a superior from the outside, but they could find no one willing to take on the job. The house was too poor, and, they claimed, its reputation had been ruined by Sœur Marguerite's indiscreet conduct and the scandal caused by her departure.

The nuns went a year with no superior before offering the position to a Benedictine from Picardy named Madeleine de Saint-Augustin, who had come to Paris on account of the wars. A sincerely devout and pious nun, she might have helped right the situation, but she lasted little more than a year. In 1652, when the battles of the Fronde drove the nuns of Notre-Dame de Liesse to take shelter with the Cistercians of Port-Royal, Mère Madeleine took a liking to her new home and decided to stay. She abandoned the poor Benedictines of Notre-Dame de Liesse and took the habit of Port-Royal. Her daughters excused her desertion on religious grounds; she wanted, they claimed, to join an order more austere than her own. And yet it is hard to avoid the conclusion that the dismal poverty, internal dissension, and troubled future of Notre-Dame de Liesse played a large part in this desertion, just as they had in the departures of Gertrude de la Trinité, Hillaire de Sainte-Thérèse, and Marguerite de Saint-Benoît.[61]

The nuns of Notre-Dame de Liesse were poor in part because of their refugee status. Forced out of their home in the Ardennes by the marauding troops common to the Thirty Years War, they did not have the leisure to ensure sound funding before setting out on their trek. But there was more to their financial difficulties than that. When they sought the king's permission to found a convent in Paris, the sisters of Notre-Dame de Liesse showed him notarial contracts signed by great aristocrats Anne de Montassié, comtesse de Soissons, and Louise de Bourbon, duchesse de Longueville, promising them an income of 2,500 livres a year, and yet the promised monies never materialized. Why was this the case? On closer inspection, it appears that the donations were fraudulent; secret countercontracts (contrelettres) invalidated the gifts from the start. The donors were merely lending their names to the foundation to satisfy the requirement that all new convents be financially self-sufficient and not dependent on alms. They never intended to pay the promised funds.

The falsehood is shocking to us today, but contrelettres were a not uncommon legal device at the time. Indeed, they had come to be used so often in the founding of new religious institutions that the archbishop of Paris formally denounced and forbade them in 1638. The preface to Archbishop Gondi's order is revealing. It states flatly that "some persons lent their names as founders for religious houses and to this end promised sums of money that they never gave, and, to protect themselves from demands for payment, they secured counterletters or quittances for the stipulated amounts, without ever having given or even intended to give the money."[62] As with other abuses the same document aimed to curb, however, there was little attempt to enforce the order. The contract between the comtesse de Soissons and the nuns of Notre-Dame de Liesse was signed two months after the archbishop's order was announced. Perhaps the parties to the contract justified their disregard for the archbishop's order on the ground that it had no validity in the faubourg Saint-Germain, where the authority of the abbot was supreme. Perhaps they merely hoped that God in his providence would make up for the missing endowment; the nuns would establish themselves, draw paying boarders, gradually improve their financial position, and ultimately thrive.

If that was their hope, in the end they were not entirely mistaken. After more than twenty years of constant struggle, Notre-Dame de Liesse finally improved its financial position. It is not clear that it thrived, but it survived down to the Revolution. Two things in particular helped. In 1660 Parlement confirmed a decision ordering the comtesse de Soissons's heirs to pay each of three surviving original nuns a pension of 300 livres a year.[63] To all appearances, the sentence was intended to make the comtesse's heirs bear some of the responsibility for her pious fraud by not letting them entirely off the hook in spite of the counterletters. More important, the convent finally began to make ends meet when, after the economy finally recovered from the effects of the Fronde, wealthy parents again began to look for boarding convents where they could place their daughters. In time, the convent's location in the increasingly prestigious faubourg Saint-Germain became in itself a draw for the daughters of the elite. The convent's troubled past receded from view.

In this respect, the Benedictines of Notre-Dame de Liesse were luckier than the Filles de Notre-Dame, who had founded their convent on the same fraudulent financial procedures. Historian Emile Raunié, researching the convent for his *Epitaphier du vieux Paris*, uncovered evidence that a 2,400 livre rente promised by Secrétaire d'Etat Henri-Auguste de Loménie and his wife, Louise de Massez, at the time of the convent's foundation was voided by counterletters two years later. Confirming from convent accounts that the house's pious benefactors never contributed a sou to the institution they were credited with founding, Raunié concluded, with good reason, that the whole purpose of the Loménies' promised donation was to satisfy the king's requirement that all new convents have substantial endowments and not be dependent on alms.[64] Crippled with debt by the end of the Fronde, the Filles de Notre-Dame were forced to sell their house to the abbess of Malnoue, and it was as the Benedictine priory of Notre-Dame de Consolation that the convent continued through the Old Regime to board the daughters of elite families in the faubourg Saint-Germain. In addition, the priory rented apartments to widows and other ladies desiring a genteel retreat. The taking in of lady pensioners—another practice strictly forbidden by the archbishop of Paris in 1638—was to become an important strategy in the financial survival of religious houses in the second half of the seventeenth century. Times were changing, and the houses that survived had to change with them.

The case of Bellechasse, though extreme, makes the point well. The cumulative impact of the convent's intractable financial difficulties meant that the nuns still owed at least 32,000 livres toward the purchase of their expensive property in 1651, when one particularly wealthy novice stepped forward to offer the convent's superiors a way out of their difficulties. The extraordinary concessions the sisters made to secure seventeen-year-old Renée de Livene de Verdille's large dowry show just how loudly money spoke. Insisting on being received as a founder, Renée de Verdille wanted to choose her own room and furnish it with her personal belongings. She wanted a prayer stool alongside the assistant prioress in the convent church, a position normally reserved for the most senior nun. She also wanted an active voice in the chapter and membership in the convent's governing council immediately on taking her vows, instead of having to prove herself worthy over a matter of years. In addition, she demanded to be exempted from performing routine chores, to have one of the convent's lay sisters serve as her personal servant, and to reserve 400 livres income from her dowry each year to cover personal expenses. It is easy to imagine the horrified reaction that Barbe Acarie and her friends would have had to these demands, which went against the grain of all of the reforms they had struggled to introduce, and yet the convent's chapter approved them without exception by a special act. That they were approved for purely financial reasons is evident from the last point enumerated in the act, which specified that if the promised dowry was not paid, Renée de Sainte-Cécile, as she was known in religion, was to enjoy none of these privileges.[65]

Just six years later, the nuns of Bellechasse elected Renée de Sainte-Cécile as their prioress, despite the fact that she was not yet twenty-five years of age, as the statutes required. She had led them to believe that, distressed by the convent's mismanagement, she was thinking of retiring elsewhere if proper discipline was not restored. Eager to protect the crucial income provided by her dowry, without which the convent's already shaky finances would collapse, the sisters convinced the prior of Saint-Germain, Dom Bernard Audibert, to seek a dispensation from Rome allowing her to serve as prioress despite her young age. What the nuns did not know, but the prior did, was that Renée Sainte-Cécile suffered an even greater impediment than her young age: she had been a married woman when she took her vows. Her husband, whom she had been forced to marry at a very young age, had subsequently died, and, knowing her vows invalid, she had secretly sought to open proceedings that would allow her to return to secular life.[66] The nuns' pleas to make her prioress interrupted this plan. Renouncing any thought of abandoning the convent, she settled in to a leadership role instead. Under her direction, Bellechasse entered into a new era of prosperity. The number of girls seeking entry took a leap, as did the size of the dowries they brought. The convent also began to gain important noble patronage.[67] Renée de Sainte-Cécile's ability to charm Parisian elites allowed her to put Bellechasse on sound financial footing at last. The nuns not only paid off their debt for the original purchase of the convent grounds, but they also filled in part of their gardens with houses whose rental would assure a steady income in years to come. With the faubourg Saint-Germain rapidly becoming Paris's most chic *quartier*, this was a sound investment strategy. The convent's fashionable location also contributed to its growing popularity as a place for elite families to send their daughters for a little polite schooling before they married. By the eighteenth century, Bellechasse was worlds away from its Counter-Reformation roots.

Whether or not Dom Audibert would have approved of this evolution, he made it possible by choosing to make a prioress out of an underage woman who was not even legitimately a nun. It is easy to imagine him struggling with his conscience and deciding that the survival of Bellechasse, in its reputation as well as its finances, justified, even required, concealment of Renée de Sainte-Cécile's irregular status. It is also easy to imagine how throughly Barbe Acarie and her ascetic friends would have disapproved of this choice. Sincerely believing that their austere vision of Catholic reform represented timeless religious truth, they would not have comprehended that their understanding of this truth had been inflected by their own experience and spiritual preferences. And yet the first generation of reformers had more in common with Dom Audibert than they would have admitted. They too had made compromises to secure funding for the institutions they founded. Lay patronage played a crucial role in the Catholic revival and sometimes shaped the institutions born of this revival in unexpected ways.

Donors who defaulted on their promises of patronage, moreover, could have as profound an impact as those whose generous gifts came with strings attached. Failures of patronage threatened all seventeenth-century foundations but proved especially crippling to cloistered communities founded during the economically troubled 1630s and 1640s with the expectation that the dowries of the novices they would attract and the pensions paid by boarding students would cover the high cost of building in Paris. In retrospect, it is clear that these expectations were naïve. Even at very successful convents like the Ursulines, the pensions paid by boarding students did not cover the convent's expenses. The nuns had to rely on a combination of outside patronage and the dowries of entering novices to make ends meet.[68]

With two houses of Ursulines already well established and enjoying great popularity among the Parisian elite, teaching convents founded later and enjoying less social cachet had a hard time competing for wealthy novices. It would appear, moreover, that the popularity of teaching convents as a choice for a religious vocation peaked early. Elizabeth Rapley found that the number of women entering convents of Ursulines and the Congrégation de Notre-Dame began to decline as early as 1630.[69] By the time the convents discussed in the previous pages were founded, they were competing with so many other options for religious life that the rush of new vocations the founders confidently expected had almost inevitably failed to materialize.

7

The Impulse to Charity

If the Wars of the League ignited a wave of penitential piety among Parisian dévotes, the battles of the Fronde half a century later prompted a very different response. Rather than taking to the streets in mystical processions, pious women organized committees to aid those impoverished or driven from their home by the rebellion and the ongoing war with Spain. They collected used clothing and redistributed it, along with money and food, among the refugees of war-torn Picardy, Champagne, and the Ile-de-France; they found shelter for orphans and whole convents of nuns fleeing invading armies; and they raised money for these and other charitable projects by distributing graphic accounts of the miseries of war among their devout friends and acquaintances. The effort pious women made to sustain the enormous flow of money and goods needed to assist the dispossessed has been overshadowed by the towering figure of Vincent de Paul, which dominates every account of seventeenth-century French charity. But Monsieur Vincent, as he was known to his friends, did not accomplish his work alone. Women were among his most important collaborators. With the exception of Louise de Marillac, who has been canonized for her role in founding the Filles de la Charité, their contributions remain little known.

This chapter attempts to repair this oversight by examining the part that elite women played in organizing, subsidizing, and administering new institutions for the care of the sick and destitute in mid-seventeenth-century Paris. These institutions included lay confraternities, or *Charités*, dedicated to the care of the sick poor, and congregations of women bound by only simple vows who served the

Visiting the Sick, by Abraham Bosse. One of a series of engravings of the canonical "Works of Mercy," the image captures well the charitable impulse of the middle decades of the seventeenth century (including the ambivalence of the young ladies on the left, who seem less than wholly engaged in their devout mother's good works). Bibliothèque nationale de France.

community as teachers, nurses, and caregivers. The chapter focuses on five key women and the institutions they helped create. I then look more broadly at the work of the Dames de la Charité. A lay confraternity founded in 1634 to assist poor patients at Paris's Hôtel-Dieu, the organization quickly expanded its membership and its activities to become the primary institution through which Parisian dévotes coordinated their charitable efforts during the troubled decades of the Thirty Years War and the Fronde.

Vincent de Paul and Marguerite de Silly

In histories of seventeenth-century French Catholicism, the word "charity" is virtually inseparable from the name of Vincent de Paul, who was indeed associated in one way or another with many of the new charitable institutions created in Paris and across much of northern France. There is, however, a tendency to credit de Paul personally with accomplishments that might more fairly be attributed to other individuals in his circle.[1] The women in particular tend to be viewed as simple foot soldiers sent out to accomplish the missions dictated by their saintly general. Vincent de Paul's letters, which are a key source of information on these activities, lend themselves well to this perspective. Full of advice and counsel on even minor matters, they show him to have been intimately knowledgeable about the good works undertaken by those in his circle. The humble respect that de Paul's female correspondents showed for his superior wisdom and their stream of requests for advice reinforce the sense that he was, if not their commanding officer, at least the éminence grise calculating every move.

We need to revise our understanding of the relationship implied in these letters by recognizing that their rhetoric of female dependence was a conventional reflection of gender relations in early modern times. Moreover, it was a rhetoric deliberately cultivated, even exaggerated, by pious women to demonstrate submissive obedience to their spiritual directors. Adopting a broader view of the many diverse enterprises in which Vincent de Paul was simultaneously engaged, we can begin to read between the lines of these letters just how much of the work that the women in his circle undertook was accomplished without his direct input or initiative.

We can start by taking seriously de Paul's own attempts to credit his female collaborators with inspiring and carrying through many of the charitable projects for which he is known, instead of joining his admirers in interpreting his self-deprecating remarks as but signs of saintly humility. The first woman whose role demands reconsideration is his patron, Françoise-Marguerite de Silly, baronne de Montmirail and comtesse de Joigny. Along with her husband, Philippe-Emmanuel de Gondi, commander general of the king's galleys, Marguerite de Silly provided the funds that established de Paul's Congrégation de la Mission in 1625. De Paul clearly acknowledged her formative role in his career in lectures delivered in 1655 and 1658 to priests of the Mission on the congregation's origins. It was, he explained, at her request that he preached his first mission. He went on to tell how, while still quite young, she observed that when she had finished making her confession her curé did not give her proper absolution but merely mumbled a few words between his teeth. Listening closely on other occasions, she realized that he did not know the correct words to say. She solved the problem by asking a visiting friar to give her the formula in writing, which she then carried with her when she went to confession. But she remained troubled by the curé's ignorance. How many other priests, she wondered, were unable properly to absolve their penitents because they did not know the necessary words? When she told Vincent de Paul about this, he too began to listen closely to the priests to whom he made his confession and so became more aware of how poorly the country folk were being served by their clergy.[2]

A second and more direct spur to action occurred in January 1617 when, visiting the Gondis' country properties, de Paul heard the confession of a dangerously sick peasant, who afterward confided to Marguerite de Silly that, in causing him to make a general confession, the priest had relieved his conscience of several mortal sins he had never before confessed. Fearing that a great many of the peasants on her estates were similarly burdened by unconfessed sins, Silly urged de Paul to seize the next possible occasion to preach a sermon that would impress on people the great need to make a general confession and explain just how to proceed. He took up her suggestion and, by his later account, it was such a success that he had to ask the Jesuits in the nearby town of Amiens to come help hear the confessions the people flocked to make. Afterward, de Paul went from village to village on the Gondis' extensive estates, preaching on the same theme with the same resounding success. Wanting to ensure that this was not a one-time effort, Marguerite de Silly offered 16,000 livres to a religious community that would promise to make a regular preaching mission on her lands. After the Jesuits and Pierre de Bérulle's newly founded company of the Oratoire turned down the offer, Vincent de Paul came to recognize in these events his own call to found a company of priests whose special service would be to missionize among the poor.[3] Marguerite de Silly and Philippe-Emmanuel de Gondi contributed 45,000 livres toward the company's foundation.

What is striking in Vincent de Paul's account of the Mission's origins is that he credits Marguerite de Silly with inspiring the congregation's purpose and not merely supplying funds to realize his own and his colleagues' vision. The point is significant because Silly, although traditionally recognized as the patron who, with her husband, made possible the foundation of the Congregation of the Mission, has not fared well at the hands of de Paul's biographers, who have placed more emphasis on her emotional dependence on the saint than on her active efforts to improve the spiritual, moral, and physical well-being of the peasants who peopled her vast estates. Although praising her piety and charity, these writers leave an unfavorable impression of Silly, whom they depict as an insecure and demanding woman whose selfish insistence on keeping de Paul at her side despite his clear calling to a broader mission was enough to try the patience of even a saint.[4] They see her unreasonable demands as the principal reason that de Paul abruptly left her household, where he was serving as preceptor to her sons, to take up service as a parish priest in a poorly served area of Bresse in the summer of 1617 and cite as evidence of his flight the emotional letter she wrote begging him to return and charging him with responsibility for the imperiled state of her abandoned soul.[5] Theodore Maynard forcefully characterizes the letter as "a form of spiritual blackmail" and the "revelation of 'angelic' egotism and hypochondria."[6] Pierre Coste is less blunt but nevertheless presents Silly's actions in a negative light by depicting de Paul's departure from the Gondi household as the thwarted commencement of his true mission to the poor and suggesting that, when he returned to the Gondis in December 1617, the missions he began to undertake on their estates were "concessions" extracted from Silly as the price for his renewed services to her husband and herself.[7]

A more objective look at contemporary sources suggests that, from the beginning, Marguerite de Silly viewed Vincent de Paul's departure as an enormous loss for her peasants, as well as for her husband, sons, and self. Deploring the abrupt end of the good he did her family but also the "seven or eight thousand souls" who inhabited her lands, she demanded rhetorically whether "these souls were not redeemed by the precious blood of Our Lord, every bit as much as those of Bresse? Were they not as dear to him?"[8] Clearly her intention in seeking de Paul's return was not just to use him as her own spiritual director and chaplain to her household but rather to continue the missions to her peasants that he had earlier begun. Philippe-Emmanuel de Gondi, moreover, was as intent on securing de Paul's return as his wife was, and yet it is only Marguerite de Silly whose pleas are derided as emotional blackmail. De Paul's return to the Gondi household is best interpreted not as capitulation to the neurotic demands of a spoiled aristocrat but as the product of his own realization that, with the support of this powerful family, he could extend the reach of his mission to the poor far beyond what he might accomplish as a simple parish priest.

During the eight years that remained of Marguerite de Silly's life, Vincent de Paul worked closely with her to found Confraternities of Charity, or Charités, as they were most often called, on her scattered estates. These Charités were patterned after the first such foundation, which de Paul had made while serving as parish priest at Châtillon-en-Bresse. This initial foundation is said to have resulted from de Paul's discovery as he prepared for mass one Sunday in August 1617 that a local family had been left destitute by unforeseen illness. He added a plea for assistance to his homily, with the result that so much food was delivered to the poor family that some inevitably went to waste. This prompted him to organize a meeting of local women to talk about how they might provide more consistent and sustainable aid to needy families. The meeting resulted in the formation of the first Charité. Structuring themselves as a devotional confraternity whose special mission was the practice of works of mercy, the women agreed to bring food and necessary supplies on a rotating basis to impoverished families in need of help.

Vincent de Paul's biographers tend to write of this foundation as if it resulted entirely from a spontaneous flash of insight, or divine inspiration, on his part. Emphasizing the saint's empathetic and very personal love of the poor, they neglect to mention that the Charité's foundational rule was quite explicitly borrowed from a similar charitable confraternity that had been founded in Rome.[9] It does not diminish the importance of the foundation—or the quality of de Paul's love for the poor—to recognize that the first French Charité was not a unique and novel creation but an adaptation of a form of assistance already being practiced in papal Rome, where de Paul had lived and studied for several years. He may have learned about the Roman confraternity at this time or only later, through his connections with French dévots. In either case, the Roman precedent for the French Charités reminds us that the Catholic revival was an international movement in which programs for reform and institutional innovations, like spiritual literature, circulated without regard to national boundaries. It also reminds us that Vincent de Paul was more sophisticated, better educated, and more closely tied in to the devout circles in which these ideas circulated than his legendary status as the humble "Apostle of Charity" might incline us to believe. By necessity, he learned early how the patronage system common to both lay and ecclesiastical society operated, and, as his sense of personal vocation deepened, he saw how this system could be made to benefit the poor people he felt a mission to aid. Just as he convinced "pious ladies" and "virtuous bourgeoises" of Châtillon-les-Dombes that working together to "assist spiritually and corporally those of their town" would be a work of mercy immensely pleasing to God, so he mobilized the energies of elites in other locations to sponsor and promote subsequent charitable foundations.[10] Within two months of his return to the Gondi family, Vincent de Paul and Marguerite de Silly had begun to erect Confraternities of Charity on one after another of her estates.

The first was officially inaugurated at Villepreux (Seine-et-Oise) on 23 February 1618. No records remain from this foundation, but the rules for subsequent Charités give a good picture of how the societies worked. Organized as religious confraternities, the Charités took Jesus as their patron and adopted a chapel in the parish church where a group meeting and confraternal mass took place once a month. They defined as their purpose the spiritual and corporal assistance of the sick poor, to whom members brought food, medicines, warm blankets, and other necessary supplies. Although the rules of some Charités focus largely on the material assistance provided the sick poor, others clearly show that the founders attached as much importance to the souls as to the bodies of their patients. Some rules, for example, urged members to bring religious images for the sick to contemplate and to read to them from pious books. Above all, the women were expected to encourage those they visited to reflect on and confess their sins and to receive absolution for them. As the rule for the Charité of Châtillon-les-Dombes put it, members were "zealously to cooperate in the salvation of souls and to lead them as if by the hand to God."[11] Many of the confraternities also undertook to offer regular instruction to local girls, either through the voluntary labors of their members or by hiring a woman to teach them.[12] This instruction was largely religious and focused on the catechism and fundamental religious obligations, but it also included lessons in reading. As such, it offered an important service to country girls, who often lacked any sort of schooling at all.

The Charités served only the "shame-faced poor" considered members of the local community. They paid local women to provide nursing care to patients living alone or otherwise requiring this special service but did not try to assist the chronically ill, which would have depleted their resources too quickly. Rather, their intention was to help out in those cases where a sudden accident or unforeseen illness threatened a poor but otherwise stable household with disaster. A superior, or prioress, elected for a two-year term by a plurality of votes, had the responsibility of determining who should receive the confraternity's services, as well as ensuring that members provided the promised services in accordance with the rules. She was aided by two counselors, one of whom also served as treasurer for the group. The Charités raised money in a variety of ways. Members took turns asking for alms outside the church and in house-to-house visits. Wherever possible, they also convinced local magistrates to assign certain fines and fees to the confraternity's benefit.[13] Gifts and bequests that promised a regular income were especially welcome.

Not surprisingly, these gifts were most often made by the dévotes associated with the confraternities' foundation. This is why, long after Marguerite de Silly's death, Vincent de Paul continued whenever possible to found new Charités in collaboration with aristocratic women. The financial assistance they offered was often crucial to the confraternities' success, but their participation in the societies was fruitful in other ways as well, as de Paul recognized from his work alongside Silly, who took a very active role in the confraternities established in towns adjoining her estates. Using the influence that came with her position as comtesse de Joigny to secure the permission of town officers and the local archbishop to found a Charité at Joigny, she joined the confraternity on the same terms as other women, in full knowledge that her participation would spur the wives and daughters of the town's most prominent citizens to take part. Records of the foundation list forty-two initial members, twenty of whom could not sign their name. We can surmise from this that the membership included a broad social mix. Given the low rate of literacy among rural women in seventeenth-century France, the twenty-two who could sign the membership roster surely represented the best families of Joigny and probably included the wives and daughters of estate managers and other rural notables. Not surprisingly, given the social values of the time, the members of Joigny's new Charité promptly elected the countess as their prioress. She accepted the office, although she can have exercised its functions only intermittently, as she did not reside permanently on this estate. She also joined the Charité established at Montmirail in Brie and, although she initially declined to hold office there because she did not often reside on her lands in this region, accepted the position of first assistant when someone else resigned shortly after the first elections were held. Apparently recognizing that other ladies would take more pride in their offices if they could claim her as one of their fellows, she agreed to the post on condition that a substitute be permitted to perform the actual functions of the office.[14]

It should not be supposed that, in joining the confraternities that she helped to found, Marguerite de Silly acted out of an impulse of egalitarian social leveling or a belief that social differences did not matter. Quite the contrary; she deliberately used her elevated status to achieve the results she desired. Her biographer, the Minim Père Hilarion de Coste, emphasizes her high social position when he tells how, when she went out to visit "all her lands in the provinces of Picardy, Brie, Champagne, and Burgundy," her subjects "paraded before her with the cross and banner in the certain hope that she would deal with them with calm meekness, as the mother of her vassals, and the support of the oppressed." He credits her with punishing the "judges and other officers who mistreated her people" and tells how she summarily fired one judge after hearing a great many complaints about his abusive behavior. But if Marguerite de Silly joined to her consciousness of high status a strong sense of social responsibility, Hilarion de Coste makes it clear that a desire to procure spiritual benefits for her peasants was even more fundamental than her desire to improve the conditions in which they lived. "Her entire passion," he informs his readers, "was to procure the advancement of the glory of God and the salvation of souls." To this end, she sponsored preaching missions on her own lands and those that adjoined them. "When she saw the happy outcome which it pleased our savior to give to the work of these good priests, in the improvement of morals which she saw in her villagers, and in the instruction of the little children in the Christian faith," he concludes, "she was overcome with happiness and indescribable peace."[15]

Louise de Marillac and the Filles de la Charité

Marguerite de Silly was just one of a number of women who aided Vincent de Paul in his mission to serve the poor and who, in turn, were aided by his spiritual counsel. Happiest when working among society's dispossessed, de Paul nevertheless recognized that the financial and logistical support of the wealthy dévotes he met through his connections with the Gondis and Bérulle were essential to his missions, and so he deliberately cultivated them, visiting their Paris mansions and country estates and showing a solicitous concern about their well-being in his letters. All the while, he pressed them to put their money and influence to work on behalf of the poor. His efforts paid off well. A number of these ladies sponsored the foundation of Charités in the villages adjoining their estates. Using their rank and influence to obtain the necessary authorizations, they supported the Charités with gifts of money and supplies and, by participating themselves in the confraternities, encouraged women in the second tier of local society to join and support them as well. It soon became evident, however, that founding new Charités was not enough. Except where local patrons remained truly devoted to the project and continued to give it their energies and funds, the Charités tended to founder after a few years. And disappointingly few dévotes proved willing to make this continued effort, however enthusiastically they had supported the initial foundation. To halt this slippage, Vincent de Paul turned to the small handful of dévotes who proved truly committed to the endeavor. With the founding of the Congregation of the Mission in 1626, he was busier than ever and, though he continued to encourage the founding of Charités wherever his preaching missions took him, he could not keep doubling back to check on them and reanimate those that had faltered. Instead, he relied increasingly on the efforts of a small group of devout women to visit the Charités and aid and instruct local women. The leading member of the group, and deservedly most famous, was Louise de Marillac (Mademoiselle Le Gras).

Although the daughter of Michel de Marillac's brother Louis, seigneur de Ferrières and Farinvilliers, Louise de Marillac remained on the margins of the elite society of which her paternal family was a part because of her illegitimate birth. Her mother never has been conclusively identified. Sent at an early age to board at the Dominican convent of Poissy, she then lived with an aunt and uncle on their estate at Attichy until her marriage in 1613 to Antoine Le Gras, a royal official and secretary to Queen Marie de Medici. By her own account, Louise de Marillac had ardently desired to become a Capucine, but when she confided her wishes to Père Honoré de Champigny he told her that she lacked the strength to endure the Capucines' austerities and that "God had another plan for her."[16] The frustrated religious vocation is a common topos in seventeenth-century pious biographies. In the case of Louise de Marillac, however, it does appear to be more than a conventional trope. Even as a young bride, she was very devout. She is said to have begun very soon after her marriage to visit the sick in her parish of Saint-Sauveur, bringing them soup and medicines, urging them to receive communion, and helping to prepare their bodies for burial. Mortifying her body with fasting and hair shirts, she sought spiritual direction from François de Sales and Jean-Pierre Camus, bishop of Belley, before taking Vincent de Paul as her spiritual director in 1625. With the death of her husband, also in 1625, she dedicated her life to serving the poor.[17]

Ever cautious and only too familiar with devout women whose initial enthusiasm for charitable projects quickly faded, Vincent de Paul nevertheless gradually came to rely more and more on Louise de Marillac to supervise and invigorate the rural Charités. First using her to channel money and supplies to confraternities he visited on his missions, he began by 1629 to ask her to inspect the Charités herself. On 6 May of that year she set out in a borrowed carriage for Montmirail, in Champagne, where one of the first confraternities had been established, bringing linens, medicines, and other supplies that she thought might be needed. This was the first of many such voyages made at her own expense or with the aid of wealthier friends. Arriving at her destination, she would assemble members of the local Charité, question them to learn how well the confraternity was functioning, and then attempt to reignite their fervor and instruct them on how better to accomplish their tasks.

It was a short step from restoring neglected Charités to helping to organize new ones, and each new charity meant one more that had to be revisited and periodically reinvigorated. By 1629, moreover, the impulse to found charitable confraternities had spread to the city. The parish of Saint-Sauveur was the first to establish a Charité. Saint-Nicolas-du-Chardonnet followed in 1630; Saint-Merry, Saint-Benoît, and Saint-Sulpice in 1631; and other parishes soon after. As the number of Charités grew, Louise de Marillac's responsibilities multiplied and her administrative talents came to the fore. She became distinctly more self-confident and self-reliant as the work progressed. Louise Sullivan, who has edited Marillac's writings, concludes that the "four years of intense activity in the service of the poor" that began for Marillac in 1629 were transformative for her. "She had found a work in which her human and spiritual gifts could flourish. . . . Although she still relied on Vincent particularly in her spiritual life, she had become his collaborator and equal, a woman of decision."[18]

Working out the details for each Charité demanded enormous patience and tact. Although a generic rule had been drawn up to serve as a model for new confraternities, each Charité was independently organized and devised its own constitution. In the cities especially, it was often difficult to get potential members to abandon their personal priorities in favor of proven methods and practices. Dealing with local authorities and aristocratic sponsors could be especially trying. Often, either the principal patron or one of the secular or ecclesiastical authorities whose consent was needed for the new institution had ideas about how the organization should function that appeared unworkable to de Paul's and Marillac's more experienced eyes, and she had to negotiate a compromise without giving offense and losing crucial support. Jeanne de Schomberg's desire to give a house to the Charité she helped establish at Liancourt in 1635 posed just such a problem. The offer was generous, but de Paul feared that, with a house from which to distribute food and medicine, the members of the Charité and the nursing sisters they employed would cease making the home visits that the founders considered essential to the Charités' mission. Marillac resolved the issue by accepting the gift of the house as a place where the confraternity's hired nurses might live but explicitly requiring these women to visit the poor twice a week, not only in Liancourt itself but in three neighboring communes.[19]

When she visited a confraternity, Louise de Marillac did not limit herself to meeting with members and local authorities. According to her first biographer, Nicolas Gobillon, she had a strong desire to serve the poor personally. After meeting with the Charité's members, she would go out into the countryside to visit patients and see to their needs. Predictably, she occupied herself with more than their bodily ailments. In Gobillon's words, after seeing to their physical illnesses, she "worked to cure the maladies of their souls, and, as ignorance was the primary one, she took every care to defeat it, and [to this end] she assembled the country girls in a local house, where she taught them the articles of faith and duties of Christian life. If there was a schoolmistress in the place, she instructed her on her duties; if there was not, she tried to establish one."[20] De Paul's letters confirm that by 1630 Marillac was catechizing girls in the villages she visited. He approved of these efforts, suggesting at one point that her work with the girls would "facilitate the means of winning their mothers over to God."[21]

The same letters show that Louise de Marillac did sometimes encounter opposition to her teaching efforts from local clerics. She had to learn to proceed cautiously and always to obtain the curé's consent before attempting to meet with local girls. A larger problem, however, was finding a way for the teaching efforts to continue after her departure. There was an almost total lack of qualified teachers. Some Charités tried to solve the problem by asking their members voluntarily to take on this task, but these efforts were seldom lasting.[22] And yet the country girls who came forward to help nurse the Charités' sick nearly always had too little education themselves to take on a teaching role. With the foundation of the urban Charités, moreover, a new problem appeared. It was one thing for women living in the country to prepare soup and personally deliver it to the poor in their villages; it was quite another to expect aristocratic ladies to take on this role in urban parishes. Both problems found a solution—and Louise de Marillac her true vocation—with the creation of the Filles de la Charité to assist with the work of the parish charities.

The new organization took shape only gradually and acquired a legal existence still more slowly. Erected as a confraternity by permission of the archbishop of Paris in 1646, the Filles de la Charité received formal approval from the king only in 1657 and Parlement in 1658.[23] Informally, however, the group dated its origins to 1630, when its first member, a simple cowherd named Marguerite Naseau, offered her services to Vincent de Paul to help with the new urban confraternities. He sent her to Marillac for training in the services she was to provide. Other girls followed, and by 1633 Louise de Marillac had taken in five or six young women and begun to form them into an orderly community. She drew up an "Order of the Day" spelling out how they were to employ their time between the first prayers that they said on rising and the examination of conscience that preceded sleep. When not occupied with their tasks of serving the sick and delivering medicines in the parishes, they were expected to return to Marillac's house to engage in study and meditation. Those

who were illiterate were given daily reading lessons after mass and expected
to practice in their later free time so as to give an account of what they had
read at the evening's recreation period.[24] Marillac believed it essential, moreover, not only to teach the girls the basic nursing skills they would need for
their work in the parishes but also to deepen their understanding of the faith.
She sought to nurture in them a distinct vocation of "service of their neighbor
in imitation of the Son of God" and to prepare them to assist their patients
spiritually as well as corporally. To this end, she composed a short catechism
for their use.

Louise de Marillac's surviving correspondence from this period is scanty,
and it is hard to piece together an exact chronology of the evolution of her
informal "family" into an organized society. Recent scholarship suggests, however, that it was she who took the initiative here. Vincent de Paul, ever cautious,
held back, urging her to slow down, continue the good work she was doing,
and wait for God to make his will known.[25] As always, she yielded to his superior wisdom, and the community was founded on 29 November 1633, following de Paul's decision in August or September of that year that this was
indeed God's plan. In many respects, however, de Paul's approval only reaffirmed something that had already taken place. Marillac's composition of the
"Order of the Day" predates the society's official foundation, and it is likely
that the orderly plans she presented for the society played a key role in convincing de Paul that this new community of servants of the poor was indeed
a part of God's design.[26]

The "little family," as Louise de Marillac frequently referred to the group,
grew rapidly. It contained a dozen members by July 1634 and about twenty by
the end of the following year. Having become too large for Marillac's house in
the Left Bank parish of Saint-Nicolas-du-Chardonnet, the community moved
to La Chapelle in Paris's northern suburbs in May 1636 and then again in
September 1641 to a house in the faubourg Saint-Denis across from the Congregation of the Mission at Saint-Lazare. By this time the community contained
between sixty and eighty members.[27] With the move to the suburbs, not all of
its members could conveniently return to the motherhouse each night, and so
some lodged in the parishes where they worked. As time passed, the Filles
were scattered more widely and their tasks diversified. By the 1640s they were
not only working in urban parishes and at the Hôtel-Dieu, but some had been
sent out to rural Charités where, in addition to helping the ladies deliver medicines, they opened schools for local girls. They opened a school at the motherhouse in 1641 and ran the foundling home, the Enfants Trouvés, established
by the Dames de la Charité. This meant placing the infants with wet nurses
in the countryside and returning to ensure they were being well cared for, as
well as running the orphanage where they were brought after having been
weaned. Beginning in 1640 the Filles de la Charité also served galley convicts
imprisoned near the Porte Saint-Bernard while awaiting transfer to the fleet at

Marseilles. They brought aid to regions devastated by the Thirty Years War and, at the urgent request of Geneviève Fayet, founder of the Dames de la Charité, took over nursing duties at the Hôtel-Dieu of Angers. This led to their establishment at hospitals in other towns as well.

As the community grew and diversified its labors, Louise de Marillac worked to transform the initial draft "Order of the Day" into a detailed set of rules. She also sought to regularize the growing community's status. As usual, it was Vincent de Paul who insisted on taking things slowly. Remembering François de Sales's experience with the Visitandines, he feared that if the Filles looked too much like a religious order, they would be forced into the cloister, rendering them useless for parish service. When Marillac and several of the Filles asked him in 1640 if they might not take vows of service to the poor, he deliberated the question for nearly two years before agreeing that they might take annual, simple vows on the model of the private vow of chastity that Marillac had already taken but not the public and irrevocable vows that might characterize them as nuns. Only in 1645 did he ask the archbishop of Paris formally to approve the institution of the Filles de la Charité as a confraternity dedicated to serving the poor. Even after the Filles received this initial approval, the path to formal recognition was slow. Perhaps because of the disruptions of the Fronde, the archbishop's approval was formally reiterated ten years later to gain the approbation of the king in 1657 and Parlement in 1658. The community received formal approval from Rome only in 1668, eight years after the deaths of both de Paul and Marillac.

These dates are significant because they nuance—indeed, correct—our understanding of the pioneering role often attributed to the Filles de la Charité, who are frequently credited with having originated the new status of filles séculaires and shown other women desiring to lead an active religious life how, by rejecting exterior signs that would mark them as nuns, they might avoid the forced enclosure mandated by the Council of Trent.[28] As we shall see, at least two other Parisian organizations, the Filles de la Croix and Filles de la Providence, achieved official recognition as uncloistered communities of women with an active religious vocation earlier than did the Filles de la Charité. Moreover, the founders of these other groups also had close connections to Vincent de Paul. They looked to him for spiritual direction and practical advice but remained less dependent on his judgment than did Louise de Marillac.

The real originality of the Filles de la Charité lay in the breadth of their vocation as "servants of the poor" and their willingness to go out into the community wherever they were needed in groups of two or three, while still remaining part of a larger organization, faithful to its rule and obedient to its superiors. It lay also in the nature of the Filles' recruitment, which initially at least drew most heavily on social groups with little education or previous exposure to religious life. Building a community that not only functioned but grew and thrived on this novel base required imagination, initiative, and considerable administrative talent. Louise de Marillac displayed all three, as well as uncommon gifts for spiritual direction and leadership.

Administering the growing operations of the Filles de la Charité was a demanding job made all the more complicated by the diverse and decentralized nature of their operations and the need to work closely with lay patrons and the Dames de la Charité, who could be imperious in commanding the services of the Filles, at the same time that they complained about their insufficiencies. Louise de Marillac was forced to spend quite a bit of time mediating between the Dames and certain Filles, who had to be taught to remain humble and submissive but at the same time not to allow themselves to be used as the ladies' personal servants. Well aware that the success of the new company depended on the quality of the girls that joined it, Marillac attentively supervised girls under her charge. She studied new recruits to be sure that they had the right personal qualities to succeed in their new lives and had not volunteered out of some worldly desire to come to the big city. Her attentive concern did not cease once a sister had been sent out from the motherhouse; she kept in close touch by letter and expected sisters who lived within two days' journey to return there once a year for a spiritual retreat.[29] She also gave spiritual retreats to elite ladies at the Filles' motherhouse. The house was too small to provide accommodation to more than a small number of extra women at any given time, but this was perceived as an advantage in that, by fully sharing the Filles' humble and disciplined life, the ladies might better learn to despise the worldly "riches and grandeur" they ordinarily enjoyed.[30]

In retrospect, it can be argued that the Filles de la Charité benefited from taking a slow track to official recognition. During the decades that elapsed between the community's initial foundation in Louise de Marillac's home and its official recognition by ecclesiastical and secular authorities, she did not cease to think about how it could best function and whom it should serve. The enduring strength of the Filles de la Charité owes much to this prolonged period of innovation and experimentation. The institution officially approved in the 1650s was markedly stronger, more flexible, and conceptually more sophisticated than the little community of country girls originally founded to do the menial work of tending the poor for elite Dames de la Charité.

Marie Luillier and the Filles de la Croix

Louise de Marillac's Filles de la Charité remain the best known of the new communities of filles séculaires founded between 1630 and 1650 but, as has already been noted, they were not alone in adopting this new form of religious life. Nor were they the first to receive permission from Paris's archbishop to live as organized communities without formal vows. This honor would appear to belong to the Filles de la Croix, who received approval from Archbishop

Jean-François de Gondi in 1640 for statutes that not only allowed them to live in community without subjecting them to the rules of enclosure but also explicitly prohibited them from "making solemn vows or a regular profession."[31]

Founded at Brie-Comte-Robert in 1640 and in Paris several years later, the Filles de la Croix defined their mission broadly as "the service of the poor of their sex in all of their spiritual needs."[32] Although this meant first and foremost the instruction of young girls in the Catholic faith, the schools run by the Filles also taught reading, writing, and basic needlework skills. In addition, the institute attempted to do for poor women what the Visitandines and, in a more limited fashion, the Filles de la Charité did for wealthy elites. That is to say, it offered grown women spiritual instruction and retreats. To train more women to carry on their mission, the Filles de la Croix established a seminary in their motherhouse in 1648.[33]

The Filles de la Croix had their origin in the Picard town of Roye, where four young dévotes—Françoise Vallet, Charlotte de Lancy, Marie Samier, and Anne de Lancy—began in 1625 to instruct local girls in their religious obligations and such useful skills as reading, writing, and sewing. When the mothers of these girls began to sit in on some lessons to enlarge their own understanding of church teachings, the "Filles" (as they were called, having as yet no formal name) expanded their activities to include Sunday afternoon gatherings where grown women could meet for pious conversation and religious instruction. As their audiences grew larger, the town's former schoolmaster, recently fired for misconduct, succeeded in stirring opposition among certain local residents. Subsequent legal proceedings brought Marie Samier and another of the Filles to Paris, where they presented a defense of their activities to the theologians of the Sorbonne. On 26 November 1630 a panel of nineteen theologians handed down a decision praising the women's work as good and useful.[34] Contrary to what one might have expected from as traditionally conservative a bastion of French Catholicism as the Sorbonne, the judgment in no way suggested that the women should form themselves into a formal religious order or retreat behind walls. Nor did it object to the idea of women offering spiritual lessons to others of their sex.

Besides clearing the women from the aspersions cast on them by a jealous competitor, the visit to Paris inadvertently served another purpose, which was to bring Marie Samier into contact with Marie Luillier de Villeneuve, a wealthy widow who, on learning of the Filles' work in Roye, was determined to found a similar institution in the Paris area. The sister of the Visitandines' founder, Hélène-Angélique Luillier, and a generous benefactor of that order, Marie Luillier, the widow of Claude Marcel, sieur de Villeneuve, lived for a number of years in the special quarters the Visitandines provided for their secular patrons while engaging in various works of charity. Devoted to François de Sales, Luillier was convinced that her own mission was to carry through the saint's frustrated plan of creating an open congregation of women who would do charitable works in the community. She convinced the Filles de Roye and their director, curé Pierre Guérin, to send Charlotte de Lancy to aid her, and the two women were busy planning and obtaining permissions for this new institute when the fall of Corbie and besiegement of Roye in 1636 brought the rest of the Filles, along with many of their pupils, in hasty flight to Paris. A friend of Luillier's offered the Filles refuge on his estate at Brie-Comte-Robert, where they reopened their school. Subsequently moving to independent quarters, they took in local pupils in addition to those who had accompanied them from Roye. When the dangers of war finally receded in 1639, the residents of Roye wanted the Filles to return, but Luillier worked out an arrangement to keep them in Brie-Comte-Robert and also to draw from this house schoolmistresses who might be sent to other locations.[35]

The agreement with the magistrates of Brie-Comte-Robert, which describes the women simply as "bonnes et dévotes Filles maîtresses d'école," makes it clear that as of this date the group had no formal institutional structure.[36] Its members took no vows, not even simple ones, and had no statutes. Although said to have been sometimes referred to as "Filles de la Croix" on account of the trials they had endured, they had no formal name. Luillier, however, was determined to change this situation. Modeling statutes for a new institute on those drawn up by François de Sales for the Visitandines in their original, uncloistered state, she presented these statutes to Archbishop Jean-François de Gondi and received his approval for them in April 1640.

The statutes, which began by placing the new society under the title and invocation of the Holy Cross, regulated its members' comportment and even their day's routine with the same specificity as religious constitutions and yet concluded by firmly stating that members were to take no solemn vow or religious profession.[37] Luillier's clear intention was to avoid any danger that the Filles de la Croix should be forced into the cloister, as the Visitandines had been. (Quite possibly, Luillier received counsel on this point from Vincent de Paul, whom she knew well in his capacity as the Visitandines' superior, but I have found no conclusive evidence to this effect.) As Luillier defined it, the community was to consist of "single women and widows who were neither nuns nor seculars, but who had the virtue of the former and the honest liberty of the latter to work for the sanctification of their fellow-beings, as well as their own advancement in perfection."[38] The unique character of the institute flowed from this desire to create a society of women who were "neither nuns nor seculars." The Filles de la Croix were not given a distinctive mode of dress but instructed merely "to wear decent and modest clothing, without following fashion." They were not to have their own church but to attend mass in their parish, where they were expected to serve as a good example and a help to other parishioners. They were to make their twice-weekly confessions to parish priests as well.[39]

Except for their daily attendance at mass, they were to leave their house as rarely as possible. Within the house, life was conducted by rules very similar to those in effect in teaching convents such as the Ursulines. Outside of the hours spent teaching and caring for boarding students and attending religious services, the Filles divided their day into periods of prayer, spiritual reading, and examination of conscience, with an hour of recreation—pious conversation—after the noon and evening meals. Just as in convents, they followed the evening recreation with a "great silence," during which they spoke only when necessary. Although the Filles did not have a formal parlor where they spoke to visitors from behind a grille, they admitted men to the house only for such necessary functions as administering last rites or doing repairs they could not make themselves. [40]

In contrast to even reformed convents, where chapter meetings at which nuns recounted their failings generally took place once a week, the Filles de la Croix met just before retiring each night to "expose to one another the day's faults." Enjoining the sisters to offer and receive this counsel with "gentleness, humility, and docility," the statutes depict the occasion as a mutual giving of advice and, unlike the constitutions of most religious orders, do not go on to prescribe penalties for each possible infraction of the rules. The character of these evening gatherings would thus appear to have been quite different from the solemn chapter meetings of traditional religious orders. The 1640 statutes suggest in other ways as well that the Filles de la Croix were more egalitarian in their structure than traditional convents. They set up no special rules for a novitiate, and all members were to be addressed simply as "Sister," even the première, as the Filles called their elected superior. There were no other officers or specially designated functions, and not only was the première expected to expose her faults and be corrected by her sisters at the nightly meetings, but she was to go first, "so as not to flatter or fool herself."[41]

As the institute grew larger and its structure more formalized, some of this egalitarian simplicity was lost. Certain changes were perhaps inevitable results of the institute's greater complexity, for example, the special provisions for postulants and novices introduced in the constitutions drawn up after Luillier's death and formally approved in 1654. Others, however, were imposed by Luillier to make the institute conform more closely to her personal ideal of an active religious life. Most controversial, in August 1641 she introduced the practice of taking perpetual and irrevocable vows by herself taking vows of charity and obedience (she could not yet, she claimed, take a vow of poverty because of the institute's precarious financial state). Luillier confidently expected the rest of the Filles to follow her lead in this. Some, however, refused, including superior Françoise Vallet. In defense of their refusal, they pointed to the line in the 1640 statutes forbidding members of the society to take solemn vows. Luillier replied that only solemn—that is to say, publicly pronounced— vows were prohibited and not the private vows she had initiated, but she failed to win over her opponents. Unable to reach an agreement, the Filles de la Croix split in two. Those who refused vows returned to Roye and Brie-Comte-Robert and in 1644 opened a school in the parish of Saint-Germain l'Auxerrois, where Pierre Guérin, one of their old superiors from Roye, had found a new position. Those who accepted vows remained at Vaugirard and also opened a house across from the Visitandines in the faubourg Saint-Antoine in 1643. This became the seminary where they trained girls to run the schools they founded in other parishes and towns. The quarrel also led to a lawsuit, as each group claimed the right to gifts and properties donated in the name of the Filles de la Sainte-Croix, and several decades passed before the Parlement of Paris finally handed down a decision entitling each group to use the name and specifying which properties belonged to each.[42]

Histories of the Filles de la Croix identify the question of vows as the unique source of the quarrel that led to the institute's split, and yet on closer examination it appears that this particular issue was merely one symptom of slowly emerging but fundamental disagreements between Luillier and at least some of the original Filles from Roye. As Luillier's biographers tell the story, she introduced the practice of simple vows and took them herself before learning that the community's elected superior and some of its members disapproved of the practice.[43] If this was the case, then she was clearly following her own lights without fully consulting those who had created and run the society for fifteen years. Convinced as she was of her own divine mission, Luillier may have failed to realize how much her expansive plans for the Filles de la Croix diverged from the more modest vision of the original Filles from Roye. She may have forgotten their close ties to their local community, the reluctance with which they had sent Charlotte de Lancy to Paris to help her found a broader congregation on their model, and the fact that, if the rest of the community soon followed, it was because they had been driven from their home by war and not because they shared the mission of creating a teaching institute that would radiate broadly across France. At least some of the sisters wanted nothing more than to return to Roye when conditions once again proved safe. Even if they endorsed Luillier's vision of seeing the society expand to benefit as many people as possible, they appear to have been happier working on a local scale, with simpler and less formal structures, supporting themselves by taking in mending rather than seeking the patronage of wealthy elites.

It is precisely on this latter point that the greatest differences emerged. To bring to fruition Luillier's expansive mission to her sex required more elaborate administrative machinery but also additional sources of funding and a much higher public profile than those enjoyed by the Filles de Roye. Although she adopted many of their daily routines and practices for the new institute, it quickly began to have a different character. In 1641, for example, when the Filles de la Croix inaugurated their new house in the Parisian suburb of Vaugirard, Luillier organized a formal entry procession, just as religious orders typically did for the founding of new convents.[44] Led by one of the Filles carrying a large cross and two bearing candles, this public procession of the entire community and their pupils sounds very foreign to the quiet ways of the Filles de Roye, who had counted on word of mouth and their own need to earn a living to spread their reputation. Accounts of the procession mention only the admiring throngs of local residents. We may suspect, however, that the procession was also intended to bring favorable notice from the Parisian dévots whose support Luillier needed if her institute was to take root and spread. Her personal fortune was small. To support the Filles de la Croix, Luillier thus found herself engaged in the same avid search for patronage as Paris's numerous underfunded convents. Times were hard by the 1640s, and competition for wealthy patrons was acute, especially with the arrival of whole convents of nuns in flight before the armies of the Thirty Years War.

When a house across from the Visitandines in the rue des Tournelles became available in 1642, Luillier struggled mightily to raise the money needed to buy it to establish a motherhouse in Paris that might also serve as a seminary for the new congregation. She secured a promise of more than 30,000 livres from the duchesse d'Aiguillon and planned to cover the balance of the 55,000 livres purchase price by selling a property given the society by another patron. Parlement nevertheless held up registration of the new foundation for more than four years because she did not have the funds to ensure the community's subsistence.[45] When she died in 1650, the community's position remained sufficiently precarious that it was nearly dissolved. Only the intervention of the Dames de la Charité, responding to an emergency appeal from Vincent de Paul, saved it. Anne Pétau (Madame de Traversay), the widow of a magistrate and founder of the Franciscan Third Order convent of the Conception, agreed to serve as the group's protector and manage its finances, for despite its economic difficulties the community was doing important work that the Dames wished to preserve and extend.[46]

The patronage of the Dames de la Charité was also essential to the Filles de la Croix's expansion into the Parisian countryside. According to Jean-Jacques Olier, wealthy ladies from the faubourg Saint-Germain offered to help support the Filles' financially struggling schools in exchange for their "conducting some short missions among the girls and women on their estates, and teaching the essential truths of the faith, the manner in which to make a good confession, and how to sanctify themselves in their estate by a truly Christian life. This zeal in fact resulted in the foundation of houses of Filles de la Croix on several estates." The house established at Rueil, where the duchesse d'Aiguillon made her country home, was especially noted for the conférences (talks) given there by Charlotte de Lancy, one of the original Filles from Roye. According to the Filles' chronicles, the crowds of women and girls who came to hear these talks quickly outgrew the room that held them. One wealthy widow thought this apostolate so important that she left 6,000 livres to endow a weekly lecture for "poor women and girls" at the Filles' seminary in the hôtel des Tournelles.[47]

In addition to their conférences, the Filles de la Croix also conducted religious retreats at their various houses.[48] Making this one of their principal missions, they opened their doors to local women, both rural and urban, and offered both individual, or solitary, and group retreats. Although the latter were directed by priests, one of the sisters played an important supporting role that included leading morning and afternoon meditations and working with each participant individually "to aid and console" her as she probed the depths of her soul in preparation for the annual or general confession that was the central purpose of the exercise. Catherine Morin, the sister specially delegated to lead these retreats at the house in the rue des Tournelles, is said to have guided more than five hundred women in preparing for a general confession by the time of her death in 1652.[49]

Marie Lumague and the Filles de la Providence

The Filles de la Providence de Dieu represent yet another pious woman's innovative attempt to aid the less fortunate members of her sex. Like a number of other dévotes, Marie Lumague aspired to be a Capucine but married instead when her parents decided that she was not strong enough to survive the Capucines' austere life. At the age of eighteen she wed François Pollalion, a diplomat and officer of the king. He died several years later, leaving her a widow and the mother of a young child. Appointed a lady-in-waiting and governess of the (as yet unborn) children of Marie de Bourbon de Montpensier, the first wife of Gaston d'Orléans, Marie Lumague retired from court when her mistress died in childbirth in 1627 with the announced intention of raising her daughter and devoting herself to good works. Although the court of Gaston d'Orléans was awash with political intrigue, there is no indication that Lumague's departure had any motive other than the desire of this Capucine *manquée* to lead a more retired and pious life. With the consent of her spiritual director, Vincent de Paul, she took the habit of the Dominican Third Order and through the rest of her life wore it underneath her regular clothes.[50]

Her desire to do good works led her to share the work that Louise de Marillac and other devout penitents of Vincent de Paul were undertaking with the rural Charités. Along with these other women, she worked to catechize peasant women and girls. Her biographers describe her as willingly going into the "most abandoned parishes of the countryside" to carry "the truths of religion" to the local women. According to another of her spiritual directors and first biographer, Dominique Le Brun, she once spent two weeks disguised as a peasant to instruct the poor inhabitants of the little village of Taverny outside of Paris.[51] An eighteenth-century biographer tells how, gathering together girls but also grown women, she taught them their catechism in a way that engaged their interest without embarrassing them by showing off their ignorance. "She instructed each, according to their ability, in the maxims of the gospel and duties of the Christian; she taught them about the greatness of God, the nothingness of the world, the state of humankind after the fall . . . and most especially, the powerful mediation of Jesus Christ, and the efficacity of the prayers of the saints."[52] She was also one of the original Dames de la Charité of the Hôtel-Dieu and served as the group's first treasurer.

Lumague's real sense of apostolic mission, however, was directed neither to educating the peasantry nor to tending poor patients in the Hôtel-Dieu but to rescuing vulnerable girls from the dangers of debauchery and prostitution. In about 1629, she began to seek out young women who, lacking other resources, were about to prostitute themselves, to convince them to save themselves before it was too late. Lumague's biographers delight in telling how this virtuous widow exposed herself to humiliation and even personal danger by descending into houses of prostitution "to chase out the crime, while covering with embarrassment the infamous corrupters that lurked there." One even compares her to Jesus driving the moneychangers from the Temple in a melodramatic narration of how she burst into the house of a madam who had disguised herself as a dévote to lure a young girl into her house of ill repute. Striking the woman two blows, she took the girl by the hand and led her off to the convent of the Madeleine, or so we are told.[53] The rhetoric is familiar; the virtuous widow descending into dens of iniquity to rescue others of her sex is a common topos in pious biography, where it serves to highlight the value placed on chastity and moral purity and to underscore the protagonist's sterling honor, which emerges untarnished by contacts that would have soiled a less pure and dedicated soul.

However familiar the topos, the rescue stories told about Lumague form the necessary background for her life's work. The big problem was what to do with the girls once she had wrested them from the arms of their would-be debauchers. She took some to the Madelonnettes, but the convent was intended for repentant prostitutes and was not, to Lumague's mind, an appropriate place for the many girls who had not yet fallen into debauchery but, lacking the support of family and friends, were in danger of doing so. With the consent of Vincent de Paul, who had been made superior of the charity hospital of the Pitié, she began to send girls there. But this was only an interim solution, and by the time she had lodged some forty girls with the Pitié, it was clear that an alternative would have to be found. Lumague's plan was to found a special institution for the girls where they might be housed, educated, and trained for gainful work. Cautious as usual, de Paul greeted the plan with less than full enthusiasm. He knew that Lumague had little personal fortune; her husband's wealth belonged by rights to her daughter and was not at Lumague's disposal.

Despite his hesitations, she went ahead with her plans, trusting that Providence would provide—hence the name for the new institution, the Filles de la Providence de Dieu. She began by taking girls into her own home outside Paris at Fontenay. Their numbers grew rapidly. By all accounts, there were eighty girls in 1641, when they moved to a larger house at Charonne, in Paris's eastern suburbs, and one hundred when they obtained letters patent from Queen Anne of Austria in 1643 officially authorizing the foundation.

With the community's rapid growth, their expenses outran their founder's income. Although in principle the girls paid a modest sum toward their board, many had no money or relatives willing to pay for their care. Lumague used her connections in Paris's devout society to supply the funds that she herself lacked. Her former position as a lady-in-waiting to the duchesse d'Orléans allowed her to present her case to aristocratic elites. As a founding member of the Dames de la Charité, she was also able to call on the assistance of other wealthy dévotes.[54] The marquise de Maignelay, the duchesse d'Aiguillon, and Madeleine Fabri, the wife of Chancellor Séguier, supplied most of the funds for the purchase of the house at Charonne.[55] All three were Dames de la Charité, as well as being generous donors to other devout causes. Maignelay in particular shared Lumague's preoccupation with rescuing girls from the street, and it is not surprising that, after having helped to found the Madelonnettes, she should have aided this new establishment for girls at risk.

Despite his initial hesitations, Vincent de Paul supported the foundation and agreed to serve as its first superior. Enjoying the favor of Anne of Austria, whom he served as spiritual director and as a member of the *conseil de conscience* established to advise on ecclesiastical appointments, he is generally credited with convincing the queen mother to declare herself protectress of the Filles de la Providence in 1647. It may also have been at his suggestion that she gave the Filles the old hospice of the Santé as a permanent home in 1651.[56] De Paul also worked with Lumague to draw up the first written constitutions for the Filles de la Providence in 1656.

The lack of earlier constitutions means that we know less about the evolution of the Filles de la Providence than we do about the Filles de la Charité or the Filles de la Croix. Like these other groups, the Filles de la Providence took only simple vows. Not waiting for girls whose honor was endangered by their poverty or other family circumstances to come to her, Lumague sought them out in the streets and taverns of the city's most sordid quarters, and she insisted that members of the community be free to move about in the same way. Despite remaining filles séculaires, the Filles de la Providence modeled their daily lives more directly on those of traditional religious orders than did either the Filles de la Charité or the Filles de la Croix. They borrowed many of their teaching practices from the Ursulines, and their cloistered buildings had all the marks of a convent. A tall balustrade divided the church to separate the sisters and their pupils from the general public, and their parlor featured a grille. Even though they were not officially subject to the rules of clausura, the Filles de la Providence accepted the sweeping definition of chastity that required religious women to isolate themselves from the world. The importance they attached to their purely religious obligations is evident in the fact that the congregation's teachers were known as "choir sisters" and not "teaching sisters." A further indication is the sisters' decision in November 1652 to begin a nightly vigil before the Blessed Sacrament reserved in their church.[57] Some contemplative convents elaborated special cults of the Blessed Sacrament, but this is not a practice we would expect to find in a teaching community of filles séculaires.

The decision to take only simple vows did not mean that standards for membership were lax. Quite the contrary. In contrast to traditional religious orders, which accepted girls at seventeen, prospective Filles de la Providence had to be at least twenty years old and spent six months as postulants and two years as novices before being admitted to the society. Lumague and de Paul apparently agreed that the responsibility for instructing young girls in good conduct and Christian virtue required greater maturity than contemplative life in a cloistered community. This became all the more important when the Filles de la Providence developed the ambition of taking their teaching beyond the walls of the motherhouse.[58] Plans to broaden the community's mission were delayed by the Fronde, which sorely tested the Filles, as it did other religious communities, but once peace was restored (and alms began again to flow), the sisters went out to teach young girls in the faubourg Saint-Germain and various Parisian parishes. Their activities soon spread outside of Paris as well.[59]

It is worth noting, moreover, that, far from wishing to force the Filles de la Providence into the cloister, the archbishop of Paris gave them his full support and even declared himself their protector. He was quick to realize the advantages of expanding their services outside the confines of their initial house, and it was on his initiative that they established themselves in several parishes of the Ile-de-la-Cité, at Saint-Germain l'Auxerrois, and in other Parisian locales.

Expanding to other dioceses at the invitation of their bishops, the Filles de la Providence were necessarily decentralized and forced to adapt to local conditions. In this they typified the active congregations that sprang up in diverse profusion in the middle and late seventeenth century. There were both advantages and disadvantages to this decentralization. The ability to be flexible and adapt to local needs and conditions came at the price of institutional stability. Lumague's death in 1657 caused a crisis for the Filles de la Providence. Although the sisters were in theory governed by a superior elected for a three-year term, Lumague had retained general oversight of all aspects of the community but especially its finances in her capacity as directress and protectress. Her role remained so crucial to the institution's success that it was very nearly disbanded on her death. To resolve the crisis, Vincent de Paul summoned the

Dames de la Charité to an emergency meeting. They agreed to take on the responsibility of supervising the community on a rotating basis. Even so, many of the girls had to be returned to their family for a time, while the institution got back on its feet.[60] Without the long-term commitment of the Dames de la Charité, it is very possible that the institution would have been forced to disband. The work of the Filles de la Providence thus remained very much the project of Parisian dévotes.

Geneviève Fayet and the Dames de la Charité

Like her friends Louise de Marillac, Marie Luillier, and Marie Lumague, Geneviève Fayet was a devout widow with a passion for good works. After the death of her husband, Antoine Goussault, a president of the Chambre des comptes, in 1631, she frequently accompanied Marillac on her visits to inspect and revitalize rural Charités. In the spring of 1633, she undertook her first solo inspection trip while journeying to visit properties she owned in Anjou. The detailed account of this trip that she sent Vincent de Paul is without parallel in its revelation of the public behavior and intimate reactions of a Parisian dévote to the situations she encountered while traveling through the French countryside on a mission of charity. For this reason, it deserves a fuller narration.

Fayet began her account with a description of the pious practices with which she and her traveling companions—her servants and household intendant—embellished every stage of their trip. Departing each morning after hearing mass in the nearest church, the travelers punctuated their day with sung and recited prayers, spiritual readings, and pious conversation. "Every time my clock struck the hour," Fayet wrote, "we would say a Hail Mary, placing ourselves again in the presence of God and asking for the accomplishment of His holy Will."[61] In every town she passed she sought out the local charity hospital, the Hôtel-Dieu, and inquired about its functioning, the religious observances of the nuns who ran it, and the financial and moral support it received from local elites. She recorded these things because she knew that de Paul was eager to learn whether the movement for establishing local charities he had begun more than fifteen years earlier had survived and spread to other localities. But Fayet was not merely a passive observer; she actively quizzed the nuns she encountered and engaged in lengthy conversations with locals to test their understanding of the fundamentals of their faith. Most important, she catechized all who would listen, sometimes individually but also in large groups.

She recounts how she quickly gauged the level of understanding of her audience and adapted her message to suit their needs. In Angerville, for example, she offered very rudimentary lessons to the locals she found gathered for mass at the church and "began by having them make the sign of the Cross, which the majority did not know how to do." Recognizing that the wife and daughters of a city official with whom she was staying in Angers were ignorant but also very proud, she did not attempt to teach them directly but instead convinced them to come along on a tour of the countryside while she cate-chized the peasants on the farms. The farm children were "fairly well in-structed," she reported to de Paul, thanks to a competent and caring local priest. But she was most pleased by the response of her hostess, who confessed after the trip that she had found it very interesting, as "she knew almost nothing about all that." Fayet also quoted her as saying, "It is quite evident that you love the poor a great deal and that you are at your heart's content among them. You looked twice as beautiful while you were talking to them." The words sound naïvely boastful, although we must realize that Geneviève Fayet was referring here not to a worldly and external beauty but an inner glow that she attributed directly to God's grace. "Father," she continued, "it is admirable that God granted me the courage to speak in the presence of their priest and at least one hundred people." Clearly, Fayet surprised herself by taking on such a public role.[62]

With a confidence born of religious faith (but also a good measure of aristocratic arrogance), Fayet appears never to have questioned whether her unannounced visits and unsolicited lectures were truly welcome. Whatever her listeners privately thought—and we have only her account to go by—the same deference to social station that allowed her freely to offer her advice to the country folk she visited ensured a respectful audience. And yet we cannot help asking whether people did receive Fayet's teachings as enthusiastically as she claimed. Were the local people really so willing to be taught by a perfect stranger, and a woman at that? Were the curés not in the least offended when this outsider, this lay woman, began to catechize their flock in their presence and even in their church? Fayet records nothing but praise from her audiences. She even quotes one priest as saying that "he would consider himself most fortunate to be able to end his days near me, without wages or reward, just to listen to the words that would come from my lips."[63] We must filter these alleged reactions through our understanding of the social hierarchies of the Old Regime. Although she claims to have dressed very simply, "with a low collar and no farthingale, like a servant," Geneviève Fayet had the bearing and diction of a noblewoman, and her identity as the widow of a president of the sovereign courts would not have escaped her local audiences, whose attentive-ness surely reflected long traditions of obeisance to a dominant nobility—and perhaps also the hope of benefiting from customary distributions of noble largesse—as much as or more than a desire to hear her expound the principles of the faith.

Whether the words of the priest who, she claimed, wanted nothing more than to end his days at her feet were more than simple flattery we will never know. Fayet's perceptions were distorted by the biases inherent in her social status but also, and most important, by an intoxicating sense of mission and the satisfaction of having assumed a new and powerful role. What she had accomplished left her both proud and humble. "I cannot tell you the graces [God] granted me here," she wrote Vincent de Paul, and she expressed her deepening commitment to bringing Christ's teachings to the poor and ignorant in apostolic terms: "I am ready to lose everything and leave everything, preferring humility to all consolations and possessions. The example of my Savior is very powerful; He left the bosom of His Father to come and practice it [humility] in poverty and self-abasement."[64] By implication, Fayet planned to do the same, taking as her model not the suffering Christ of the passion, so dear to previous generations of dévots, but rather Jesus the teacher and friend of the poor.

Of course, Geneviève Fayet did not abandon rank, fortune, and station to wander the French countryside catechizing peasants, but she did dedicate the years that remained of her life to the service of the poor. Organizing a cadre of elite women known as the Dames de la Charité, Fayet launched a concerted program to bring well-born women who shared her sense of apostolic mission into the charity wards of Paris's ancient Hôtel-Dieu to catechize the sick and ensure that the dying made a final confession and received the last rites before they died. In a fixed rotation, groups of women came each day to visit the hospital's patients and deliver an afternoon snack intended largely as a means of gaining entry and persuading the sick to listen to the moral and spiritual counsels that were in fact the principal object of the visits.[65]

Historians have generally assumed that the Dames de la Charité represented a new approach to charitable assistance characteristic of the Catholic Reformation in general and Vincent de Paul in particular. Indeed, so closely does the organization fit with de Paul's other works that there is a tendency to credit him and not Geneviève Fayet with the foundation.[66] He did contribute to the Dames in important ways. His willingness to speak periodically to their assemblies must have lent a special prestige to the organization and encouraged the growth of its membership. He also assisted them with sound practical advice. At one 1636 assembly, for example, he explained just how the ladies designated to visit the hospital each week should prepare the patients to make a general confession. So that they would not "appear to be preaching" in the religious instruction they offered, he composed a little booklet that covered the principal points the ladies should make. When we look to the actual circumstances of the foundation, however, we find that, not only was it not initiated by de Paul, but he attempted to discourage Fayet when she went to him with her idea for the organization, just as he initially discouraged the plans of Louise de Marillac and Marie Lumague. Only after Fayet took her case directly to Archbishop Jean-François de Gondi did de Paul change his mind and agree not only to support the Dames de la Charité but also to serve as the group's spiritual guide.[67]

Crediting Geneviève Fayet and not Vincent de Paul with initiating the plan for the Dames de la Charité is important because it sets the record straight but also because, freeing us from unwarranted assumptions about the organization's novelty, it allows us to recognize that the Dames had important precedents in long (if only intermittently effective) traditions of Parisian ladies offering charitable assistance at the Hôtel-Dieu. We have already seen that Marie Du Drac was visiting the Hôtel-Dieu in the 1570s and that the visits Barbe Acarie and her friends made during the wars of the League were a revival of earlier practices.[68] Such visits continued, at least on an individual basis, to 1634.[69] There were also, however, earlier attempts to organize a confraternity that would provide this service on a regular and consistent basis, and it appears quite possible, even probable, that Fayet was familiar with one of these attempts, either from her own visits to the Hôtel-Dieu or from her friendships in devout circles. In the collective biography of notable women that he published in 1647, Minim Hilarion de Coste tells how a devout widow named Suzanne Habert brought Parisian ladies to serve in the Hôtel-Dieu, and he reproduces the detailed rule that she drew up to guide their service. The document is undated, but internal evidence suggests that it was composed sometime between 1611 and 1615, when Habert retired to the convent of Ville-l'Evêque in Paris's northern suburbs, where she lived as a lay boarder until her death in 1633.[70] Parisian dévotes frequently visited Ville-l'Evêque, and it is possible that Fayet encountered Habert there, though she may also have learned about the earlier project from mutual acquaintances.

Whether or not there was a direct connection between the two women, the practices of the Dames de la Charité echo those described in the earlier rule in ways that appear more than coincidental.[71] Like Geneviève Fayet's Dames de la Charité, Suzanne Habert's ladies selected their most willing and pious members to serve on a rotating basis at the Hôtel-Dieu. Arriving in the morning, the ladies designated for the day's service were expected to stop in the hospital's chapel to pray and then spend the morning assisting the nuns with a variety of useful, and often menial, tasks, including cooking the patients' soup, cleaning their rooms, and spreading scented herbs to freshen the air. The afternoon was devoted to visiting with the patients in their wards, where the ladies were to gently exhort them to receive the sacraments and generally aid them in "both body and soul." The entire membership was to meet every three months to talk about how best to accomplish their work. Members would also, as in a traditional confraternity, attend fellow members' funerals and say prayers for their dead. Habert's vision for the society was an expansive one. The ladies were not just to help out at the Hôtel-Dieu but also to visit poor prisoners in jail, help establish reformed convents, and employ themselves in other good works.[72]

It is not clear whether this confraternity was ever more than a fond dream on Habert's part. Hôtel-Dieu records indicate that in 1608 Parisian ladies offered to assist with the patients' meals. The offer was accepted, but the experiment lasted at most four years. Within six months the hospital's directors had to warn the ladies not to interfere with the nuns' work, and in 1612 they discontinued all charitable gifts of food and wine for the patients on the ground that the practice was causing too much confusion.[73] Evidence connecting the failed initiative with Habert's plan is, however, tenuous. Delivering food to charity patients was only a very small part of Habert's project, which appears in any event to have been composed in 1611 at the earliest. It may thus have been a response to the failed initiative of 1608, rather than representing the initiative itself.

Whether or not Habert's plan was ever put into effect, it foreshadows the activities of the Dames de la Charité in important ways. The biggest difference is that the Dames did not offer the same assistance with menial tasks but focused more exclusively on the spiritual well-being of the patients. In most other respects, their program of charitable service at the Hôtel-Dieu and their broader plan for good works closely echoed the earlier project. There is good reason, then, to believe that when Geneviève Fayet pressed Vincent de Paul to found the Dames de la Charité at the Hôtel-Dieu, she did not view the organization as a new departure so much as the realization of a charitable impulse long familiar to Paris's devout elites, if only irregularly exercised by them. Even if she did not know of Habert's specific initiative, her own service at the Hôtel-Dieu (which began years before the Dames de la Charité were organized) would have taught her that visits to hospital charity wards by well-born ladies were an old tradition, and her central concern would have been to revive this tradition in ways that made it most serviceable and ensured its continuing success. Moreover, she would have seen the work of the Dames as beneficial for their own souls and not just the poor patients they visited. Recalling the sense of empowerment and spiritual blessing she derived from her own attempts to catechize the poor, she would have imagined other Dames de la Charité enjoying the same rewards. Inscribing the work of the Dames at the Hôtel-Dieu in a long tradition of lay women's apostolic service, she would have applauded the broadening of their mission to other forms of charitable service. If she did not play much part in the Dames' other enterprises, it is because she died in 1639, just five years after the organization was founded.

The Work of the Dames de la Charité

Even before Geneviève Fayet's death, the Dames de la Charité had decided to expand their mission to help tend the foundlings who, following an age-old tradition, were left in a chapel or on the steps of the cathedral Notre-Dame in the hope that God would provide. Appalled to learn that virtually all of the three or four hundred babies so abandoned each year died from lack of care, the

Infirmary of the Hôpital de la Charité, by Abraham Bosse. Founded in 1602 by disciples of Saint John of God, the Hôpital de la Charité in Paris's faubourg Saint-Germain was independent of the Hôtel-Dieu. The pious women depicted here helping the monks to serve the sick patients' meals were nevertheless engaged in an activity similar to that performed by the Dames de la Charité of the Hôtel-Dieu. Bibliothèque nationale de France.

Dames joined with the Filles de la Charité to see if they could not improve the foundlings' survival rate. Deciding to start small, the Dames placed two or three infants with the Filles de la Charité in 1636 and expanded the group to a dozen two years later. Pleased with the results of these first experiments, in 1640 they decided to establish a home where the foundlings, once weaned, might be nurtured, educated, and trained for gainful jobs. The project was an expensive one. By one estimate, the new foundling home, the Enfants Trouvés, cost 40,000 livres a year by 1644. Although Louis XIII and his mother donated rentes worth 12,000 livres a year and the queen mother offered the abandoned castle of Bicêtre as a home and school for the children, the responsibility for supplying the remainder of the funds fell to the Dames de la Charité, who supplemented the alms they collected from the general public with their own donations.[74]

Raising the large sums needed to support the Enfants Trouvés was a continuing challenge for the Dames de la Charité, but it was by no means the only financial burden they assumed. They paid stipends to the priests who heard confessions at the Hôtel-Dieu, aided prisoners condemned to the galleys, raised money for foreign and internal missions, and provided considerable financial support to the Filles de la Providence and other charity hospitals. The single greatest effort during the first two decades of their existence, however, went into war relief. Disturbed by reports of the miseries brought on by the fighting on France's northeastern borders, they began in 1639 to raise funds and organize aid for those left homeless and destitute on account of the wars. Forming a new subgroup called the Charité de Lorraine, the Dames collected alms and held meetings to decide how best to help orphaned girls and nuns forced out of their convents by approaching armies. They also raised money to help support the priests of the Mission and Filles de la Charité sent to the front to nurse the wounded and run soup kitchens and camps for refugees.[75]

Between 1650 and 1652, war relief again dominated the Dames' agenda, as Frondeur princes and their Spanish allies, who had refused to sign the 1648 Peace of Westphalia and remained at war with France, made battlegrounds of Picardy, Champagne, and the Ile-de-France. Moved by distressing reports of starving families left destitute by rapacious armies, the Dames engaged in a concerted effort to come to their aid. They helped to publicize the disastrous state of affairs in war-torn regions by distributing pamphlets that graphically recounted news from the front to charitably minded acquaintances and the public at large. Consisting largely of extracts of letters from priests of the Congregation of the Mission working at the front, these *Relations* appeared on a monthly basis between September 1650 and April 1651, only somewhat less regularly through 1652, and occasionally thereafter. Each concluded by telling how many thousand livres the relief effort was costing each month and urging sympathetic persons to bring their donations to their parish priests or to the president and treasurer of the Dames de la Charité.[76] In addition to cash contributions, the Dames collected used clothing and blankets for homeless refugees, tools and seeds for farmers returning to devastated lands, liturgical vessels and missals for clergy whose churches had been pillaged, and other useful items for those in need. Madeleine de Lamoignon, the unmarried daughter of the Dames' third president, turned her Parisian townhouse into a vast store where she sold off donated items such as paintings and jewels to benefit the cause.[77] Unfortunately, financial accounts for these transactions have not survived. However, the effort was enormous. In 1657 Vincent de Paul credited the Dames with having raised more than 350,000 livres to send to war-torn areas, not counting donations in kind.[78]

Previous historians have tended to be dismissive in their assessment of the Dames de la Charité. Focusing on their activities at the Hôtel-Dieu, they portray the Dames as self-important busybodies who disrupted hospital routines by trying to tell the nuns how to do their job and as snobs who, unused to hard work, turned the nitty-gritty tasks of charitable assistance over to the sturdy country girls recruited into the new secular institute of the Filles de la Charité. This harsh judgment overlooks the fact that seventeenth-century conceptions of charity were quite different from modern ones. The principal aim of the Dames de la Charité was to bring comfort and assistance to the souls of poor hospital patients. The afternoon snacks they brought the sick were not intended to substitute for hospital fare but rather to give the ladies the opportunity to speak to patients about religious matters. Most important, to dismiss the Dames' contribution because they turned the physical care of Hôtel-Dieu patients over to the Filles de la Charité is to willfully ignore the administrative talent they displayed in directing charity hospitals, organizing war relief, and, above all, raising vast sums of money to support a wide variety of charitable causes. These activities were not incidental but central to the organization's purpose. During the first several decades of their existence, the Dames' record was in fact an impressive one.

From the beginning the organization was envisioned not just as a group of elite ladies who condescended periodically to visit the sick poor but as a much broader and more ambitious charitable confraternity. Its very structure testifies to this. Although service at the Hôtel-Dieu was considered beneficial for the Dames' own souls, as well as for those they aided, not all members were expected to volunteer for this work. The other ladies, the "Dames de l'Assemblée," contributed instead by helping to raise money for the organization's projects. They attended the general assemblies the Dames held at least annually, heard reports on actual and potential projects, and discussed how best to accomplish these aims. The notes Vincent de Paul's associates made of his addresses to these assemblies show how much they were focused on fund raising. As with any charitable association, the Dames' energies periodically slackened, and we can see in de Paul's conferences how he used his role as the Dames' spiritual adviser to reignite their fervor and urge them to sustain and increase the contributions that funded their good work. Although praising them for their accomplishments, he reminded them repeatedly of the continuing needs of society's unfortunate and did not hesitate to chide, scold, and even threaten them with perdition should they allow their good works to lapse. In one conference, for example, he set before them the image of the two gates to the afterlife, one wide and the other narrow, reminding them that only a few would be chosen. To pass through the narrow gate, they must separate themselves from all worldliness and "declare themselves members of the party of God and of charity." There must not be the least division here, he warned: "God cannot tolerate a divided heart." He went on to urge them to use the fellowship provided by their confraternity to keep themselves on the narrow path of virtue and inspire others by their example. This impromptu sermon on moral reform was tightly interwoven with a financial report that emphasized how much the Dames' revenues had fallen off since the prior meeting and how necessary it was to remedy this situation.[79]

As de Paul clearly recognized, the assemblies of the Dames de la Charité provided a ready forum for promoting pious behavior among Parisian elites. But even more important, the organization served as a clearinghouse for information on actual and potential works of mercy and a place where the competitive instincts of socially conscious women might be turned to good benefit by encouraging them to emulate leading dévotes in works of charity instead of aspiring to more worldly accomplishments. With a membership of two or three hundred women during its first several decades, the Dames de la Charité served as a rich repository of social and economic capital with which to sustain existing charitable activities and sponsor new ones.[80] From the beginning, the organization's leadership was provided by socially prominent women. In addition to Geneviève Fayet, the widow of a president of the Chambre des comptes, early members included the widows of two presidents of Parlement, Charlotte de Ligny (Madame de Herse) and Marie Deslandes (Madame de Lamoignon), and Madeleine Fabri, the devout wife of Chancellor Pierre Séguier. Marie Deslandes served as the society's president from 1643 until her death in 1651 and with Charlotte de Ligny headed the war relief campaign begun in 1650. Another prominent early member was Marie de Vignerot, duchesse d'Aiguillon, who was a member from at least 1639, when she joined with Charlotte de Ligny to assume responsibility for organizing the Charité de Lorraine. The duchesse d'Aiguillon served as president for more than twenty years after the death of Deslandes and often held the society's meetings at her home.

The Dames' rapid growth—they are said to have had a hundred members within a year of their foundation—is in large measure due to the active role these prominent Parisiennes played in the organization. Their high social status however, was not uncharacteristic of the society as a whole. The single surviving membership list, compiled in the early eighteenth century but purporting to list members since the organization's foundation in 1634, names more than five hundred Dames de l'Hôtel-Dieu and Dames de l'Assemblée. The titled nobility is well represented in both categories. If only one member was a princess, there were ten duchesses, three countesses, and twenty-three marquises. The highest ranks of the magistracy were an even stronger presence and included the wives or widows of three French chancellors and twenty-four presidents of the sovereign courts, along with another twenty-three women whose husbands were counselors of state or other royal officials of sufficient distinction that their offices were noted on the list.[81] The high social standing of the group as a whole is also evident in the fact that members accorded the honorific "Madame" traditionally reserved for noblewomen far outnumbered those designated "Mademoiselle," the honorific used for the higher levels of the bourgeoisie.

Of course, not all of the elite women whose names appear on the list participated equally in the Dames' affairs. Just as certainly, not all were equally devout. Some undoubtedly joined more out of social ambition than true piety. We cannot know how many, any more than we can divine how many alternated bouts of sincere piety with the sorts of worldly occupations that Vincent de Paul so thoroughly condemned or how many developed an avocation for charity only with widowhood and advancing age. Reputations were fragile things in the seventeenth century, and many widows found it seemly to occupy themselves with good works, just as they found it seemly to retire to convents. We cannot penetrate the hearts of the roughly five hundred women who served as Dames de la Charité during the seventeenth century to know just why they joined and whether they found what they sought in the organization. We can, however, judge them by their collective achievements, and here the record is strong. In addition to the activities already discussed of the group as a whole, many of the Dames can be identified as patrons of reformed convents, sponsors of Charités in the localities where they had their country estates, and founders or key supporters of the new institutes of filles séculaires established to aid needy members of their sex. The administrative talent and commitment shown by the Dames de la Charité made it natural, for instance, for Vincent de Paul to turn to them for help in rescuing the Filles de la Croix after the death of Marie Luillier and the Filles de la Providence on the death of Marie Lumague. Anne Pétau (Madame de Traversay), who assumed the leadership of the Filles de la Croix, and Madeleine Deffita (Mademoiselle Viole) and Marie de Maupeou (Madame Fouquet), who took over as directors of the Filles de la Providence, were among the earliest and most active Dames de la Charité.[82]

By the mid-seventeenth century, the Parisian dévote was no longer a solitary figure, moving silently among religious services, meditative devotions, and her personal and private charities. Rather, she was enmeshed in collaborative efforts on a new scale. If some of the motivation and encouragement she received to engage in these projects came from such admired male leaders as Vincent de Paul, she was nevertheless working in the company of other women who had seized the initiative to create institutions that responded to their own perceptions of society's needs.

If women's prominent role in pioneering new forms of charity between the 1630s and the Fronde remains little known today, it is because women's contributions were overshadowed by the mid-1650s with the founding of the male-directed Hôpital Général. An ambitious attempt to conquer the still growing problem of urban poverty by enclosing vagrants in workhouses, where they might be catechized and perform work that would help pay for their care but also learn skills useful for earning a living, the Hôpital Général was established on the initiative of the secret confraternity of dévots known as the Compagnie du Saint-Sacrement. Although many of the Dames de la Charité had spiritual directors (including Vincent de Paul), spouses, sons, and other kinsmen who were members of the Compagnie, the organization's rule of secrecy—and its repeated refusal to create a women's auxiliary—meant that women were closed out of the plan, discussed as early as 1640, to replace the ineffective system of outdoor relief administered by the Grand Bureau des Pauvres with asylums where religious instruction would produce moral reform and reshape the idle poor into "productive subjects."[83] The royal edict that established the Hôpital Général in 1656 put it under the direction of the first president of the Parlement of Paris and the king's solicitor general. Beneath them, a board composed of more than two dozen magistrates and members of the civic elite supervised the hospital's finances and functioning. Women contributed funds, collected linens, and visited hospital wards but had no organized or official role.

Scholars have tended to be critical of the Hôpital Général, viewing it as a radical departure from earlier charitable initiatives and an attempt on the part of narrow-minded elites to discipline the popular classes and repress their culture.[84] There is indeed much to criticize about the institution's functioning, but it is important to recognize the fundamentally religious aims of the Hôpital's founders, who were moved by an ardent desire to save souls and not just preoccupied with public order or determined to get beggars, prostitutes, and other undesirables out of sight and off the street. There was nothing novel about the conception of poverty, its origins and potential cure, that prompted the establishment of the Hôpital Général in 1656. The women whose works of charity have been the subject of this chapter shared the same confidence that religious instruction would encourage the poor to become hard-working, moral individuals, as well as helping to save their souls. The Dames de la Charité even discussed the idea of founding a new confinement hospital where the vagrant poor might be provided with manual labor on several occasions in 1653. When Louise de Marillac took the idea to Vincent de Paul, he did not tell her that plans to found such an institution were already well advanced, even though, as a member of the Compagnie du Saint-Sacrement, he must have been well aware of this fact. Preserving the Compagnie's vow of secrecy, he merely cautioned the ladies that they should proceed slowly, taking time for reflection and prayer. He also recommended that they start small, with one to two hundred indigents who entered of their own free will, instead of attempting to forcibly intern all of the beggars in the capital, as some of the women proposed.[85]

De Paul's caution was well founded. The establishment of a confinement hospital that aimed to intern all of the vagrant poor did result in a radical change in the character of Parisian poor relief. Whatever the validity of the initial idea of reforming and educating the poor so that they would become productive members of society, the problem of poverty proved simply too enormous and intractable to solve in this way. As de Paul foresaw, an institution that aimed to take all of Paris's mendicants off the streets would need to house and care for enormous numbers of people. It would, moreover, draw people from outside the capital as well as within. The founders of the Hôpital Général badly underestimated both the population the new institution would need to serve and the cost of providing this service. Entranced by the idea of a spiritually revitalized and morally reformed French society, devout members of the Compagnie du Saint-Sacrement envisioned a vast network of charity hospitals spread across the landscape of France. This was an impossible dream. Most towns found it easier—and far less expensive—simply to let the indigent drift toward Paris in search of relief. Economic crisis, especially a broad wave of famine in 1662, brought hordes of people to the capital. The governors of the Hôpital Général found themselves trying to feed an estimated eight to ten thousand hungry mouths each day, which put an enormous strain on the underfunded and already indebted institution. Although the king issued an edict in December 1662 requiring every French town to establish its own Hôpital Général, Parisian magistrates recognized that this was at best a long-term solution to the crisis. To resolve the more immediate problem of the influx of poor, they banished nonnative beggars from the city entirely and threatened even locally born vagrants with deportation to the galleys if they did not report immediately to the Hôpital Général. This was just the beginning of increasingly repressive legislation that, contradictorily, aimed at reducing the hospital's population at the same time that it made an ever broader spectrum of social undesirables susceptible to incarceration in the Hôpital Général.[86] The conditions of confinement became more and more punitive, while the pedagogical goals of educating and reforming the poor receded ever further from view.

Underestimating the number of people who would seek the services of the Hôpital, the governors also grossly underestimated the revenue the new institution would require. The asylum quickly outstripped its original funding sources, which combined voluntary donations from pious Parisians, endowment funds from several older charity hospitals now incorporated into the new Hôpital Général, and a sales tax on wine initially authorized to support the Grand Bureau des Pauvres. As new taxes were added, the willingness of wealthy dévots to fund the Hôpital Général with their personal gifts and legacies declined. Poor relief came to be seen more as a broad public responsibility than as a particular burden and religious obligation of the rich.

This did not mean the end of pious women's charitable endeavors. The Dames de la Charité continued their good works, though their money-raising efforts inevitably trailed off after the crisis of the Fronde had passed. Pious women also continued to direct the orphanages, charity hospitals, and other institutions they had helped to found and even established additional orphans' homes, asylums for endangered girls, and parish schools. Most famously, Marie Bonneau (Madame de Miramion), married and widowed in 1645 at the age of sixteen, founded the orphanage of the Sainte-Enfance in her home parish of Saint-Nicolas-du-Chardonnet. She also founded the Refuge for delinquent girls and in 1661 established a community of lay dévotes known as the Sainte-Famille dedicated to teaching and nursing the poor. Still under Bonneau's direction, this community was later joined to a similar community of lay dévotes, the Filles de Sainte-Geneviève, and expanded its mission to include conducting religious retreats for working-class and other women. In addition, Bonneau took over as lay director of the Filles de la Providence when Madeleine Deffita, the successor to Marie Lumague, died.[87] Bonneau's charitable career was exceptionally lengthy (she died in 1696), intense, and diverse, but many pious women engaged in similar sorts of activities on a smaller scale. Their efforts to assist society's outcasts and the poor were eclipsed by the greater publicity given the Hôpital Général, but they were not abandoned. To many minds, the latter institution's seemingly futile struggle to make significant inroads into the problems of poverty must only have proved the sad truth that "ye have the poor always with you" (Matthew 26:11) and reinforced the conviction that private as well as public efforts were needed to succor the dispossessed.

Conclusion

For more than twenty-five years, Madeleine de Lamoignon regularly accompanied her mother, Marie Deslandes, on her charitable rounds. Rising early to attend matins at 4 A.M. in summer and 5 in winter, the women spent long days carrying food and medicine to needy families, collecting money and goods that could be resold for their benefit, and organizing the broader work of the Dames de la Charité, for which Deslandes served as president from 1643 until her death in 1651. So intense were the women's efforts that Madeleine's father and brother, magistrates in the Parlement of Paris, are said to have commonly discovered when they returned home to eat that there was nothing to put on the table because the women had given everything away. Although they worked long hours together in their common devotion to the poor, it was only when Deslandes fainted one day from wounds caused by the spiked iron bands she wore beneath her clothes that Madeleine learned her mother's painful secret: even in old age, she routinely wore a hair shirt and constricting bands to mortify her flesh. That Marie Deslandes should have kept her bodily mortifications a secret, rather than raising her children to share the penitential spirituality that prompted these private practices, symbolizes well the generational difference between the pious women whose spirituality was shaped by the crisis of the Holy League and their daughters, who were raised with a quite different religious sensibility.[1]

Born in 1576, Marie Deslandes belonged to the generation of pious women who came of age at a time when France was still engaged in a desperate civil war. No information survives about which political faction she personally favored, but the fact that her father sided with the League and served in its Parlement makes it likely that she remained in Paris during the siege.[2] Whether or not she took part in the League's processions and experienced firsthand the frenzied religiosity of the times, her ascetic piety closely resembles that of Marie Sévin, Marie de Tudert, and others who, interpreting the conflict as a sign of God's wrath, vowed to spend their lives expiating their own sins and those of their society. Perhaps, like Sévin and Tudert, Deslandes would have become a Carmelite had the hazards of fortune left her a young widow and not the wife of a rising magistrate and mother of a growing family at the time of the convent's foundation in 1604.

By contrast, Madeleine de Lamoignon, born in 1610, developed a very different set of spiritual values. François de Sales, who prepared her for her first communion when he visited Paris in 1619, was a formative influence. While de Sales much admired Marie Deslandes, whom he considered one of the saintliest women of her generation, he impressed on Madeleine a gentler and more confident faith, in which love of God was expressed through compassionate service to others rather than bodily mortifications and self-imposed suffering. Madeleine's sisters, in common with many others of their generation, were also strongly influenced by de Sales. The eldest, marrying a colleague of her father in the Parlement of Paris, consciously modeled herself on de Sales's devout Philothée in seeking "sanctification in the world," and the middle daughter embraced a Salesian religious vocation and insisted on becoming a Visitandine nun. Madeleine's life choice was less conventional. After much deliberation, she rejected both marriage and the cloister, deciding to remain in the world as an unmarried woman to devote her entire life to serving the poor. In a time when elite women were traditionally viewed as having only two choices—a husband or the veil—this was an extraordinary decision, especially for a woman who was healthy, comely, and financially secure. Using tropes common to saints' lives, Madeleine's biographer depicts her as heroically embracing a difficult path, one that would set her at odds with social conventions and potentially even endanger her family's good name. Clearly, he intended her life to inspire admiration rather than direct imitation. And yet the very fact that a cleric could write admiringly of Madeleine de Lamoignon's vocation, praising both her private efforts to assist the poor and her more public role raising funds for war relief and the Dames' other charitable causes, underscores the legitimacy that a life of determined Christian service had acquired by the second half of the seventeenth century.[3]

The example of Marie Deslandes and Madeleine de Lamoignon reminds us of the importance of understanding the spiritual currents of the Catholic Reformation in a historical context that embraces changing social values and political realities. Although Deslandes and a handful of other stalwart members of the generation that came of age during the wars of the League continued to exercise leading roles in the Dames de la Charité through midcentury, the younger women who worked alongside them and under their direction had a different spiritual orientation.[4] Penitential asceticism by no means disappeared. Nevertheless, as the century progressed, there was a tendency for lay dévotes, like nuns, to favor internalized mortifications—the willful sacrifice of personal inclination—over ritualized punishments of the body, such as scourging and excessive fasts. Authors of late seventeenth-century pious biographies continued to include a chapter on the subject's mortifications and often still used such phrases as "crucifying her flesh." But where earlier biographies told of self-starvation, flagellation, and bleeding bodies, later ones were more likely to say only that the devout lady worked very long hours, neglected to eat regularly, and did not get enough sleep. Mortifications were depicted as by-products of the subject's dedicated service and not as a self-punishing regimen adopted for its own spiritual ends.

Like their mothers, the younger women remained profoundly Christocentric in their piety, and yet they tended to attach themselves more to the example of the living Christ as teacher and friend to the poor than to the agonies of his passion that had been the favorite subjects of meditation for Barbe Acarie and her peers. The transition was a gradual one. However important the experience of the League may have been in shaping the characteristically ascetic and penitential spirituality that dominated in the initial stages of the Catholic revival, actually living through the League was not essential if a girl's parents or her first teachers and spiritual guides impressed on her their own penitential faith. For example, Catherine de Jésus Nicolas, born in 1589, was too young to have had more than vague childhood memories of the disruptions caused by the wars of the League. This childhood experience may nevertheless have reinforced her precocious preference, at the age of seven or eight, for reading and imitating the lives of ascetic saints. Taking a Feuillant as her spiritual director at the same tender age, she began the life of self-denial and self-mortification that would take her to an early grave.[5] Her characteristic devotion to Christ crucified and desire for atonement through suffering was formed early, and, although it found new forms of expression after she became a Carmelite nun at the age of nineteen, it underwent little fundamental change.

By contrast, Louise de Marillac's spirituality continued to evolve much later in life. Born in 1591, only two years after Catherine Nicolas, Marillac also engaged in vigils and fasts, wore a hair shirt to mortify her body, and wanted nothing more than to become a Capucine nun. Marriage and motherhood disrupted this plan but also kept her in the world and open to a variety of spiritual influences—including the counsels of François de Sales and Jean-Pierre Camus, bishop of Belley, as well as Vincent de Paul—so that her mature spirituality had acquired a quite different character by the time she began to offer guidance to the Filles de la Charité and the dévotes who joined them for religious retreats. Consider, for example, how Louise de Marillac's devotion to the unborn infant Jesus differed from that cultivated by Catherine de Jésus

Nicolas. Where the latter focused obsessively on Christ's suffering as he was deprived for nine long months of the use of his perfect senses, Marillac, although also depicting Jesus as "imprisoned" in Mary's womb, meditated joyously on the communications that passed between the "Divine Infant" and his mother during the time when "she alone possessed him." A mother herself, Marillac may have drawn on personal experience in describing the little movements that Mary would have felt in her womb, but the "divine communications," the "secrets revealed," and even Christ's "dearest caresses" were products of her religious imagination and not her own pregnancy. Stressing the courage Mary would have drawn from her precious charge, Marillac's meditation reflects a notion of Christ as an interiorized guide and loving source of strength very different from Catherine de Jésus's idea of a suffering God who could be approached only through the imitation of his suffering.[6]

Close attention to the changing spiritual climate of the Catholic revival in France gives us a fresh picture of the movement's evolution and dynamics. Traditional histories, focusing on the so-called positive phase of France's Catholic Reformation considered to have begun only after Henri IV's death in 1610, have tended to ignore the movement's difficult birth amid the agonies of the sixteenth-century Wars of Religion and to dismiss the penitential spirituality that dominated its initial stages as a bizarre and fortunately brief aberration.[7] This book has argued, to the contrary, that the Catholic revival was deeply rooted in the traumas of religious war and in the apocalyptic and penitential spirituality to which the wars gave birth. Even after the wars ended, pious Catholics nurtured a profound desire to engage in acts of atonement to appease the wrath of God, end heresy, and save lost souls. This penitential enthusiasm was not a bizarre aberration but a natural expression of the relationship between physical suffering and divine reward inherent in Christianity's core doctrine of the redemption gained by Christ's death on the cross. As such, it fed a desire for the foundation of reformed religious orders where women might retreat from a sinful world into mortified lives believed to embody participation in Christ's sacrifice and ultimately lead to union with him. The heroic asceticism of the women who first rushed to join the newly founded orders inspired emulation and hence new vocations; it also prompted admiring benefactors to make the generous donations that permitted the movement's rapid spread. In this way, the ascetic impulse that grew out of the religious wars served as the very motor for the Catholic revival.

However natural an expression of Christian ideals, the penitential spirituality that characterized the first stages of the Catholic Reformation was a self-limiting phenomenon. Like any movement born of the extreme emotions produced in moments of crisis, its ardor was bound to fade. In the end, it proved easier to build ascetic convents than to continue to fill them with aspiring saints. But the character of reformed Catholic spirituality gradually changed for other reasons as well. Most important, the introspection the new teachings encouraged led their focus to shift from exteriorized gestures of corporal discipline to interiorized mortifications of the will. Intense self-scrutiny and self-denial came to replace flagellation, excessive fasting, and other dramatic behaviors in the practice of devout piety. The same process of interiorization encouraged pious Catholics to repress the mystical raptures through which they had sought union with God during the initial stages of the penitential enthusiasm in favor of a more internalized form of union thought to occur in just the higher spirit, or soul. In this way, devout Catholics believed, they could be possessed with God and still active in the world.

Often expressed as "leaving God for God," the notion that the highest form of union with God might best be achieved not through prostrating raptures but through an active life of Christian service was essential to the French Catholic Reformation's turn from penitence to charity. As we have seen, this active mysticism was first cultivated in the devout circle around Barbe Acarie, who was herself frequently described as being continually preoccupied in God, even as she went about her most humble tasks. Acarie and her friends brought this same spirit to Paris's Carmelites and other contemplative convents, where it valorized the routine acts of community life. It was also transmitted to the new active communities of filles séculaires. Vincent de Paul paraphrased the idea of leaving God for God when he reminded the Filles de la Charité in one of his first conferences that "when you leave prayer and Holy Mass to serve the poor, you are losing nothing, because service to the poor is going to God and you should see God in them."[8]

Lay dévotes who dedicated their lives to charitable activities, whether individually or, from the 1630s, as members of organized Charités, likewise took to heart Jesus' injunction that whatever you do for another, you do for me (Matthew 25:40). They took as their model the evangelical Jesus—healer, teacher, and friend to the poor—and looked for God in those they served. Moreover, their impulse to charity was rooted in an apostolic desire to assist the souls and not just the bodies of society's unfortunates. As we have seen, lay dévotes felt a mission to catechize the peasants on their estates, the sick and dying patients of the Hôtel-Dieu, and the urban poor of their parishes. Although many preferred to teach only girls or other women, others did not limit their instruction to their own sex. Moreover, women engaged in this mission to save souls with the full knowledge and even approval of male clerics, who, far from resenting women's intrusion into the clergy's monopoly, encouraged their efforts to teach fundamental Christian doctrines as a necessary supplement to a priesthood inadequate in numbers and often education as well.

If the spirituality of the Catholic revival evolved in response to an internal dynamic, it also evolved in response to the external forces of economic depression and war. The rush to found ascetic contemplative convents that dominated the first third of the seventeenth century tapered off by the mid-1630s.

The ascetic impulse had largely spent itself, but other forces were at work as well. The economic recovery that helped finance the first foundations gave way by the 1620s to increasingly troubled times. Taxes rose precipitously on account of France's covert and, after 1635, open participation in the Thirty Years War. Already squeezed between rising rents and stagnant or declining prices, peasants were forced into extremity. Unemployment rose and with it vagrancy and vagabondage. As depression spread to the cities, poverty took on an increasingly visible face. Under these circumstances, it was natural that elites who had the money and will for charitable giving should find it more urgent to help ease the popular misery than to support the voluntary poverty of contemplative nuns. As the problem was obviously too great to solve with individual handouts, pious elites tried instead to address it through the creation of charitable confraternities, hospitals, orphanages, and asylums.

The disruptions of the Fronde—the sacking and pillaging by rival armies, as well as the interruption of the normal agricultural cycle—came hard on the heels of these earlier troubles. The Fronde was not a religious war and so, for all the damage it caused, did not prompt apocalyptic visions and acts of penitential atonement. Rather, its devastations prompted an extraordinary fundraising campaign on the part of the elite Dames de la Charité. But it was not just the poor who suffered as a consequence of the rebellion. The Fronde posed an important break in religious life. In 1649 and again in 1652, nuns from convents located outside Paris's walls scrambled to take refuge in the city, where they crowded into other convents or accepted the hospitality of lay patrons. When the danger receded, they returned to their homes and tried to put their affairs in order. For many communities, however, life was never quite the same. Even religious houses lucky enough to escape the wars unscathed experienced a serious drop in revenues. Families were slow to pay promised pensions, and almsgiving was interrupted—or deflected to other ends. At the same time, the new options for religious life increased competition for girls with handsome dowries, as even girls from elite families began to consider congregations engaged in charitable service instead of the traditionally more prestigious contemplative houses.

The Fronde did not put an end to the revival of Catholic religious life. New religious communities continued to be founded. They included a few contemplative convents, though the greater number were uncloistered teaching congregations or charity hospitals. The next decades were nevertheless difficult ones for contemplative and active congregations alike. A few of the contemplative houses recovered relatively quickly from the vicissitudes of the Fronde. The Visitandines of the faubourg Saint-Jacques, for example, although forced to admit a dozen girls as boarders in 1652 to solve pressing financial problems, had grown strong enough by 1660 to sponsor a new foundation in the rue Montorgueil.[9] But many convents, particularly those established with small endowments during the troubled 1630s and 1640s, struggled to hold on. A few disappeared in the 1650s; others were shut down by order of Parlement, which mandated the closure of a number of "irregularly founded" convents in 1670.[10] Many survived only by adjusting their way of life to the new realities. The Fronde marked the beginning of a new era in which Parisian convents would distinguish themselves by the genteel finishing they gave socially prominent young ladies and the elegant retreat they offered wealthy widows rather than the austerities practiced by their nuns. The change progressed unevenly and overtook different convents at different times. The first signs, however, are clearly visible in the compromises many convents were forced to make in the wake of the Fronde.[11]

Several of the teaching congregations founded in the 1630s also disappeared, and many if not most of the charitable orders struggled against a rising tide of economic difficulty. Lay confraternities suffered the same malaise. The Dames de la Charité appear to have exhausted their initial zeal with the ladies' extraordinary efforts to aid those left destitute on account of the Fronde. The organization continued to exist, but the members' social and economic engagement declined. Many of the ladies had doubtless tired of the heavy demands on their time and money, but a larger change was also taking place in attitudes toward society's unfortunates. The widespread misery that followed the Fronde reinforced the conviction of pious elites that they needed to abandon piecemeal private charity in favor of a new public institution, where the poor would be fed and clothed but also subjected to moralizing sermons and the discipline of regular work. The foundation of the new Hôpital Général in 1656 radically altered the scale and nature of charitable assistance, which became less an expression of Christian compassion and more a campaign for moral reform as mendicants and vagabonds—but also prostitutes, abandoned children, and the mentally ill—began to be rounded up off the streets and forcibly incarcerated, if they did not voluntarily present themselves at the hospital's gates. At the same time that the provision of charitable assistance shifted from the private to the public domain, it ceased being a largely female concern and became instead a male responsibility. Elite women continued to direct the institutions founded earlier in the seventeenth century, but the dominant institution in the era after the Fronde, the new Hôpital Général, was placed entirely under the direction of men.

As with convent life, the Fronde thus marked a watershed in the provision of charity. The changes occurring after this time exceed the bounds of this book, which focuses on the renewal of Catholic religious life that occurred between the wars of the League and the Fronde and, in particular, on women's contributions to this project. Traditional histories have obscured women's active part in shaping the institutions, spirituality, and value system that characterized the Catholic Reformation in France by concentrating too narrowly on the achievements of a handful of great men. Even those women whose names have made it into the standard texts appear as subordinate partners charged with executing the designs of brilliant men. Jeanne de Chantal stands in the shadow of François de Sales, Louise de Marillac of Vincent de Paul; the male saints receive more credit than do the female for founding the religious orders their collaborations produced. In a similar fashion, Barbe Acarie is depicted as animating the devout circle that gathered at her Paris townhouse through her mystical visions rather than her forceful personality, hard work, and organizational skills. Far from restoring women to their proper place in the history of the Catholic Reformation, revisionist historians working outside the confessional traditions that long dominated religious history have tended to diminish this place still further by interpreting the Catholic Reformation as the product of a misogynistic clergy intent on controlling women and locking them behind high convent walls. Their insistence on casting their narratives as stories of frustrated vocations has only reinforced the image of the Catholic Reformation as not only inhospitable to female initiatives but actively hostile to women themselves.

This study of the renewal of Catholic institutions and spirituality that took place in early seventeenth-century Paris has revealed the inadequacy of these interpretive generalizations. The Catholic revival was the product of a vast collaboration between clerics and lay people, women and men. It was not the church but individual donors who built the convents of the Catholic Reformation, and, in Paris, most of the principal benefactors were lay women, the wives or (more often) widows of wealthy aristocrats and officers of the king. Some lay donors merely financed new buildings for established houses, but others played a far more active part in initiating new foundations. They brought reformed nuns from other towns to establish daughter houses, chose at least some of the convents' first novices, and in other ways helped shape the institutions founded with their gifts. In addition to fostering the spread of reformed contemplative orders, pious lay women invented new forms of religious association to serve society's disadvantaged members, especially those of their own sex. They created uncloistered communities of teaching and nursing sisters, ran orphanages and homes for endangered girls, founded charitable confraternities dedicated to serving the poor in their rural and urban parishes, and engaged in extensive fund-raising campaigns to keep the new institutions running and provide relief for victims of war. They did these things with the support and assistance of male collaborators, but the initiative and much of the planning and effort came from the women themselves.

Pious women also contributed to the spiritual side of the Catholic Reformation in ways that are often overlooked. Lay dévotes catechized their children but also their household servants, patients in urban hospitals, and peasants on their estates. A few exceptional lay women even gained a broader reputation for their spiritual wisdom and offered advice and guidance to spiritual "daughters" and "sons." It is the superiors of Paris's reformed convents, however, who offer especially striking examples of spiritual leadership and authority. Prioresses and mistresses of novices played an important pastoral role through the exhortations and lessons they gave their daughters. They served as spiritual guides to the nuns in their communities and directed their conscience in all matters not explicitly reserved for the confessional. The spiritual teachings of distinguished prioresses even extended beyond convent walls through the counsel they offered the lay women and men who frequented their parlors. Some religious communities also adopted a more formal pedagogical role in offering regular lectures for pious lay women and providing them the opportunity to engage in multiday religious retreats. In sum, women were not the victims of a male establishment operating to limit and restrict their roles but full participants and even leaders in the spiritual revival that lay at the heart of the Catholic Reformation in Paris.

To what extent were the conditions that allowed women this prominent role in the Catholic Reformation peculiar to Paris? The question deserves to be asked, though it can be answered only in part, given the current state of knowledge and the problems of generalization. The timing, pace, and thoroughness of Catholic reform differed greatly from one place to another, on account of their disparate political situations and the character of the individuals who assumed a leadership role. A recent study of the career of one Counter-Reformation archbishop in the Spanish Netherlands, for example, has suggested that proximity to Protestant lands caused the prelate to moderate his demand for strict enclosure of religious women. He pragmatically allowed the many active congregations of nursing sisters that existed in his diocese to continue their work in hospitals and private homes unimpeded, because he recognized that they performed essential services and an attempt to force them into the cloister might undermine the Catholic allegiance of the entire community. He also backed off when his demands for strict enclosure of a Benedictine convent met with determined opposition from well-connected nuns: "As he explained later to the nuncio, it was difficult to go 'from one extreme to another' when dealing with such strong-minded well-connected women. It was also imprudent, because unlike in Italy, the nearness of heretics in the Dutch Republic made apostasy—a worse alternative than compromise—attractive to disgruntled nuns."[12] The archbishop's recognition that, despite their vows of obedience, women from prominent families could mount effective opposition to changes imposed from above shows a pragmatic recognition of political realities that most ecclesiastics would have shared. On the other hand, the danger that religious women might choose apostasy over submission was something only bishops in borderlands or areas with significant Protestant minorities would have had to consider.

As this example shows, the implementation of monastic reforms mandated by the Council of Trent had repercussions in the broader community and should not be viewed as a matter that concerned only bishops and the women who owed them obedience. Even in the cities of Italy and Spain, where the repressive power of the church was effectively marshaled to eliminate the challenge posed by Luther's revolt and where clerical authority was enhanced by a new emphasis on order and orthodoxy, reforming bishops met with sometimes surprising levels of resistance on the part of civic leaders and well-connected nuns. Even Carlo Borromeo, the epitome of the Counter-Reformation bishop, had to compromise in his attempt to impose strict enclosure on the convents in his diocese on account of resistance from both stubborn nuns and elite families whose patronage was essential to the convents' financial success. Although he generally succeeded in regulating the external forms of monasticism—imposing strict rules to ensure that the walls were high and the grilles small and heavily barred—he had much less success in altering the internal dynamics of convent life. He forced some outsiders from the cloister by constraining widows, who had traditionally been able to spend many years in a convent without taking vows, to make their profession or return to secular life. He nevertheless found it impossible to shut out the lay world entirely, as most convents depended on the fees paid by the girls they boarded to supplement their inadequate endowment funds. The need to please influential patrons meant that boarders were allowed to receive visitors, come and go from the cloister, and generally disrupt the nuns' reclusive life far more often than the archbishop might have liked.[13] As in Paris, even reformed convents were not sealed off from the world outside but remained rooted in the local community through a multitude of social, economic, and political ties.

From one perspective, the inability of Counter-Reformation bishops to isolate religious women in their cloisters can be seen as a failure of the reforms imposed by the Council of Trent. However, it can be more fruitfully interpreted as a sign of the successful integration of religious life into the larger society of which its members remained a part, despite the vows that proclaimed them dead to the secular world. Early modern convents were not simply warehouses where superfluous daughters could be retired from the marriage market and secluded from view. All but the poorest convents represented concentrations of wealth and social power that could exert important leverage on the secular community that surrounded them, and important questions still need to be answered about the ways this wealth and power were used and how these uses changed over time. Will we not find many nuns who, like Milanese Angelics Paola Antonia and Agata Sfondrati, made effective use of their position to aid their families' social and political ambitions?[14] Or nuns whose patronage of the arts created lasting monuments in their community, as well as adding to the glory of their family name?

Will we also find nuns who used their influence for more purely spiritual ends, sponsoring sermons by charismatic preachers, catechizing the daughters of townspeople, and offering guidance to women, and possibly also men, who visited their parlors? Perhaps the greatest gap in the current literature concerns this question of women's exercise of spiritual authority. Did women in other parts of Europe display the same leadership qualities as the women discussed in this book, or was the Catholic Reformation in Paris unique in this regard? I am confident that we can generalize from the Parisian case to other French cities. The close communication and overlap of personnel between new Counter-Reformation houses founded in the capital and their sister houses in other French towns suggest that the women who led the religious revival in provincial cities, whether native to these cities or sent from Paris, were just as respected for their spiritual insights and authority as their Parisian sisters were. Whether the same can be said of women in other countries remains to be seen.

We know that on the Italian peninsula and in Spain gender roles were more restricted and the church's political and social authority less subject to challenge than in France. Historians of both regions have credited the church with successfully silencing "holy women" who assumed too public a role. The Italian case is particularly interesting because the circumstances that allowed women to assume an active religious role at the start of the sixteenth century bear a strong resemblance to the situation in France at the century's end. The shock of the French invasions of Italy and the trauma of warfare on an unprecedented and terrifying scale awakened an anguished religiosity characterized by asceticism, apocalyptic visions, and fear of divine judgment. In the unsettled conditions, some women assumed an unusual public role as charismatic figures, objects of devotion, and even political prophets. The mystical and often ecstatic spirituality that characterized these "living saints" closely parallels that of French dévotes who came of age during the wars of the League, as does their vision of a reformed and invigorated church and their enthusiasm for apostolic service. And yet, the moment of opportunity for Italian women was brief. By the 1540s, political circumstances had stabilized and the threat posed by Luther's revolt had awakened the repressive forces of the institutional church. Placing a new premium on orthodoxy and order, church leaders put a speedy end to women's public mission, silencing prophetic voices and forcing innovative communities into the decorum of the cloister.[15]

In Spain, too, fear of heresy prompted a relentless insistence on orthodoxy and a suspicion of "holy women" who assumed public roles. Although Protestantism itself represented only a very small danger on the Iberian peninsula, Spanish clerics mounted a campaign against "illuminism" that threatened even doctrinally orthodox Catholics if they were inclined toward mysticism, because they were seen as following their own lights instead of bowing to the superior authority of the hierarchical church. Even Teresa of Avila was twice brought before the Inquisition to defend her orthodoxy. The policy was not gender-specific; Ignatius of Loyola had to defend himself before the Inquisition as well. The gender biases common at the time nevertheless operated to ensure that the voices of female mystics were silenced even more firmly than those of men.[16]

It would be wrong, however, to equate women's spiritual leadership with dramatic prophecies and public missions. As we have seen, French women exercised spiritual authority in much quieter but nonetheless effective ways. Only more research will show the extent to which women in other parts of Europe performed the same roles. Was the losing battle Ana de Jesús and other Carmelite prioresses fought in Spain to direct the consciences of their nuns symptomatic of a widespread disapproval of women's spiritual leadership? Were women in other Counter-Reformation orders able to exhort, instruct, and probe the consciences of their nuns? Did they offer spiritual advice to lay women, and potentially even men, in their parlors? And what role did new active orders in other parts of Europe play in catechizing girls and instructing their mothers through public conferences and guided retreats? Vincent de Paul founded his first Charité on a Roman model. What were the precedents for this sort of female engagement in charity, and who else followed this lead?[17] Much work remains to be done before we have adequate answers to these and other questions.

It is possible, even probable, that circumstances were more favorable to women's independent action in Paris than in most other parts of Europe. The city had the largest concentration of well-educated, wealthy, and cultured women on the continent. With a prominent role at court, especially under the regencies of Marie de Medici and Anne of Austria, and in Parisian salons, elite women were unusually visible on the public scene. Wives of magistrates and other royal officers enjoyed a relatively large sphere of independent action, as their husbands' professional obligations frequently caused the men to abandon the management of domestic affairs, including supervision of the often extensive estates they owned in the countryside, to the women of the family. Legal traditions that permitted daughters to inherit significant wealth, along with a common tendency to appoint widows as the guardians of minor children and administrators of their husband's estates, also played a part.[18] It is no coincidence that many of the women who founded new religious and semireligious communities were wealthy widows with experience in managing both money and people. Nor is it coincidental that many of the prioresses most celebrated for their spiritual counsel were women who entered religious life not as girls but as widows with some experience of the world and its ways.

All of these factors contributed to the active part women played in the Catholic revival in Paris, and they combine to suggest that opportunities for female initiative here were indeed unparalleled. This does not mean, however, that women were merely objects of repression elsewhere in Europe. There is good reason to suspect that, though unique in scale, women's contributions to the revival of both religious institutions and spirituality in Paris were not unique in kind. Pious biographies poured forth from printing presses in Italy, Spain, and other Catholic regions of Europe, just as they did in France, offering a variety of models of holiness for women to admire and imitate. Do these lives not reveal the possibilities open to women, as well as the limits on their roles?[19] The Catholic Reformation was a complex movement that changed and evolved over time. Despite the church's efforts to control and direct the movement from above, a vast grassroots effort was required to fund and administer new religious institutions, catechize an ignorant populace, fortify believers, and revivify the faith. Surely Paris is not the only city in which pious women played an essential role in these tasks.

LIBRARY, UNIVERSITY OF CHESTER

Biographical Appendix

Absolu, Jeanne (1557–1637). Daughter of Nicolas Absolu, receveur du roi in the county of Dreux and later in Paris. Married in 1575 to Antoine Hotman, a lawyer who served as avocat général in Parlement and as an échevin during the time of the League but shifted his allegiance to Henri IV in good time and worked for peace. The mother of four children, she adopted the life of a lay dévote after her husband's death in 1596. Drawn to religious life, she briefly entered the Capucines but, finding herself spiritually arid, returned to pursue spiritual enlightenment in the world before eventually finding her true vocation at the abbey of Hautes-Bruyères, where her eldest daughter was already a nun. She made her vows at the age of sixty. Her mystical spirituality, much influenced by Benoît de Canfield, inspired Jean Auvray (or Aubray), the spiritual director at Hautes-Bruyères, to publish a pious biography in 1640.[1]

Acarie, Barbe (Blessed **Marie de l'Incarnation**) (1566–1618). Daughter of Nicolas Aurillot, seigneur de Champlâtreux, conseiller du roi et maître ordinaire en sa Chambre des comptes, and Marie Luillier, daughter of Christophe Luillier, seigneur de la Malmaison. Married in 1582 to Pierre Acarie, conseiller du roi et maître ordinaire en sa Chambre des comptes, with whom she had three daughters and three sons. Active supporters of the Holy League, for which Pierre Acarie was exiled from Paris from 1594 until 1598, after which the Acaries' house on the rue des Juifs became a center of dévot action. Encouraged the reform of Montmartre and other convents; most celebrated as founder of the Discalced

Carmelites in Paris, but also aided the foundation of the Ursulines in Paris. Active as a lay dévote until her husband's death in 1613, after which she took religious vows as a Carmelite lay sister at Amiens in 1614, later moving to Pontoise, where she died in 1618. Her *Vrays exercices* were published in 1622. Beatified in 1791[2]

Acarie, Marguerite (Mère **Marguerite du Saint-Sacrement**) (1590–1660). Daughter of Pierre Acarie, conseiller du roi et maître ordinaire en sa Chambre des comptes, and Barbe Aurillot. Entered the Carmelite monastery of the Incarnation in Paris in 1605 and made her profession in 1607. Served as prioress in Tours and the second Paris convent, the Couvent de la Mère de Dieu, among other positions.[3] Her advice for "Christian and religious conduct" has been published, as have many of her letters.

Aiguillon, Marie de **Vignerot** du Pont de Courlay, duchesse d' (1604–1675). Daughter of René de Vignerot, seigneur du Pont de Courlay, and Françoise du Plessis de Richelieu, a sister of the cardinal de Richelieu. Married against her will in 1620 to Antoine du Roure, seigneur de Combalet (d. 1622), a nephew of the royal favorite Luynes. Entered Carmelite convent in 1623 but left in 1624 in obedience to her uncle the cardinal, who attached her to Marie de Medici as dame d'atours. Said to have been very powerful at court during Richelieu's lifetime, she remained close to the royal family even after his death. An important patron of Counter-Reformation convents and very devout, however worldly her activities during Richelieu's period of power. Her gifts helped fund the Filles du Calvaire du Marais, the Bernardines Réformées du Précieux Sang, the second Paris convent of the Filles de la Croix, the Filles de Saint-Joseph, the Madelonnettes, and the Filles de Notre-Dame de la Miséricorde, among others. An early member of the Dames de la Charité, she served as president of the organization from 1652 until 1675 and was one of the members convoked by Vincent de Paul to discuss the future of the Filles de la Providence after the death of Marie Lumague in 1657. Buried in a Carmelite habit when she died in 1675.

Arbouze, Marguerite d' (Mère **Marguerite de Sainte-Gertrude**) (1580–1626). Daughter of Gilbert de Veni d'Arbouze, chevalier, seigneur de Villemont, gentilhomme ordinaire de la Chambre du roi Henri III and lieutenant de cent hommes d'armes, and Jeanne de Pinac. Destined for religious life from childhood, she entered a convent in Lyons at the age of nine and took her vows there but later insisted on moving to a convent where the rule would be more exactly observed. Rejected by the Capucines and Carmelites, whose rule forbade taking women who had made vows at other convents, but accepted at Montmartre, where she did a second novitiate and was subsequently named prioress of the new daughter house at Ville-l'Evêque. Named abbess of Val-de-Grâce by the king in 1618, she undertook a much needed reform of the abbey, which she had transferred to

Paris in 1621. Anne of Austria served as patron of the splendid new convent of Val-de-Grâce. Left Paris in 1626 to found a convent in La Charité.

Arnauld, Jacqueline (Mère **Marie-Angélique**) (1591–1661). Daughter of Antoine Arnauld, a famous lawyer, and Catherine Marion, daughter of Simon Marion, avocat général au Parlement de Paris. Raised as a Protestant, Antoine Arnauld is thought to have converted to Catholicism after the Saint-Bartholomew's Day Massacre. He acquired the position of coadjutrice of the Abbey of Port-Royal for his second daughter, Jacqueline, when she was eight, but the pope refused to confirm the position because of her age. Arnauld nevertheless placed Jacqueline as a novice at the Cistercian abbey of Maubuisson, where she took her vows in 1600 at the age of nine, adopting the name Marie-Angélique. In 1601, Arnauld applied for papal bulls under his daughter's new name, giving her age as seventeen. The bulls arrived in July 1602, and eleven-year-old Angélique Arnauld took up her position as coadjutrice at Port-Royal. She began the convent's reform in 1609. The success of her efforts caused her to be called to aid in restoring Maubuisson to regular observance of its rule in 1618. She returned to Port-Royal in 1622, bringing with her some of the nuns from Maubuisson. A gift from Catherine Marion allowed the nuns of Port-Royal to construct a new convent in Paris in 1626. Mère Angélique left Port-Royal again in 1633 to try to establish a new institute dedicated to the Saint-Sacrement, but the institute failed for a variety of reasons and she returned to Port-Royal, where the nuns continued the cult of the Blessed Sacrament to which the failed institute had been dedicated. While at the convent of the Saint-Sacrement, Mère Angélique met and took as her spiritual director Jean Duvergier de Hauranne, abbé de Saint-Cyran. Her fidelity to his ideas led Port-Royal into the Jansenist quarrels.[4]

Aurillot, Barbe. See **Acarie**, Barbe.

Aurillot, Mademoiselle. See **Du Drac**, Marie.

Beauvilliers, Marie de (1574–1657). Daughter of Claude de Beauvilliers, comte de Saint-Aignan, and Marie Babou de la Bourdaisière. Placed in a convent at the age of seven, she asked for the habit at twelve, began her novitiate at fifteen, and took vows at sixteen in the abbey of Beaumont. A brother-in-law procured the position of abbess of Montmartre for her in 1598. She undertook a long and difficult reform of the abbey, publishing new constitutions and returning it to regular observance of its rule, and died there after serving as abbess for sixty years. Her *Conférences spirituelles* have been published.

Bonneau, Marie (Madame de **Miramion**) (1629–1696). Daughter of Jacques Bonneau, seigneur de Rubelles, conseiller et secrétaire du roi. Married in 1645 to Jean-Jacques de Beauharnais, seigneur de Miramion, conseiller du roi en sa cour du Parlement de Paris, and widowed the same year. Mother of one daughter, who was put to board at the convent of the Visitation, where Marie Bonneau also resided part of the year. Made a vow of chastity in 1649 after a retreat at the motherhouse of the Filles de la Charité and took up the life of a lay dévote. Formed a group of twelve girls to teach school and care for the sick in her parish, later joining them with another group of dévotes under the name of the Filles de Sainte-Geneviève. Also founded an orphanage, a refuge for endangered girls (later absorbed into the Hôpital Général), and a retreat house, and after 1678 served as lay superior of the Filles de la Providence.

Breauté, Charlotte **Harlay de Sancy**, marquise de (Mère **Marie de Jésus**) (1579–1652). Daughter of Nicolas de Harlay de Sancy, who served as ambassador to England, maître d'hôtel du roi et surintendant de ses finances, and in other ministerial positions under Henri IV, and Marie de Moreau. Harlay was a Protestant who converted after Henri IV's conversion, but the daughters of the marriage were raised Catholic like their mother. Married at eighteen to Pierre de **Breauté**, who died eighteen months later fighting in Flanders. Their only son was turned over to his grandfather to raise. After her husband's death she adopted the life of a lay dévote, frequenting the devout circle around Barbe Acarie. Entered the Carmelite monastery of the Incarnation in December 1604 and took her vows a year later. Contributed 10,000 livres toward foundation of the Pontoise convent. Elected assistant prioress of Paris's convent of the Incarnation in 1607, she subsequently served several terms as prioress.

Brienne, Louise de **Béon de Massez**, comtesse de (?–1665). Daughter of Bernard de Béon, gouverneur of Saintonge, Angoulême, and the Aunis, and Louise de Luxembourg. Married to Henri-Auguste de Loménie, comte de Brienne and de Montbron, seigneur de la Ville-aux-Clercs. Active Dame de la Charité and one of those convoked to determine the future of the Filles de la Providence on the death of Marie Lumague in 1657. Founded a house of Filles de la Charité at Brienne. Said to have been a confidante of Anne of Austria, accompanying her on her visits to convents, and also serving as spokeswoman for the poor to queen. Founder of the Carmelite convent of Saint-Denis; also with her husband promised a 50,000 livre gift toward the Congrégation de Notre-Dame's foundation in the rue du Chasse-Midi, though it appears that the latter donation was never actually made.[5]

Brûlart, (?–?) Madeleine. Daughter of Pierre Brûlart, seigneur de Sillery et de Berny, conseiller du roi et président en sa cour de Parlement, and Marie Cauchon. Married in 1587 to Guichard Faure, maître d'hôtel ordinaire du roi et conseiller en le conseil d'Etat (d. 1623). Principal patrons of the hospital of the Charité Notre-Dame; also made a large donation to the Récollets, in whose church she and her husband were buried.

Caumont, Anne de. See **Saint-Paul**, comtesse de.

Combalet, Madame de. See **Aiguillon**, duchesse d'.

Condé, Charlotte-Marguerite de **Montmorency**, princesse de (1594–1650). Daughter of Henri de Montmorency, connétable de France, and Louise de Budos. Wife of Henri II de Bourbon, prince de Condé, first prince of the blood, and mother of Louis II de Bourbon, duc de Condé (le Grand Condé); Armand de Bourbon, prince de Conti; and Anne-Geneviève de Bourbon-Condé, duchesse de Longueville. Important patron of the Carmelite monastery of the Incarnation, where she had her own apartment. Also active in other dévot causes, including being a member of the Dames de la Charité from at least 1640.

Dauvaine, Marie-Agnès (1602–1665). Daughter of Antoine Dauvaine, gouverneur of Brie, and Anne de Salignac. From the age of thirteen lived with the comtesse de Salme, who brought her to the ducal court of Nancy. Refusing her parents' plans to marry her, entered convent of the Annonciades Célestes at Nancy in 1618 and made her profession the following year. Came to Paris in 1622 to help found the Annonciades' new convent there, serving first as mistress of novices and after 1635 as prioress.

Deslandes, Marie (Madame de **Lamoignon**) (1576–1651). Married to Chrétien de Lamoignon, conseiller du roi et président en sa cour de Parlement (d. 1636), by whom she had one son and three daughters who survived to adulthood. With her husband, gave generously to the Visitandines. Helped the Récollettes of Verdun establish a Paris convent in 1627. One of the early members of the Dames de la Charité and their president from 1643 until her death in 1651. Also formed an association of clerics and lay people who agreed to visit, assist, and console prisoners and to work to free those imprisoned for debt.

Du Drac, Marie (Mademoiselle **Aurillot**) (1544–1590). Daughter of Adrien Du Drac, vicomte d'Ay, seigneur de Beaulieu and Mareuil, conseiller du roi dans son Parlement de Paris, and Charlotte Raponnel, dame de Bandeville and Vignolles. Married at seventeen to Jacques Aurillot, also a conseiller au Parlement de Paris, by whom she had five children who survived to adulthood. A Minim tertiary, she lived the retired life of a lay dévote between her husband's death in 1572 and her own in 1590. A strong supporter of the Holy League. Some of her spiritual exercises and letters were published after her death by her spiritual director, Antoine Estienne.[6]

Faure, Madame de. See **Brûlart**, Madeleine.

Fayet, Geneviève (Madame **Goussault**) (ca. 1582–1638). Married in 1613 to Antoine Goussault, seigneur de Souvigny, conseiller du roi et président en sa Chambre des comptes de Paris (d. 1634). Engaged in charitable good works with Louise de Marillac and Marie Lumague from at least 1632; founder of the Dames de la Charité at the Hôtel-Dieu, she served as the group's president until her death in September 1638.

Fontaines, Madeleine du Bois de (Mère **Madeleine de Saint-Joseph**) (1578–1637). Daughter of Antoine du Bois, seigneur de Fontaines, and Marie

Prudhomme. Recognized her religious vocation early and debated whether to enter the Capucine or Carmelite convents being planned for Paris. Chose the Carmelites and became one of their first novices. Took her vows in November 1605 and was immediately named mistress of novices. First elected prioress in 1608, she was the first French prioress and subsequently served a number of terms in this position. A book of advice for the conduct of novices, a spiritual biography of one of her nuns, and many of her spiritual letters have been published.[7]

Gallois, Louise (Mademoiselle **Jourdain**; in religion Mère **Louise de Jésus**) (1569–1628). Daughter of Charles Gallois and Claude Riom. Married Guillaume Jourdain, described in her biographies only as a "God-fearing and virtuous man," by whom she had several children. Adopted the life of a secular dévote after Jourdain's death and was introduced by her confessor to Barbe Acarie's circle. Went to Spain to help escort the Carmelite nuns coming to establish the new French order and entered the convent of the Incarnation among the first group of novices. Helped make the new Pontoise foundation and, after briefly returning to Paris, made her profession at Pontoise in 1605. Assisted with the Dijon foundation and became prioress there when Ana de Jesús left for Flanders. Also served as prioress at Dôle and Besançon.[8]

Gobelin, Anne, dame de **Plainville** (?–1627). Daughter of Balthasar Gobelin, conseiller du roi et président en sa Chambre des comptes, and Anne Abra de Raconis. Married Charles d'Estournel, chevalier and seigneur de Plainville, gouverneur of Corbie and capitaine de la première des quatre compagnies des gardes du corps de sa majesté. Principal founder of the Feullantines' Paris convent.[9]

Gondi, Charlotte-Marguerite de. See **Maignelay**, marquise de.

Gondi, Madame de. See **Silly**, Marguerite de.

Goussault, Madame. See **Fayet**, Geneviève.

Hannivel, Marie d' (Mère **Marie de la Trinité**) (1579–1647). Daughter of Robert d'Hannivel, chevalier and seigneur de Saint-Etienne de Rouvray, near Rouen, and Marie Aubery, daughter of Jean Aubery, conseiller et secrétaire du roi. Precociously devout, she refused marriage and, after briefly debating whether to join the Carmelites or Capucines, decided on the Carmelites, where she became one of the first novices. Fluent in Spanish, she was especially close to the Spanish mothers and often served as their interpreter. She aided in the foundation of the Pontoise and Dijon convents, taking her vows at the latter in November 1605. Subsequently served as prioress of Pontoise, Amiens, Rouen, and Caen, and as founding prioress for two convents in Troyes; she also assisted with the foundation of Châtillon.[10]

Jourdain, Mademoiselle. See **Gallois**, Louise.

La Grange, Jeanne (Madamoiselle de) (?–1630). Daughter of Louis de La

Grange, écuyer, sieur de Trianon, and Louise Guybert. Principal donor and founder of the Franciscan Third Order Penitent convent of Sainte-Elisabeth. Also made gifts to Franciscan Third Order Penitent friary of Franconville.

Lamoignon, Madame de. See **Deslandes**, Marie.

Lamoignon, Madeleine (Mademoiselle de) (1609–1687). Daughter of Chrétien de Lamoignon, conseiller du roi et président en sa cour de Parlement, and Marie Deslandes. Chose not to marry or enter a convent, instead becoming one of the most active Dames de la Charité. Opened a store in the family home where people could contribute clothing and other goods for the poor and devoted her life to charitable service.

Le Gras, Mademoiselle. See **Marillac**, Louise de.

Longueville, Antoinette d'**Orléans**, princesse de (1572–1618). Daughter of Léonor d'Orléans, duc de Longueville, a descendant of Charles V through the illegitimate line of Dunois, the "Bastard of Orléans," and Marie de Bourbon, duchesse d'Estouteville and comtesse de Saint-Paul. Married in 1588 to Charles de Gondi, marquis de Belle-Isle, who died in 1596. Left her two young sons with family and ran away to join the Feuillantine convent at Toulouse in 1599; ordered by the pope to become coadjutrice to her aunt, Eléonore d'Orléans, abbesse de Fontevraud, in 1605, but delayed taking up the position until 1607. Left Fontevraud when her aunt died in 1611, renouncing her right to be abbess. As her family still refused to allow her to return to Toulouse, instead reformed the convent of Lencloître with some nuns from Fontevraud. Wanting to live under a still stricter observance of the Benedictine rule, she and some of the nuns of Lencloître moved to Poitiers, where she founded a new convent dedicated to Notre-Dame du Calvaire in 1617. Although she died before the new house was fully established, its practices became the basis of the new order of Calvary founded by Capuchin Père Joseph de Paris in 1621.[11]

Longueville, Catherine d'**Orléans**, princesse de (ca. 1565–1638). Daughter of Léonor d'Orléans, duc de Longueville (1551–1573), a descendant of Charles V through the illegitimate line of Dunois, the "Bastard of Orléans," and Marie de Bourbon, duchesse d'Estouteville and comtesse de Saint-Paul. Held captive by the Holy League in Amiens. Refused to marry and became an important religious patron, most famously as founder of the Carmelite monastery of the Incarnation.

Luillier, Hélène-Angélique (1592–1650). Daughter of François Luillier, seigneur d'Interville, and Anne Brachet, dame de Frouville. Married at the age of sixteen to Thomas Gobelin, seigneur du Val, maître ordinaire en la Chambre des comptes, but the marriage was nullified in 1620, at which time she retired to the Visitandines' Paris convent. Took the Visitandine habit in February 1621, making a founder's gift of 45,000 livres, but arranging that her sister, Marie Luillier, dame de Villeneuve, enjoy the privi-

leges of founder in her place. Made her vows one year later and served as
superior of the convent almost continually between 1627 and 1649.

Luillier, Madeleine (Madame de **Sainte-Beuve**) (1562–1620). Youngest daughter of Jean Luillier, seigneur de Boulancourt, conseiller du roi et président
en sa Chambre des comptes (d. 1563), and Renée de Nicolay, a widow by
her first marriage to Dreux Hennequin. Married at nineteen to Claude III
Le Roux, seigneur de Sainte-Beuve, conseiller du roi en son Parlement de
Paris, who died three years later. Participated actively in Holy League politics, along with her Hennequin kin; made lengthy retreats in the convents
of Chelles and Saint-Pierre de Reims after the League, returning to Paris
to take up charitable good works in the company of Barbe Acarie and
other dévotes in 1598. Worked actively for return of the Jesuits to Paris
and served as cofounder of their noviciate house before founding the Ursulines.[12]

Luillier, Marie (Madame de **Villeneuve**) (1597–1650). Daughter of François
Luillier, seigneur d'Interville, and Anne Brachet, dame de Frouville. Married in 1613 to Claude Marcel, seigneur de Villeneuve-le-Roi, conseiller du
roi et maître des requêtes ordinaires, by whom she had two daughters. Enjoyed founder's privileges at the Visitandines' first Paris convent, on account of her sister Hélène-Angélique's large donation to the house; engaged in charitable works with the poor and was a member of the Dames
de la Charité. Principally known as founder of the Congrégation des Filles
de la Croix.[13]

Lumague, Marie (Mademoiselle **Pollalion**) (1599–1657). Married in 1617 to
François Pollalion, gentilhomme ordinaire du Roi and conseiller d'Etat,
but soon widowed. Named dame d'honneur of the duchesse d'Orléans but
quit court when her husband died. Founded the Filles de la Providence de
Dieu in 1630 to shelter and educate girls whose poverty was a threat to
their chastity and continued to direct the house until her death in 1657.
Member of the Dames de la Charité from the organization's beginning.

Luxembourg, Marie de. See **Mercœur**, duchesse de.

Maignelay, Charlotte-Marguerite de **Gondi**, marquise de (1570 or 1571–1650).
Daughter of Albert de Gondi, duc and maréchal de Retz, a favorite of
Catherine de Medici, and Catherine de Clermont, a clever and wealthy
heiress, whose literary salon was a precursor to the more celebrated salons
of the seventeenth century. Married at seventeen to Florimond Halwuin,
duc and pair de France and marquis de Maignelay (d. 1591), by whom she
had one son, who died in childhood, and one daughter. According to one
source, she dragged her husband into the Holy League, despite the fact
that most of her family and his were royalists, but at the point of his death
he was preparing to deliver la Fère, for which he served as military governor, to Henri de Navarre.[14] Refused to remarry and devoted the rest of her
life to pious good works. Her powerful family prevented her from becom-

ing a Capucine, but she aided the convent financially and made frequent retreats there and at the Carmelites. A ubiquitous presence in devout society, she began working with Barbe Acarie to aid the poor around 1600 and continued to take part in a wide variety of charitable projects until her death at the age of eighty. Most noted as a founder of the congregation of the Oratoire and the principal donor for the Filles de la Madeleine, she contributed to a variety of causes and is said to have had a special avocation for rescuing girls from the street.[15]

Marillac, Saint Louise de (Mademoiselle **Le Gras**) (1591–1660). The natural daughter of Louis de Marillac (1556–1604) and a woman who has never been identified. Married to Antoine Le Gras, secrétaire des commandements de Marie de Medicis (d. 1625), by whom she had one son, Michel Le Gras (b. 1613). Took Vincent de Paul as her spiritual director in 1625 and dedicated her life to charitable service, having vowed not to remarry. Founded the parish Charité of Saint-Nicolas-du-Chardonnet in 1630 and spent much of her time visiting and revitalizing rural and urban Charités. Principally known as founder of the Filles de la Charité, which she directed until her death in 1660.

Mercœur, Marie de **Luxembourg**, duchesse de (1563–1623). Daughter of Sébastien de Luxembourg, duc de Penthièvre and pair de France (d. 1569), and Marie de Beaucaire, dame de Puyguillon (d. 1613). Married in 1575 to Philippe-Emmanuel de Lorraine, duc de Mercœur (d. 1602), by whom she had two children, a son who died young and a daughter, who married César, duc de Vendôme, an illegitimate son of Henri IV. Took charge of the foundation of the Capucines after the death of her sister-in-law Louise de Lorraine, the widow of Henri III, and the duc de Mercœur. In the end, her donations considerably outweighed Louise de Lorraine's original bequest.

Miramion, Madame de. See **Bonneau**, Marie.

Montmorency, Charlotte-Marguerite. See **Condé**, princesse de.

Neuvillette, Madeleine **Robineau**, baronne de (1610–1657). Daughter of Guy Robineau and Marie de Mogorny. Married at twenty-five to Christophe de Champagne, baron de Neuvillette, who died at the siege of Arras (1640). Converted to the devout life by Gaston de Renty shortly before her husband's death. Remained a lay dévote, visiting prisons and engaging in other works of charity. Bremond calls Robineau's letters "unreadable" on account of their "solemn emptiness," and characterizes her as having "something about her of the précieuse, something of the dévote, in the worst sense of the word, and something of the saint. A curious and rare mix."[16]

Nicolas, Catherine (Sœur **Catherine de Jésus**) (1589–1623). Daughter of a Bordelais merchant named Charles Nicolas. Precociously pious, she was brought to Paris in 1608 by Marie Séguier and her husband, Marc-

Antoine de Gourgues, founders of the Carmelites' Bordeaux convent, and remained some time in the home of Barbe Acarie before entering the Carmelite convent of the Incarnation without a dowry. Her penitential asceticism contributed to her early death, but her piety so impressed Madeleine de Saint-Joseph de Fontaines that she wrote a pious life of Catherine de Jésus, which was first published in 1631.[17]

Plainville, Madame de. See **Gobelin**, Anne.

Pollalion, Mademoiselle. See **Lumague**, Marie.

Robineau, Madeleine. See **Neuvillette**, baronne de.

Saint-Paul, Anne de **Caumont**, comtesse de (1574–1642). Daughter of Geoffroy de Caumont, a Protestant (d. 1574), and Marguerite de Lustrac. Converted from Protestantism in 1587. Married in 1595 to François d'Orléans de Longueville, comte de Saint-Paul (d. 1631), who served as gouverneur of Picardy, then lieutenant général in Orléans. Contributed to foundation of the Carmelite convent and Jesuit collège in Amiens, but most important as founder of the Dominican convent of the Filles de Saint-Thomas in Paris. Said to have been generous in her charity to the Hôtel-Dieu, Enfants Trouvés, and other institutions and to have taken a monthly turn personally serving the poor in the Hôtel-Dieu.[18]

Sévin, Marie (Mère **Marie de la Trinité**) (1571–1656). Daughter of François Sévin, seigneur de Villeran, conseiller du roi et président dans sa Cour des aides, and Antoinette Rebours. Married Jacques de Pincé, seigneur du Coudray, conseiller du roi et maître en sa Chambre des comptes, who died only a year later in 1598. Lived as a lay dévote until entering the Carmelite monastery of the Incarnation, where she made her profession in 1605. Served as prioress at Rouen and Pontoise and went on to serve as founding prioress of nine Carmelite convents before dying at Auch. The autobiographical memoirs she composed on the instructions of her spiritual director were subsequently assembled into a book but not published until 1930.[19]

Silly, Marguerite de, dame de Montmirail (Madame de **Gondi**) (1580–1625). Daughter of Antoine de Silly, comte de Rochepot, baron de Montmirail, seigneur de Commercy, chevalier des ordres du roi, and gouverneur d'Anjou, ambassador to Spain, and Marie de Lannoy. Married in 1604 to Philippe-Emmanuel de Gondi, comte de Joigny, marquis des Iles d'Or, chevalier des ordres du roi, and general of the galleys of France, third son of Albert de Gondi, duc de Retz, peer and marshal of France, and Claude-Catherine de Clermont de Vivonne and brother of Henri de Gondi, the first cardinal de Retz. Mother of three sons, one of whom was Jean-François-Paul de Gondi, the second cardinal de Retz. With Vincent de Paul's aid, sponsored Charités on her extensive estates and, with her husband, served as patron for the Congrégation de la Mission.[20]

Sublet des Noyers, Madeleine (Mère **Madeleine de Saint-Jean**) (1584–?).

Daughter of Jean Sublet des Noyers, conseiller du roi et maître en sa Chambre des comptes, and Madeleine Bochart, daughter of Jean Bochart, seigneur de Champigny, and sister of Capuchin Père Honoré de Champigny. Entered the Feuillantine convent at Toulouse in 1599 and made her profession the following year. Returned to Paris in 1622 as one of the original nuns at the Feuillantines' new Paris convent.[21]

Sublet des Noyers, Marie (Mère **Marie de Saint-Benoît**) (ca. 1588–?). Daughter of Jean Sublet des Noyers, conseiller du roi et maître en sa Chambre des comptes, and Madeleine Bochart, daughter of Jean Bochart, seigneur de Champigny, and sister of Capuchin Père Honoré de Champigny. Entered the Feuillantine convent at Toulouse in 1600 at the age of twelve and made her profession in 1604. Returned to Paris in 1622 as one of the original nuns at the Feuillantines' new Paris convent.[22]

Tixier, Marie du, baronne de Veuilly. See **Veuilly**, baronne de.

Tudert, Marie de (Mère **Marie de Jésus**) (1566–1638). Daughter of Claude de Tudert and Nicole Hennequin. Married first to Mathurin Roigne, seigneur de Boisvert, conseiller du roi en son Parlement de Paris; remarried in 1586 Jean Séguier, seigneur d'Autry, lieutenant civil de la prévôté de Paris, bringing 58,000 livres to the marriage. Mother of five children by the second marriage, among them Pierre Séguier (b. 1588), chancellor of France, and Jeanne de Jésus Séguier (b. 1596), a Carmelite nun. Adopted the life of a lay dévote after the death of her husband in 1596 and entered the Carmelite convent of the Visitation in 1613, after her children were grown. Took her vows in 1615, subsequently serving as prioress in Bordeaux before returning to Paris, where she died at the age of sixty-two.[23]

Verdille, Renée de Livenne de (Mère **Renée de Sainte-Cécile**) (ca. 1634–?). Orphaned young, she was married at thirteen to Jean de Besançon, the second son of her guardian. She fled after several years of marriage and entered the priory of the Saint-Sépulchre (Bellechasse) in Paris, where she was received as a founder and took vows in 1652, concealing the fact that she was married. In 1657, her husband having died, she confessed her married state to the prior's canonical superior and began proceedings to leave religious life but ceased her proceedings when the nuns of Bellechasse expressed their desire to elect her as prioress, despite the fact that she was underage (and married, though the other nuns did not know this). The pope granted the necessary dispensations in 1658, allowing for her election. She subsequently led the financially troubled convent into a new period of prosperity, largely through boarding the daughters of rich residents of the faubourg Saint-Germain and renting of properties the convent owned.

Veuilly, Marie du **Tixier**, baronne de (Mère **Marie de Saint-Charles**) (1593–1665). Daughter of Amos du Tixier, seigneur de Maisons and Brie, gentilhomme ordinaire de la chambre du roi Henri IV, and Françoise Hurault.

A Protestant, Tixier converted on his deathbed, after which Hurault adopted the life of a lay dévote until her children were reared and then became a Récollette at the convent of Sainte-Claire in Verdun, where one of her daughters was already a nun. The eldest of the five children who survived to adulthood, Marie was raised by her maternal grandmother and married at the age of fifteen to Charles Ripault, baron de Veuilly. He died seven years later, when she was pregnant with her first child. A year later, she entered the Franciscan Third Order Penitent convent of Sainte-Elisabeth clandestinely, to avoid family opposition and pressure to re-marry. She took the habit in January 1617 and made her vows in March 1618. Elected superior in December 1622. The pious biography by Carmelite Jean Macé contains some of her spiritual writings; a fictionalized version of her life was published by Jean-Pierre Camus, bishop of Belley, under the title *La pieuse Julie* in 1625.[24]

Vignerot, Marie de. See **Aiguillon**, duchesse d'.

Ville-aux-Clercs, Madame. See **Brienne**, comtesse de.

Villeneuve, Madame de. See **Luillier**, Marie.

Viole, Anne (Mère **Anne du Saint-Sacrement**) (1584–1630). Eldest child of Nicolas de Viole, seigneur d'Auxeraux, conseiller du roi et maître des requêtes de son hôtel, and Philippe de Pétremol, who is said to have played a role in ensuring Henri IV's entry into Paris during the Holy League. Orphaned young, she was raised in the household of an uncle and showed strong tendencies toward devotion from an early age. Hesitated between the Capucines and Carmelites but chose the latter, delaying her entry until she could ensure a substantial donation of her properties, which went to found the Carmelite convent of Amiens. Took her vows at the Paris convent of the Incarnation in 1606 and was elected mistress of novices in 1608, when Madeleine de Saint-Joseph became prioress. Elected prioress of the convent of Amiens in 1616, she aided the foundation of a house of the Oratoire in that city and gained a reputation for her spiritual counsel.[25]

NOTES TO BIOGRAPHICAL APPENDIX

1. Auvray, *Modèle de la perfection religieuse;* see also the more recent biography by Augereau, *Jeanne Absolu, une mystique du grand siècle.*

2. See Duval, *Vie de Marie de l'Incarnation;* Bruno de Jésus-Marie, *La belle Acarie.*

3. See [Tronson de Chenevière], *Vie de Marguerite Acarie.*

4. See the bibliography listed in *DS*, vol. 1, cols. 879–81.

5. Raunié, *Epitaphier du vieux Paris*, 3:98–99n.

6. Estienne, *Oraison funèbre.*

7. Madeleine de Saint-Joseph, *Avis pour la conduite des novices, Vie de Catherine de Jésus*, and *Lettres spirituelles.*

8. *Chroniques des Carmélites*, 2:491–528.

9. "Les feuillantines de Paris," 208; Raunié, *Epitaphier du vieux Paris*, 4: 232–36.

10. *Chroniques des Carmélites*, 3:409–88.

11. Bazy, *Vie de Jean de la Barrière*, 337–63; Hélyot, *Dictionnaire des ordres religieux*, 6:355–70.

12. Leymont, *Madame de Sainte-Beuve*.

13. See Salinis, *Madame de Villeneuve*.

14. Leymont, *Madame de Sainte-Beuve*, 85.

15. See Senault, *Oraison funebre de la Marquise de Maignelay*; Bauduen, *Vie de Marguerite de Gondy, marquise de Maignelais*; *Testament de Madame la Marquise de Maignelay*.

16. Bremond, *Histoire du sentiment religieux*, 6:388.

17. Madeleine de Saint-Joseph, *Vie de Catherine de Jésus*.

18. Hilarion de Coste, *Les éloges et les vies des reynes*, 1:90–119.

19. Marie de la Trinité [Sévin], *Une glorieuse fille de Sainte Thérèse*.

20. Rybolt, "Madame de Gondi: A Contemporary Seventeenth-Century Life."

21. *Histoire des religieuses feuillentines*, 71.

22. Ibid.

23. Richet, "Une famille de robe: les Séguier avant le chancelier," in his *De la Réforme à la Révolution*, 215, 262; *Chroniques des Carmélites*, 1:535–47.

24. Macé, *Vie de Marie de Saint-Charles*; Camus, *La pieuse Julie*. See also Jean-Marie de Vernon's biography of her mother, *Vie de Françoise de Saint-Bernard*, and Antoine de Saint-Martin de la Porte's biography of her sister Anne, *Vie de Madame de Beaufort Ferrand*.

25. *Chroniques des Carmélites*, 4:142–205.

List of Abbreviations

AAP   Archives de l'Assistance publique
ACC   Archives du Carmel de Clamart
ACP   Archives du Carmel de Pontoise
AL   Archives lazaristes, Maison Mère de la Congrégation de la Mission
AN   Archives nationales
BMaz   Bibliothèque mazarine
BNF   Bibliothèque nationale de France
BSG   Bibliothèque Sainte-Geneviève
DS   *Dictionnaire de la spiritualité ascétique, doctrine et histoire.* Edited by M. F. Viller, F. Cavallera, J. de Guibert, et al. 17 vols. Paris, 1937–95.

Notes

I have used the King James Bible when citing scripture. All other translations are my own except where noted. In citing sixteenth- and seventeenth-century sources, I have retained original spellings but added an occasional accent or punctuation mark for purposes of clarity.

PROLOGUE

1. Estienne, *Oraison funebre*, fol. 32r.
2. L'Estoile, *Journal pour le règne de Henri IV*, 1:74.
3. Estienne, *Oraison funebre*, fols. 11–14.
4. She did, however, join the Minim Third Order, an association founded half a century earlier for lay men and women who wished to lead a more devout life. Thuillier, *Diarium ordinis minimorum*, 127–28. I am grateful to Cynthia Cupples for this reference.
5. Estienne, *Oraison funebre*, fols. 34–37, 42.
6. Ibid., fols. 15–17, 22–24, 49.
7. Ibid., fols. 16, 28, 48–49.
8. On medieval mystics and food, see Bynum, *Holy Feast and Holy Fast* and *Fragmentation and Redemption*.
9. Estienne, *Oraison funebre*, fol. 52.
10. Ibid., fols. 27–28.
11. L'Estoile, *Journal pour le règne de Henri IV*, 1:74.
12. Memoirist Pierre de L'Estoile wrote of Estienne's sermon that "by reading this lovely book, any thinking man would learn the difference between superstition and religion, in order to embrace the one and reject the other as vain and stupid in all ways" (ibid.).

INTRODUCTION

1. *Histoire des religieuses feuillentines*, 26.

2. The question of appropriate terminology for describing the experience of early modern Catholics has provoked considerable controversy, with some historians objecting to the term "Counter-Reformation" because it implies that change in the Catholic church came only in response and opposition to the Protestant Reformation. Although I generally use the more neutral "Catholic Reformation" and prefer "Catholic revival" or "Catholic renewal" to describe the energetic extension of institutions and piety that are the subject of this book, the term Counter-Reformation also has its place in describing a Catholic milieu that was profoundly concerned with winning back souls from its Protestant opponents. See Venard, "Réforme, Réformation," in *Le catholicisme à l'épreuve*, 9–26, on the quarrels over terminology in France, and O'Malley, *Trent and All That*, on their international dynamics.

3. Hsia, *The World of Catholic Renewal*, 33–39 and 138–51, and Wiesner, *Women and Gender in Early Modern Europe*, 195–203, exemplify the depiction of the Catholic Reformation as hostile to women in recent texts. The literature on monastic enclosure on which this interpretation largely rests includes Liebowitz, "Virgins in the Service of Christ"; Rapley, *The Dévotes*; Sperling, *Convents and the Body Politic in Late Renaissance Venice*; Medioli, "An Unequal Law"; and Evangelisti, " 'We Do Not Have It, and We Do Not Want It.' " Norberg, "The Counter-Reformation and Women Religious and Lay"; King, *Women of the Renaissance*, 81–156; Cavallo, *Charity and Power in Early Modern Italy*; and Lehfeldt, "Discipline, Vocation, and Patronage," offer more nuanced views of the requirement for religious enclosure and its impact on women. Strasser, "Cloistering Women's Past," offers perceptive insights into the problems surrounding strict cloistering but accepts without question the assumption that religious women longed for an active apostolate after Trent.

4. On the events that led up to this massacre, see Diefendorf, *Beneath the Cross*.

5. "Pasquil de la court pour apprendre à discourir," in *Le changement de la court*, 23–31, especially 24, 25.

6. See for example, *Le miroir du temps passé*.

7. Jacquart, *La crise rurale en Ile-de-France*, 605–36.

8. Ibid., 677–80.

9. Benedict, "French Cities from the Sixteenth Century to the Revolution: An Overview," in his *Cities and Social Change*, 24; de Vries, *The Economy of Europe in an Age of Crisis*, 156.

10. Diefendorf, *Paris City Councillors*, 176–77, 286–87; Diefendorf, "Women and Property in *Ancien Régime* France," 177–79.

11. The law permitted daughters to waive this right in their marriage contract, but in practice this was rare. I discuss women's legal position in Parisian law and practice in more detail in *Paris City Councillors*, chapters 7, 8, 9, and "Women and Property in *Ancien Régime* France."

12. On widows and the management of family properties, see Diefendorf, *Paris City Councillors*, chapter 9.

13. On medieval women's ascetic practices, see, among others, Bynum, *Holy Feast and Holy Fast* and *Fragmentation and Redemption*; Kieckhefer, *Unquiet Souls*.

14. See Le Brun, "Mutations de la notion de martyre" and "A corps perdu"; Bre-

mond, *Histoire littéraire du sentiment religieux*, 1:239–54; H.-J. Martin, *Livre, pouvoir et société à Paris au XVIIᵉ siècle*, 1:154–60; Burkardt, "Les vies des saints et leurs lectures," 214–33, especially 214–15.

15. Duval, *Vie de Marie de l'Incarnation*, 399. A parallel incident occurs in chapter 8 of the *Life and Doctrine of Saint Catherine of Genoa*, a favorite book of Acarie's (ACP, Acarie beatification, testimony of André Duval, fol. 322r).

16. The term "discalced" (literally, "barefoot") refers to the practice of wearing only sandals as a gesture of humility and sign of strict observance of a monastic rule.

CHAPTER I: WOMEN IN THE NEW JERUSALEM

1. The notion that the world began with an "Age of Gold," a time of innocence and earthly perfection, and subsequently decayed into a corrupt iron age dates back to ancient times. The trope was a common one in the Renaissance, particularly among Christian humanists who envisioned their projects for renewal and reform as leading to a new golden age. The quotation comes from the testimony of Sr. Marie du Saint-Sacrement (Valence de Marillac) in the proceedings for the beatification of Sr. Marie de l'Incarnation (Barbe Acarie): ACP, Acarie beatification, fol. 644r. Similar statements occur in the testimony of André Duval, fol. 322v; Françoise de Jésus de Fleury, fol. 339v; Marie de Jésus de Breauté, fol. 619v; and other witnesses. I wish to thank the Carmelites of Pontoise for graciously making this and other precious manuscripts available to me.

2. L'Estoile, *Journal pour le règne de Henri IV*, 1:70. See also the *Brief traité des misères de la ville de Paris*, especially 281–82. For an ultra-Catholic perspective on the siege, see Corneio, *Bref discours*.

3. L'Estoile, *Journal pour le règne de Henri IV*, 1:68.

4. On the failure of the French kings to suppress the Protestant movement, see especially Monter, *Judging the French Reformation*.

5. Carroll, *Noble Power during the French Wars of Religion*, 161–63, convincingly argues that the Guises did not organize this League, though many of their clients were early supporters of it.

6. These paragraphs borrow from my essay "The Religious Wars in France," which gives a more complete account of the Wars of Religion than can be offered here.

7. This summary of events draws on a variety of primary sources, most notably the *Journal de François*; *Coppie de la response faicte par un politique*; and L'Estoile, *Registre-journal pour le règne de Henri III*, vol. 3, in his *Mémoires-journaux*.

8. *Journal de François*, 51, 54.

9. *Coppie de la response faicte par un politique*, 274.

10. *Journal de François*, 25; Richet, "Politique et religion: Les processions à Paris en 1589," in his *De la Réforme à la Révolution*, 72.

11. *Journal de François*, 63.

12. Ibid., 44–45, n. 2; Richet, "Politique et religion," in *De la Réforme à la Révolution*, 77–78.

13. *Journal de François*, 19.

14. *Coppie de la response faicte par un politique*, 275; the tract is dated 30 January 1589.

15. Estienne, *Remonstrance charitable*, fols. 2–4, 32. The first *privilège*, or permission to publish the book, is dated 5 November 1570; the fourth printing was completed 25 August 1585.

16. Estienne, *Oraison funebre*, fols. 13v–14r.

17. *Journal de François*, 85, says that curates forbade parishioners to take part in future processions in anything other than their usual clothes, but he gives no reason for the order.

18. Constant, *La Ligue*, 247.

19. L'Estoile, *Journal pour le règne de Henri IV*, 1:48.

20. Franklin, *Journal du siège de Paris*, especially 133–34, 154–55, is very clear about the perceived dangers of internal sedition.

21. Dufour, "Histoire du siège de Paris," 216–17. In the final days of the siege, the ground bones of slaughtered animals are said to have been used to stretch the flour. Pigafetta, "Relation du siège," 78–79; this appears to be taken from Corneio's *Bref discours*, 262.

22. On the collection of domestic pets for the common soup, see *Brief traité des misères de la ville de Paris*, 277. On rising prices and shortages, see Corneio, *Bref discours*, 261–63; Pigafetta, "Relation du siège," 77–78 (again, much of this description appears to be taken from Corneio, even though Pigafetta was in Paris through the siege); Franklin, *Journal du siège de Paris*, 177–89; L'Estoile, *Journal pour le règne de Henri IV*, 1:52, 58–59, 70. Some descriptions of the horrors of the siege, including L'Estoile's (70), recount acts of cannibalism. The rumors of cannibalism appear to have had their origins in polemics, however, and I have chosen to discount them here. I find more plausible the denial made by the anonymous author of the manuscript "Histoire de la Ligue"(BNF, Ms. fr. 23296, 273–74), who wrote that, despite the extremities to which famine pushed the Parisians, those fighting for their religion were not so lacking in feeling as to eat their own children. Those who wrote otherwise did not know the truth. The author is emphatic about the importance attached at this time to the maintenance of order as part and parcel of the aim of conserving religion.

23. Dufour, "Histoire du siège de Paris," 209, 213, 220. The anonymous memoirist estimates the number of children participating at 10,000. See also Pigafetta, "Relation du siège," 80–81. He estimates the number of participants at "several thousand" and notes that they were barefoot and robed in coarse cloth but doubtless exaggerates when he says that the oldest participants were at most seven years old. See also L'Estoile, *Journal pour le règne de Henri IV*, 1:54, 655.

24. L'Estoile, *Journal pour le règne de Henri IV*, 1:70–71, 93–94, 104–5, 162, 165, 170, 211, 250. His food having given out, L'Estoile had received a passport to leave on 30 August 1590 (and paid a bribe of 50 écus to guarantee a safe departure).

25. Pigafetta, "Relation du siège," 56. See also Franklin, *Journal du siège*, 318–25, which views the siege as a necessary purging not just of heresy but also of sensuality, luxury, presumption, and other sins that had come to Paris with prosperity and riches.

26. Pigafetta, "Relation du siège," 56.

27. Carroll, "The Guise Affinity," 139–40, notes that the Guise women regularly resided in Paris in the 1580s to "oversee family affairs." This included raising money for war and ensuring the delivery of armaments to the duke's army.

28. L'Estoile, *Mémoires-journaux*, 3:200, 246. According to L'Estoile, she arrived in Paris on 10 February 1589; François places the date at 11 February (*Journal de François*, 54). See also Viennot, "Des 'femmes d'Etat' au XVIᵉ siècle," and "Les femmes dans les 'troubles' du XVIᵉ siècle."

29. See, for example, L'Estoile, *Journal pour le règne de Henri IV*, 1:139, 140, 142, 193, 260, 316, 338; Corneio, *Discours du siège*, 242, 259.

30. See, for example, L'Estoile, *Mémoires-journaux*, 3:53–54, 66, 242, 275; L'Estoile, *Journal pour le règne de Henri IV*, 1:52–53.

31. L'Estoile, *Mémoires-journaux*, 3:302.

32. L'Estoile, *Journal pour le règne de Henri IV*, 1:19.

33. Ibid., 1:19, 72; *L'Estoile Mémoires-journaux*, 3:164, 97.

34. L'Estoile, *Mémoires-journaux*, 3:248, 259. A very similar account of Sainte-Beuve's behavior appears in the royalist pamphlet *Conseil salutaire d'un bon Françoys aux Parisiens*, 97–98.

35. L'Estoile, *Mémoires-journaux*, 3:291–93, citing a "Lettre du Président Dassi à Monsr. le Duc de Maienne," dated 18 May 1589. The letter is not mentioned in Leymont, *Madame de Sainte-Beuve.*

36. ACP, Acarie beatification, testimony of Jeanne de Jésus Séguier, fol. 822r. According to the testimony of Nicolas Pinette de Charmoy (fol. 486r), who knew the Acaries at least from 1593, Pierre Acarie lost more than 30,000 écus on account of the League.

37. Duval, *Vie de Marie de l'Incarnation*, 85, on her acquaintance with Dom Beaucousin, the Carthusians' vicar. Pierre Acarie spent his exile after the League with the Carthusians of Bourgfontaine. See also BNF, Ms. fr. 3996: "Deliberations, arrests, actes & memoires de ce qui se passa à Paris durant la Ligue," vol. 1, fols. 195–202.

38. According to Marguerite de Gondi, marquise de Maignelay, Pierre Acarie, "having recognized [his wife's] abilities, depended on her for the management of all his affairs and did not meddle at all in them" (ACP, Acarie beatification, fol. 403). See also the testimony of Michel de Marillac about how she handled accounts of kinsfolk for whom Pierre Acarie was named guardian (ACP, Acarie beatification, fols. 803v–804r).

39. ACP, Acarie beatification, Marie de Jésus de Breauté, fol. 619v. See also Duval, *Vie de Marie de l'Incarnation*, 24, and, more generally on League processions, Richet, "Les processions à Paris," in *De la Réforme à la Révolution.*

40. ACP, Acarie beatification, Agnès de Jésus de Lyons, fol. 9r; Françoise de Jésus de Fleury, fol. 339v; Marie de Jésus de Breauté, fols. 619v–20r.

41. Duval, *Vie de Marie de l'Incarnation*, 68. See also ACP, Acarie beatification, Marie de Saint-Joseph Fournier, fol. 112v; Michel de Marillac, fol. 781; Marguerite de Gondi, marquise de Maignelay, fol. 396v; Marie de Jésus Séguier, fol. 553; Marie de Jésus Acarie, fol. 516r.

42. See especially the testimony of Marie de Jésus Séguier, ACP, Acarie beatification, fol. 553.

43. In fact, the practice had its roots in hospital visits begun at least a generation earlier. In 1578, Acarie's kinswoman Renée de Nicolay, the widow of a president in the Chambre de Comptes (and mother of Madeleine Luillier de Sainte-Beuve), was asked by the supervisors of the Hôtel-Dieu to help organize the visits that Parisian ladies wished to make to the hospital (AAP, Hôtel Dieu 1438, "Registre pour 1574–

1578," 611–12). It appears that the initiative was not pursued, though there is evidence that Acarie's devout aunt, Marie Du Drac (also a kinswoman of Renée de Nicolay), began to visit Paris hospitals at about this time (Estienne, *Oraison funebre*, fol. 37v). According to Acarie's eldest daughter, moreover, she did not go to the Hôpital Saint-Gervais alone but in the company of her mother-in-law, Marguerite Lottin (ACP, Acarie beatification, testimony of Marie de Jésus Acarie, fol. 516r). It is probable that other devout ladies were beginning to do the same thing. Even if they were not actually ministering to patients in Paris hospitals, they were collecting linens and other donations to serve the Hôtel-Dieu in this time of crisis (BNF, Ms. fr. 3996: "Deliberations, Arrests, Actes et Memoires de ce qui se passa à Paris durant la Ligue," fol. 143).

44. I am following here the chronology set out by Acarie's most important twentieth-century biographer, Bruno de Jésus-Marie, *La belle Acarie*, 48n, 125–27. On the frequency with which Spanish mystics were alleged to have received stigmata in the early seventeenth century, see Poutrin, *Le voile et la plume*, 98–100.

45. Marie de la Trinité [Sévin], *Une glorieuse fille de Sainte Thérèse*, 31. The autobiographical writings themselves have disappeared, but the biography based on it by M. d'Aignan du Sendat, vicar general of Auch, is simply a recopying and assemblage of first-person statements. The biography was abandoned in 1669 (thirteen years after Marie de la Trinité's death), probably because the compiler had gone blind, and not published until 1930. I am grateful to Cynthia Cupples for first calling it to my attention.

46. Ibid., 32.

47. Ibid.

48. Ibid., 32–35.

49. Ibid., 36.

50. I include as opponents to the League women who were considered to be royalists because their husbands had fled Paris and joined the royalist camp, even if there is no direct evidence of their personal political sentiments.

51. Documentation of these practices can be found in AN, H² 1882² and 1882³: Bureau de la Ville de Paris, 1591–1594; also Z¹ʰ 91: Sentences du Bureau de la Ville de Paris for January–June 1591.

52. Département de la Somme, Amiens, *Inventaire sommaire*, 3:148–49 (proceedings of the Bureau de la Ville for 26 and 27 December 1588) and 161 (letters of 4 and 6 March 1589).

53. Ibid., 3:164 (deliberations of 27 April 1589), 157 (deliberations of 30 January 1589), and 184–85 (meetings of 30 September and 1 and 6 October 1589). See also the *Discours veritable sur l'inique emprisonnement*, 141–53. The presumed author of this tract is Louis de Gonzague, duc de Nevers, the father of the young duchesse de Longueville.

54. See, for example, Département de la Somme, Amiens, *Inventaire sommaire*, 3: 166–67, 171–72 (meetings of 6, 10, and 17 May); 181–83 (meetings of 29 July and 1, 4, and 23 September 1589); 196–97 (proceedings of 26 February 1590); 203 (proceedings of 18 June 1590); 216–18 (letter of 31 August and proceedings of 3, 5, 10, 12, 16, 17, and 23 September); 219–20 (meetings of 11 and 22 November 1591); 222 (meeting of 21 January 1592).

55. Ibid., 3:222.

56. Ibid., 3:172 (meetings of 19 and 21 June 1589); 177 (discussions of 13 July

1589); 194 (letter of 18 January 1590); 201 (proceedings of 17, 18, and 22 May 1590); 208 (29 October 1590); 209 (21 November 1590).

57. Jean Séguier, the most outspokenly royalist among the men in the family, was replaced as *lieutenant civil* in February 1589. His brothers Antoine, *avocat général* in the Parlement of Paris, and Pierre, a president of Parlement, followed him into exile. See Richet, "Une famille de robe: Les Séguier avant le chancelier," in his *De la Réforme à la Révolution*, 238-48. The month of Jean Séguier's replacement is supplied by Descimon, *Qui étaient les Seize?*, 127.

58. AN, Z¹ʰ 86: Sentences du Bureau de la Ville (14 April 1589); AN, H² 1882²: 17 September 1591: order from the *prévôt des marchands.*

59. L'Estoile, *Journal pour le règne de Henri IV*, 1:220, 279, 321, 360. Louise Boudet had been on bad terms with Aubery at least since May 1588, when she had confronted him about the knifing of a fellow parishioner set upon by two other locals, who claimed he was a heretic even though he had taken communion at Saint-André just two days earlier (L'Estoile, *Mémoires-journaux*, 3:156-57).

60. AN, Y156, fol. 26: Donation by Marie de Tudert (Marie de Jésus-Christ) to the Carmelite convent of the Incarnation (27 December 1614).

61. *Chroniques des Carmélites*, 1:536-37.

62. Duval, *Vie de Marie de l'Incarnation*, 80-83.

63. Marie de la Trinité [Sévin], *Une glorieuse fille de Sainte Thérèse*, 51. This image of the body as food recalls the practices of medieval female saints discussed in Bynum, *Holy Feast and Holy Fast.*

64. See, for example, Bauduen, *Vie de Marguerite de Gondy, marquise de Magnelais*, especially 124-40.

65. ACP, Acarie beatification, fol. 644r, testimony of Valence de Marillac.

66. On these responsibilities, see Diefendorf, *Paris City Councillors*, 176-77.

CHAPTER 2: THE ASCETIC IMPULSE

1. It is unclear just what role the League played in forming Antoinette's religious convictions. By taking her out of her mother's household, her wedding in March 1588 to Charles de Gondi, marquis de Belle-Isle, saved her from being held captive in Amiens with her mother and sisters during the League. On the other hand, she was subjected to the stress of divided loyalties during this period, which she appears to have spent largely on the Gondi estates in Brittany. To the great distress of his royalist family, the marquis de Belle-Isle went over to the League and was killed in its service in 1596, leaving Antoinette a widow at the age of twenty-four. Whether or not she shared the marquis's Leaguer sympathies, surely she was emotionally torn, seeing her husband serve the party that held her mother and sisters prisoner. She also witnessed the strains on her mother-in-law, the spirited Claude-Catherine de Clermont, duchesse de Retz, who, finding her Breton properties threatened by her eldest son's defection to the League, raised troops to defend them and at the same time set about reassuring Henri IV of her continued loyalty to his cause. Pommerol, *Albert de Gondi*, 201-204; Hilarion de Coste, *Les éloges et les vies des reynes*, 152-53; Pasquier, *Lettres familières*, 208-11: Book 14, letter 3: "à Madame la Duchesse de Rez"; Tallement des Réaux, *Historiettes*, 1:29.

2. "La vie de Madame d'Orléans, ditte de Sainte-Scholastique, fondatrice de

l'Ordre du Calvaire, composé par le R.P. Dom Damien Lerminier, religieux de l'Ordre de Saint-Benoît et la congregation de Saint-Maur, 1656": Manuscript of the Bibliothèque de la ville de Toulouse, as cited in Bazy, *Vie de Jean de la Barrière*, 339–42, 356–57. On her wedding, see L'Estoile, *Mémoires-journaux*, 2:123.

3. *Histoire des religieuses feuillentines*, 71.

4. Henry de Calais, *Vie de Honoré de Champigny*, 199.

5. *Histoire des religieuses feuillentines*, 26.

6. Duval, *Vie de Marie de l'Incarnation*, 7; Bruno de Jésus-Marie, *La belle Acarie*, 16n.

7. Biver and Biver, *Couvents de femmes à Paris*, 69–70: notarial contracts of 1577 and 1600; AN, L 1053: Filles-Dieu, *rente* contracts from 24 September 1577 and 1 August 1600.

8. François de Sales, *Œuvres*, 12:136–52: letter of 22 November 1602.

9. Biver and Biver, *Couvents de femmes à Paris*, 143.

10. Ibid., 480–81.

11. Blaisdell, "Religion, Gender, and Class," 149, 151.

12. Biver and Biver, *Couvents de femmes à Paris*, 482–83; L'Estoile, *Journal pour le règne de Henri IV*, 1:60.

13. Hélyot, *Dictionnaire des ordres religieux*, vol. 2, cols. 1084–85: "Montmartre."

14. Blaisdell, "Religion, Gender, and Class," 151–52; Biver and Biver, *Couvents de femmes à Paris*, 144.

15. Dufour, "Histoire du siège de Paris," 220.

16. L'Estoile, *Journal pour le règne de Henri IV*, 1:60.

17. Duval, *Vie de Marie de l'Incarnation*, 3–7; Bruno de Jésus-Marie, *La belle Acarie*, 4–10; Vincent de Paul, *Correspondence, Conferences, Documents*, 4:483–87: letter of 25 October 1652 to Cardinal Antonio Barberini.

18. AN, S 4207, fol. 197, as cited in Raunié, *Epitaphier du vieux Paris*, 4:248–49n.

19. Chaussy, *Les Bénédictines et la réforme catholique*, 1:70, 76, 81.

20. This tendency may have been reinforced by a Tridentine decree that, recognizing how vulnerable rural convents had proved in periods of war and brigandage, permitted bishops and superiors, if they deemed it wise, to move nuns from exposed areas into cities or towns (*Canons and Decrees of the Council of Trent*, 220–21 and 488–89: Twenty-Fifth Session, "On Regulars and Nuns," chapter 5). Although the decrees issued by the Council of Trent were never officially accepted in France, the clergy agreed to abide by them in 1615. Contrary to what some historians have rather carelessly written, the decrees of Trent permitted bishops and superiors to move convents into cities but did not require them to do so.

21. Chaussy, *Les Bénédictines et la réforme catholique*, 1:76.

22. Ferté, *La vie religieuse dans les campagnes parisiennes*, 118–19, 119n; Alliot, *Histoire de l'abbaye de Notre-Dame du Val de Gif*, 159–61, 165.

23. Arnauld, *Relation sur Port-Royal*, 30, 32–35, 39–40.

24. For example, Alliot, *Histoire de l'abbaye du Val de Gif*, 159–60.

25. Raunié, *Epitaphier du vieux Paris*, 1:267–71; Biver and Biver, *Couvents de femmes à Paris*, 97–100.

26. ACC, ms. "Vie de la Mere Marie de Jesus [de Breauté], Carmélite," 22–23.

27. Haton, *Mémoires*, 1:214–20; Paschal, *Journal de ce qui s'est passé*, 113; also Diefendorf, *Beneath the Cross*, 61, 145.

28. The Jesuits, who figure prominently in most accounts of Catholic Reformation religious congregations, did not place the same stress on asceticism, either in their own lives or those of their penitents. Ignatius of Loyola went through a period of extreme asceticism following his religious conversion but later decided that rigorous mortifications, by damaging his health, only hampered his ability to serve the church effectively. He and his followers encouraged self-discipline but opposed the penitential practices that caused people to admire the Minims, Capuchins, and Feuillants. Equally important, because they were accused (however unfairly) of preaching regicide, the Jesuits were expelled from France between 1594 and 1603, crucial years for the events discussed in this chapter. The expulsion was not enforced in parts of France outside the reach of the Parlement of Paris, but the Jesuits were forced to leave the capital and surrounding areas and thus could not serve as spiritual directors or counselors to Parisian dévotes.

29. Whitmore, *The Order of Minims*, 13.

30. Robert Fiot, "Saint François de Paule," *DS*, vol. 5 (Paris, 1964), cols. 1040–49; Raymond Darricau, "Minimes," ibid., vol. 10 (1980), cols. 1239–50.

31. Cargnoni, *I frati cappuccini*, vol. 1, contains the essential documents on their founding.

32. Mauzaize, *Le rôle et l'action des Capucins*, 1:40–45; Godefroy de Paris, *Les frères-mineurs capucins*, 1:38–41.

33. BNF, Ms. fr. 25046 "Eloges historiques des Capucins," 19–20.

34. Caluze, *Annales des freres mineurs capucins*, 348–49, 131; more extensively: BNF, Ms. fr. 25044, 48–51: "Chronologie historique de ce qui s'est passé de plus considerable dans la Province de Paris depuis l'an 1574 jusques a lannee [blank]," reproduced in Cargnoni, *I frati cappuccini*, 4:99–105.

35. BMaz, Ms. 2418: "Annales des Reverends Peres Capucins," 23–30. In 1580, forty-one joined as regulars and eleven as lay brothers.

36. Cargnoni, *I frati cappuccini*, 4:26.

37. *Histoire des religieuses feuillentines*, 11–13, citing letter of Jean de la Barrière, 13–16. From the feast day of the Holy Cross in September until Easter, the monks took only one meal a day; during Lent, this meal was limited to bread and water.

38. Antoine de Saint-Pierre, *Vie d'Eustache de Saint-Paul Asseline*, 95.

39. *Histoire des religieuses feuillentines*, 20, 26.

40. Ibid., 47.

41. "La vie de Madame d'Orléans," as cited in Bazy, *Vie de Jean de la Barrière*, 339–49.

42. Ibid., 357.

43. Still rebuilding after their own devastating religious divisions during the League, Paris's Feuillants had other preoccupations. They told the Longueville princesses, as they had already told Jean Sublet des Noyers, that they did not wish to take responsibility for the cure of female souls. Hélyot, *Dictionnaire des ordres religieux*, 2:274–81, "Feuillantes, dites incorrectement Feuillantines."

44. This paragraph and the next summarize themes developed at greater length in Diefendorf, "Give Us Back Our Children," especially 305–6, 274–75.

45. L'Estoile, *Journal pour le règne de Henri IV*, 2:207.

46. ACC, ms. "Vie de la Mere Marie de Jesus [de Breauté]," 22, 31–32.

47. Ibid., 26–27, 30.

48. *Chroniques des Carmélites*, 3:410–11, 412, 413–14; "Eloge de la V.M. Marie de Hanivel de la Sainte Trinité," in Gallement, *Vie de Jacques Gallement*, 331–32. Marie d'Hannivel's Carmelite biographer says that these events took place when Marie was not yet seventeen and identifies the Capuchin who so influenced her as Père Ange de Joyeuse, but either the date or the identification is wrong. When Marie was sixteen, that is to say in 1596 or 1597, Ange de Joyeuse had not yet returned to the Capuchin fold. The "Eloge de la V.M. Marie de Hanivel de la Sainté Trinité, carmélite" appended to Placide Gallement's *Vie de Jacques Gallement* dates Marie's conversion to about 1599, which would make the identification of the Capuchin as Père Ange more plausible.

49. *Chroniques des Carmélites*, 2:493–95.

50. Marie de la Trinité [Sévin], *Une glorieuse fille de Sainte Thérèse*, 51–52, 53.

51. Ibid., 53.

52. Henry de Calais, *Vie de Honoré de Champigny*, 206, 214–15.

53. *Chroniques des Carmélites*, 2:497.

54. Duval, *Vie de Marie de l'Incarnation*, 465.

55. ACC, ms. "Vie de la Mere Marie de Jesus [de Breauté]," 29.

56. Jean-Marie de Vernon, *Vie de Françoise de Saint Bernard*, 104–105.

57. Marie de la Trinité [Sévin], *Une glorieuse fille de Sainte Thérèse*, 57–58.

58. François de Sales, *Introduction à la vie dévote*, 24–25. The first edition of this work dates from 1608.

59. Duval, *Vie de Marie de l'Incarnation*, 51, 44; Senault, *Vie de Catherine de Montholon*, 16–17.

60. ACP, Acarie beatification, testimony of Marie de Jésus Acarie, fols. 500r, 502r; Marguerite du Saint-Sacrement Acarie, fol. 425v.

61. Ibid., Marie de Jésus Acarie, fol. 501.

62. [Tronson de Chenevière], *Vie de Marguerite Acarie*, 13.

63. Duval, *Vie de Marie de l'Incarnation*, 41; ACP, Acarie beatification, testimony of Marguerite du Saint-Sacrement Acarie, fols. 424v–425v.

64. ACP, Acarie beatification, testimony of Marguerite du Saint-Sacrement Acarie, fols. 424v, 425v; Marie de Jésus Acarie, fols. 500r, 501r.

65. Ibid., testimony of Marguerite du Saint-Sacrement Acarie, fol. 427r; Marguerite de Gondi, marquise de Maignelay, fol. 403; Michel de Marillac, fol. 752v, 753r, 754v.

66. Ibid., testimony of Anne de Saint-Laurent de Saint-Leu, fol. 55v; also Marguerite de Gondi, marquise de Maignelay, fol. 403r–v; Marguerite de Saint-Joseph (Langlois), fol. 756v; Marie de Saint-Joseph (Fournier), fol. 86r; Marguerite du Saint-Sacrement (Acarie), fol. 427r; Marie de Jésus (de Tudert), fol. 539r, Michel de Marillac, fol. 754r.

67. My thinking here has benefited from Rudolph M. Bell's analysis of the complex relationship between obedience and autonomy, will and denial of will, in the self-mortifying behavior of the late medieval and early modern holy women who are the subject of *Holy Anorexia*.

68. [Tronson de Chenevière], *Vie de Marguerite Acarie*, 16–19, 30–32, 50, 65–68, 80–81, 89–94.

69. Ibid., 80–81, 92–93.

70. Bynum, *Fragmentation and Redemption*, 222, 235.

CHAPTER 3: MADEMOISELLE ACARIE'S CIRCLE

1. A good brief account of this assembly and the negotiations that followed is given by Morgain, *Pierre de Bérulle et les Carmélites de France*, 83–90. See also Duval, *Vie de Marie de l'Incarnation*, 118–28; ACP, Acarie beatification, testimony of Michel de Marillac, fol. 764.

2. Brétigny, *Lettres*, 67.

3. ACP, Acarie beatification, testimony of René Gaultier, fols. 76–77; Marguerite de Gondi, marquise de Maignelay, fols. 396–97; Michel de Marillac, fols. 778–82; Jeanne de Jésus Séguier, fols. 833–35; Jeanne L'Espervier, fol. 580v; Bruno de Jésus-Marie, *La belle Acarie*, 199–201.

4. ACP, Acarie beatification, testimony of Edmond de Messa, fols. 383v–384; Jeanne L'Espervier, fol. 580r; Michel de Marillac, fol. 779v.

5. Morgain, *Pierre de Bérulle et les Carmélites de France*, 69.

6. Schoote, "La Perle évangélique," 87–88.

7. Marie de la Trinité [Sévin], *Une glorieuse fille de Sainte Thérèse*, 57; ACC, ms. "Vie de la Mere Marie de Jesus [de Breauté]," 31, 33.

8. The Carthusians had tried to send Beaucousin to Nantes for the same reason in 1598 but relented on the appeal of many distinguished dévots. In 1602, however, there was no appeal. Dom Beaucousin continued to work for monastic reform in the south of France. In particular, he played a key role in convincing Antoinette d'Orléans to move to Fontevraud to take up the reform of that order, but his role in the Parisian revival effectively ended. Schoote, "La Perle évangélique," 86–89.

9. Dagens, *Bérulle et les origines de la restauration catholique*, 111.

10. Duval, *Vie de Marie de l'Incarnation*, 103.

11. Descimon, *Qui étaient les Seize?*, 187–88.

12. Among the many accounts of this incident in the beatification testimony for Barbe Acarie, see ACP, Acarie beatification, testimony of Pierre Coton, fols. 741–42; Marie de Jésus de Breauté, fols. 635–37; Michel de Marillac, fols. 819–21.

13. Ibid., testimony of Michel de Marillac, fols. 804–805; Anne de Saint-Laurent de Saint-Leu, fol. 60; Jeanne de Jésus Séguier, 348.

14. Pierre de Bérulle's formative contributions to seventeenth-century French devotion came later. In the 1590s he was still more student than teacher, influenced by, rather than influencing, Beaucousin, Benoît, and Acarie, with whom he was intimately acquainted from at least late adolescence. Barbe Acarie lived with Pierre de Bérulle's mother during the period of Pierre Acarie's exile after the League (1594–98), and he continued to visit her frequently in her own home after she returned there.

15. Chaix, "Contributions cartusiennes aux débuts de la Réforme catholique," 115–23; Dagens, *Bibliographie chronologique*.

16. Benoît de Canfield sought Dom Beaucousin's approval for his *Règle de Perfection*, which, although published only in 1609, circulated in manuscript from at least

1593. Similarly, Pierre de Bérulle sought his approbation for the *Bref discours de l'abnégation intérieure* that he published in 1597, and Beaucousin's influence on the work is, in Jean Dagens's words, "incontestable." Dagens, *Bérulle et les origines de la restauration catholique*, 115, 139–40.

17. Morgain, *Pierre de Bérulle et les Carmélites de France*, 69.

18. Schoote, "La Perle évangélique," 86, citing J.-B. Boucher, *Vie de la Bienheureuse Sœur Marie de l'Incarnation* (Paris, 1800), 61.

19. Ibid.

20. Optat de Veghel, *Benoît de Canfield*, 381–99.

21. Optat de Veghel, "Aux sources d'une spiritualité des laïcs: Le P. Benoît de Canfield et l'Exercice de la volunté de Dieu," 38.

22. Optat de Veghel, *Benoît de Canfield*, 348–55, on conformity to God's will as the central premise of all virtue, all perfection.

23. Renaudin, *Un maître de la mystique française, Benoît de Canfield*, 220, as cited in Optat de Veghel, "Aux sources d'une spiritualité des laïcs," 35.

24. See especially Optat de Veghel, *Benoît de Canfield*, 328–44.

25. Ibid., 363–75. The edition of the *Breve compendio di perfezione cristiana* published by Mario Bendiscioli (Florence, 1952) attributes authorship of the work to the Jesuit Achille Gagliardi, Isabella Bellinzaga's spiritual director, on the title page of the book. In his introduction to the work, he concedes that it was the product of close collaboration between Bellinzaga and Gagliardi, but he believes that the former contributed largely her experiences as a mystic and the latter recorded and interpreted these experiences.

26. Dagens, *Bérulle et les origines de la restauration catholique*, 135–49.

27. There is debate about when Barbe Acarie first made Benoît's acquaintance. Several witnesses for Acarie's beatification proceedings recall her crediting a Capuchin friar with having been the first person to assure her that her raptures were divine in origin, and many historians have identified this friar (who remains unnamed in the testimony) as Benoît, even though he is never named in contemporary sources. I remain skeptical about this identification, which presupposes that Acarie first made Benoît's acquaintance in late 1592 or 1593. Benoît remained in Italy studying theology until sometime in 1592. Although it is possible that he returned to Paris in time to take part in the provincial assembly that named him to office in Orléans in September 1592 and met Acarie at this time, there is no certain evidence of this, and it seems improbable, given the political situation in Paris at that time. The Paris Capuchins had only recently repaired the internal schism provoked by the League and were holding aloof from further political entanglements. The Acaries, by contrast, remained thoroughly enmeshed in the most radical faction of the League. It was not a propitious moment for a young Capuchin, recently returned from theological studies, to go calling on the Acaries. Moreover, even if Benoît did meet Barbe Acarie and provide reassurance at this moment of crisis, he spent most if not all of the five years between September 1592 and 1598 not in Paris but in Orléans. His duties first as master of novices and then as *gardien* (superior) of the Capuchin friary in that city would have made continued contact with Acarie intermittent at best. It thus appears unlikely that he served as her spiritual director in any concerted or prolonged way before his return to Paris in 1598. Barbe Acarie herself appears to date her acquaintance with Benoît to 1597 or 1598 in a letter of 1615 to Bérulle. Historians who prefer

the date of 1592 or 1593 simply ignore this letter (cf. Morgain, *Pierre de Bérulle et les Carmélites de France*, 63n).

28. ACP, Acarie beatification, testimony of Françoise de Jésus de Fleury, fol. 331; Marguerite de Saint-Joseph Langlois, fol. 786.

29. *Les vrays exercices de la bienheureuse sœur Marie de l'Incarnation composez par elle même* (Paris, 1623, 2nd ed.), 19–20, as reproduced in Bruno de Jésus-Marie, *La belle Acarie*, 727–47; cited passage 735–36.

30. Optat de Veghel, without doubting that Benoît served as Acarie's spiritual director at a crucial moment in her life, failed to find "any special rapport between the directed and the director with regard to spiritual doctrine" (*Benoît de Canfield*, 382).

31. Estienne, *Oraison funebre*, fols. 52–53.

32. Orcibal, *La rencontre du Carmel thérésien*, especially 9–15; Minton, "Bérulle's Christic Vision," 5–6. The thesis has also passed more broadly into the literature. See, for example, Taveneaux, *Le catholicisme dans la France classique*, 2:403–404; Vidal, *Critique de la raison mystique*, 55–58; Martin, *The French Book*, 17. Dagens, *Bérulle et les origines de la restauration catholique*, 304–21, is more nuanced where Benoît de Canfield, Barbe Acarie, and others of her circle are concerned, but he nonetheless accepts the notion that an abstract mysticism that bypassed Christ predominated in the late sixteenth century and that Bérulle's Christocentrism was developed only after about 1601. Mauzaize, *Le rôle et l'action des Capucins*, 2:658–64, also identifies Mademoiselle Acarie's circle with "abstract mysticism," though he attributes to Benoît rather than the Carmelites the key role in imparting a new focus on Christ's passion to the group.

33. I use here the English translation given by Minton, "Bérulle's Christic Vision," 5–6, citing Jean Dagens, ed., *Correspondance du Cardinal de Bérulle*, vol. 1 (Paris, 1937), viii. The same passage is cited by Orcibal in *La rencontre du Carmel thérésien*, 13–14.

34. Dagens, *Bérulle et les origines de la restauration catholique*, 205–10, is good on this subject. Other evidence suggesting that the practice of an abstract mysticism dominated in French devotional circles is equally flawed. François de Sales warned against such practices, as did Jean-Pierre Camus and other distinguished theologians, it is true. But the only possible hint that they intended to direct these warnings against the devotional practices encountered in Mademoiselle Acarie's circle comes in a letter from François de Sales to Jeanne de Chantal following a visit that the latter made to the Carmelites' new Dijon convent in June 1606, where she was apparently told by Marie de la Trinité Hannivel and one of the superiors, probably Gallement, that it was not necessary to "use the imagination to represent the sacred humanity of the Savior." Orcibal (*La rencontre du Carmel thérésien*, 14–15) cites this letter as evidence that Hannivel and Gallement were teaching abstract mysticism, a conclusion that seems much too broad to base on a single quotation. The Spanish mother Ana de Jesús was prioress of the Dijon convent at this time. Hannivel was a special favorite of hers, in large part because she spoke Spanish, and came to Dijon at her express wish. It is highly improbable that Hannivel should not only stubbornly maintain but also expound to others doctrines that her prioress did not approve (see *Chroniques des Carmélites*, 3:418–19). Furthermore, Gallement's spirituality was demonstrably Christocentric, and such a teaching would be inconsistent with everything known about his devotional practices as well (see Gallement, *Vie de Jacques Gallement*, especially 198–

200). There appears to be some misunderstanding or missing context here; the advice Jeanne de Chantal reported getting from Hannivel and Gallement was not representative of their broader spiritual views.

35. Marie de la Trinité [Sévin], *Une glorieuse fille de Sainte Thérèse*, 24.

36. *Chroniques des Carmélites*, 3:413. The "Eloge de la V.M. Marie de Hanivel de la Sainte Trinité, Carmelite" included in Placide Gallement's *Vie de Jacques Gallement*, 329–39, also attributes her conversion to the reading of Bonaventura and moves immediately into a discussion of her new abnegations.

37. Dagens, *Bibliographie chronologique*, 131–72.

38. Marie de la Trinité [Sévin], *Une glorieuse fille de Sainte Thérèse*, 26–27.

39. François de Sales, *Œuvres*, 12:267–71, letter of 3 May 1604 to "la présidente Brulart"; François de Sales, *Introduction à la vie dévote*, 28, 86.

40. L'Estoile, *Journal pour le règne de Henri IV*, 2:194 on Teresa of Avila's *Life* and 266 on Granada. See also 2:195, 250, 322, 328, 365, 370, 486–87 for other derogatory comments on spiritual works prized by dévots.

41. Ibid., 2:402.

42. An interesting example of this incorporation of Christ into even the highest forms of union with God in northern mysticism occurs in *The Evangelical Pearl*, the work of a Flemish mystic translated by Dom Richard Beaucousin in 1602. *The Evangelical Pearl* not only posits Christ, considered in both his humanity and his divinity, as the unique means to union with God. It also describes this union as consisting dialectally of five distinct "moments": adhesion to God, to the three persons of the Trinity, to Christ made man, to the eucharistic moment, and to the "moment immediately preceding exterior action of God by the soul." All five "moments" represent distinct aspects of one "introversion," or act of being filled with God. See Schoote, "La perle évangélique," 296, 301.

43. Preface to the *Rule of Perfection* as cited by Dagens, *Bérulle et les origines de la restauration catholique*, 147.

44. Minton, "Bérulle's Christic Vision," 5.

45. *Les vrays exercices*, 7–8, as reproduced in Bruno de Jésus-Marie, *La belle Acarie*, 730. Although not published until later, the *Vrays exercices* were composed sometime prior to 1600 (Morgain, *Pierre de Bérulle et les Carmélites de France*, 62n).

46. The *Vrays exercices* that constitute Acarie's only surviving writing is an extended meditation enlarging on one of Louis de Blois's spiritual exercises. A comparison between the two texts shows how Acarie read and used her favorite spiritual works as a basis for meditation. Focusing on her favorite passages, she borrows them literally or paraphrases them but at the same time builds around them her own invocations and prayers. That this was a standard practice with her is suggested by Marie de Saint-Joseph's account of how Acarie, while visiting the Carmelites one time on Good Friday, asked to borrow a little treatise on the passion. When Marie de Saint-Joseph remarked that she did not believe Acarie needed a book to inspire thoughts about the passion on such a day, the latter replied that "she needed [to make use of] everything possible in order to try to follow our Lord. Then she began to speak on this subject with such ardor that she was entirely enraptured" (ACP, Acarie beatification, testimony of Marie de Saint-Joseph Fournier, fol. 148). The borrowed book, obviously one familiar to Acarie, thus served more as a point of departure for her own

meditations than as a text to be studied or dissected. Marguerite de Saint-Joseph, a lay sister at Pontoise, gave similar testimony in recounting how, asked to speak to the novices in the convent, Acarie (by this time Sœur Marie de l'Incarnation) would at first appear embarrassed and reluctant, but then, reaching for a book, "she would tell us very graciously, 'But, my sisters, I have nothing to say to you; let's see if this little book will teach us something.' In saying that, she would take out the little book on spiritual combat that she ordinarily carried on her and would ordinarily read us some passage and afterwards begin to speak about it, but so fervently that she was all inflamed and, no longer having that bashful look, remained as if enraptured" (ACP, Acarie beatification, testimony of Marguerite de Saint-Joseph Langlois, fol. 786).

A nun at Amiens also commented on Acarie's tendency to pull out the *Spiritual Combat* when asked to address the novices on some inspirational theme and particularly mentioned how important Acarie considered the chapters on the need for defiance of oneself and confidence in God (ACP, Acarie beatification, testimony of Françoise de Jésus de Fleury, fol. 331). The little book that was Acarie's constant companion during her life as a Carmelite was a work popular among members of her circle two decades earlier. Written by the Italian Theatine Lorenzo Scupoli, the *Spiritual Combat* was first published in French in 1594. It went through multiple editions and served as a popular guide to the devout life. Indeed, it is one of the books that François de Sales recommends to his Philothée (*Introduction à la vie dévote*, 86–89). Other nuns who knew Acarie at Amiens and Pontoise tell how she read and reread the Gospels, extracting from them and from the epistles of Saint Paul and the Psalms of David maxims that she would write out onto little slips of paper and hand to the nuns as themes for meditation. Mère Jeanne de Jésus Séguier explained how Acarie "founded her doctrine of the need for religious souls to work toward abnegation on the text *'qui vult venire post me, etc.'* " and how she used the line from the Twenty-First Psalm *Ego sum vermis et non homo* to teach how we should "love and embrace debasement and abjection following the example of Our Lord" (ACP, Acarie beatification, testimony of Jeanne de Jésus Séguier, fol. 815). Barbe Acarie's way of reading was meditative and not analytical.

47. ACP, Acarie beatification, testimony of Marie de Jésus de Tudert, fol. 568v; Pierre Coton, fol. 736; Anne de Saint-Laurent de Saint-Leu, fol. 58.

48. ACP, Acarie beatification, testimony of Pierre Coton, fol. 736.

49. AN, M 233, no. 3: "Poincts notables."

50. Prat, *Recherches sur la Compagnie de Jésus en France*, 2:369; also ACP, Acarie beatification, testimony of Pierre Coton, fol. 736.

51. ACP, Acarie beatification, Anne de Saint-Laurent de Saint-Leu, fol. 74; similarly, Marguerite de Saint-Joseph Langlois, fol. 791; Père Pacifique, Capucin, fol. 75.

52. AN, M233, no. 3, "Poincts notables."

53. See Bynum, *Holy Feast and Holy Fast*; Bynum, *Fragmentation and Redemption*; also Kieckhefer, *Unquiet Souls*.

54. BNF, NA fr. 82–83: Le Fèvre de Lezeau, "Vie du garde des sceaux de Marillac," fols. 259–65.

55. Gallement, *Vie de Jacques Gallement*, 22, 233–34, 335–36.

56. Ibid., 19–21, 185–86.

57. Henry de Calais, *Vie de Honoré de Champigny*, 68–69.

58. Bynum, *Fragmentation and Redemption*, 93–114.

59. Optat de Veghel, *Benoît de Canfield*, 77, citing Benoît's autobiography, 85–88, 108–109.

60. Gallement, *Vie de Jacques de Gallement*, 23, 30, 92.

61. Gallement, for example, founded a school for girls and reformed the Dominican tertiaries in Aumale before becoming part of Acarie's circle. In later life he refused nomination as bishop of Senlis to continue to work with Carmelites and Ursulines (ibid., 39, 82, 104).

62. ACC, Duval, "Vie de Maître André Duval," 71.

63. Borrowing a writing from an earlier scholar was a standard way of adding authority to one's own opinion in the sixteenth century. Estienne's use of the technique in this case suggests that he was well aware that, far from approving his praise of Marie Du Drac's devout piety, many of his peers would denigrate his funeral sermon, as Pierre de L'Estoile was to do, calling it a work of "superstition" rather than religion (L'Estoile, *Journal pour le règne de Henri IV*, 1:74).

64. Estienne, *Oraison funebre*, unpaginated preface.

65. Petroff, *Medieval Women's Visionary Literature*, 34.

66. Teresa of Avila, *The Book of Her Life*, 215, 216.

67. Teresa of Avila, *Book Called Way of Perfection*, 3.

68. Sérouet, *Jean de Brétigny*, 132–33.

69. ACC, Duval, "Vie de Maître André Duval," 89–90.

70. Duval, *Vie de Marie de l'Incarnation*, 103.

71. Morgain, *Pierre de Bérulle et les Carmélites de France*, 69, credits Dom Beaucousin with the initiative for the reform but gives no further details. It is possible that it was in Beaucousin's parlor at Vauvert that Cardinal Sourdis charged Benoît de Canfield with directing Marie de Beauvilliers's conscience and aiding her in the abbey's reform, but I have discovered no direct evidence that this was the case.

72. Blémur, *Eloges*, 1:155–58, as cited in Optat de Veghel, *Benoît de Canfield*, 132.

73. Beauvilliers, *Conférences spirituelles*, 14, 45, 204.

74. Blémur, *Eloges*, 1:155–58, as cited in Optat de Veghel, *Benoît de Canfield*, 131–33.

75. Chaussy, *Les Bénédictines et la réforme catholique*, 1:30–38; Optat de Veghel, *Benoît de Canfield*, 130–34.

76. François de Sales, *Œuvres*, 12:171–74, "A Madame de Beauvilliers" (Annecy, [January] 1603).

77. Chaussy, *Les Bénédictines et la réforme catholique*, 1:176, citing Blémur, *Eloges*.

78. Sérouet, *Jean de Brétigny*, 138.

79. Chaussy, *Les Bénédictines et la réforme catholique*, 176, identifies her as visiting Sully with her sister. Despite the fact that Sully was a Protestant, the visit is entirely plausible. The abbess's elder sister, Louise de L'Hôpital, dame de Simiers, worked closely with Sully to ensure the surrender of the League's governor of Rouen (Barbiche and Dainville-Barbiche, *Sully*, 54–55). The position of abbess for the younger Louise de L'Hôpital was a reward for this cooperation and assistance, and Madame de Simiers might well have wished to have her younger sister meet Sully and thank him for any personal role he may have played in recommending the award of the abbey to the L'Hôpitals. Chaussy does not further identify the "abbé de Beaulieu," however. This information is provided by Pierre Sérouet in *Jean de Brétigny*, 138.

80. Chaussy, *Les Bénédictines et la réforme catholique*, 1:176, citing the "Registre journalier" kept by the abbey's confessor.

81. Louise de L'Hôpital's admiration for Jacques Gallement comes through clearly in the letter Placide Gallement cites in his *Vie de Jacques Gallement*, 57–58.

82. Chaussy, *Les Bénédictines et la réforme catholique*, 1:177, citing the "Registre journalier" kept by the abbey's confessor.

83. Ibid., 1:177–78.

CHAPTER 4: FIRST FOUNDATIONS

1. *Chroniques des Carmélites*, 1:116.

2. Capuchins Pacifique de Souzy and Archange de Pembroke may also have attended the meeting, but their presence is not verified in contemporary sources. The best secondary account of this meeting is Morgain, *Pierre de Bérulle et les Carmélites de France*, 84–90.

3. Duval, *Vie de Marie de l'Incarnation*, 122–23.

4. ACP, Acarie beatification, testimony of André Duval, fol. 352r.; Duval, *Vie de Marie de l'Incarnation*, 123.

5. AN, L 1046, pièce no. 70: lettres patentes du roi Henri IV (St-Maur, July 1602); verified in Parlement 1 October 1602; Raunié, *Epitaphier du vieux Paris*, 2:158n, reproducing notarial contract of 22 January 1603 before Jean Le Normand and François Herbin.

6. François de Sales, *Œuvres*, 2:131–34: letter from Thorens, beginning of November 1602.

7. The bull "In supremo" is reproduced in Morgain, *Pierre de Bérulle et les Carmélites de France*, 490–504, from the version in AN, L 1047, no. 121.

8. The most complete account of Acarie's supervision of the convent's construction is given in Duval, *Vie de Marie de l'Incarnation*, 133–35. Many other witnesses also testified to Pierre Acarie's demands on his wife's time. See for example, ACP, Acarie beatification, testimony of Marie de Saint-Joseph Fournier, fols. 109–10.

9. The figure of 80,000 livres in debts is given by Marie de Tudert Séguier (ACP, Acarie beatification, fol. 548). Michel de Marillac tells how Barbe Acarie arranged letters of credit and advanced the funds necessary for the trip to Spain, even though she had to borrow to do so. He also praises her utter confidence in sending off to Spain even before the necessary papal permissions were assured (ACP, Acarie beatification, fols. 766–67). Other sources suggest, however, that it was Jean de Brétigny, with close ties in the Spanish mercantile community, who assumed financial responsibility for the trip to Spain (AN, L 1046, "L'arrivee des reverendes meres carmelites d'Espagne en France," by Jean Navet, 4, 5). Navet, who accompanied Brétigny to Spain, does, however, give Barbe Acarie credit for giving everyone a great deal of advice about the trip, which she was especially insistent must be kept secret (7).

10. ACP, Acarie beatification, testimony of Maris de Jésus de Tudert, fol. 548; Michel de Marillac, fol. 764.

11. ACP, Acarie beatification, testimony of Marie de Saint-Joseph Fournier, fol. 109.

12. Duval, *Vie de Marie de l'Incarnation*, 135–38. This testimony is particularly

important because Duval cites specific cases of Acarie's insights into the vocations of potential novices. See also ACP, Acarie beatification, testimony of Anne de Saint-Laurent de Saint-Leu, fol. 60; Jeanne L'Espervier, fol. 581; Marguerite de Gondy, marquise de Maignelay, fol. 397.

13. *Chroniques des Carmélites*, 1:22–23.

14. Ibid., 1:119–22.

15. Eriau, *L'ancien Carmel du Faubourg Saint-Jacques*, 56.

16. Ibid., citing Ana de Jesús's letter of 8 March 1605; also Morgain, *Pierre de Bérulle et les Carmélites de France*, 156.

17. Eriau, *L'ancien Carmel du Faubourg Saint-Jacques*, 83, citing Ana de Jesús's letter of 8 March 1605.

18. The church was a Gothic structure remaining from the old priory of Notre-Dame des Champs; its basic size and configuration were thus not the product of recent designs. The interior, however, was thoroughly redesigned and refurbished when the Carmelites moved in.

19. *Chroniques des Carmélites*, 3:426, 431–32, 418, 1:130.

20. Ibid., 1:130, 129. Pierre de Bérulle in particular seems to have encouraged restraint and solemnity among the French novices. He disapproved, for example, of the informality shown by Spanish nuns, who within the cloister normally wore their heavy outer veils only during religious services. Finding this practice "quite contrary to French mores," he ordered the French nuns always to wear their outer veils except when engaged in manual labor. He was careful not to make this change, however, until after Ana de Jesús had departed from France (1:128).

21. Ibid., 1:123.

22. Ibid., 1:124, 127, 2:126–30. See also Ana de San Bartolomé, *Autobiographie*, 137, on the beginnings of the convent at Pontoise. I use the French version of Ana de San Bartolomé's memoirs out of convenience, because I own a copy. The translation is based on the critical edition published by Julián Urkiza in 1981 from the autograph manuscript in the Carmel of Antwerp, and comparisons with the Spanish edition show it to be entirely scrupulous.

23. *Chroniques des Carmélites*, 1:134, 139. In March 1606, Ana de Jesús petitioned the pope to allow the Paris convent to have thirty-three nuns instead of the twenty-one permitted by the constitutions. If the French chronicles are to be believed, the convent already exceeded this number. See Ana de Jesús, *Cartas*, 55–56, letter from Dijon, 2 March 1606.

24. According to Concepción Torres, both Ana de Jesús and Ana de San Bartolomé considered themselves direct heirs to Teresa and custodians of her legacy, which made relations between them difficult. The most important disagreement between them concerned the order's constitutions. Although both women wanted the French Carmelites placed under the direction of Carmelite fathers, Ana de Jesús disagreed with Ana de San Bartolomé's unquestioning allegiance to Carmelite general Nicolás Doria, because he had changed the constitutions in ways that deprived the nuns of too much autonomy. Ana de Jesús wanted the Carmelites as superiors, but with Teresa's original constitutions and not Doria's subsequent revisions (Ana de Jesús, *Cartas*, 23).

25. The most recent account is Morgain, *Pierre de Bérulle et les Carmélites de France*; see also Dagens, *Bérulle et les origines de la restauration catholique*, 207–14.

26. Ana de San Bartolomé, *Obras completas*, 1:177–221.

27. Ana de San Bartolomé, *Autobiographie*, 142–45; cf. Ana de San Bartolomé, *Obras completas*, 1:189–90.

28. Ana de San Bartolomé, *Autobiographie*, 145, 146–49; cf. Ana de San Bartolomé, *Obras completas*, 1:191, 199.

29. Morgain, *Pierre de Bérulle et les Carmélites de France*, 192–211; Ana de San Bartolomé, *Lettres et écrits spirituels*, especially 79–81: letter of 15 February 1610 to Pierre de Bérulle, and 87–97: letters 41 and 43 to Bérulle and letter 42 to Michel de Marillac, all written early in 1611.

30. Ana de San Bartolomé, *Autobiographie*, 151–52; similarly, Ana de San Bartolomé, *Obras completas*, 212.

31. Ana de San Bartolomé, *Autobiographie*, 157.

32. When Ana de San Bartolomé arrived in Paris, she found it necessary to correct the novices on behavior they claimed was permitted by Ana de Jesús that she nevertheless found contrary to the constitutions. Ana de San Bartolomé, *Lettres et écrits spirituels*, 53–55: letter 21 to Jean de Brétigny, 1605. See also Morgain, *Pierre de Bérulle et les Carmélites de France*, 196.

33. Ana de San Bartolomé, *Autobiographie*, 152.

34. Bilinkoff, *The Avila of Saint Teresa*, 159–66; see especially chapters 2 and 5, on Teresa's rejection of traditions of aristocratic dominance in monastic foundations.

35. Dagens, *Bérulle et les origines de la restauration catholique*, 211; see also the bull "In supremo" of 1603 reproduced in Morgain, *Pierre de Bérulle et les Carmélites de France*, 501.

36. Superior Guillaume Gibieuf sent a letter to all of the Carmelite convents in 1646 in which he repeatedly reproached them for letting standards of cloistering slip from the strict practices instituted by the Spanish nuns. See BNF, Ms. fr. 17719: Gibieuf, "Lettre generalle," fols. 229–35.

37. *Chroniques des Carmélites*, 1:118, 154–55.

38. Ibid., 1:121.

39. L'Estoile, *Journal pour le règne de Henri IV*, 2:170.

40. *Chroniques des Carmélites*, 1:138.

41. Ibid., 2:123–26, 134, 137–39.

42. Ibid., 2:131–32.

43. Sérouet, *Jean de Brétigny et les Carmélites de France*, 211; AN, L 1046, pièce 56, p. 6, testimony of Marie de La Trinité d'Hannivel concerning Ana de Jesús.

44. Coming first to make the acquaintance of Mother Ana de Jesús, Jeanne de Chantal soon developed an enduring spiritual friendship with Marie de la Trinité d'Hannivel, who was serving as the prioress's translator. Sérouet, *Jean de Brétigny et les Carmélites de France*, 212; *Chroniques des Carmélites*, 3:463–65.

45. *Chroniques des Carmélites*, 1:292–93: Table des années de chaque fondation de l'ordre.

46. To cite just two examples, Tours was founded by Antoine du Bois de Fontaines, father of Madeleine de Saint-Joseph de Fontaines, brother-in-law through his wife, Marie Prudhomme, of chancellor Nicolas Brûlart de Sillery, and closely tied by blood and marriage to other Parisian elites. The first Bordeaux convent was founded by maître des requêtes Antoine de Gourgues and his wife, Marie Séguier, the daughter of Jean Séguier d'Autry and Marie de Tudert.

47. Morgain, *Pierre de Bérulle et les Carmélites de France*, 196, citing letter to Jean de Brétigny, late October 1605.

48. On the Spanish nuns' defense of the constitutions of Alcalá, see Morgain, *Pierre de Bérulle et les Carmélites de France*, especially 161–78, 240. See also Weber, "Spiritual Administration," 123–46, especially 142–46, on the implications of the changes Nicolás Doria made in the constitutions.

49. ACC, ms. "Vie de la Mere Marie de Jesus [de Breauté]," 71–72.

50. Finley-Croswhite, *Henry IV and the Towns*, 69–70, 70n; Tingle, "Nantes and the Origins of the Catholic League," 109.

51. Buisseret, *Henry IV, King of France*, 69.

52. L'Estoile, *Journal pour le règne de Henri IV*, 2:489.

53. Raunié, *Epitaphier du vieux Paris*, 2:118n.

54. Malet, *Sommaire narration*, 1229. Except where otherwise cited, I have followed Malet's account, which gives the fullest account of this foundation. Malet was Marie de Luxembourg's confessor and may have embellished her role somewhat out of a desire to flatter her, but he was well positioned to know her actual contributions.

55. Mauzaize, *Histoire des Frères Mineurs Capucins*, 78–79; Mauzaize, *Le rôle et l'action des Capucins*, 2:883–85.

56. Denis, "Les clarisses capucines de Paris," 202. The Capuchins' annals credit Ange de Joyeuse in particular with prompting the foundation of the Capucines (BMaz, Ms. 2418: "Annales des Reverends Peres Capucins," 323).

57. Malet, *Sommaire narration*, 1224; [Bauduen], *Vie de Marguerite de Gondy, marquise de Magnelais*, 146–47.

58. Malet, *Sommaire narration*, 1222.

59. Denis, "Les clarisses capucines de Paris," 196.

60. Malet, *Sommaire narration*, 1226.

61. Ibid., 1223–24.

62. Denis, "Les clarisses capucines de Paris," 197.

63. Malet, *Sommaire narration*, 1225.

64. BMaz, Ms. 2418: "Annales des Reverends Peres Capucins," 326.

65. Denis, "Les clarisses capucines de Paris," 200–201.

66. Ibid., 201, 203.

67. On contemporary interest rates, see Ultee, *The Abbey of Saint Germain des Prés*, 75.

68. Malet, *Sommaire narration*, 1238.

69. Ibid., 1233.

70. BMaz, Ms. 2418: "Annales des Reverends Peres Capucins," 326.

71. Denis, "Les clarisses capucines de Paris," 402.

72. On Marie de la Trinité d'Hannivel: *Chroniques des Carmélites*, 3:414–16; on Marie de Jésus de Breauté: ACC, ms. "Vie de la Mere Marie de Jesus [de Breauté]," 33; on Madeleine de Saint-Joseph de Fontaines: Senault, *Vie de Magdeleine de S. Joseph*, 42.

73. Gallement, *Vie de Jacques Gallement*, 38–39, 45–46, 98–99.

74. Leymont, *Madame de Sainte-Beuve*, 147–50.

75. Ibid., 162–63.

76. Pommereuse, *Chroniques des Ursulines*, 128.

77. Leymont, *Madame de Sainte-Beuve*, 64–66, 76–81.

78. Ibid., 4–5; more generally on the Luillier family, Diefendorf, *Paris City Councillors*.

79. ACP, Acarie beatification, testimony of Michel de Marillac, fols. 768–69; Leymont, *Madame de Sainte-Beuve*, 168–69.

80. Leymont, *Madame de Sainte-Beuve*, 177. The papal bull issued in 1612 authorizing foundation of the Paris Ursulines specifies that Madeleine Luillier had promised rentes yielding 2,000 livres annually in revenue to endow the new convent, along with rentes yielding 500 livres promised by another, unnamed donor. The original convent was to be limited to twelve persons. These specifications are almost identical to those set out in the bulls establishing the Carmelites and Capucines. Twenty-five hundred livres was to be a standard sum for endowing new convents. The bull is published in Leymont, *Madame de Sainte-Beuve*, 403–419, cited at 405.

81. Pommereuse, *Chroniques des Ursulines*, 129, 106.

82. Ibid., 106, 129.

83. On Sainte-Avoye: Raunié, *Epitaphier du vieux Paris*, 1:305–306; on the Haudriettes: Sauval, *Histoire et antiquites de la ville de Paris*, 1:598–600.

84. Raunié, *Epitaphier du vieux Paris*, 1:305–307; Leymont, *Madame de Sainte-Beuve*, 275–77.

85. Leymont, *Madame de Sainte-Beuve*, 92.

86. See introduction, n. 3.

87. Leymont, *Madame de Sainte-Beuve*, 185–203, 404–5, citing the papal bull of Paul V.

88. Gallement, *Vie de Jacques Gallement*, 82, 102–3.

89. Pommereuse, *Chroniques des Ursulines*, 133.

90. Prat, *Recherches sur la compagnie de Jésus en France*, 3:540–41, 727–28.

91. Pommereuse, *Chroniques des Ursulines*, 134, 135.

92. See also Jégou, *Les Ursulines du Faubourg St-Jacques*, chapter 2, especially p. 57, on the "originality" of the Ursulines' blend of contemplation with a teaching apostolate.

93. Ibid., 26; Leymont, *Madame de Sainte-Beuve*, 173–74.

94. Pommereuse, *Chroniques des Ursulines*, 136; Leymont, *Madame de Sainte-Beuve*, 249–51.

95. Papal bull of Paul V erecting the monastery of Saint Ursula in Paris, as published in Leymont, *Madame de Sainte-Beuve*, 416.

96. Pommereuse, *Chroniques des Ursulines*, 106, 136.

97. Ibid., 113.

98. Denis, "Les clarisses capucines de Paris," 196n, but see also 203 for a first expansion of this privilege in 1615, when the duchesse de Mercœur and her daughter got permission to bring a secular person with them into the convent, as long as this person remained no longer than one night.

99. Ibid., 400–401. The duchesse de Mercœur was one of the principal patrons of the house in Tours. The other was Marie de Bragelonne, a member of a distinguished Parisian family and the widow of Claude Bouthillier, a secretary of state and surintendant des finances.

100. Leymont, *Madame de Sainte-Beuve*, 233–38.

101. Senault, *Vie de Catherine de Montholon*, 33–54.

CHAPTER 5: THE CONTEMPLATIVE REVIVAL

1. The number is difficult to calculate because some groups of women lived together informally for a number of years before seeking papal bulls and letters patent from the king permitting their formal erection as a religious house. In other cases, legal permissions were acquired well before recruits were sought and assembled into a community. I have tried to count only groups that had official recognition and for which there is evidence that a community, even if only four or five members large, actually existed by 1650. I have not counted the several convents of English Catholics established in Paris because the evidence suggests that, during this period at least, they recruited only from the British Isles and remained quite apart from the currents of French Catholicism that are the subject of this book.

2. On the creation of active orders, see especially Rapley, *The Dévotes* and *A Social History of the Cloister*.

3. Dufour, "Histoire du siège de Paris," 210–27.

4. Malet, *Sommaire narration*, 1222.

5. Arnauld, *Relation sur Port-Royal*, 129, 145.

6. *Histoire des religieuses*, 71–74.

7. Raunié, *Epitaphier du vieux Paris*, 4:237.

8. Fagniez, *Le Père Joseph*, 2:90.

9. BNF, Ms. fr. 13884: "Constitutions generalles des soeurs de Saincte Elizabeth," fol. 1.

10. Ferraige, *Vie de Marguerite d'Arbouze*, 100, describes how, when Marguerite d'Arbouze was installed as abbess of Val-de-Grâce in a ceremony at the Carmelites' church, Anne of Austria came to examine her habit and found that she was wearing a shift not of linen but of wool, "which caused her . . . thereafter to hold [Marguerite] in high esteem."

11. BNF, Ms. fr. 13884: "Constitutions generalles des soeurs de Saincte Elizabeth," fols. 26–31. Récollettes could wear shoes only by special permission of the Récollet provincial who served as their superior. See BMaz, Ms. 3338: "Statuts et reglements des religieuses recollettes Ste Claire," 28.

12. See, for example, Ferraige, *Vie de Marguerite d'Arbouze*, 106, which tells how the very first thing that Marguerite d'Arbouze did when shown into the abbess's room on her arrival at Val-de-Grâce was to order the sumptuous tapestries, embroidered bed hangings, and silken bed coverings removed. Reducing her new quarters to "the poverty in which a Benedictine should live" was a way of announcing that a new regime had begun. See also *Vie de Marie Agnes Dauvaine*, 89, on her willing participation in the convent's most burdensome chores.

13. BNF, Ms. fr. 13884: "Constitutions generalles des soeurs de Saincte Elizabeth," fols. 51–55, 59–62. See also BMaz, Ms. 3338: "Statuts et reglements des religieuses recollettes Ste Claire."

14. *Vie de Marie Agnes Dauvaine*, 264, 282.

15. Rapley, *A Social History of the Cloister*, 111–18, does call attention to the "highly positive case" for enclosure made in the nuns' own writings, though she seems to suggest that this was largely a case of the nuns making the best of a poor deal: "Whether by choice or necessity, the cloister was the place where these women were going to spend their lives, and it was up to them to decide whether they would

do so as prisoners or as true lovers of Jesus Christ" (117). At the same time, Rapley sees the public perception of religious enclosure as very strongly negative. It made the women "safe in the one respect that really mattered: their chastity," but, beyond that, "the life within it was assumed to be largely meaningless" (117). The sources cited for this judgment, however, date from the late seventeenth and eighteenth centuries, and whatever its validity for this later period, it should not be projected back on the earlier stages of the Catholic Reformation.

16. This is spelled out with unusual explicitness in *Vie de Marie Agnes Dauvaine*, 19. Significantly, this biography was composed by the nuns themselves.

17. Macé, *Vie de Marie de Saint-Charles*, 48–49. See also ACC, ms. "Vie de la Mère Marie de Jesus [de Breauté]," 45.

18. *Vie de Marie Agnes Dauvaine*, 264, 18.

19. Gazier, *Jeanne de Chantal et Angélique Arnauld*, 128: letter of August 1620.

20. See, for example, the constitutions of the Franciscan Third Order Penitents of the convent of the Conception Notre-Dame, which explain that, having consecrated their bodies "and all the affections of the heart" to God, along with their souls, the nuns must avoid anything not only that "soils the whiteness" but even that "dims the luster" of their virtue. BMaz, Ms. 3324: "Constitutions du Monastere de la Conception Notre-Dame," 5–7.

21. That lesbian relationships could and did exist in early modern convents has been documented in Brown, *Immodest Acts*. My point is rather that, for reformed nuns, the concept of chastity encompassed far more than sexual continence, and even friendships untouched by homosexual desire were seen as disruptive of the monastic community.

22. BNF, Ms. fr. 13884: "Constitutions generalles des soeurs de Saincte Elizabeth," fols. 1–2, 87–88. By contrast, the nuns of the Conception Notre-Dame, although also Franciscan Third Order Penitents, scourged themselves only once a week, after Friday matins and only for "the time it takes to say one Miserere" (BMaz, Ms. 3324: "Constitutions du Monastere de la Conception Notre-Dame," 41).

23. Jean-Marie de Vernon, *Histoire du Tiers Ordre de S. François*, 2:636–40.

24. Macé, *Vie de Marie de Saint-Charles*, 110–11.

25. See Le Brun, "Mutations de la notion de martyre," 77–90.

26. Madeleine de Saint-Joseph, *Vie de Catherine de Jesus*, 44, 48, 86–87, 96.

27. Madeleine de Saint-Joseph de Fontaines, for example, used the image of the baby Jesus to teach her novices humility. "Mixing Calvary with the manger," she urged them to acquire the virtues of Christ's infancy "so as to profit more abundantly from the effects of his death" ([Senault], *Vie de Magdeleine de S. Joseph*, 90–91). On the cult more generally, see Le Brun, "A corps perdu," 397–98. See also Bremond, *Histoire littéraire du sentiment religieux*, 3:522–47; Bérulle, *Œuvres complètes*, vol. 2: *Œuvres de piété*, chapters 37–40, 47–48.

28. Madeleine de Saint-Joseph, *Vie de Catherine de Jesus*, 75–76, 162–63.

29. Macé, *Vie de Marie de Saint-Charles*, 111–12. See, for example, Ferraige, *Vie de Marguerite d'Arbouze*, 63, on the strength d'Arbouze drew from Teresa's teachings.

30. *Vie de Marie Agnes Dauvaine*, 19.

31. Macé, *Vie de Marie de Saint-Charles*, 178–84.

32. Madeleine de Saint-Joseph, *Lettres spirituelles*, 33: undated letter to a Carmelite prioress, in which Mère Madeleine advises her "conduire les âmes avec douceur"

and says she has not herself given any penitence greater than a "mortification au re-
fectoire" in over six years and yet has never received more respect from her nuns.

33. The only sustained discussion of women's role as spiritual directors is in
Timmermans, *L'accès des femmes à la culture*, chapter 4, which places more emphasis
on the limits placed on this role and the suspicion with which women's spiritual insights were viewed than does the interpretation presented here.

34. BNF, Ms. fr. 13884: "Constitutions generalles des soeurs de Saincte Elizabeth," fols. 17, 71. Thomas Carr's recently published "Les abbesses et la Parole" discusses the strategies nuns used to skirt Pauline prohibitions against women speaking
on religious subjects.

35. Macé, *Vie de Marie de Saint-Charles*, 173, 174.

36. Ibid., 86. This rhetorical tactic is discussed in Mack, *Visionary Women*, 23–
24, 32–33.

37. Macé, *Vie de Marie de Saint-Charles*, 167–68.

38. See, for example, the "Vie de la mère Marie de Jésus, Mme de Bréauté," by
Agnès de Bellefond, as published in Cousin, *La Jeunesse de Madame de Longueville*, 433–
52: "When she spoke to her daughters to instruct them, she ordinarily had her hands
joined and her eyes raised toward heaven and appeared so filled with God that everyone seeing her believed that it was from this divine source that everything she told
them came, which had a great effect on their advancement in perfection" (448). See
also [Catherine de Saint-François Mallet], "Vie de Madeleine Bochart de Saron," 7:
"She inspired in almost the entire community [the Annonciades du Saint-Esprit at Po-
pincourt] the desire to return to the noviciate under her in order to hear the celestial
eloquence and the surprising things that this infused doctrine made shine. The gifts
that her humility had until this time kept hidden appeared all of a sudden with such
force, this ease of expressing in a manner that was at once both elevated and intelligi-
ble the greatest secrets of spiritual life."

39. Ferraige, *Vie de Marguerite d'Arbouze*, 692, 694, 693, 194; more generally
692–705. See also the lengthy discussion of Ferraige's biography of Marguerite
d'Arbouze in Bremond, *Histoire littéraire du sentiment religieux*, 2:485–536, especially
489–90.

40. *Exercice journalier pour les religieuses bénédictines de Nostre-Dame du Val-de-
Grâce, par la Révérende Mère Marguerite de Veni d'Arbouze, abbesse et réformatrice de
l'Abbaye de Nostre-Dame du Val-de-Grâce, avec un traité de l'oraison mentale par la meme*
(Paris, 1676), as cited in *DS*, vol. 1 (1937), col. 838; Beauvilliers, *Conférences spirituelles*;
Madeleine de Saint-Joseph, *Avis pour la conduite des novices*. In addition, Bremond,
Histoire littéraire du sentiment religieux, 2:345, cites a posthumous collection of letters
of direction and spiritual advice by Marguerite du Saint-Sacrement Acarie, the *Conduite chrétienne et religieuse selon les sentiments de la V.M. Marguerite*, published by Father J. M. de Vernon, which he calls "one of the best books of [spiritual] direction"
that he knows.

41. The reformed Dominicaines de Saint-Thomas were brought from Toulouse,
where the reform originated, to establish a Paris convent in 1627.

42. [Lantages], *Vie de Françoise des Seraphins*.

43. Jeanne de Chantal, *Correspondance*; Madeleine de Saint-Joseph, *Lettres spirituelles*.

44. Madeleine de Saint-Joseph, *Lettres spirituelles*, 263–64: letter 244, undated and addressed only to "une Prieure de Carmel."

45. Ferraige, *Vie de Marguerite d'Arbouze*, 285.

46. Ibid., 282, 286.

47. Macé, *Vie de Marie de Saint-Charles*, 85.

48. *Regles et constitutions pour les sœurs de la Visitation* (as approved at Annecy in 1618), 211.

49. Jeanne de Chantal, *Correspondance*, 1:374–76: letter of May–June 1619 to Mère Anne-Marie Rosset at Bourges.

50. Madeleine de Saint-Joseph, *Avis pour la conduite des novices*, 26, 31, 56–57. Carmelite Anne du Saint-Sacrement Viole went a step further in stressing that the good prioress must be sure to nurture in her spiritual daughters the "firm virtues" that tie them to Jesus Christ and not to herself: "The grace is not attached to the person but rather to the charge." *Chroniques des Carmélites*, 4:168–69.

51. See chapter 4; also Weber, "Spiritual Administration," 123–46.

52. ACC, ms. "Vie de la Mere Marie de Jesus [de Breauté]," 71–72; also Weber, "Spiritual Administration," 142–46, on the implications of the changes made in the constitutions, and Morgain, *Pierre de Bérulle et les Carmélites de France*, 161–78, 240, on the Spanish nuns' defense of their earlier constitutions. Unfortunately, Morgain does not address the question of the prioress's spiritual authority.

53. Duval, *Vie de Marie de l'Incarnation*, 136–38, 146–52.

54. "Déposition autographe de Madame de Longueville," as published in Cousin, *La jeunesse de Madame de Longueville*, 415, 416, more generally 414–20.

55. Madeleine de Saint-Joseph, *Lettres spirituelles*, 216–18: letter 207, undated and addressed simply to "une Prieure de Carmel." Similarly, 266–69: letter 246, also undated and addressed simply "à une prieure de Carmel."

56. *Chroniques des Carmélites*, 4:180.

57. Marie de Medici and the princesse de Condé apparently unburdened themselves to Mère Marie-Angès Dauvaine at the Annonciades Célestes, as well as to various Carmelite mothers, and Mère Dauvaine's biographer is quick to explain that when these great ladies began to complain about their mistreatment by persons close to them at court, the sage prioress deftly returned the conversation to a pious track by reminding them of the great difference between the favors of heaven and those of the world. *Vie de Mere Marie Agnes Dauvaine*, 276–77, 284, 285.

58. *Chroniques des Carmélites*, 3:428, 453.

59. Madeleine de Saint-Joseph, *Lettres spirituelles*, 249–63: letters 236–43.

60. [Tronson de Chenevière], *Vie de Marguerite Acarie*, 170–73, 177–80.

61. *Chroniques des Carmélites*, 4:193.

62. One Parisian prioress who rejected demands for spiritual counsel from men was Angélique Arnauld. Although at one point she did engage in this practice, she later decided that it was not proper for women "to meddle in the teaching of men and priests." Significantly, however, it was her own decision to refuse men's requests for spiritual guidance and not something forced on her by her male directors (Arnauld, *Relation écrite sur Port-Royal*, 155–56).

63. AN, S 4692, contract of 6 May 1623, as given in Raunié, *Epitaphier du vieux Paris*, 4:234–35.

64. Ibid., 4:236.

65. Boulenger, *Traitez de la closture*, 307.

66. Raunié, *Epitaphier du vieux Paris*, 4:236.

67. AN, L 1053, no. 62: "Les fondateurs et bienfacteurs de la monastere du Calvaire de la Compassion, rue de Vaugirard," fols. 6–7.

68. The key contracts are reproduced in Raunié, *Epitaphier du vieux Paris*, 4:231–43.

69. The constitutions for the nursing sisters of the Charité Notre-Dame published by Archbishop Jean-François de Gondi in 1635 specify that, in order that the nuns not become a burden on their families and friends, the convent must possess for each nun an annual income equal to 200 pounds "in large cities where it is expensive to live, such as in Paris" (*Constitutions de la Charité nostre Dame*, 11).

70. "Les feuillantines de Paris," 207–22; see especially the list of expenses, 219.

71. Ibid.

72. Ibid., 222.

73. AN, S 4691, contract of 31 October 1613, as cited in Raunié, *Epitaphier du vieux Paris*, 3:540–41, 539.

74. Hélyot, *Dictionnaire des ordres religieux*, vol. 3, cols. 211–12: "Pénitents du Tiers Ordre de Saint-François."

75. AN, L 957, contract of 5 August 1616, as cited in Raunié, *Epitaphier du vieux Paris*, 3:543–44. The donor, Jeanne de La Grange, also owned property at Franconville, where Père Vincent initially established his reform, and it is quite probable that she first encountered his preaching there.

76. AN, S 4691, contract of 31 October 1613, as cited in Raunié, *Epitaphier du vieux Paris*, 3:540–41.

77. Louis XIII took the title of patron and founder of the convent, promising it his "special and particular protection and safeguard." So did his mother, but neither gave any money toward the foundation.

78. Raunié, *Epitaphier du vieux Paris*, 3:542–43.

79. "Whenever and as often as it pleases the aforesaid damoiselle Jeanne de La Grange to enter the aforesaid convent to live and reside with its nuns, the convent will be obligated to receive her to live there in whatever habit and manner she desires, without being obligated to follow the rules of the aforesaid convent, as long as the convent is not harmed or its [devotional] activities disturbed on account of her residing there." AN, L 957, contract of 5 August 1616, and S 4691, contract of 20 January 1628, as cited in Raunié, *Epitaphier*, 3:543–45.

80. At the rates cited in the contract, the 14,000 livres promised in payment of bequests and debts on Jeanne de La Grange's death would have translated into 700 livres of rentes, or annuities. Adding this hypothetical amount to the 300 livres annually promised to the Picpus friars for coming to say mass at the convent and the 200 livre rente promised to the young woman admitted at de La Grange's request, should she decide to leave the convent, the nuns would have been required by the contract to pay out 1,200 livres each year. Whether or not the 110 arpents of donated farmland would have covered these costs would have depended on the income that could be drawn from them. Farm rents varied greatly. Jean Jacquart's study of the agricultural communities southwest of Paris suggests, however, that, during the first third of the seventeenth century, such lands might have yielded somewhere between 3

and 6 livres per arpent *(La crise rurale en Ile-de-France*, 130–31, 332–35, 772). At the high rate of 6 livres per arpent, the lands would have yielded 660 livres per year, which, along with the 650 livres promised in rentes, would have totalled 1,310 livres annual income, a sum sufficient to cover the promised payments. At 5 livres per arpent, the nuns would have just broken even. Anything less than 5 livres per arpent would have produced too little revenue to pay the claims against the estate.

81. Over the course of the next ten years, the nuns purchased another four properties for a total cost of 1,200 livres in rentes plus 2,400 livres in cash. AN, S 4691, contracts of 12 November 1616, 29 December 1617, 27 February 1626, and 11 March 1626, as cited in Raunié, *Epitaphier du vieux Paris*, 3:545–47. I have included here also the fees demanded of the nuns by the monks of Saint-Martin-des-Champs, who had extensive seigneurial rights to the purchased properties.

82. Jean-Marie de Vernon, *Histoire du Tiers-Ordre de S. François*, 2:636–41.

83. Macé, *Vie de Marie de Saint-Charles*, 36.

84. Jean-Marie de Vernon, *Histoire du Tiers-Ordre de S. François*, 2:640–41.

85. AN, S 4690, memorandum of 20 April 1626, as cited in Raunié, *Epitaphier du vieux Paris*, 3:547.

86. Jean-Marie de Vernon, *Histoire du Tiers-Ordre de S. François*, 2:641–42; Macé, *Vie de Marie de Saint-Charles*, 101.

87. Raunié, *Epitaphier du vieux Paris*, 3:548–52.

88. Macé, *Vie de Marie de Saint-Charles*, 158–59, 200–202. Among the patrons allowed entry to the convent were the duchesses d'Angoulême and Sully and the marquise Danton. Again, the convent's increasing appeal to elites is evident.

89. Macé, *Vie de Marie de Saint-Charles*, 157–58.

90. On the Annonciades des Dix-Vertus: Raunié, *Epitaphier du vieux Paris*, 1:103–4. Founded by Jeanne de France at the start of the sixteenth century, the Annonciades des Dix-Vertus were a separate order from the Annonciades Célestes. On the Bernardines: Hélyot, *Dictionnaire des ordres religieux*, vol. 3, cols. 451–52; AN, L 773, Bernardines du Précieux Sang. In fact, a far more extensive reform occurred only after the Bernardines' founding in Paris. When they arrived in the city, their manner of life, religious practices, and even the shape of their habits were modeled more closely on those of the Visitandines than on the strict Cistercian observances they claimed to wish to adopt. A threat by the Cistercians (spurred on, it would seem, by Cardinal Richelieu, who was, among other positions, abbot of Cîteaux) to eject them from the fold appears to have served as a wake-up call, setting the nuns on the path to a more rigorously Cistercian—and more rigorously ascetic—reform. Taking as their ideal "the austerity of the primitive spirit of Cîteaux," they slowly but surely revised their practices to conform to this spirit, eliminating the refinements in their dress, instituting new fasts and regular abstinence, returning to a schedule of devotions that required them to rise in the night for matins, and incorporating mental prayer and spiritual readings into the day's schedule. Their example reminds us that the reform impulse did not follow a simple and fixed chronology but inspired different communities at different times. On the Augustinian canonesses from Rheims: Raunié, *Epitaphier du vieux Paris*, 1:147–48; Félibien and Lobineau, *Histoire de la ville de Paris*, 2:1371.

91. The patron and chief benefactor of the new foundation, Anne Pétau, dame de Traversay, justified the new convent on the ground of the "exemplary lives and dis-

cipline" of the nuns from Toulouse. There is, however, no reason to believe that the lives of these nuns were any more exemplary than those of the Filles de Sainte-Elisabeth. They were favored by the archbishop because they accepted him as their superior, rather than subjecting themselves to the Third Order Franciscan friars, as was the case for the Filles de Sainte-Elisabeth, but the constitutions of the two houses were in other respects very similar. BNF, Ms. fr. 14475: "Constitutions du Monastere de la Conception N. Dame"; cf. BNF, Ms. fr. 13884: "Constitutions generalles des soeurs de Saincte Elizabeth."

92. The correspondence of Madeleine de Saint-Joseph de Fontaines, prioress of the Carmelites' convent of the Incarnation between 1624 and 1635, reveals no signs of this alleged jealousy, so it is possible that the opposition came from other quarters.

93. Orcibal, *Jean Duvergier de Hauranne*, 307–9, 312; Arnauld, *Relation écrite sur Port-Royal*, 120.

94. Arnauld, *Relation écrite sur Port-Royal*, 121–22. Zamet's biographer, Louis Prunel, offers a very different perspective on his motives and actions—and a vigorous critique of Arnauld's. See Prunel, *Sébastien Zamet*, 210–83, especially 240–41.

95. Arnauld, *Relation écrite sur Port-Royal*, 125–26, 126–27; also 161–62.

96. Prunel, *Sébastien Zamet*, 230–36, is strongly critical of Arnauld's later account of her differences with Zamet and insists that the two were on the best of terms until Saint-Cyran entered the picture in 1635. Though there may be some justice to his claim that Arnauld's ideas of religious perfection shifted under Saint-Cyran's influence, Prunel's strong bias against Arnauld renders his account of events suspect.

97. On Saint-Cyran's place in the dévot community, see Orcibal, *Jean Duvergier de Hauranne*, 380–433.

98. Orcibal, *Jean Duvergier de Huranne*, is the essential work on Saint-Cyran's friends and enemies.

99. Sauval, *Histoire et recherches des antiquités de Paris*, 1:661–62, 663–64.

100. Madeleine de Saint-Joseph, *Lettres spirituelles*, 212–13: letter 204, undated and addressed only to "une Prieure de Carmel."

101. Arnauld, *Relation écrite sur Port-Royal*, 170, 173–74. Marie le Prévost de Saint-Germain was separated from her husband, Nicolas Le Camus de Pontcarré, when she negotiated a retreat at Port-Royal in exchange for a gift of 24,000 livres late in 1626. She remained faithful to Zamet when Arnauld, preferring Saint-Cyran's more ascetic spirituality, tried to return Port-Royal to a more austere life and theology in 1636. See also Prunel, *Sébastien Zamet*, 206–7, 259–60.

102. Marguerite du Saint-Sacrement Acarie, *Lettres spirituelles*, 79–81: letter 25 to Madame de Cabriès, 3 July 1654.

103. See, for example, Biver and Biver, *Couvents de femmes à Paris*, 382–85, on the difficulty that the Religieuses Bénédictines de l'Adoration perpétuelle du Saint-Sacrement had establishing themselves in Paris after taking flight from the wars in Lorraine.

CHAPTER 6: BOTH MARY AND MARTHA

1. Duvignacq-Glessgen, *L'ordre de la Visitation à Paris*, 23–24.

2. Ibid., 25–29, 37, 79.

3. Ibid., 92, 184, 174.

4. Ms. "Règles et constitutions de la Congrégation des sœurs dédiées à Dieu sous l'invocation de N.-D. de la Visitation," as cited in Salinis, *Madame de Villeneuve*, 338. The account of Mary's visit to her cousin Elizabeth in the Gospel of Luke (1:39–56) was commonly used to credit her with authorship of the "Magnificat," which very early found its way into the Catholic liturgy.

5. Ibid., 331–32, citing *Œuvres de Saint François de Sales*, vol. 13, letter 158 (Annecy, 16 August 1607).

6. Letter of Denis Simon de Marquemont, archbishop of Lyons (20 January 1616), as published in *Œuvres de Saint François de Sales*, 17:405–7. See also Duvignacq-Glessgen, *L'ordre de la Visitation à Paris*, 15–16.

7. M. Descargues, "Aux origines de la Visitation," *Nouvelle Revue théologique* 73 (1951): 483–513, as cited in Burns, "Aux origines de la Visitation," 669.

8. Hsia, *The World of Catholic Renewal*, 38. Rapley, *The Dévotes*, 34–41, also depicts the enclosure of the Visitandines as a serious defeat for François de Sales.

9. Although Jeanne de Chantal spent ten months in Lyons (January to October 1615) preparing for the new foundation and must have had discussions with Archbishop Marquemont in which he raised the question of making the Visitandines a formal religious order during this time, her letters give no indication of the proposed changes until after her return to Annecy. She first mentions the matter in a letter written in January 1616 to Mère Marie-Jacqueline Favre, who had been left in charge of the Lyons foundation. This and later letters to Mère Favre consistently maintain that the women's posture should be one of humble obedience and acceptance of whatever organizational forms their male superiors agreed on. Reading between the lines, we might infer from the very fact that Chantal felt it necessary to reassure Mère Favre and instruct her on the appropriate response to Marquemont's proposed changes that the women were unhappy with these changes. Their response was nevertheless one of religious obedience and not strenuous objection. Chantal's letter of 6 June, moreover, explicitly states that it matters little whether they are called a congregation or an order, so long as the special aims of the institute are maintained. See Jeanne de Chantal, *Correspondance*, 1:134–35, 138–40, 148–49, 174–77: letters of 17 January, 2 February, 14 March, and 6 June 1616 to Mère Marie-Jacqueline Favre in Lyon.

10. *Œuvres de Saint François de Sales*, 17:137–42: letter of 2 February 1616 to Mère Favre; 238–48: letter of 10 July [1616] to Cardinal Robert Bellarmine; see also Burns, "Aux origines de la Visitation," 667.

11. *Œuvres de Saint François de Sales*, 17:238–48: letter to Bellarmine.

12. Jeanne de Chantal, *Correspondance*, 1:29; Fichet, *Les sainctes reliques de l'érothée*, 199. Archbishop de Marquemont proposed a different solution to the problem of admitting widows. He would have them take the habit but prolong their novitiate until they could free themselves of any worldly ties that might make it necessary to leave the cloister (*Œuvres de Saint François de Sales*, 17:406: letter of 20 January 1616 from Denis de Marquemont to François de Sales).

13. Burns, "Aux origines de la Visitation," 663, citing constitutions of 1613.

14. On the criticisms, see Fichet, *Les sainctes reliques de l'érothée*, 261–63.

15. *Regles et constitutions pour les soeurs de la Visitation*, 38–40, from the preface by François de Sales.

16. See for example, her letter of 20 January 1616 to Mère Marie-Jacqueline

Favre in Lyons, in which she urges the latter in the very strongest terms to eat well and get plenty of rest, "for your health is entirely necessary to the service of our Lord for the time being, which is why it is necessary to recover it and then preserve it with care" (Jeanne de Chantal, *Correspondance*, 1:134).

17. Ibid., 1:146–48: letter of 29 February [1616] to Mère Marie-Jacqueline Favre.

18. Ibid., 1:154–55: letter of 30 April [1616] to Mère Marie-Jacqueline Favre.

19. Arnauld, *Relation écrite sur Port-Royal*, 101–2.

20. BMaz, Ms. 3324: "Constitutions ajoutees a la regle de Saint Augustin, faites pour les religieuses de l'Assomption," 28. The discussion of accepting widows with children (2–4), for example, is taken almost verbatim from Visitandine constitution 43.

21. Marie de Maupeou, widow of counselor in Parlement François Fouquet, whose five daughters all became nuns at the Visitation, was one of the leading members of the Dames de la Charité. So was Marie Deslandes, who, along with her husband, Chrétien de Lamoignon, was counted among the benefactors of the Visitandines' second Paris convent. One of the daughters of Chrétien de Lamoignon and Marie Deslandes joined the Visitandines. The youngest, Madeleine de Lamoignon, was schooled for her first communion by François de Sales. Coste, *Monsieur Vincent*, 1:364–69.

22. Salinis, *Madame de Villeneuve*, 327–30.

23. Coste, *Monsieur Vincent*, 1:358–60.

24. Coste, *Saint Vincent de Paul et les Dames de la Charité*, 86–89.

25. *Œuvres de Saint François de Sales*, 13:373–74: letter of 29 or 30 April 1619 to Jeanne de Chantal.

26. Hélyot, *Dictionnaire des ordres religieux*, vol. 2, cols. 812–20: "Madelonnettes"; also BNF, Ms. fr. 14486: "Erection et institution des filles de Ste Marie Magdaleine à Paris"; on the number of Visitandines who served there, see Duvignacq-Glessgen, *L'ordre de la Visitation*, 266–67.

27. *Collection de lettres circulaires des religieuses de la Visitation*, letter of 12 April 1676.

28. Montry, *Relation veritable*, 17–89.

29. Ibid., 42–43, 49, 93, 112–20, 138–41. See also BNF, Ms. fr. 14486: "Erection et institution des Filles de Ste Marie Magdaleine à Paris," 1–5; [Senault], *Oraison funèbre de la marquise de Maignelay*, 60–63; *Testament de Madame la marquise de Maignelay*, 10–12; *Estat pitoyable des pauvres filles du monastère de Ste Magdaleine*.

30. Montry, *Relation veritable*, 70–71, 76–77.

31. Ibid., 72–74.

32. Ibid., 89–94.

33. Duvignacq-Glessgen, *L'ordre de la Visitation à Paris*, 264.

34. See Jeanne de Chantal, *Correspondance*, 3:686–87: letter of 12 June 1630 to Anne-Marie Bollain at the Madeleine, which suggests that Bollain played an active role in drawing up the constitutions.

35. BNF, 500 Colbert, Ms. 159, fols 154–65: "Reglement et constitutions pour les filles et femmes qui sont au second rang soubz l'invocation de Ste Marthe."

36. BNF, Ms. fr. 14486: "Erection et Institution des Filles de Ste Marie Magdaleine," 7–8.

37. Duvignacq-Glessgen, *L'ordre de la Visitation*, 266, citing letter of 8 February 1647 conserved in the Visitation's Annecy archives.

38. BNF, 500 Colbert, ms. 159, fols. 154–65: "Reglement et constitutions pour les filles et femmes qui sont au second rang soubz l'invocation de Ste Marthe," fols. 155–56.

39. That Montry regretted this is evident from the tone he adopts in reminiscing about the goodwill, docile behavior, and eagerness to learn godly ways of the initial members of the community, who all came voluntarily and were never held there by violence or force. Montry, *Relation veritable*, 70–71.

40. BNF, Ms. 13880: "Vie de Françoise de la Croix," 10, 12–13, 21. This was true of both Catherine Le Bis, the widow of Jean Hennequin, a procureur au Chambre des comptes in Rouen, who established an initial hospital with Françoise de la Croix at Louviers, and Guichard Faure, maître d'hôtel ordinaire du roi, who founded the Paris hospital with his wife, Madeleine Brûlart, in 1625.

41. *Constitutions de la Charité nostre Dame*, 17, 13.

42. Ibid., 21, 33.

43. Ibid., 17.

44. Biver and Biver, *Couvents de femmes à Paris*, 377–81.

45. The purpose is given in the provisional rule established by Pierre Fourier in 1598, as cited in Rohan-Chabot, "L'œuvre pédagogique de saint Pierre Fourier," 67.

46. Rapley, *The Dévotes*, 61–73, tells how the Congrégation de Notre-Dame was forced to accept clausura.

47. Pommereuse, *Les chroniques des Ursulines*, 136; Fourier, "Mémoire qu'il donna aux deux religieuses qu'il envoya aux Ursulines de Paris."

48. Paul and Marie Biver insist that all three foundations were made by Filles from Laon, but they do not even attempt to explain why the Laonnais convent would send out three apparently unrelated groups of nuns to found convents in a single city within a ten-year period, when combining their resources would have given each a far better chance to survive (Biver and Biver, *Couvents de femmes à Paris*, 229). A history entitled *Le troisième monastère de la Congrégation de Notre-Dame à Paris* sounds promising but offers little solid information on any of the foundations. Its suggestion that the ultimately unsuccessful convent founded at Charonne was established by nuns from the convent of Saint-Nicolas in Lorraine under the protection of Marguerite de Lorraine, the second wife of Gaston d'Orléans, is plausible (20), but the date of 1636 offered for the foundation is not. Louis XIII did not recognize Gaston's marriage to Marguerite of Lorraine or invite her to Paris until shortly before his death in 1643. It is unlikely that she would have founded a Parisian convent under these circumstances.

49. BSG, Ms. 1686, "Constitutions des religieuses de la Congregation Notre-Dame," part 3: "De l'instruction des filles seculières." This manuscript is undated but appears to predate the final version of the congregation's constitutions published in 1649. See Fourier, *Les vrayes constitutions des religieuses de la congregation de Notre-Dame*, 3, 70–73, 88.

50. Raunié, *Epitaphier du vieux Paris*, 3:95–97n, reproducing contracts of 13 May and 14 August 1634 (from AN, S 4590), and 99n "Sommaire de la recepte depuis le mois d'avril de l'an 1635 jusques au 10 septembre 1644."

51. Ibid., 100n, citing AN, L 1044.

52. This conclusion is speculative and based on descriptions of the convent in Raunié, *Epitaphier du vieux Paris*, 3:101, 102n, which makes no mention of external classrooms.

53. Ranum, *Paris in the Age of Absolutism*, 111.

54. AN, L 770: Couvent du St Sepulchre à Bellechasse: letters patent of 13 May 1637 and undated "Mémoire" on the establishment of the convent.

55. AN, L 1016: contracts for professions of nuns at Bellechasse.

56. AN, L 771: Notre-Dame de Liesse: 3 January 1639: summary of documents presented to the prior of Saint-Germain for establishment of the convent, including a contract for 500 livres from the duchesse de Longueville (14 May 1637) and another from the comtesse de Soissons for 2,000 livres (9 September 1638); letters patent from the king (October 1638); also 14 April 1642: request from Sister Gertrude de la Trinité, mother superior of the convent, to return to Rethel, giving an account of the foundation.

57. This episode is described at greater length in Diefendorf, "Contradictions of the Century of Saints," 469–70. The charges against Mère Hillaire de Sainte-Thérèse are given in AN, L 771, 26–27 July and 2–3 August 1644.

58. AN, L 771, documents dated 5 September and 15 December 1644, 22 December 1645, and 7 September 1647.

59. *Factum pour les Religieuses Benedictines*.

60. AN, L 771, request of 14 April 1642.

61. The chronology outlined here is drawn from the *Factum pour les Religieuses Benedictines*, 4–7, 9–10.

62. BNF, 500 Colbert, no. 160, item 8: "Ordre que Monseigneur l'illustrissime et reverendissime Archevesque de Paris veut estre gardé en toutes les maisons des religieuses de son diocèse" (Paris, 18 July 1638).

63. AN, L 771, extract from the registers of Parlement dated 13 February 1660.

64. Raunié, *Epitaphier du vieux Paris*, 3:99n.

65. AN, L 770, Bellechasse, *acte capitulaire* of 7 May 1652; the income from the dowry is given in a list dated 1651 in the same *liasse*.

66. AN, L 770, Bellechasse, documents concerning "Madame de Verdille, ditte Ste-Cecille," especially extract from the registers of the official of Saint-Germain des Près, *procès-verbaux* of 10 and 11 May 1658 and 11 May 1659, and papal dispensation of 23 November 1658. The events surrounding Renée de Verdille's marriage and subsequent election as prioress of Bellechasse are recounted in more detail in Diefendorf, "Contradictions of the Century of Saints," 495–98.

67. Already in May 1659, the wife of the duc de Saint-Simon promised the convent 300 livres a year in exchange for the privilege of having a room in the cloister with a garden view where she could retreat whenever she liked. The duchess gave as the reason for her donation the great affection she had for the convent and her "particular affection for the Lady de Verdille, our prioress and founder." AN, L 770, Bellechasse, gift of 7 May 1659.

68. Rapley, *The Dévotes*, 181. Teaching convents were forbidden to charge their pupils tuition (which would have been considered a form of simony) and tried to make up for this by the pensions they received from boarders. As a result, however,

many lavished most of their attention on the paying boarders at the expense of day students, which some convents did not accept at all.

69. Ibid., 200. Rapley's table is based on 743 cases drawn from registers of the Ursulines of Paris, Rouen, Blois, Lille, Valenciennes, and Saumur; the Congrégation de Notre-Dame of Nancy, Provins, Reims, and Châteauroux; and the very similar Filles de Notre-Dame of La Flèche.

CHAPTER 7: THE IMPULSE TO CHARITY

1. See, for example, Gager, *Blood Ties and Fictive Ties*, 121–22, which credits Vincent de Paul rather than the Dames de la Charité with "taking over" the foundling hospital that became the Enfants Trouvés.

2. Coste, *Monsieur Vincent*, 1:88–90, citing conferences of 25 January 1655 and 17 May 1658. Marguerite de Silly's biographer, Hilarion de Coste, concludes his account of her life with the same story about how, as a young girl, she was troubled by her priest's inability to pronounce the formula for absolution and says he was told the story by Vincent de Paul himself. Hilarion de Coste, *Les éloges et les vies des reynes*, as translated by John Rybolt in "Madame de Gondi: A Contemporary Seventeenth-Century Life," 41–42.

3. Coste, *Monsieur Vincent*, 1:88–90.

4. This discussion of Marguerite de Silly draws on my introduction to "Madame de Gondi: A Contemporary Seventeenth-Century Life."

5. The letter is published in Vincent de Paul, *Correspondance, entretiens, documents*, 1:21–22: Madame de Gondi à Saint Vincent (September 1617).

6. Maynard, *Apostle of Charity*, 77, 78.

7. Coste, *Monsieur Vincent*, 1:114–15. See also Bertière, *Vie du Cardinal de Retz*, 46–49, 52, which typifies the view, not only that Marguerite de Silly was a difficult and self-centered woman, but that the initiative for de Paul's charitable projects came uniquely from him, with the Gondis' role limited to financing the projects.

8. Coste, *Monsieur Vincent*, 1:111.

9. Vincent de Paul, *Correspondance, entretiens, documents*, 13:423: "Charité des femmes de Châtillon-les-Dombes" (November and December 1617).

10. Ibid.

11. Ibid., 429. Significantly, this rule was approved in November 1617 by Denis Simon de Marquemont, archbishop of Lyons, just a year after his refusal to permit the Filles de la Visitation to be established as anything other than a cloistered religious order. This is further evidence that Marquemont's insistence on cloistering the Visitandines derived from his understanding of what constituted a valid religious community and his worry about the legal problems that might be encountered by uncloistered religious women rather than a misogynistic desire to protect their endangered virtue or a refusal to believe them capable of instructing others in the faith.

12. Ibid, 422–23n, citing the rule for the Charité of Neufchâtel-en-Bray, founded in 1634.

13. The rules of a number of these confraternities are published in Vincent de Paul, *Correspondance, entretiens, documents*, 13:417–537. See also Coste, *Monsieur Vincent*, 1:118–23.

14. Coste, *Monsieur Vincent*, 1:123–24. See also Mathieu, *Monsieur Vincent chez les Gondy*, 24–26, which reproduces several documents concerning the foundation of the Charité of Montmirail.

15. Hilarion de Coste, *Les éloges et les vies des reynes*, as translated by John Rybolt in "Madame de Gondi: A Contemporary Seventeenth-Century Life," 41.

16. Gobillon, *Vie de Mademoiselle Le Gras*, 9.

17. Even before her husband's death, she convinced Camus to allow her to make a vow to remain a widow if Antoine Le Gras predeceased her. Garreau, *Jean-Pierre Camus*, 80.

18. Louise Sullivan, "Louise de Marillac: A Spiritual Portrait," in Ryan and Rybolt, *Vincent de Paul and Louise de Marillac*, 44.

19. Vincent de Paul, *Correspondence, Conferences, Documents*, 1:99–100: undated letter from 1630 or 1631 to Louise de Marillac; 286–88: letters to Louise de Marillac [1635]; 294–96: letter of Louise de Marillac to Vincent de Paul (4 September [1635]).

20. Gobillon, *Vie de Mademoiselle Le Gras*, 32–36.

21. Vincent de Paul, *Correspondence, Conferences, Documents*, 1:82–83: letter to Louise de Marillac at Villepreux, 4 May [1630]; 119–21: letters to Louise de Marillac and the pastor of Bergères, 2 September 1631; 158–59: letter to Louise de Marillac, June 1632(?).

22. Ibid., 1:161: letter to Louise de Marillac at Villeneuve-Saint-Georges, 10 July 1632; 13:422n, citing rule for the Charité of Neufchâtel-en-Bray.

23. The relevant documents are reproduced in Vincent de Paul, *Correspondance, entretiens, documents*, 13:557–65, 578–87. On the evolution of the community, see Dinan, "Confraternities as a Venue for Female Activism."

24. Louise de Marillac, *Spiritual Writings*, 726–27.

25. See especially Vincent de Paul, *Correspondence, Conferences, Documents*, 1:113–14: undated letter to Louise de Marillac; 200–201: letter to Louise de Marillac [May 1633].

26. Ryan and Rybolt, *Vincent de Paul and Louise de Marillac*, 167.

27. Charpy, *Petite vie de Louise de Marillac*, 29.

28. For example, Wiesner, *Women and Gender in Early Modern Europe*, 202–3.

29. Ryan and Rybolt, *Vincent de Paul and Louise de Marillac*, 186.

30. Gobillon, *Vie de Mademoiselle Le Gras*, 79.

31. AN, LL 1671: Congrégation de la Sainte-Croix, permission of 27 April 1640; also reproduced in Salinis, *Madame de Villeneuve*, 539. They received permission from Louis XIII to expand where they wished in the diocese of Paris in 1642 (AN, LL 1673: Registre). The Filles de Saint-Joseph, who arrived from Bordeaux to establish a girls' orphanage in 1638, took only simple vows by permission of the archbishop of Bordeaux, Henri d'Escoubleau de Sourdis. Their status in Paris as filles séculaires however, was made official only several years later. They received letters patent from the king in May 1641, permission from the abbot of Saint-Germain des Prés, in whose territory the new house lay, in June 1641, and letters from the archbishop of Paris in January 1642. See AN, L 775, Filles de Saint-Joseph, letters of 28 January 1642. See also AN, H⁵ 4120: Etat et compte que rend Marie Delpech de Lestang [1645]. On their foundation in Bordeaux, see Peyrous, *La réforme catholique à Bordeaux*, 1:488–90.

32. Salinis, *Madame de Villeneuve*, 452, citing the manuscript "Constitutions des Filles de la Croix."

33. AN, LL 1671: Registre, 4 January 1648.

34. The decision is reproduced in Salinis, *Madame de Villeneuve*, 284–89.

35. Ibid., 304–14; see especially chapters 8 and 14. The hagiographical nature of this work makes it tedious reading, but the inclusion of many important documents cited verbatim renders it more useful than it might at first appear. Despite the author's determination to give all of the credit for the shape the Filles de la Croix were eventually to take to Marie Luillier, François de Sales, and divine inspiration, it is possible to read through these documents the important role that the original Filles of Roye, especially Charlotte de Lancy, maintained in the Paris foundation.

36. Ibid., 527–29, reproducing AN, L 1659, "Délibérations des habitants de Brie-Comte-Robert," 1 August 1639.

37. AN, LL 1671, Registre des Filles de la Sainte-Croix, 27 April 1640.

38. Salinis, *Madame de Villeneuve*, 315, citing a manuscript life of Marie Luillier.

39. AN, LL 1671, Registre des Filles de la Sainte-Croix, 27 April 1640. Also reproduced in Salinis, *Madame de Villeneuve*, 529–39.

40. AN, LL 1671, Registre.

41. Ibid., fol 4; Salinis, *Madame de Villeneuve*, 537.

42. AN, LL 1673: Registre des Filles de la Croix, 1 July 1644. The claims of the group that Pierre Guérin continued to direct are clearly expressed in the registers of the community in the parish Saint-Gervais.

43. Salinis, *Madame de Villeneuve*, 361–67.

44. Ibid., 360.

45. AN, L 1055, "fondation" of 25 October 1643; LL 1671, fols. 8–9, citing registers of Parlement from 3 September 1646. See also Salinis, *Madame de Villeneuve*, 415–33.

46. Coste, *Monsieur Vincent*, 1:359–60.

47. Salinis, *Madame de Villeneuve*, 482–83, citing manuscript "Mémoires authentiques de M. Olier" [1643], 307 (Olier was the founder of the Society of Saint-Sulpice for the training of the clergy); 482–83, citing manuscript "Histoire des Filles de la Congrégation de la Croix"; 480–81, citing AN, L 1055, no. 30.

48. Ibid., 468–69; see also BMaz, Ms. 3333: Constitutions de la Congregation des Sœurs de la Croix, 5–6.

49. Salinis, *Madame de Villeneuve*, 472–78, reproduces the instructions for exercises of solitude and for retreats from the manuscript "Constitutions des Filles de la Croix."

50. These details on her life are taken from Collin, *Vie de Marie Lumague*, 1–36.

51. Ibid., 50–54, citing the funeral sermon of Dominique Le Brun. See also Marie de l'Enfant-Jésus, "Mademoiselle Pollalion et la Providence de Dieu," 155n.

52. Collin, *Vie de Marie Lumague*, 56–57.

53. Ibid., 44.

54. The duchesse d'Aiguillon, for example, gave them a rente of 500 livres in 1643. Biver and Biver, *Couvents de femmes à Paris*, 316.

55. AN, H⁵ 3714, "Memoire," fol. 23.

56. Bergin, *The Making of the French Episcopate*, 505–12, on the *conseil de conscience*. Biver and Biver, *Couvents de femmes à Paris*, 316, specify that the queen gave the institution 63,000 livres plus an annual income of 1,500 livres. On her death, Louis XIV continued to pay them an annual stipend.

57. Coste, *Saint Vincent de Paul et les Dames de la Charité*, 60, 249–50, reproducing Lumague's letter of 3 November 1652 to Vincent de Paul.

58. Even before they started parish schools, Filles de la Providence were dispatched from the motherhouse to run the Maison des Nouvelles Catholiques, established by Marie Lumague in 1634 to provide a secure retreat for girls from Protestant families who had abjured or at least promised to take instruction in the Catholic faith. The Filles directed the institution until a separate congregation was established several decades later.

59. Biver and Biver, *Couvents de femmes à Paris*, 313–18; Coste, *Monsieur Vincent*, 1:346–50.

60. Coste, *Monsieur Vincent*, 1:351–53.

61. Vincent de Paul, *Correspondence, Conférence, Documents*, 1:192: Madame Goussault to Saint Vincent, Angers, 16 April 1633.

62. Ibid., 193, 195.

63. Ibid., 195.

64. Ibid.

65. Vincent de Paul describes the first meeting of the group in an undated letter to Louise de Marillac, written sometime between January and March 1634 (*Correspondance, entretiens, documents*, 13:229–30). See also his letter of 25 July 1634 to François du Coudray in Rome (ibid., 253).

66. See, for example, Hufton, *The Prospect before Her*, 386.

67. Coste, *Saint Vincent de Paul et les Dames de la Charité*, 7–10, 111–14, 4–7. Coste suggests that de Paul's objections to Fayet's plan may have stemmed from his knowledge that an earlier attempt by devout Parisians to bring food to the Hôtel-Dieu had to be discontinued because the ladies were causing "confusion" and interfering with the work of the nuns. But the theory is tenuous, given that the earlier initiative began in 1608 and was apparently discontinued by 1612.

68. AAP, fonds de l'Hôtel-Dieu, liasse 1438, "Registre pour les annees 1574–1578," 610–12, entry of 31 December 1578.

69. Hélyot, *Dictionnaire des ordres religieux*, vol. 2, col. 473, says that princesses and "persons of quality" were commonly seen assisting with even the "most vile" tasks in the Hôtel-Dieu and recounts specifically that Marthe d'Oraison, the daughter of a distinguished Provençal family, died there in 1627 from an illness contracted while serving the poor.

70. Hilarion de Coste, *Les éloges et les vies des reynes*, 2:781–82, 788, 796. A textual reference to the Reformed Jacobins, whose Paris monastery was founded in 1611, would seem to determine the earliest date at which it could have been composed. The latest date is 1618, to judge from a reference to Cardinal Jacques Davy du Perron, who died in that year.

71. It is also possible that, like the rural Charités, the confraternities were based on an as yet undiscovered common model, but the level of communication that occurred in devout circles makes this appear less likely than a direct connection between the two known Parisian initiatives.

72. Coste, *Les éloges et les vies des reynes*, 2:783–88.

73. AAP, Hôtel-Dieu, liasse 1438, "Registres pour les années 1608–1615": 25 January and 16 July 1608.

74. Coste, *Saint Vincent de Paul et les Dames de la Charité*, 18–33. On the found-ling home, see Gager, *Blood Ties and Fictive Ties*, 112–23.

75. Abelly, *Vie de S. Vincent de Paul*, 2:41, 53; Coste, *Saint Vincent de Paul et les Dames de la Charité*, 35.

76. These relations were subsequently collected and republished in 1655 (*Recueil des relations . . . pour l'assistance des pauvres*). Féron, *La vie et les œuvres de Charles Maignart de Bernières*, 258–60, establishes the dévot Charles Maignart de Bernières as the probable author of the *Relations*. He also shows that Maignart paid for the publication of the *Relations* and that of the 80,000 livres he collected for the war effort between January 1651 and September 1652, he turned 35,000 over to the Dames de la Charité (255–56). The rest presumably went to other agencies engaged in the relief effort.

77. Coste, *Saint Vincent de Paul et les Dames de la Charité*, 66–67.

78. Abelly, *Vie de S. Vincent de Paul*, 2:43.

79. Ibid., 2:42–54, especially 49–50; more generally, Coste, *Saint Vincent de Paul et les Dames de la Charité*, 115–50; Saint Vincent de Paul, *Correspondance, entretiens, documents*, 13:787–97.

80. The figure is given in Vincent de Paul's conference of 11 July 1657; he re-gretted that the membership had since fallen to only 150 (Abelly, *Vie de S. Vincent de Paul*, 2:45).

81. AL, Dossiers compiled by Pierre Coste (G/5.III.2), Dames de la Charité: "Noms des premières Dames de la Charité, 1634–1660." Eliminating identifiable du-plicate entries, the list contains approximately 543 names but is not limited to the twenty-six-year period announced in its title. The total is necessarily approximate on account of unidentifiable duplicate entries; although street names are given for the Dames de l'Hôtel-Dieu, some uncertainties as to identity remain. The list is undated and its provenance is unknown, so its accuracy and completeness cannot be guaranteed. It nevertheless represents the best information we have on the society's membership. I am grateful to the Congrégation de la Mission for kind access to this and other docu-ments in their archives.

82. On Pétau, see Coste, *Saint Vincent de Paul et les Dames de la Charité*, 73; on Deffita and Maupeou, see AN, H^5 3714, fols. 23–31: "Memoire"; also AN, S 6144, con-tract of 24 August 1658, which lists them as directors.

83. McHugh, "The Hôpital Général," 249. Tallon, *La Compagnie du Saint-Sacrement*, 47–49, points out that some women, especially the wives of the Compag-nie's members, certainly were aware of the organization's existence and were used in different ways in its projects, even though the members refused to create organized female affiliates.

84. Tallon, *La Compagnie du Saint-Sacrement*, 141–46, offers a good corrective to the argument that the Hôpital Général was largely an attempt at social discipline.

85. Coste, *Saint Vincent de Paul et les Dames de la Charité*, 44–48. Coste implies that the Dames de la Charité actually initiated the plan for the Hôpital Général, only to be displaced by men when the project was confided to male governors in 1656. The work for which the women had so labored was no longer theirs, he tells us, but they continued to support the institution with the "same zeal and generosity." This inter-pretation of events overlooks the fact that members of the Compagnie du Saint-Sacrement discussed the idea of establishing such a hospital as early as 1631 and even

appointed a committee of eight to work on the project in 1636. Realization of the project was delayed for a number of reasons, but it never was entirely dropped. Specific plans were drawn up during the Fronde, and only Parlement's indecision over whether to try to reform existing charity hospitals or create an entirely new institution prevented the foundation from taking place within a year or two of the Fronde's end. See Argenson, *Annales de la Compagnie du St-Sacrement*, especially 26–27; McHugh, "The Hôpital Général," 238–39.

86. McHugh, "The Hôpital Général," 244–49.

87. Biver and Biver, *Couvents de femmes à Paris*, 214–16; Coste, *Saint Vincent de Paul et les Dames de la Charité*, 86–89.

CONCLUSION

1. BN, Ms. fr. 14342: "Vie de Mademoiselle de Lamoignon," especially 4–6, 28–29.

2. Maugis, *Histoire du Parlement de Paris*, 2:279.

3. BN, Ms. fr. 14342, "Vie de Mademoiselle de Lamoignon," 6–25.

4. Most prominently, Marguerite de Gondi, marquise de Maignelay, continued to play a very public role in Parisian charities until shortly before her death in 1650 at the age of eighty. As late as 1640, she was working to reestablish Charités on her estates in war-torn Picardy, even though, as she wrote to Vincent de Paul, she now had to employ young women to tend the poor in their houses because her declining health prevented her from doing this herself (letters of 21 and 26 August 1640, in Vincent de Paul, *Correspondence, Conférences, Documents*, 2:109–11).

5. Madeleine de Saint-Joseph, *Vie de sœur Catherine de Jesus*, 32–36.

6. Gobillon, *Vie de Mademoiselle Le Gras*, 14, 197–98, reproducing Marillac's meditation on Christ "dans le sein de la Vierge."

7. Taveneaux, *Le catholicisme dans la France classique*, 1:8, 27. By contrast, Denis Richet and Marc Venard have emphasized the sixteenth-century roots of the Catholic Reformation.

8. Vincent de Paul, "Explanation of the Rule," in Ryan and Rybolt, *Vincent de Paul and Louise de Marillac*, 204.

9. Duvignacq-Glessgen, *L'ordre de la Visitation à Paris*, 46.

10. All of the convents included in the order were in dire straits financially, and their fiscal difficulties were in truth more responsible for their inclusion on the list than any alleged "irregularities" in their foundation.

11. Jean de Viguerie finds signs that a broader malaise and worry about declining standards for religious life set in by about 1660. The rigorist tendencies of Jansenist clerics may have been responsible for some of the accusations of laxity and decline, but some abbesses clearly were relaxing the strict rules of poverty, community, and enclosure that had once been their convent's pride ("Y a-t-il une crise de l'observance régulière?," 140–44).

12. Harline and Put, *A Bishop's Tale*, 235–36, 219. Counter-Reformation clerics in Münster, which had returned to the Catholic fold after the failed attempt to establish a radical Anabaptist Kingdom there in 1535, similarly found it necessary to compromise when town magistrates opposed their plan to force the town's beguines into the cloister and place them under the direction of strict Poor Clares in 1613. Although

supportive of a moderate Catholicism, civic leaders resisted the threats to local autonomy they perceived in the more militant Counter-Reformation church. Too much
pressure to conform might backfire by alienating moderate Catholics and pushing
them into the Lutheran camp (Hsia, *Society and Religion in Münster*, 142–45).

13. Baernstein, *A Convent Tale*, 79–111.

14. Ibid., especially 138–44.

15. Zarri, "Living Saints," especially 248–54. Zarri dates the end of the public
role of the "living saints" to 1530. I find more convincing the turning point of the
1540s suggested by Baernstein in her study of the Angelics (*A Convent Tale*, 6–7). Pol-
izzoto, "When Saints Fall Out," also deals with women's reform initiatives and their
subsequent repression.

16. Schutte, *Aspiring Saints*, 42–59.

17. Venice's Casa delle Zitelle has much in common with Paris's Filles de la
Providence, including the purpose of providing a secure home for endangered girls
but also the leadership role exercised by elite women in founding and administering
the home. By contrast, elite women played an important role in founding the Pietà
and several other residential communities for girls in Florence, but their active administrative role declined as the initial generation of pious founders disappeared and
more formal structures were put into place under male supervision. See Chojnacka,
"Women, Charity and Community in Early Modern Venice"; Terpstra, "Mothers, Sisters, and Daughters." Philip Gavitt's current research on Tuscany and Lance Lazar's
on Rome should help round out our understanding of women's charitable initiatives
in Italy.

18. Samuel Cohen's important essay "Women and the Counter Reformation in
Siena: Authority and Property in the Family" in his *Women in the Streets* suggests that
the transmission of property in Sienese families changed significantly in the wake of
the Council of Trent, and in ways that opened new possibilities for women to participate both in parish life and in the management of patrimonial properties. Cavallo,
Charity and Power in Early Modern Italy, 167–75, identifies a contrary trend in Turin,
where legislation increasingly restricted women's control over property. Clearly further research is needed on the impact of the Catholic Reformation on women's position in marriage and the family.

19. The bibliography of writings by and about early modern nuns is large and
growing, even if the questions asked in these studies still remain in many ways limited. For Spain, see especially Poutrin, *La voile et la plume*, and Sanchez Lora, *Mujeres,
conventos y formas de la religiosidad barroca*. For Italy, a useful starting point is the
lengthy bibliography in Zarri, *Donna, disciplina, creanza cristiana*. On the need to
broaden our understanding of gender in early modern Catholicism, see Bilinkoff,
"Navigating the Waves (of Devotion)."

Bibliography

MANUSCRIPT SOURCES

Archives de l'Assistance publique (AAP)
  Fonds de l'Hôtel-Dieu, liasse 1438: Registres pour les années 1574–1578,
    1608–1615.
Archives du Carmel de Clamart (ACC)
  Duval, Robert. "La vie de Maître André Duval."
  "Extractum seu Transsumptum ex Originalibus Attestationibus circa Vita
    Sanctitatem & Miracula Ancillae Dei Matris Magdalena a Ste Jo-
    seph . . ." (1647)
  Ms. Lettres de Marie de Jésus
  Ms. "Vie de la Mere Marie de Jesus [de Breauté], Carmélite"
Archives du Carmel de Pontoise (ACP)
  Procès informatif and Procès apostolique de Marie de l'Incarnation (Man-
    uscript copy of testimony for the beatification of Barbe Acarie)
Archives Lazaristes, Maison Mère de la Congrégation de la Mission (AL)
  Dossiers compiled by Pierre Coste on "les Dames de la Charité" (G/
    5.III.2), "la Misère au XVIIe siècle," and "Saint-Vincent de Paul et les
    ordres religieux féminins"
Archives nationales (AN)
  H^2 1882^2 and 1882^3 Bureau de la Ville de Paris, 1591–1592, 1593–1594
  H^5 3714, fols. 23–31: "Memoire pour servir d'archives" (Filles de la Provi-
    dence)
  H^5 4120: "Etat et compte que rend Marie delpech de lestang" (Filles de
    Saint-Joseph)
  L 770: Couvent du Saint Sepulchre à Bellechasse
  L 771: Notre-Dame de Liesse; Annonciades des Dix Vertus
  L 773: Religieuses du Verbe Incarné; Bernardines du Precieux Sang
  L 775: Filles de Saint Joseph

L 1016: Bellechasse

L 1041: Congrégation Notre-Dame

L 1043: Haudriettes, puis Filles de l'Assomption

L 1046: Carmélites de la rue Saint-Jacques

L 1047: Carmélites de Pontoise et de la Rue Chapon

L 1053: Filles Dieu

L 1055: Filles de la Croix

L 1057, pièce 4: "Recueil des actions . . . de Jean Anthoine Le Vachet"

LL 1638: Augustines du Verbe Incarné

LL 1671 and LL 1673: Filles de la Sainte Croix

M 233, pièce 3: "Poincts notables de la vie de la bienheureuse sœur Marie de l'Incarnation," by Dom Sans de Sainte-Catherine, 12 September 1619

S 6144: Filles de la Providence

Y 143, fol. 361; Y144, fols. 386v–87v; Y 156, fol. 26: donations to Carmelites

Z¹ʰ 86 and 91: Sentences du Bureau de la Ville, 1589–1590, 1591

Bibliothèque mazarine (BMaz)

Ms. 1206: Letters of Père Joseph de Paris

Ms. 1802: "Vie de Jeanne de Jesus Chésard de Matel" (Verbe Incarné)

Ms. 2418: "Annales des Reverends Peres Capucins," by Maurice d'Epernay

Ms. 3324: Constitutions of the Religieuses de l'Assomption and the Conception Notre-Dame

Ms. 3333: Constitutions of the Sœurs de la Croix

Ms. 3338: "Statuts et reglements des Religieuses Recollettes Ste Claire"

Ms. 3344: "Abregé du reglement de la communauté des Filles de Ste Genevieve"

Bibliothèque nationale de France (BNF)

Ms. fr. 3996: "Deliberations, Arrests, Actes et Memoires tirez des Registres du Parlement, de ce qui se passa à Paris durant la Ligue," vol. 1: 1588–1594

Ms. fr. 11565: "Recit de quelques actions" of Jean de la Barrière

Ms. fr. 13880: "Vie de . . . Françoise de la Croix, institutrice des religieuses hospitalières de la Charité Notre-Dame, Ordre de St Augustin" (1744)

Ms. fr. 13883: "Constitutions et reglemens pour les religieuses du tiers ordre sainct François"

Ms. fr. 13884: "Constitutions generalles des soeurs de Saincte Elizabeth" (1625, 1628)

Ms. fr. 13886: "Constitutions du Monastere du S. Sacrement à Port Royal"

Ms. fr. 14342: "La vie de Mademoiselle de Lamoignon ecrite par le R. P. **** de la C. D. Jesus"

Ms. fr. 14475: "Constitutions pour la direction et conduicte du Monastere de la Conception N. Dame du tiers ordre de S. François, . . . rue S. Honoré"

Ms. fr. 14486: "Erection et Institution de la maison et monastere des Filles de Ste Marie Magdeleine a Paris"

Ms. fr. 17719, fols. 229–235: "Lettre generalle . . . pour renouveller les anciens usages," by Père Gibieuf (1646)

Ms. fr. 17808: Letters to Angélique Arnauld at Port Royal

Ms. fr. 23295 and 23296: "Histoire de la Ligue" (anonymous, 17th c. ms.; the first part was published by Charles Valois in 1914; the second has never been published)

Ms. fr. 25046: "Eloges historiques" of notable Capucins of the Province de Paris, vol. 2

Ms. fr. 25054: "Escrit du R. P. Caussin . . . sur la vocation de la R. M. Louise Angelique de la Fayette, religieuse de la Visitation de Ste. Marie"

Ms. fr. 25069: "Projet d'établissement d'une maison de jeunes orphelines dans l'hôtel Couppeaulx, anciennement de la Petite-Bretagne à Paris" (16th–17th c. ms.)

Ms. fr. 25077: "Histoire de la vie de plusieurs veuves qui ont vêcu en grand vertu dans l'Ordre de la Visitation Sainte-Marie"

NA fr. 82–83: "Vie du garde des sceaux de Marillac," by Nicolas Le Fèvre de Lezeau

500 Colbert, Ms. 159, fols. 154–65: "Reglement et constitutions pour les filles et femmes . . . soubz l'invocation de Ste Marthe de la maison de Ste Marie Magdelaine"

500 Colbert, Ms. 160: Documents concerning various convents and monasteries, especially fol. 244: "Ordre que Monseigneur l'illustrissime et reverendissime archevesque de Paris veut estre gardé en toutes les maisons religieuses de son diocese" (1638)

Bibliothèque Sainte-Geneviève (BSG)

Ms. 1686: "Constitutions des religieuses de la Congrégation Notre-Dame"

Ms. 3030, fol. 18: Biographical note on Madeleine de Saint-François, abbesse des Capucines

PUBLISHED PRIMARY SOURCES

Abelly, Louis. *Vie de S. Vincent de Paul, instituteur et premier supérieur général de la Congrégation de la Mission.* Paris, 1854.

Amelote, Denis. *La vie de sœur Marguerite du Saint-Sacrement, Religieuse, Carmélite du monastère de Beaune*, composée par un prêtre de la congrégation de l'Oratoire. Paris, 1655.

Ana de Jesús. *Cartas (1590–1621): Religiosidad y vida cotidiana en la clausura femenina del Siglo de Oro.* Edited by Concepción Torres. Salamanca, 1995.

Ana de San Bartolomé. *Autobiographie.* Translated by Pierre Sérouet. Ghent, n.d. (based on the critical edition published in 1981 by Julián Urkiza, from the autograph manuscript in the Carmel of Antwerp).

———. *Lettres et écrits spirituels de la Bienheureuse Anne de Saint-Barthélemy.* Translated by Pierre Sérouet. Paris, 1964.

———. *Obras Completas.* Edited by Julián Urkiza. 2 vols. Rome, 1981–85.

Antoine de Saint-Martin de la Porte. *L'idee de la veritable et solide devotion en la vie de Madame de Beaufort Ferrand.* Paris, 1650.

Antoine de Saint-Pierre Lejeune. *La vie du Réverend Père Dom Eustache de Saint-Paul Asseline, docteur de Sorbonne & religieux de la Congregation de Notre-Dame de Fueillens [sic]. Ensemble quelques opuscules spirituels utiles aux ames pieuses & religieuses.* Paris, 1646.

Archives curieuses de l'histoire de France depuis Louis XI jusqu'à Louis XVIII. Edited by L. Cimber [pseud. of Louis Lafaist] and Félix Danjou, 30 vols. Paris, 1834–1841.

Argenson, René de Voyer d'. *Annales de la Compagnie du St-Sacrement.* Edited by H. Beauchet-Filleau. Marseille, 1900.

Arnauld d'Andilly, Angélique de Saint-Jean. *Mémoires pour servir à l'histoire de Port-Royal et à la vie de la Reverende Mere Marie Angélique de Sainte Magdelaine Arnauld, reformatrice de ce monastere.* 3 vols. Utrecht, 1743.

Arnauld, Jacqueline Marie Angélique. *Relation écrite par la Mère Angélique Arnauld sur Port-Royal.* Edited by Louis Cognet. [Paris], 1949.

Auvray, Jean. *Modele de la perfection religieuse en la vie de la venerable mere Jeanne Absolu, dite de S. Sauveur, religieuse de Hautes-Bruyeres de l'Ordre de Fontevrault.* Paris, 1640.

[Bauduen, Marc de]. *La vie admirable de très haute, très puissante, très illustre et très vertueuse dame Charlote Marguerite de Gondy, marquise de Magnelais, fait par le P.M.C.P.* Paris, 1666.

Bazy, Annoncia. *Vie du vénérable Jean de la Barrière, abbé et réformateur de l'abbaye des Feuillants, fondateur de la congrégation des Feuillants & des Feuillantines, etc., et ses rapports avec Henri III, roi de France.* Toulouse, 1885.

Beauvilliers, Marie de. *Conférences spirituelles d'une supérieure à ses religieuses.* Edited by L. Gaudreau. Paris, n.d.

Benoît de Canfield. *La règle de perfection.* Edited by Jean Orcibal. Paris, 1982.

Bérulle, Pierre de. *Correspondance.* Edited by Jean Dagens. 3 vols. Louvain, 1937–39.

———. *Œuvres complètes.* Reproduction of the Édition Princeps (1644). 2 vols. Montsoult, n.d.

Biesse, René. *La vie de la Venerable Mere Marie Alvequin, dite de Jesus, Superieure & Reformatrice du Monastere des Religieuses Penitentes de Paris, Ordre de S. Augustin, rue S. Denis.* Paris, 1649.

Blémur, Jacqueline Bouette de. *Eloges de quelques personnes illustres en piété de l'ordre de saint Benoît.* 2 vols. Paris, 1679.

Boulenger, Florent. *Traitez de la closture des religieuses: leur enseignant l'obligation que toutes y ont, pourquoy elles en peuvent sortir; qui y entrer, & avoir accez aux parloirs.* Paris, 1629.

Brétigny, Jean de. *Quintanadueñas. Lettres de Jean de Brétigny, 1556–1634.* Edited by Pierre Sérouet. Bibliothèque de la Revue d'histoire ecclésiastique, 53. Louvain, 1974.

Brief traité des misères de la Ville de Paris. N.p., 1590. In *Archives curieuses,* 1st. ser, 13: 271–85.

Caluze, Antoine. *Les annales des freres mineurs capucins,* vol. 2. Paris, 1677.

Camus, Jean-Pierre, bishop of Belley. *La pieuse Julie.* Paris, 1625.

Canons and Decrees of the Council of Trent: Original Text with English Translation. Translated by Henry Joseph Schroeder, St. Louis, 1941.

Cargnoni, Costanzo, ed. *I frati Cappuccini: Documenti e testimonianze del primo secolo.* 5 vols. in 6. Perugia, 1988–93.

[Catherine de Saint-François Mallet]. *Vie de la Révérende Mère Madeleine Bochart de Saron, morte 17 mars 1688.* N.p., n.d.

Ceremonial des vestures et professions. Pour les religieuses de Sainte Ursule de la Congregation de Paris. New ed. Paris, 1681.

Le changement de la court. N.p., 1614.

Chaugy, Françoise-Madeleine de. *Les vies de VIII venerables veuves religieuses de l'ordre de la Visitation Sainte Marie.* Annecy, 1659.

Chroniques de l'ordre des Carmélites de la réforme de Sainte Thérèse depuis leur introduction en France. 5 vols. Troyes, 1846–65.

Collection de lettres circulaires émanées des religieuses de la Visitation Sainte Marie. Paris, n.d. (BNF, Ld173-2-104).

Collin, M. *Vie de la vénérable servante de Dieu Marie Lumague, veuve de M. Pollalion, gentilhomme ordinaire du Roi, institutrice des Filles de la Providence, sous la conduite de S. Vincent de Paul, morte en odeur de sainteté en 1657.* Paris, 1744.

Conseil salutaire d'un bon Françoys aux Parisiens. Contenant les impostures & monopoles des faux Predicateurs. Avec un discours veritable des actes plus memorables de la Ligue, depuis la journee des Barricades. N.p., 1590.

Constitutions des religieuses hospitalieres de la Charité nostre Dame, de l'Ordre de Sainct Augustin, establies à Paris par l'authorité de Monseigneur l'Illustrissime & Reverendissime Messire Jean François de Gondy, Archevesque de Paris. Paris, 1635.

Constitutions pour la maison des nouvelles catholiques de Paris. Paris, 1675.

Coppie de la response faicte par un polytique de ceste ville de Paris. Paris, 1589. In *Archives curieuses,* 12:251–81.

Corneio, Pierre. *Bref discours et veritable des choses plus notables arrivees au siege memorable de la renommee ville de Paris.* Paris, 1590. In *Archives curieuses,* 1st ser., 13: 227–70.

Discours veritable sur l'inique emprisonnement & detention de mes-Dames les Duchesses & Damoiselles de Longue-ville, & de Monseigneur le Comte de sainct Pol. Par ceux de l'Union. N.p., 1590.

Dufour, Adolphe, ed. "Histoire du siège de Paris sous Henri IV en 1590 d'après un manuscrit nouvellement découvert." *Mémoires de la Société de l'histoire de Paris* 7 (1880): 175–270.

Duval, André. *La vie admirable de la bienheureuse sœur Marie de l'Incarnation, religieuse converse de l'ordre de Notre-Dame du Mont-Carmel et fondatrice de cet ordre en France, appelée dans le monde Mademoiselle Acarie.* New ed. of Paris, 1893; reproducing edition of Paris, 1621.

Eloge funebre de tres-illustre et tres-religieuse Dame Charlotte de Harlay, abbesse de l'abbaye de Sainte Perrine à la Villette lez-Paris. Prononcé dans l'eglise de la meme abbaye le dix-septiéme jour de fevrier 1688, qui estoit le trentiéme après son decês. Paris, 1688.

Estat pitoyable des pauvres filles du monastère de Ste Magdaleine. Paris, 1675.

Estienne, Antoine. *Oraison funebre, faicte sur le trespas de noble & vertueuse Damoiselle Marie du Drac, en son vivant, veufve de feu noble homme, maistre Jacques Aurillot, jadis Conseiller du Roy, en son Parlement de Paris, en laquelle sont amplement declarees plusieurs choses admirables, avec les rares vertus & graces speciales dont la dessus-dicte Damoiselle a esté douée de Dieu, par sa tresgrande liberalité & bonté infinie.* Paris, 1590.

———. *Remonstrance charitable aux dames et demoyselles de France sur leurs ornemens dissolus.* Paris, 1585. 1st ed., 1570.

Factum pour les Religieuses Benedictines, composant la plus grande & principale partie du Monastere de Nostre Dame de Liesse, située aux Faux-bourg S. Germain, demanderesses en requeste. N.p., n.d. [approximately 1654].

Félibien, Michel, and Guy-Alexis Lobineau. *Histoire de la ville de Paris.* 5 vols. Paris, 1725.

Ferraige, Jacques. *La vie admirable, et digne d'une fidele imitation, de la B. Mere Margue-rite d'Arbouze, ditte de Saincte Gertrude*. Paris, 1628.

"Les feuillantines de Paris, 1622–1792. Journal d'une religieuse de ce monastère, pub-lié d'apres le manuscrit original par F.-H. Mabille." *Bulletin de la Montagne de Sainte-Geneviève et ses abords* 3 (1899–1902) (Paris, 1902): 207–22.

Fichet, Alexandre. *Les fleurs de la parfaicte contemplation, ou se voient les institutions du Tiers Ordre du Cordon S. François, ensemble les vies des saincts et sainctes dudit tiers ordre*. 2nd ed. Paris, 1619.

———. *Les sainctes reliques de l'érothée, en la saincte vie de la mere Jeanne Françoise de Fremiot, Baronne de Chantal, Premiere Superieure, & Fondatrice de L'Ordre de La Visitation Saincte Marie*. Paris, 1643.

[Fortin, Thomas]. *La vie de damoiselle Elizabeth Ranquet, femme de Monsieur de Cheu-reul, sieur d'Esterville*. 2nd ed. Paris, 1660.

Fourier, Pierre. "Mémoire qu'il donna aux deux religieuses qu'il envoya aux Ursulines de Paris." In *La Pastorale, l'éducation, l'Europe chrétienne*, edited by René Tave-neaux, 55–58. Paris, 1995.

———. *Les vrayes constitutions des religieuses de la congregation de Notre-Dame. Faites par le Tres Reverend Pere Pierre Fourier, leur instituteur et general des Chanoines re-guliers de la Congregation de Nostre Sauveur, approuvées par Nostre Sainct Pere le Pape Innocent X*. N.p., 1649.

François de Sales, Saint. *Introduction à la vie dévote*. Paris, [1934]. 1st ed., 1608.

———. *Œuvres. Edition complète d'apres les autographes et les éditions originales*. 22 vols. Annecy, 1892–.

Franklin, Alfred, ed. *Journal du siège de Paris en 1590 rédigé par un des assiégés*. Paris, 1876.

Gallemant, Placide. *La vie du venerable prestre de J.C. M. Jacques Gallemant, docteur en théologie de la Faculté de Paris, premier superieur des Carmelites en France, etc., conduite dans toutes les expressions de la sagesse & perfection chrestienne*. Paris, 1663.

Gobillon, Nicolas. *La vie de Mademoiselle Le Gras, fondatrice et premiere superieure de la Compagnie des Filles de la Charité, servantes des pauvres malades*. Paris, 1676.

Haton, Claude. *Mémoires contenant le récit des événements accomplis de 1553 à 1582*. Ed-ited by Félix Bourquelot. 2 vols. Paris, 1857.

Henry de Calais. *Histoire de la vie, de la mort et des miracles du R. P. Honoré Bochart de Champigny, Capucin*. New ed. Paris, 1864.

Hilarion de Coste. *Les éloges et les vies des reynes, des princesses, et des dames illustres en pieté, en courage & en doctrine, qui ont fleury de nostre temps, du temps de nos Peres*. 2 vols. Paris, 1647.

———. *Histoire catholique, ou sont descrites les vies, faicts et actions heroiques et signalees des hommes & dames illustres, qui par leur pieté ou saincteté de vie se sont rendus recommandables dans les XVIe & XVIIe siecles. Divisee en quatre livres*. Paris, 1625.

Histoire de la fondation du monastère des religieuses feuillentines [sic] de Toulouse; avec les éloges de plusieurs religieuses de cette maison, remarquables par leurs vertus. Par un religieux feuillent [sic]. Bordeaux, 1696.

Jean-Marie de Vernon. *Histoire generale et particuliere du Tiers Ordre de S. François d'Assize*. Vol. 2: *Les vies des personnes illustres qui ont fleury dans les siecles xv, xvi & xvii*. Paris, 1667.

————. *La vie de la venerable mere Françoise de Saint Bernard, religieuse de Ste Claire à Verdun; nommee dans le monde Madame de Maisons.* Paris, 1657.

Jeanne-Françoise Fremyot de Chantal, Saint. *Correspondance de Jeanne-Françoise Frémyot de Chantal.* 6 vols. Edited by Marie-Patricia Burns. Paris, 1986–96.

Journal de François, bourgeois de Paris. 23 décembre 1588–30 avril 1589. Edited by Eugène Saulnier. Paris, 1913.

[Lantages, Charles-Louis de]. *La vie de la v. Mere Françoise des Seraphins, religieuse de l'ordre de S. Dominique au monastère de S. Thomas d'Aquin, à Paris.* Clermont, 1669.

Léonard de Paris. *La regle du Tiers Ordre des Penitens, instituée par le Patriarche & Seraphique Pere S. François, pour les personnes seculieres qui desirent vivre en peniten. Ensemble les annotations & reglemens sur la mesme regle par un Pere Capucin, pour la conduite de ceux qui la professent sous leur direction.* Paris, 1663.

L'Estoile, Pierre de. *Journal de l'Estoile pour le règne de Henri IV et le début du règne de Louis XIII.* Edited by Louis-Raymond Lefèvre and André Martin. 3 vols. Paris, 1948–60.

————. *Mémoires-journaux.* Edited by Gustave Brunet, Aimé-Louis Champollion-Figeac, Eugène Halphen, Paul Lacroix, Charles-Alexandre Read, Philippe Tamizey de Larroque, and Edouard Tricotel. 12 vols. Paris, 1875–99.

Louise de Marillac, Saint. *Spiritual Writings of Louise de Marillac: Correspondence and Thoughts.* Edited and translated by Louise Sullivan. Brooklyn, 1991.

Macé, Jean. *La vie de la vénérable mère Marie de Saint-Charles, religieuse de sainte Elizabeth dite au siècle Madame la baronne de Veuilly.* Paris, 1671.

Madeleine de Saint-Joseph. *Avis de la venerable mere Madeleine de S. Joseph, pour la conduite des novices.* Paris, 1672.

————. *Lettres spirituelles.* Edited by Pierre Sérouet. Paris, 1965.

————. *La vie de sœur Catherine de Jesus, religieuse du premier monastere de l'Ordre de Nostre-Dame du Mont-Carmel, estably in France selon la reforme de Sainte Therese de Jesus.* 4th ed. Paris, 1656. Reproduced in J.-B. Eriau, ed., *Une mystique du XVIIe siècle: Sœur Catherine de Jésus, Carmélite (1589–1623): Sa vie et ses écrits,* 1–102. Paris, 1929.

Malet, Antoine. *Sommaire narration du premier establissement qui a esté fait en France de l'Ordre des Capucines, dites Filles de la Passion.* Paris, 1609.

Marguerite du Saint-Sacrement [Acarie]. *Lettres spirituelles, suivies de treize lettres de la mère Marthe de l'Incarnation à Mme de Cabriès.* Edited by Pierre Sérouet. Paris, 1993.

Marie de la Trinité [Sévin du Coudray]. *Une glorieuse fille de Sainte Thérèse d'Avila: "Mère Sainte," fondatrice du Carmel d'Auch, 1570–1656: Vie et écrits.* Edited by M. d'Aignan du Sendat. Paris, 1930.

Marillac, Michel de. *De l'érection et institution de l'ordre des religieuses de Notre Dame du Mont-Carmel, selon la réformation de Sainte Thérèse en France; des troubles et différends excités en cet ordre et du jugement rendu par Notre Saint Père le Pape sur iceux.* Paris, 1622.

Le miroir du temps passé à l'usage du present; à tous bons peres religieux et vrais catholiques non passionnez. Paris?, 1625?

Montry, Robert de. *Relation veritable de la naissance et progrez du Monastere de Saincte Marie Magdaleine.* Paris, 1649.

Ordre a tenir pour la visite des pauvres honteux. N.p., n.d.

Paschal, Pierre de. *Journal de ce qui s'est passé en France durant l'année 1562, principalement dans Paris et à la cour.* Edited by Michel François. Paris, 1950.

Pasquier, Étienne. *Lettres familières.* Edited by Dorothy Thickett. Paris, 1974.

Pigafetta, Filippo. "Relation du siège de Paris par Henri IV." Edited by A. Dufour. *Mémoires de la Société de l'histoire de Paris* 2 (1875): 1–105.

Pommereuse, Marie de. *Les chroniques de l'ordre des Ursulines, recueillies pour l'usage des religieuses du mesme ordre.* Paris, 1673.

Recueil des relations contenant ce qui s'est fait pour l'assistance des Pauvres. Entre autres ceux de Paris, & des environs, & des Provinces de Picardie & Champagne, pendant les années 1650, 1651, 1652, 1653 & 1654. Paris, 1655.

Reglemens de la Compagnie de la Charité de Saint André des Arcs. Paris, 1662.

Reglemens de la Companie instituée pour le restablissement des pauvres familles honteuses de la paroisse S. Eustache. Paris, 1654.

Regles de Sainct Augustin et constitutions pour les soeurs religieuses de la Visitation Saincte Marie. Lyons, 1645.

Renty, Jean-Baptiste Gaston de. *Correspondance.* Edited by Raymond Triboulet. [Paris], 1978.

Requeste au Roy, et a Messeigneurs de son Conseil en faveur des pauvres mendians. Paris, 1618.

Sauval, Henri. *Histoire et recherches des antiquités de la ville de Paris.* 3 vols. Paris, 1724.

[Senault, Jean-François]. *Oraison funebre de . . . Charlotte-Marguerite de Gondy, Marquise de Maignelay, prononcée en présence de Mgr. l'archevêque de Corinthe, coadjuteur de Paris, célébrant pontificalement dans l'église des prêtres de l'Oratoire de Jésus.* Paris, 1650.

———. *La vie de Madame Catherine de Montholon, veuve de Monsieur de Sanzelles, maistre des requestes, et fondatrice des Ursulines de Dijon.* Paris, 1653.

———. *La vie de la Mere Magdeleine de S. Joseph, religieuse Carmélite Déchausée, de la premiere regle selon la reforme de Sainte Therese.* 2nd ed. Paris, 1670.

Tallement des Réaux, Gédéon. *Historiettes.* 2 vols. Edited by Antoine Adam. Paris, 1960.

Teresa of Avila. *The Collected Works.* Vol. 1: *The Book of Her Life.* Translated by Kieran Kavanaugh and Otilio Rodriguez. Washington, DC, 1976.

———. *The Complete Works of St. Teresa of Jesus.* Vol. 2: *Book Called Way of Perfection.* Translated and edited by E. Allison Peers. London, 1946.

Testament de Madame la Marquise de Maignelay. Paris, 1659.

Thuillier, René. *Diarium patrum, fratrum et sororum ordinis minimorum, provinciae franciae.* Geneva, 1972; reprint of Paris edition, 1709.

[Tronson de Chenevière]. *La vie de la venerable mere Marguerite Acarie, dite du S. Sacrement, religieuse Carmelite dechausée.* Paris, 1689.

Vie de la mere Antoinette de Jesus, religieuse chanoinesse de l'Ordre de S. Augustin en l'Abbaie Royale de Sainte Perrine à la Villette proche Paris. Paris, 1685.

Vie de la venerable mere Marie Agnes Dauvaine, l'une des premieres fondatrices du monastere de l'Annonciade celeste de Paris. Recueillie sur les memoires des religieuses du mesme monastere et composée par un père de la Compagnie de Jesus, amy de l'ordre. Paris, 1675.

[Vincent de Paul]. *Saint Vincent de Paul: Correspondance, entretiens, documents.* Edited by Pierre Coste. 14 vols. Paris, 1920–25. [An enlarged and updated English translation is in progress: *Saint Vincent de Paul: Correspondence, Conferences, Documents*, edited by Jacqueline Kilar. 8 vols. as of 2003. Brooklyn, 1985–.]

SECONDARY SOURCES

Alliot, J. M. *Histoire de l'abbaye et des religieuses bénédictines de Notre-Dame du Val de Gif (au diocèse actuel de Versailles)*. Paris, 1892.

———. *Histoire de l'abbaye et des religieuses bénédictines de Notre-Dame d'Yerres (au diocèse actual de Versailles)*. Paris, 1899.

Anaert, Philippe. *Le salut par les femmes: L'œuvre des Ursulines aux XVIIe et XVIIIe siècles*. Paris, 1992.

Arenal, Electra, and Stacey Schlau. *Untold Sisters: Hispanic Nuns in Their Own Words*. Albuquerque, NM, 1989.

Augereau, Joseph. *Jeanne Absolu, une mystique du grand siècle*. Paris, 1920.

Baernstein, P. Renée. *A Convent Tale: A Century of Sisterhood in Spanish Milan*. New York, 2002.

Barbiche, Bernard, and Ségolène de Dainville-Barbiche. *Sully*. [Paris], 1997.

Bazy, Annoncia. *Vie du vénérable Jean de la Barrière, abbé et réformateur de l'abbaye des Feuillants, fondateur de la congrégation des Feuillants & des Feuillantines, etc., et ses rapports avec Henri III, roi de France*. Toulouse, 1885.

Bell, Rudolph M. *Holy Anorexia*. Chicago, 1985.

Benedict, Philip, ed. *Cities and Social Change in Early Modern France*. London, 1989.

Bergin, Joseph. *Cardinal de La Rochefoucauld: Leadership and Reform of the French Church*. New Haven, 1987.

———. *The Making of the French Episcopate, 1589–1661*. New Haven, 1996.

Bertière, Simone. *La vie du Cardinal de Retz*. Paris, 1990.

Biddick, Kathleen. "Genders, Bodies, Borders: Technologies of the Visible." *Speculum* 68 (1993): 389–418.

Bilinkoff, Jodi. *The Avila of Saint Teresa: Religious Reform in a Sixteenth-Century City*. Ithaca, 1989.

———. "Navigating the Waves (of Devotion): Toward a Gendered Analysis of Early Modern Catholicism." In *Crossing Boundaries: Attending to Early Modern Women*, edited by Jane Donawerth and Adele Seeff, 161–72. Newark, DE, 2000.

Biver, Paul, and Marie-Louise Biver. *Abbayes, monastères, couvents de femmes à Paris, des origines à la fin du XVIIIe siècle*. Paris, 1975.

Blaisdell, Charmarie. "Religion, Gender, and Class: Nuns and Authority in Early Modern France." In *Changing Identities in Early Modern France*, edited by Michael Wolfe, 147–68. Durham, NC, 1997.

Boislisle, Arthur Michel de. *Histoire de la Maison de Nicolay*. 2 vols. Nogent-le-Rotrou, 1873.

Boucher, J. B. A. *Vie de la bienheureuse sœur Marie de l'Incarnation, dite dans le monde Mademoiselle Acarie, converse professe et fondatrice des Carmélites réformées de France*. Paris, 1800.

Bremond, Henri. *Histoire littéraire du sentiment religieux en France depuis la fin des guerres de religion jusqu'à nos jours*. 11 vols. Paris, 1924–33.

Briggs, Robin. *Communities of Belief: Cultural and Social Tensions in Early Modern France.* Oxford, 1989.

Brown, Judith C. *Immodest Acts: The Life of a Lesbian Nun in Renaissance Italy.* Oxford, 1986.

Bruneau, Marie-Florine. *Women Mystics Confront the Modern World: Marie de l'Incarnation (1499–1672) and Madame Guyon (1648–1717).* Albany, 1998.

Bruno de Jésus-Marie, François. *La belle Acarie: Bienheureuse Marie de l'Incarnation.* Paris, 1942.

Buisseret, David. *Henry IV, King of France.* London, 1984.

Burkardt, Albrecht. "Les vies des saints et leurs lectures au début du xviiᵉ siècle." *Revue d'histoire moderne et contemporaine* 43 (1996): 214–33.

Burns, Marie-Patricia. "Aux origines de la Visitation: La vraie pensée de Saint François de Sales." In *Les religieuses dans le cloître et dans le monde des origines à nos jours,* 659–70. Actes du Deuxième Colloque International du Centre Européen de Recherches sur les Congrégations et Ordres Religieux, Poitiers, 29 September–2 October 1988. Saint-Etienne, 1994.

Bynum, Caroline Walker. *Fragmentation and Redemption: Essays on Gender and the Human Body in Medieval Religion.* New York, 1991.

———. *Holy Feast and Holy Fast: The Religious Significance of Food to Medieval Women.* Berkeley, 1987.

Camporesi, Piero. *The Incorruptible Flesh: Bodily Mutation and Mortification in Religion and Folklore.* Translated by Tania Croft-Murray and Helen Elsom. Cambridge, UK, 1988.

Carmel de l'Incarnation [Clamart]. *La Vénérable Madeleine de Saint-Joseph: Première prieure française du premier monastère des Carmélites Déchausées en France (1578–1637).* Clamart, 1935.

Carr, Thomas M., Jr. "Les abbesses et la Parole au dix-septième siècle: les discours monastiques à la lumière des interdictions pauliniennes." *Rhetorica* 21 (2003): 1–23.

Carroll, Stuart. "The Guise Affinity and Popular Protest during the Wars of Religion." *French History* 9 (1995): 125–52.

———. *Noble Power during the French Wars of Religion: The Guise Affinity and the Catholic Cause in Normandy.* Cambridge, UK, 1998.

Cavallo, Sandra. *Charity and Power in Early Modern Italy: Benefactors and Their Motives in Turin.* Cambridge, UK., 1995.

Certeau, Michel de. "Crise sociale et réformisme spirituel au début du XVIIᵉ siècle." *Revue d'ascétique et de mystique* 41 (1965): 339–86.

———. "L'énonciation mystique." *Recherches de science religieuse* 64 (1976): 183–215.

———. *La fable mystique: XVIᵉ–XVIIᵉ siècle.* [Paris], 1982.

———. "L'histoire religieuse du XVIIᵉ siècle: Problèmes de méthode." *Recherches de science religieuse* 57 (1969): 231–50. Reprinted in Michel de Certeau, *The Writing of History,* translated by Tom Conley, 125–47. New York, 1988.

———. "Politique et mystique: René d'Argenson (1596–1651)." *Revue d'ascétique et de mystique* 39 (1963): 45–82.

Chaix, Gérald. "Contributions cartusiennes aux débuts de la Réforme catholique dans les pays de langue française." *Revue d'histoire de l'Eglise de France* 75 (1989): 115–23.

Charpy, Elisabeth. *Petite vie de Louise de Marillac*. Paris, 1991.

Châtellier, Louis. *L'Europe des dévots*. Paris, 1987.

———. *La religion des pauvres: Les missions rurales en Europe et la formation du catholicisme moderne, XVIᵉ–XIXᵉ siècle*. Paris, 1993.

Chaussy, Yves. *Les Bénédictines et la réforme catholique en France au XVIIᵉ siècle*. 2 vols. N.p., 1975.

Chaussy, Yves, et al. *L'Abbaye royale Notre-Dame de Jouarre*. Paris, 1961.

[Chérot, Henri]. *Une grande chrétienne au XVIIᵉ siècle. Anne de Caumont, Comtesse de Saint-Paul, duchesse de Fronsac (1574–1642), fondatrice des Filles Saint-Thomas à Paris (1626)*. Paris, 1896.

Chevalier, Alexis. *L'Hôtel-Dieu de Paris et les sœurs augustines (650–1810)*. Paris, 1901.

Chojnacka, Monica. "Women, Charity and Community in Early Modern Venice: The Casa delle Zitelle." *Renaissance Quarterly* 51 (1998): 68–91.

Cognet, Louis. *De la dévotion moderne à la spiritualité française*. Paris, 1958.

———. *Les origines de la spiritualité française au XVIIᵉ siècle*. Paris, 1949.

———. *La réforme de Port-Royal (1591–1618)*. N.p., 1950.

Cohen, Samuel K., Jr. *Women in the Streets: Essays on Sex and Power in Renaissance Italy*. Baltimore, 1996.

Cohen, Sherrill. *The Evolution of Women's Asylums Since 1500: From Refuges for Ex-Prostitutes to Shelters for Battered Women*. New York, 1992.

Constant, Jean-Marie. *La Ligue*. Paris, 1996.

Coste, Pierre. *Le grand saint du grand siècle: Monsieur Vincent*. 2nd ed. 3 vols. Paris, 1934.

———. *Saint Vincent de Paul et les Dames de la Charité*. Paris, 1918.

Cousin, Victor. *La jeunesse de Madame de Longueville*. 7th ed. Paris, 1869.

Dagens, Jean. *Bérulle et les origines de la restauration catholique (1575–1611)*. Paris, 1952.

———. *Bibliographie chronologique de la littérature de la spiritualité et de ses sources (1501–1610)*. Paris, n.d.

DeJean, Joan. *Tender Geographies: Women and the Origins of the Novel in France*. New York, 1991.

Delumeau, Jean. *Le Catholicisme entre Luther et Voltaire*. 2nd ed. Paris, 1978.

———. *La peur en Occident (XIVᵉ–XVIIIᵉ siècles): Une cité assiégée*. Paris, 1978.

Denis, M. "Les clarisses capucines de Paris (1602–1792)." *Etudes franciscaines* (1911): 191–203, 400–407.

Departement de la Somme. Ville d'Amiens. *Inventaire sommaire des archives communales antérieures à 1790*. Vol. 1: *Série AA*, edited by Georges Durand. Amiens, 1891. Vol. 3: *Série BB (39 à 323)*, edited by Georges Durand. Amiens, 1897.

Descimon, Robert. *Qui étaient les Seize? Mythes et réalités de la Ligue parisienne. Paris et Ile-de-France: Mémoires*. Vol. 34. Paris, 1983.

Dessert, Daniel. *Fouquet*. Paris, 1987.

Deville, Raymond. *L'Ecole française de spiritualité*. Paris, 1987.

De Vries, Jan. *The Economy of Europe in an Age of Crisis, 1600–1750*. Cambridge, UK, 1976.

Diefendorf, Barbara B. *Beneath the Cross: Catholics and Huguenots in Sixteenth-Century Paris*. New York, 1991.

———. "Contradictions of the Century of Saints: Aristocratic Patronage and the Convents of Counter-Reformation Paris." *French Historical Studies* 24 (2001): 469–99.

———. "Give Us Back Our Children: Patriarchal Authority and Parental Consent to Religious Vocations in Early Counter-Reformation France." *Journal of Modern History* 68 (1996): 265–307.

———. Introduction to "Madame de Gondi: A Contemporary Seventeenth-Century Life," translated and annotated by John E. Rybolt. *Vincentian Heritage* 21 (2000): 25–31.

———. *Paris City Councillors in the Sixteenth Century: The Politics of Patrimony.* Princeton, 1983.

———. "The Religious Wars in France." In *A Companion to the Reformation World*, edited by Ronnie Po-chia Hsia, 150–68. Oxford, 2003.

———. "Women and Property in *Ancien Régime* France: Theory and Practice in Dauphiné and Paris." In *Early Modern Conceptions of Property*, edited by John Brewer and Susan Staves, 170–93. London, 1995.

Dinan, Susan Eileen. "Confraternities as a Venue for Female Activism during the Catholic Reformation." In *Confraternities and Catholic Reform in Italy, France and Spain*, edited by John Patrick Donnelly and Michael W. Maher, 189–214. Kirksville, MD, 1999.

———. "Overcoming Gender Limitations: The Daughters of Charity and Early Modern Catholicism." In *Early Modern Catholicism*, edited by Kathleen M. Comerford and Hilmar M. Pabel, 97–113. Toronto, 2001.

Dinet, Dominique. *Vocation et fidelité: Le recrutement des réguliers dans les diocèses d'Auxerre, Langres et Dijon (XVIIe–XVIIIe).* Paris, 1988.

Dirvin, Joseph I. *Louise de Marillac.* New York, 1970.

Dompnier, Bernard. "Un aspect de la dévotion eucharistique dans la France du XVIIe siècle: Les prières des quarante-heures." *Revue d'histoire de l'Église de France* 70 (1981): 5–31.

Dupront, Alphonse. *Du Sacré: Croisades et pèlerinages, images et langages.* Paris, 1987.

Duvignacq-Glessgen, Marie-Ange. *L'ordre de la Visitation à Paris aux XVIIe et XVIIIe siècles.* Histoire religieuse de la France. Paris, 1994.

Eriau, Jean-Baptiste. *L'ancien Carmel du Faubourg Saint-Jacques, 1604–1792.* Paris, 1929.

———. *Une mystique du XVIIe siècle. Sœur Catherine de Jésus, carmélite (1589–1623). Sa vie et ses écrits.* Paris, 1929.

———. *La vénérable Mère Madeleine de Saint-Joseph, première prieure française du Carmel de l'Incarnation (1578–1637): Essai sur sa vie et les lettres inédites.* Paris, 1921.

Evangelisti, Silvia. "We Do Not Have It, and We Do Not Want It": Women, Power, and Convent Reform in Florence." *Sixteenth Century Journal* 34 (2003): 677–700.

Fagniez, Gustave. *Le Père Joseph et Richelieu (1577–1638).* 2 vols. Paris, 1894.

Féron, Alexandre. *La vie et les œuvres de Charles Maignart de Bernières (1616–1662): L'organisation de l'Assistance publique à l'époque de la Fronde.* Paris, 1930.

Ferté, Jeanne. *La vie religieuse dans les campagnes parisiennes (1622–1695).* Paris, 1963.

Finley-Croswhite, S. Annette. *Henry IV and the Towns: The Pursuit of Legitimacy in French Urban Society, 1589–1610.* Cambridge, UK, 1999.

Fosseyeux, Marcel. *L'Hôtel-Dieu de Paris.* Paris, 1912.

Gager, Kristin Elizabeth. *Blood Ties and Fictive Ties: Adoption and Family Life in Early Modern France*. Princeton, 1996.

Garreau, Albert. *Jean-Pierre Camus, parisien, évêque de Belley (3 novembre 1584–26 avril 1652)*. Paris, 1968.

Gazier, Augustin. *Jeanne de Chantal et Angélique Arnauld, d'après leur correspondance (1620–1641): Etude historique et critique suivie des lettres*. Paris, 1915.

Godefroy de Paris. *Les frères-mineurs capucins en France: Histoire de la province de Paris*. 2 vols. Rouen, 1937–50.

Gueudré, Marie de Chantal. "La femme et la vie spirituelle." *XVIIᵉ siècle*, nos. 62–63 (1964): 47–77.

———. *Histoire de l'ordre des Ursulines en France*. Vol. 2: *Les monastères d'Ursulines sous l'ancien régime*. Paris, 1960.

Gutton, Jean-Pierre. *La société et les pauvres en Europe, XVIᵉ–XVIIIᵉ siècles*. Paris, 1974.

Harline, Craig. *The Burdens of Sister Margaret: Private Lives in a Seventeenth-Century Convent*. New York, 1994.

Harline, Craig, and Eddy Put. *A Bishop's Tale: Mathias Hovius among His Flock in Seventeenth-Century Flanders*. New Haven, 2000.

Harpham, Geoffrey Galt. *The Ascetic Imperative in Culture and Criticism*. Chicago, 1987.

Hélyot, Pierre. *Dictionnaire des ordres religieux, ou Histoire des ordres monastiques, religieux et militaires, et des congrégations séculières de l'un et de l'autre sexe, qui ont été établies jusqu'à présent*. 8 vols. Paris, 1721. Reprinted in l'Abbé Migne, *Encyclopédie théologique*, vols. 20–23. Paris, 1849.

Hillairet, Jacques. *Connaissance du vieux Paris*. 2nd ed. Paris, 1994.

Hsia, R. Po-Chia. *Society and Religion in Münster, 1535–1618*. New Haven, 1984.

———. *The World of Catholic Renewal, 1540–1770*. Cambridge, UK, 1998.

Hufton, Olwen. *The Prospect before Her: A History of Women in Western Europe, 1500–1800*. New York, 1996.

Jacquart, Jean. *La crise rurale en Ile-de-France, 1550–1670*. Paris, 1974.

Jégou, Marie-Andrée. *Les Ursulines du Faubourg Saint-Jacques à Paris (1607–1662): Origine d'une monastère apostolique*. Paris, 1981.

Kieckhefer, Richard. "Holiness and the Culture of Devotion: Remarks on Some Late Medieval Male Saints." In *Images of Sainthood in Medieval Europe*, edited by Renate Blumenfeld-Kosinski and Timea Szell, 288–305. Ithaca, 1991.

———. *Unquiet Souls: Fourteenth-Century Saints and Their Religious Milieu*. Chicago, 1984.

King, Margaret L. *Women of the Renaissance*. Chicago, 1991.

Lambeau, Lucien. *Un vieux couvent parisien: Les dominicaines de la Croix de la rue Charonne (1639–1904)*. Procés-verbal de la Commission du Vieux Paris, annexe. Paris, 1908.

Laven, Mary. *Virgins of Venice: Broken Vows and Cloistered Lives in the Renaissance Convent*. New York, 2002.

Le Brun, Jacques, "Les biographies spirituelles françaises du XVIIème siècle: Écriture féminine? Écriture mystique?" In *Esperanza religiosa et scritture femminili tra Medioevo ed età moderna*, edited by Marilena Modico Vasta, 135–51. Palermo, 1992.

———. "A corps perdu: Les biographies spirituelles féminines du XVIIᵉ siècle." *Le temps de la réflexion* 7 (1987): 389–408.

————. "Mutations de la notion de martyre au XVIIᵉ siècle d'après les biographies spirituelles féminines." In *Sainteté et martyre dans les religions du Livre*, edited by Jacques Marx, 77–90. Brussels, 1989.

Lehfeldt, Elizabeth A., "Discipline, Vocation, and Patronage: Spanish Religious Women in a Tridentine Microclimate." *Sixteenth Century Journal* 30(1999): 1009–30.

Leymont, Henri de. *Madame de Sainte-Beuve et les Ursulines de Paris, 1562–1630: Etude sur l'éducation des femmes en France.* 2nd ed. Lyon, n.d.

Liebowitz, Ruth. "Virgins in the Service of Christ: The Dispute over an Active Apostolate for Women during the Counter-Reformation." In *Women of Spirit: Female Leadership in the Jewish and Christian Traditions*, edited by Rosemary Ruether and Eleanor McLaughlin, 131–52. New York, 1979.

Lierheimer, Linda. "Preaching or Teaching? Defining the Ursuline Mission in Seventeenth-Century France." In *Women Preachers and Prophets through Two Millenia of Christianity*, edited by Beverly Mayne Kienzle and Pamela J. Walker, 212–25. Berkeley, 1998.

Lottin, Alain. *Lille: Citadelle de la Contre-Réforme (1598–1668).* Westhoek, 1984.

Lougee, Carolyn C. *Le Paradis des Femmes: Women, Salons, and Social Stratification in Seventeenth-Century France.* Princeton, 1976.

Lussana, Fiamma. "Rivolta e misticismo nei chiostri femminili del Seicento." *Studi Storici* 28 (1987): 243–60.

Mack, Phyllis. *Visionary Women: Ecstatic Prophecy in Seventeenth-Century England.* Berkeley, 1992.

Marie de l'Enfant Jésus. "Mademoiselle Pollalion et la Providence de Dieu (1630–1657)." *Mission et charité: L'esprit et les œuvres*, 31–32 (July–December 1968): 144–83.

Martin, Henri-Jean. *The French Book: Religion, Absolutism, and Readership, 1585–1715.* Translated by Paul Saenger and Nadine Saenger. Baltimore, 1996.

————. *Livre, pouvoir et société à Paris au XVIIᵉ siècle (1598–1701).* 2 vols. Paris, 1969.

Martin, Victor. *Le Gallicanisme et la réforme catholique: Essai historique sur l'introduction en France des décrets du concile de Trente (1563–1615).* Geneva, 1975; reprint of Paris, 1919 edition.

Mathieu, (Madame) Robert. *Monsieur Vincent chez les Gondy: Les Missionnaires et les Filles de la Charité à Montmirail.* N.p., 1966.

Maugis, Édouard. *Histoire du Parlement de Paris.* 3 vols. Geneva, 1977; reprint of Paris, 1913–16 edition.

Mauzaize, Jean. *Histoire des Frères Mineurs Capucins de la Province de Paris (1601–1660).* Blois, 1965.

————. *Le rôle et l'action des Capucins de la province de Paris dans la France religieuse du XVIIᵉ siècle.* Thesis presented at the University of Paris-Sorbonne, 1977. 3 vols. Lille, 1978.

Maynard, Theodore. *Apostle of Charity: The Life of St. Vincent de Paul.* New York, 1939.

McHugh, Timothy J. "The Hôpital Général, the Parisian Elites and Crown Social Policy During the Reign of Louis XIV." *French History* 15 (2001): 235–53.

Medioli, Francesca. "An Unequal Law: The Enforcement of *clausura* before and after the Council of Trent." In *Women in Renaissance and Early Modern Europe*, edited by Christine Meek, 136–52. Dublin, 2000.

Minton, Anne Mansfield. "Bérulle's Christic Vision." *Studia Mystica* 13 (1990): 4–21.

Monter, William. *Judging the French Reformation: Heresy Trials by Sixteenth-Century Parlements.* Cambridge, MA, 1999.

Morgain, Stéphane-Marie. *Pierre de Bérulle et les Carmélites de France: La querelle du gouvernement, 1583–1629.* Paris, 1995.

Norberg, Kathryn. "The Counter-Reformation and Women Religious and Lay." In *Catholicism in Early Modern History: A Guide to Research,* edited by John W. O'Malley, 133–46. St. Louis, 1988.

———. *Rich and Poor in Grenoble, 1600–1814.* Berkeley, 1985.

Notter, Marie-Thérèse. "Le Carmel de Blois (1625–1790): Essai de sociologie religieuse." *Annales de Bretagne et du pays de l'Ouest* 85 (1978): 53–65.

———. "Les religieuses à Blois (1580–1670)." *Annales de Bretagne et du pays de l'Ouest* 97 (1990): 15–38.

O'Malley, John W. *Trent and All That: Renaming Catholicism in the Early Modern Era.* Cambridge, MA, 2000.

Optat de Veghel. "Aux sources d'une spiritualité des laïcs: Le P. Benoît de Canfield et L'Exercice de la volonté de Dieu." *Etudes franciscaines* 15 (1965): 33–44.

———. *Benoît de Canfield (1562–1610): Sa vie, sa doctrine et son influence.* Rome, 1949.

Orcibal, Jean. *Jean Duvergier de Hauranne, abbé de Saint-Cyran et son temps.* Vol. 2: *Les origines du jansénisme.* Louvain, 1947.

———. *La rencontre du Carmel thérésien avec les mystiques du Nord.* Paris, 1959.

Petit, Louis. *Vie de la mère Antoinette d'Orléans, fondatrice de la congrégation de Notre-Dame du Calvaire.* Paris, 1880.

Petroff, Elizabeth Avilda. *Medieval Women's Visionary Literature.* New York, 1986.

Peyrous, Bernard. *La réforme catholique à Bordeaux (1600–1789): Le renouveau d'un diocèse.* 2 vols. Bordeaux, 1995.

Pillorget, René. *Nouvelle histoire de Paris: Paris sous les premiers Bourbons, 1594–1661.* Paris, 1988.

———. "Vocation religieuse et état en France aux XVIᵉ et XVIIᵉ siècles." In *La vocation religieuse et sacerdotale en France, XVII–XIXᵉ siècles,* 9–18. Actes de la deuxième rencontre d'Histoire Religieuse organisée à Fontevraud le 9 octobre 1978. [Angers, 1979.]

Polizzotto, Lorenzo. "When Saints Fall Out: Women and the Savonarolan Reform in Early Sixteenth-Century Florence." *Renaissance Quarterly* 46 (1993): 486–525.

Pommerol, Marie-Henriette de Montety de. *Albert de Gondi: Maréchal de Retz.* Geneva, 1953.

Poutrin, Isabelle. *Le voile et la plume: Autobiographie et sainteté féminine dans l'Espagne moderne.* Bibliothèque de la Casa de Velázquez, 11. Madrid, 1995.

Prat, Jean-Marie. *Recherches historiques et critiques sur la Compagnie de Jésus en France au temps du P. Coton, 1564–1626.* 5 vols. Lyons, 1876–78.

Prunel, Louis. *Sébastien Zamet, évêque duc de Langres, pair de France (1588–1655): Sa vie et ses oeuvres, les origines du jansénisme.* Paris, 1912.

Ramsey, Ann W. *Liturgy, Politics, and Salvation: The Catholic League in Paris and the Nature of Catholic Reform, 1540–1630.* Rochester, NY, 1999.

Ranum, Orest. *Paris in the Age of Absolutism: An Essay.* Rev. ed. University Park, PA, 2002.

Rapley, Elizabeth. *The Dévotes: Women and Church in Seventeenth-Century France*. Montreal, 1990.

———. *A Social History of the Cloister: Daily Life in the Teaching Monasteries of the Old Regime*. Montreal, 2001.

———. "Women and the Religious Vocation in Seventeenth-Century France." *French Historical Studies* 18 (1994): 613–31.

Raunié, Émile, continued by Max Prinet and Hélène Verlet. *Epitaphier du vieux Paris. Recueil général des inscriptions funéraires des églises, couvents, collèges, hospices, cimetières et charniers depuis le Moyen Âge jusqu'à la fin du XVII*ᵉ *siècle*. Histoire générale de Paris. 8 vols. Paris, 1890–1996.

Renaudin, Paul. *Un maître de la mystique française, Benoît de Canfield*. Paris, 1955.

Reynes, Geneviève. *La vie des religieuses cloîtrées dans la France des XVII*ᵉ *et XVIII*ᵉ *siècles*. Paris, 1987.

Richet, Denis. *De la Réforme à la Révolution: Etudes sur la France moderne*. Paris, 1991.

Rocher, Yves, ed. *L'art du dix-septième siècle dans les Carmels de France*. Catalogue of the exhibition held at the Petit Palais (Paris), 17 November 1982–15 February 1983. Paris, 1983.

Rohan-Chabot, Alix de. "L'œuvre pédagogique de saint Pierre Fourier." In *Saint Pierre Fourier, La Pastorale, l'éducation, l'Europe chrétienne*, edited by René Taveneaux, 67–71. Paris, 1995.

Rubin, Miri. *Corpus Christi: The Eucharist in Late Medieval Culture*. New York, 1991.

Ryan, Frances, and John E. Rybolt, eds., *Vincent de Paul and Louise de Marillac: Rules, Conferences, and Writings*. New York, 1995.

Rybolt, John E., ed. and trans. "Madame de Gondi: A Contemporary Seventeenth-Century Life." *Vincentian Heritage* 21 (2000): 25–43.

Salinis, A. de. *Madame de Villeneuve, née Marie Lhuillier d'Interville, fondatrice et institutrice de la Société de la Croix*. 2nd ed. Paris, 1918.

Sallmann, Jean-Michel. "Image et fonction du saint dans la région de Naples à la fin du XVII*ᵉ* et au début du XVIII*ᵉ* siècle." *Mélanges de l'Ecole française de Rome* 91 (1979): 827–74.

Salmon, John H. M. *Renaissance and Revolt: Essays in the Intellectual and Social History of Early Modern France*. Cambridge, MA, 1987.

Sanchez Lora, José Luis. *Mujeres, conventos y formas de la religiosidad barroca*. Madrid, 1988.

Sauzet, Robert. *Contre-réforme et réforme catholique en bas-Languedoc: Le diocèse de Nîmes au XVII*ᵉ *siècle*. Brussels, [1979].

———. "Le milieu dévot tourangeau et les débuts de la réforme catholique." *Revue d'histoire de l'Eglise de France* 75 (1989): 159–66.

Sauzet, Robert, and Bernard Chevalier, eds. *Les Réformes: Enracinement socio-culturel*. XXV*ᵉ* Colloque international d'études humanistes, Tours, 1–3 juillet 1982. Paris, [1985].

Scattigno, Anna. "Jeanne de Chantal, la fondatrice." In *Barocco al Femminile*, edited by Giulia Calvi, 153–90. Rome, 1992.

Schneider, Robert A. "Mortification on Parade: Penitential Processions in Sixteenth- and Seventeenth-Century France." *Renaissance and Reformation/Renaissance et réforme*, n.s. 10 (1986): 123–46.

Schoote, J.-P. van. "La Perle évangélique." *Revue d'ascétique et de mystique* 37 (1961): 79–92, 291–313.

Schulte van Kessel, Elisja, ed. *Women and Men in Spiritual Culture (XIV–XVII Centuries)*. The Hague, 1986.

Schutte, Anne Jacobson. *Aspiring Saints: Pretense of Holiness, Inquisition, and Gender in the Republic of Venice, 1618–1750*. Baltimore, 2001.

Sérouet, Pierre. *Jean de Brétigny, 1556–1634: Aux origines du Carmel de France, de Belgique et du Congo*. Louvain, 1974.

——. *De la vie dévote à la vie mystique: Sainte Thérèse d'Avila [et] Saint François de Sales*. Paris, 1958.

Sperling, Jutta Gisela. *Convents and the Body Politic in Late Renaissance Venice*. Chicago, 1999.

Strasser, Ulrike. "Cloistering Women's Past: Conflicting Accounts of Enclosure in a Seventeenth-Century Munich Nunnery." In *Gender in Early Modern German History*, edited by Ulinka Rublack, 221–46. Cambridge, UK, 2002.

Tallon, Alain. *La Compagnie du Saint-Sacrement (1629–1667): Spiritualité et société*. Paris, 1990.

Taveneaux, René. *Le catholicisme dans la France classique (1610–1715)*. 2 vols. Paris, 1980.

——. "Port-Royal, les pauvres et la pauvreté." In *Actes du colloque sur le jansénisme (Rome, November 1973)*, 65–88. Louvain, 1977.

Terpstra, Nicholas. "Mothers, Sisters, and Daughters: Girls and Conservatory Guardianship in Late Renaissance Florence." *Renaissance Studies* 17 (2003): 201–29.

Thuau, Etienne. *Raison d'Etat et pensée politique à l'époque de Richelieu*. Paris, 1968.

Timmermans, Linda. *L'accès des femmes à la culture (1598–1715): Un débat d'idées de Saint François de Sales à la Marquise de Lambert*. Paris, 1993.

Tingle, Elizabeth. "Nantes and the Origins of the Catholic League of 1589." *Sixteenth Century Journal* 33 (2002): 109–28.

Le troisième monastère de la Congrégation de Notre-Dame à Paris, Religieuses chanoinesses regulières de Saint-Augustin. Notice historique sur la maison dite du Roule. Paris, 1892.

Ubald d'Alençon. "Les frères mineurs capucins et les débuts de la réforme à Port-Royal des Champs (1609–1626)." *Etudes franciscaines* 24 (1910): 46–62, 249–65, 665–79.

Ultee, Maarten. *The Abbey of St. Germain des Prés in the Seventeenth Century*. New Haven, 1981.

Vauchez, André. "Lay People's Sanctity in Western Europe: Evolution of a Pattern (Twelfth and Thirteenth Centuries)." In *Images of Sainthood in Medieval Europe*, edited by Renate Blumenfeld-Kosinski and Timea Szell, 21–32. Ithaca, 1991.

——. *La sainteté en Occident aux derniers siècles du moyen âge d'après les procès de canonisation et les documents hagiographiques*. Rome, 1981.

Venard, Marc. *Le catholicisme à l'épreuve dans la France du XVIᵉ siècle*. Paris, 2000.

——. *Réforme protestante, réforme catholique dans la province d'Avignon au XVIᵉ siècle*. Paris, 1993.

Vidal, Daniel. *Critique de la raison mystique: Benoît de Canfeld; possession et dépossession au XVIIᵉ siècle*. Grenoble, 1990.

Viennot, Eliane. "Des 'femmes d'Etat' au XVIᵉ siècle: Les princesses de la Ligue et l'écriture de l'histoire." In *Femmes et pouvoirs sous l'ancien régime*, edited by Danielle Hasse-Dubosc and Eliane Viennot, 77–97. Paris, 1991.

———. "Les femmes dans les 'troubles' du XVIᵉ siècle." *CLIO* 5 (1997): 79–96.

Viguerie, Jean de. "La vocation sacerdotale et religieuse aux XVIIᵉ et XVIIIᵉ siècles: La théorie et la réalité." In *La vocation religieuse et sacerdotale en France, XVII–XIXᵉ siècles*, 27–39. Actes de la deuxième rencontre d'Histoire Religieuse organisée à Fontevraud le 9 octobre 1978. [Angers, 1979.]

———. "Y a-t-il une crise de l'observance régulière entre 1660 et 1715?" In *Sous la règle de Saint Benoît: Structures monastiques et sociétés en France du Moyen Age à l'époque moderne*, 135–47. Geneva, 1982.

Voaden, Rosalynn. *God's Words, Women's Voices: The Discernment of Spirits in the Writing of Late-Medieval Women Visionaries*. Suffolk, UK, 1999.

Weaver, F. Ellen. *The Evolution of the Reform of Port-Royal: From the Rule of Cîteaux to Jansenism*. Paris, 1978.

Weber, Alison. "Spiritual Administration: Gender and Discernment in the Carmelite Reform." *Sixteenth Century Journal* 31 (2000): 123–46.

Weinstein, Donald, and Rudolph Bell. *Saints and Society: The Two Worlds of Western Christendom, 1000–1700*. Chicago, 1982.

Whitmore, Patrick J. S. *The Order of Minims in Seventeenth-Century France*. International Archives of the History of Ideas, vol. 20. The Hague, 1967.

Wiesner, Merry E. *Women and Gender in Early Modern Europe*. Cambridge, UK, 1993.

Wright, Wendy M. "The Visitation of Holy Mary: The First Years (1610–1618)." In *Religious Orders of the Catholic Reformation*, edited by Richard L. DeMolen, 216–50. New York, 1994.

Zarri, Gabriella. "Living Saints: A Typology of Female Sanctity in the Early Sixteenth Century," trans. Daniel Bornstein. In *Women and Religion in Medieval and Renaissance Italy*, edited by Daniel Bornstein and Roberto Rusconi, 219–303. Chicago, 1996.

———. "Monasteri femminili e città (secoli XVI–XVIII)." In *Stori d'Italia. Annali 9: La Chiesa et il potere politico dal Medioevo al'età contemporanea*, edited by Giorgio Chittolini and Giovanni Miccoli, 377–98. Turin, 1986.

———. *Le sante vive: Cultura et riligiosità feminile nella prima età moderna*. Turin: 1990.

———, ed. *Donna, disciplina, creanza cristiana dal xv al xvii secole: Studi et testi a stampa*. Temi et testi, n.s., no. 36. Rome, 1996.

Index

LIBRARY, UNIVERSITY OF CHESTER

Lightning Source UK Ltd.
Milton Keynes UK
UKOW04f0404240315

248406UK00001B/23/P